European Business

Four Centuries of Foreign Expansion

This is a volume in the Arno Press collection

European Business

Four Centuries of Foreign Expansion

See last pages of this volume for a complete list of titles.

BRITISH OVERSEAS INVESTMENTS
1907-1948

Edited by Mira Wilkins

ARNO PRESS

A New York Times Company

New York / 1977

Editorial Supervision: ANDREA HICKS

Reprint Edition 1977 by Arno Press Inc.

EUROPEAN BUSINESS:
Four Centuries of Foreign Expansion
ISBN for complete set: 0-405-09715-8
See last pages of this volume for titles.

Manufactured in the United States of America

Library of Congress Cataloging in Publication Data
Main entry under title:

British overseas investments, 1907-1948.

(European business)
Reprint of the sixteen articles published in London between 1909 and 1950 by various publishers.
CONTENTS: Paish, G. Our new investments in 1908.--Paish, G. Great Britain's capital investments in other lands.--Paish, G. Great Britain's capital investments in individual colonial and foreign countries. [etc.]
1. Investments, British--History--Addresses, essays, lectures. I. Wilkins, Mira. II. Series.
HG4538.B69 1977 332.6'7341 76-29782
ISBN 0-405-09783-2

CONTENTS

Kindersley, Robert [M.]
BRITISH FOREIGN INVESTMENTS IN 1930. (Reprinted from *The Economic Journal,* Vol. XLII, No. 166), London, June, 1932

Kindersley, Robert [M.]
BRITISH OVERSEAS INVESTMENTS IN 1931. (Reprinted from *The Economic Journal,* Vol. XLIII, No. 170), London, June, 1933

Kindersley, Robert [M.]
BRITISH OVERSEAS INVESTMENTS IN 1932 AND 1933. (Reprinted from *The Economic Journal,* Vol. XLIV, No. 175), London, September, 1934

Kindersley, Robert [M.]
BRITISH OVERSEA INVESTMENTS IN 1933 AND 1934. (Reprinted from *The Economic Journal,* Vol. XLV, No. 179), London, September, 1935

Kindersley, Robert [M.]
BRITISH OVERSEAS INVESTMENTS IN 1934 AND 1935. (Reprinted from *The Economic Journal,* Vol. XLVI, No. 184), London, December, 1936

Kindersley, R[obert] M.
BRITISH OVERSEA INVESTMENTS IN 1935 AND 1936. (Reprinted from *The Economic Journal,* Vol. XLVII, No. 188), London, December, 1937

Kindersley, R[obert] M.
BRITISH OVERSEA INVESTMENTS, 1937. (Reprinted from *The Economic Journal,* Vol. XLVIII, No. 192), London, December, 1938

Kindersley, R[obert] M.
BRITISH OVERSEAS INVESTMENTS, 1938. (Reprinted from *The Economic Journal,* Vol. XLIX, No. 196), London, December, 1939

Bank of England
UNITED KINGDOM OVERSEAS INVESTMENTS, 1938 TO 1948. London, 1950

OUR NEW INVESTMENTS IN 1908

[George Paish]

OUR NEW INVESTMENTS IN 1908.

The vast amount of new capital which has been subscribed by British investors in the year 1908 bears eloquent testimony to the thrift, wealth, and permanent prosperity of the country. In a single year £203,000,000 of new capital has been subscribed in this country for new loans and enterprises. This sum does not contain capital raised for conversions or amounts of new issues known to be unsuccessful. Never before has so vast an amount of capital been publicly raised in this country. Doubtless other countries have participated to some extent in issues specially reserved for the British market, but the amount of these participations does not appreciably reduce the total. Were we to estimate that the actual amount of capital subscribed for by British investors has been at least £175,000,000, we should probably be below the mark. Of course, the whole of the capital that has been placed has not yet been paid up, for many of the calls upon issues made in the last few months extend into 1909. But allowing for the payment in the early part of 1908 of instalments on capital placed in 1907, it is evident that the actual amount of publicly issued capital paid up in 1907 has been at least £150 millions, and it has probably been greater than this. A nation that is able to put down £150,000,000 of new money for publicly issued loans and companies, and a great deal of money for loans and companies not publicly issued, is in a very sound and strong position.. Beyond the savings placed in new securities, both publicly and privately, there is a vast amount of new capital every year embarked in the erection of houses, in the building of ships, in the construction and equipment of factories, in the decoration and stocking of shops, in extending British enterprise of a private character in other countries, and employed in other ways too numerous to detail. For several years past the construction of new houses has been on a relatively small scale in comparison with the new construction in the later nineties. Nevertheless, in the five years from 1902 to 1907 the income from houses assessed to taxation increased from £184 millions to £210 millions, or by £26 millions—an average increase of £5 millions per annum. On a 16-year basis of valuation, the amount of capital placed in new houses in this country has been at the rate of about £80 millions a year. The period of dear money at the end of 1907 especially affected the operations of builders, and in 1908 the number of new houses constructed has been below the normal. Nevertheless, it is evident that upwards of £50,000,000 has been expended in the past year upon new houses. There can, indeed, be little doubt that the nation's expenditures for reproductive purposes—its savings—has appreciably exceeded £300,000,000.

A few years ago it was thought and stated that it was no longer of any use for other countries to apply to England for any appreciable amount of new capital. At that time we were spending money with the greatest possible liberality upon adding to our comforts regardless of whether or not our savings were being profitably and productively employed. This condition of things caused us to bring home from other countries the interest upon the capital we had previously lent to them, and prevented us from investing any appreciable amount of fresh capital. Hence our imports showed enormous increase, and relatively our exports were stationary.

As a result of the vast growth in imports and the smallness of the increase in our exports, our imports exceeded our exports in 1903 by a sum of no less than £183 millions, and the average excess for several

Table A.—Showing Amount of Capital Subscribed (a) *by Great Britain for use at Home and for India, the Colonies and Foreign Countries in* 1907 *and* 1908.

	Home.		Foreign.		Indian.		Colonial.		Total Foreign, Indian and Colonial.		Total Capital Subscribed (a) by Great Britain.	
	1908.	1907.	1908.	1907.	1908.	1907.	1908.	1907.	1908.	1907.	1908.	1907.
	£	£	£	£	£	£	£	£	£	£	£	£
Government Securities (For further details see Table B)	4,475,000	Nil	19,363,937	7,330,767c	4,950,000	3,447,500	14,942,614b	11,973,383	39,256,551b	22,751,650c	43,731,551b	22,751,650c
Corporation stocks (For further details see Table B)	7,386,659	7,432,976	4,485,512	313,830	Nil	Nil	4,652,905	1,436,732	9,138,417	1,750,562	16,525,076	9,183,538
Railways ... ... (For further details see Table B)	16,930,488	6,559,164	42,344,634	30,959,555	6,894,250	2,200,000	14,335,776	2,978,565	63,574,660	36,133,220	80,565,148	42,697,384
Banks	130,000	693,912	2,572,500	4,359,333	Nil	800,000	250,000	300,000	2,822,500	5,459,333	2,952,500	6,153,245
Breweries and Distilleries	Nil	Nil	120,000	47,120	Nil	Nil	Nil	Nil	120,000	47,120	120,000	47,120
Canals and Docks...	382,500	Nil	117,200	Nil	935,000	Nil	Nil	Nil	1,102,200	Nil	1,484,700	Nil
Commercial, Industrial, &c.	12,209,991	8,061,669	2,899,845	1,915,161	100,000	250,000	2,985,892	489,000	5,985,737	2,654,161	18,195,727	10,715,830
Electric Lighting and Power	1,762,943	797,040	39,625	488,169	100,000	Nil	1,080,646	471,000	1,220,271	959,169	2,983,214	1,756,209
Financial Land, Investment and Trust...	1,549,850	2,318,000	9,399,060	2,309,280	Nil	Nil	1,693,694	336,500	11,092,754	2,645,780	12,642,604	4,963,780
Gas and Water	861,008	368,567	1,218,938	255,000	Nil	Nil	12,000	180,000	1,230,938	435,000	2,091,946	803,567
Insurance	1,702,369	2,201,403	Nil	Nil	Nil	Nil	Nil	Nil	Nil	Nil	1,702,369	2,201,403
Iron, Coal, Steel and Engineering	4,396,673	2,058,667	212,316	270,847	Nil	60,000	742,180	183,750	954,496	514,597	4,751,169	2,573,264
Mines	207,658	13,600	2,081,865	1,905,211	154,577	137,717	3,158,757	1,497,834	5,395,199	3,540,762	5,602,857	3,554,362
Motor Traction and Manufacturing	1,825,016	1,869,106	58,000	302,000	Nil	25,000	Nil	10,000	58,000	337,000	1,883,016	2,206,106
Nitrate	Nil	Nil	215,700	370,250	Nil	Nil	Nil	Nil	215,700	370,250	215,700	370,250
Shipping	1,549,250	2,931,000	776,000	450,000	Nil	Nil	200,000	Nil	976,000	450,000	2,525,250	3,381,000
Tea, Coffee and Rubber	Nil	Nil	113,300	964,300	319,710	207,870	397,002	314,500	830,012	1,486,670	830,012	1,486,670
Telegraphs and Telephones	250,000	1,000,000	150,000	7,940,000	Nil	Nil	Nil	Nil	150,000	7,940,000	400,000	8,940,000
Tramways	605,118	346,000	2,525,931	1,195,402	56,250	150,000	1,271,600	394,000	3,853,781	1,739,402	4,458,899	2,085,402
Grand Total	55,684,523	36,651,204	88,694,363	61,376,225	13,559,787	7,278,087	45,723,066	20,565,364	147,977,216	89,219,676	203,651,739	125,870,880

(a) Amount calculated at the prices of issue, and exclusive of loans raised to repay former loans. (b) Exclusive of £7,370,500 raised by Canada in 1908 to repay previous loans.
(c) Exclusive of Conversion loans as follows: Japan Five per Cent., £11,442,500: Argentine Five per Cent., £2,515,500.

years was in the neighbourhood of £180 millions. The change—the welcome change—that has come over the country in recent years has brought about an entirely different state of affairs. We are now receiving a much larger income from investments in other countries and from shipping and other services rendered than ever before, and our imports have shown fresh expansion ; at the same time, we are providing the new countries with the capital they need for the development of their resources, and in consequence our exports have shown great expansion. For the whole of 1907 our imports exceeded our exports by about £133 millions, and for 1908 the excess will again be about £133 millions, against £183 millions in 1903. We calculate that we have remitted about £100,000,000 of capital to other countries in the past twelve months, and that we shall send about as much in 1909. Of the £203 millions of new capital our investors have subscribed in 1908, £55 millions was for the British Government and for British Municipal Corporations, railways, and industrial companies, and £148 millions was for Indian, Colonial, and foreign enterprise. These are the amounts calculated at the prices of issue. In 1907 the amounts of capital subscribed for home enterprises was £37 millions, and for Indian, Colonial, and foreign about £90 millions. The amounts of capital subscribed in the British market for home and foreign enterprises in 1907 and 1908 are set out in Table A.

We would point out that the public subscriptions for home enterprises represent only a portion of the total amount of capital raised for these purposes. Of course, it is as yet impossible to ascertain the vast amount of capital that merchants, shipbuilders, traders and others have privately expended, but there can be no doubt that the amount has been large.

With respect to the British Government loan of £4,475,000, the amount realised from the loan, we would point out that this was not a new expenditure of capital. It was raised to enable the Irish farmers to acquire land from landlords and was merely a transference of wealth, and ought, therefore, to be ignored. On the other hand, we would note that the new capital fund of the nation in the past year has been enhanced by the action of the Government in devoting about £15 millions to the redemption of Government debt.

The amount of capital we have raised for Indian and Colonial and foreign countries has been about £148 millions. Of this sum £39 millions was invested in Government loans, £9 millions in Corporation stocks, and £63 millions in railways. A very large part of the Government loans were also for railway purposes. If allowance be made for the Government expenditures upon railways Great Britain has in 1908 provided nearly £90 millions sterling for railway construction in other countries. The investment of this stupendous sum upon new railways in our Colonies, in Argentina, in India, in the United States, in Mexico, and elsewhere cannot fail to cause an enormous extension of the area of land devoted to the production of foodstuffs, and cannot fail to bring about that bountiful supply of food upon which the prosperity of this and every other country so largely rests. In the past two years nearly £150 millions of new money has been subscribed in this market for the construction of new railways, either by direct subscriptions to issues of railway capital or by subscriptions to Government loans raised for railway purposes. When we realise the effect upon prices of food-stuffs of our failure to provide any appreciable amount of new capital for railway construction in the 10 years ended with 1904, we shall realise the beneficial effect in the future upon prices of food-stuffs and upon the general prosperity of our ability and of our willingness to provide the capital so urgently required for railway construction in the new countries. The fact that Great Britain has resumed the policy which it has pursued so profitably of providing the world with the capital it needs for the development of its wealth ensures the continued remarkable growth in our own wealth, in our commerce, in our population, and in our prosperity which we have enjoyed for three generations.

Below we set out in greater detail particulars of capital we have subscribed for other countries in 1908 and 1907.

Table B.—Capital Subscribed (a) by Great Britain for Indian, Colonial & Foreign Countries in 1907 & 1908.

	Year 1908. £	Year 1907. £
GOVERNMENT SECURITIES—		
Foreign:		
Brazil	9,125,000	3,415,000
China	5,031,125	2,150,000
Greece	194,000	Nil
Liberia	101,000	Nil
Russia	1,112,812	Nil
Salvador	860,000	Nil
Siam	Nil	1,102,500
Sweden	2,940,000	Nil
Switzerland	Nil	663,267
Total Foreign	**19,363,937**	**[c]7,330,767**
India	**4,950,000**	**3,447,500**
Colonial:		
Canada	6,343,760[b]	1,500,000
Cape of Good Hope	2,454,354	3,864,633
Natal	477,500	688,750
New South Wales	1,500,000	Nil
South Nigeria	3,000,000	Nil
Straits Settlements	Nil	4,950,000
Tasmania	197,000	Nil
Western Australia	970,000	970,000
Total Colonial	**[b]14,942,614**	**11,973,383**
Total Government Securities ...	**[b]39,256,551**	**[c]22,751,650**
CORPORATION STOCKS—		
Foreign:		
Brazil	731,200	Nil
Denmark	2,101,000	Nil
Japan	Nil	313,830
Russia	1,653,312	Nil
Total Foreign	**4,485,512**	**313,830**
Colonial:		
Canada	3,844,688	689,902
Cape of Good Hope	144,000	89,280
Natal	Nil	285,000
New Zealand	590,717	202,000
Orange River Colony	73,500	170,550
Total Colonial	**4,652,905**	**1,436,732**
Total Corporation Stocks ...	**9,138,417**	**1,750,562**
RAILWAYS—		
Foreign:		
Argentina	13,257,090	9,802,750
Brazil	179,380	800,000
Chili	1,102,285	1,472,500
Colombia	601,695	Nil
Cuba	Nil	1,036,000
Japan	3,910,000	3,880,000
Mexico	3,443,968	Nil
Paraguay	186,900	Nil
Philippines	1,819,393	Nil
Turkey	204,800	Nil
United States	17,099,123	13,568,305
Uruguay	540,000	400,000
Total Foreign Railways ...	**42,344,634**	**30,959,555**
India	**6,894,250**	**2,200,000**
Colonial (Canadian)	**14,335,776**	**2,978,665**
Total Railways	**63,574,660**	**36,138,220**
Total Government, Corporation and Railways	**[b]111,969,628**	**[c]60,640,432**
MISCELLANEOUS—		
Banks	2,822,500	5,459,333
Breweries and Distilleries	120,000	47,120
Canals and Docks	1,102,200	Nil
Commercial, Industrial, &c.	5,985,892	2,654,161
Electric Lighting and Power ...	1,220,271	959,169
Financial Land, Invest. and Trust ...	11,092,754	2,645,780
Gas and Water	1,220,938	435,000
Insurance	Nil	Nil
Iron, Coal, Steel and Engineering ...	954,496	514,597
Mines	5,395,199	3,540,762
Motor Traction and Manufacturing ...	58,000	337,000
Nitrate	215,700	370,250
Shipping	976,000	450,000
Tea, Coffee and Rubber	830,012	1,486,670
Telegraphs and Telephones	150,000	7,940,000
Tramways	3,853,781	1,739,402
Total Miscellaneous	**36,007,588**	**28,579,244**
Total Capital Subscribed for Foreign, Indian & Colonial Countries ...	**147,977,216**	**89,219,676**

(a) Amount calculated at the prices of issue, and exclusive of loans raised to repay former loans.

(b) Exclusive of £7,370,500 raised by Canada in 1908 to repay previous loans.

(c) Exclusive of Conversion loans as follows: Japan Five per Cent., £11,412,500; Argentine Five per Cent., £2,515,500.

GREAT BRITAIN'S CAPITAL INVESTMENTS IN OTHER LANDS

George Paish

Vol. LXXII.] [Part III.

JOURNAL

OF THE ROYAL STATISTICAL SOCIETY.

SEPTEMBER, 1909.

Great Britain's Capital Investments *in* Other Lands.

By George Paish.

[Read before the Royal Statistical Society, 15th June, 1909.
The Rt. Hon. Sir Charles W. Dilke, Bart., M.P., President, in the Chair.]

For some years past unusual attention has been paid to questions concerning the extent of the nation's wealth, the amount of the national income and the sources from which that income is derived. The discussions of these questions have brought into prominence the relatively meagre amount of information available concerning them. Fortunately we have one source of information of great value—the incomes assessed to income tax. From this datum it is possible to calculate with a fair degree of accuracy the extent of the national wealth, its growth from period to period and the income derived therefrom.

Information about incomes assessed to income tax is, as you all know, contained in the Report of the Commissioners of Inland Revenue. This document is of such great value to students of the progress of the nation that those of us who constantly study its pages desire to see the data contained therein greatly amplified. One of the objects of this paper is to indicate one direction in which the information could be extended without difficulty and with great advantage.

The investors of this country have, during the past three centuries, placed several thousand millions of capital in other lands, and the capital thus placed abroad yields a great annual income to the country. The Commissioners of Inland Revenue recognise the importance of the matter, and set out in detail the amount of income derived from certain of our capital investments in other lands; but their statement is far from comprehensive, and it is with the double object of drawing attention to the matter and of endeavouring to give a more complete statement that I have undertaken to read this paper.

The Commissioners give particulars of the income which our investors draw from their holdings in government bonds—Indian, colonial and foreign. Their statement is an interesting one and I append it below :—

Income of British investors from capital lent to Indian, colonial and foreign governments.

Countries, etc.	Amount of dividends and annuities charged to Income Tax.
Indian :—	£
India Government stocks and loans	4,204,278
Indian Guaranteed Railways	4,531,871
Bettiah Raj and other similar State loans	32,088
Total—Indian	8,768,237
Colonial, &c., viz.—	
Antigua	4,134
Bahamas	1,662
Barbados	13,352
British Guiana	19,762
British Honduras	1,305
Canada	1,487,744
Cape Colony	1,462,122
Ceylon	155,243
Dominica	2,475
Fiji	3,623
Gold Coast	26,422
Grenada	4,947
Hong Kong	87,936
Isle of Man	8,189
Jamaica	103,128
Lagos	69,536
Mauritius	45,942
Montserrat	425
Natal	679,930
Newfoundland	138,130
New South Wales	2,266,480
New Zealand	1,829,719
Queensland	1,281,719
St. Kitts	2,716
St. Lucia	6,808
Sierra Leone	46,144
South Australia	863,543
Straits Settlements	3,062
Tasmania	294,768
Transvaal	906,836
Trinidad	87,870
Victoria	1,609,387
West Australia	514,663
Zanzibar	3,000
Total—Colonial	13,932,722

Countries, etc.	Amount of dividends and annuities charged to Income Tax.
Foreign, viz.:—	
Europe :	£
Austria-Hungary	74,171
Belgium	385
Bulgaria	30,266
Denmark	28,432
Germany	44,541
Greece	139,425
Italy	124,927
Netherlands	3,797
Norway	44,410
Portugal	40,075
Russia	429,908
Servia	686
Spain	75,402
Sweden	76,913
Switzerland	1,392
Turkey	353,125
Total—Europe	1,467,855
Asia—	
China	869,004
Japan	1,617,361
Siam	30,228
Total—Asia	2,516,593
Africa—	
Egypt	507,504
Liberia	3,245
Total—Africa	510,749
America—	
Argentine Republic	1,357 563
Brazil	992,410
Chili	614,811
Colombia	66,485
Costa Rica	383
Cuba	59,191
Ecuador	2,071
Guatemala	238
Mexico	294,331
Nicaragua	9,171
Paraguay	8,623
Peru	1,596
Salvador	36
Uruguay	372,185
Venezuela	63,833
Total—America	3,842,927
„ —Foreign	8,338,124

SUMMARY.	£
Indian	8,768,237
Colonial	13,932,722
Foreign	8,338,124
TOTAL	31,039,083

A supplementary table showing in a condensed form the assessments on the income from Indian, colonial, and foreign Government securities is also given in the report of the Commissioners.

Year.	Indian.	Colonial.	European.	Asiatic.
	£	£	£	£
1897-98	8,168,258	10,812,176	1,563,344	728,595
'98-99	8,258,820	11,079,341	1,675,417	1,003,911
'99-1900	8,281,704	11,275,965	1,689,960	1,226,803
1900-01	8,567,639	11,529,608	1,613,042	1,333,100
'01-02	8,880,908	11,832,716	1,552,083	1,304,208
'02-03	9,018,777	12,369,514	1,486,178	1,324,585
'03-04	8,695,929	12,869,426	1,435,232	1,445,560
'04-05	8,760,185	13,553,540	1,324,476	1,651,687
'05-06	8,862,807	13,906,601	1,307,106	2,454,268
'06-07	8,768,237	13,932,722	1,467,855	2,516,593

Year.	African.	American.	Total.
	£	£	£
1897-98	691,360	3,410,459	25,374,192
'98-99	703,621	3,771,139	26,492,249
'99-1900	736,435	3,465,227	26,676,094
1900-01	655,477	3,554,183	27,253,049
'01-02	631,003	3,925,878	28,126,796
'02-03	620,598	4,134,768	28,984,420
'03-04	579,331	3,933,523	28,959,001
'04-05	574,054	3,777,080	29,641,022
'05-06	541,986	3,859,299	30,932,067
'06-07	510,749	3,842,927	31,039,083

Thus the British people are receiving an income of upwards of 31,000,000*l.* a year from their loans to Indian, colonial, and foreign governments. The income from this source has rapidly expanded in recent years in consequence mainly of new loans to our colonies and to our ally Japan. It will be noted that our investments in the loans of continental countries are tending to decline. This tendency may be checked if events cause the British market for capital to be again opened freely to Russian borrowings. That country needs to raise capital from year to year for the extension of its railway system.

Beyond setting out the income derived from loans to the Indian, the colonial and foreign governments, the Commissioners of Inland Revenue ascertain and set out the income we derive from—

(1.) "Indian, colonial and foreign securities,"

(2.) "From coupons,"

(3.) "From railways out of the United Kingdom."

The income from the first of these is 16,017,000*l*, from the second 13,767,000*l*., and from the third 18,736,000*l*., making a total of 48,521,000*l*.

The Commissioners add this income to that received from Government loans, and summarise the whole as follows:—

	£
Income disclosed by agents for payment of interest on foreign and colonial government securities	31,039,083
Income disclosed by agents for payment of dividends and interest of foreign and colonial companies and corporations	15,568,813
Income disclosed by bankers and coupon dealers in connection with the realisation of foreign and colonial coupons	13,767,315
Income declared by persons, firms, or public companies as received in respect of investments abroad without taxation at the hands of agents, bankers, or coupon dealers	6,947,482
Profits of those railways abroad which are owned and worked by British *companies* with the seat of management in the United Kingdom	12,237,423
Total	79,560,116

Further, the Commissioners compare this total of nearly 80,000,000*l*. with the income received from similar sources in previous years since 1886-87.

Income of British investors from Indian, colonial, and foreign government bonds and stocks; municipal stocks, and railway securities

1	2	3	4	5
Year.	India Government stocks, loans, and guaranteed railways.	Colonial and foreign Government securities.	Colonial and foreign securities (*other* than Government) and possessions, "coupons" and railways out of the United Kingdom, other than those included in column 2.	Total.
	£	£	£	£
1886-87	7,793,097	16,243,321	20,471,584	44,508,002
'87-88	7,972,606	16,757,736	22,248,029	46,978,371
'88-89	8,026,310	17,388,562	24,584,936	49,999,808
'89-90	7,811,310	17,528,582	26,970,320	52,310,212
'90-91	8,028,524	16,608,700	30,851,608	55,488,832
'91-92	7,784,370	14,949,017	31,995,383	54,728,770
'92-93	7,790,642	15,333,817	32,046,043	55,170,502
'93-94	7,856,721	15,950,233	31,311,075	55,118,029
'94-95	8,021,797	15,927,769	29,556,692	53,506,258
'95-96	8,019,720	16,419,933	30,461,426	54,901,079
'96-97	8,065,866	16,790,472	31,462,629	56,318,967
'97-98	8,168,258	17,205,934	31,265,474	56,639,666
'98-99	8,258,820	18,233,429	33,217,654	59,709,903
'99-1900	8,281,704	18,394,390	33,590,792	60,266,886
1900-01	8,567,639	18,685,410	33,078,476	60,331,525
'01-02	8,880,908	19,245,888	34,432,683	62,559,479
'02-03	9,048,777	19,935,643	34,844,295	63,828,715
'03-04	8,695,929	20,263,072	36,906,305	65,865,306
'04-05	8,760,185	20,880,837	36,421,087	66,062,109
'05-06	8,862,807	22,069,260	42,967,198	73,899,265
'06-07	8,768,237	22,270,816	48,521,033	79,560,116

The Commissioners are careful to point out that this income from capital invested abroad is by no means the total received. They say:

"Beyond this earmarked figure there exists a large amount of "income from abroad which in many cases cannot (in the absence of "details which the taxpayer alone could furnish) be identified as such "in the assessments and which is therefore included in the sum of "373,057,495*l.* appearing under the head of 'Businesses, profes- "sions, &c., not otherwise detailed.' The fact that this unidentified "income from foreign countries and British colonies and possessions "is of some magnitude will be appreciated when it is considered that "it includes the profits derived from the following sources":—

"Concerns (other than railways) situate abroad but having their "seat of direction and management in this country, *e.g.*, mines, gas- "works, waterworks, tramways, breweries, tea and coffee plantations, "nitrate grounds, oil fields, land and financial companies, &c."

"Concerns jointly worked abroad and in this country, such as "electric telegraph cables, and shipping."

"Foreign and colonial branches of banks, insurance companies, "and mercantile houses in the United Kingdom."

"Mortgages of property and other loans and deposits abroad "belonging to banks, insurance companies, land, mortgage and "financial companies, &c., in this country."

"Profits of all kinds arising from business done abroad by "manufacturers, merchants, and commission agents resident in the "United Kingdom."

In brief, the income which the Commissioners earmark as coming from abroad is that received from Indian, colonial and foreign government stocks, municipal securities and railways, and the great additional income the country derives from its investments in a vast number of miscellaneous undertakings of all kinds is excluded.

Before proceeding farther, may I digress for one moment in order to direct your attention to the expansion in the income from capital invested abroad that is earmarked by the Commissioners? I have already indicated the governments to which we have lent large sums in recent years. The income contained in column 4 of the foregoing tabular statement is derived partly from municipal stocks and partly from railways, chiefly the latter, and the immense expansion has arisen mainly from the very large amounts of capital we invested in the railway undertakings of the United States, of Argentina, of Canada, of Mexico and of other countries in the eighties and early nineties. A great deal of the capital we then placed abroad was for several years relatively unproductive in consequence of the severe trade depression in the new countries during the nineties. The expansion in trade of recent years, especially in the agricultural countries, has brought with it large profits for the railways and a greatly increased income for the investors of this country. You will recollect that a few years ago many of the railways of the United States, of Canada and of Argentina and of other countries paid no dividends whatever on their share capitals and that in recent years many of these railways have paid dividends of 7 per cent.—hence the great expansion in income we have derived. In a small degree the expansion in the income shown to have occurred in 1905 and 1906 was the result of fresh investments of capital, a new period of active investment of British capital in other lands having commenced in the summer of 1904.

To return.—It is impossible for anyone to ascertain the income from the capital our merchants, our manufacturers, and others have privately placed abroad, but it is possible to collect a great deal of information in addition to that compiled by the Commissioners.

There are several thousand public companies operating abroad that have raised capital publicly in this country, and these companies issue statements of their capital and of their profits.

To amplify the statement of the Commissioners, I have obtained the reports of as many of these companies as it is possible for a private person to secure. I have classified them, and have ascertained the amount of their capital and of their profits in the aggregate and by groups.

Further, I have sought to analyse the income of 79,000,000*l.* which the Commissioners have earmarked, in order to obtain a comprehensive picture both of the sources of the income we receive and of the capital publicly subscribed in this country for investment in other lands.

I will now set out the results of my investigations as regards income, and will leave the question of the amount of capital we have embarked abroad to a later stage, in order not to create confusion.

The income derived from Indian government loans issued and held in this country is 5,017,000*l.*, from colonial government loans 13,933,000*l.*, from foreign government loans 8,338,000*l.*

Beyond lending to governments, we have lent large sums to municipalities. Our income from this source is 2,500,000*l.*, of which 1,500,000*l.* is derived from colonial and 1,000,000*l.* from foreign cities. The latter include a number of South American municipalities growing rapidly in population, notably Rio de Janeiro, Buenos Ayres, Montevideo, Rosario and Santa Fé. We have also lent money to several cities in the United States, to the city of Mexico and to several Japanese towns.

In providing capital for railway construction this country has performed a great work. Most of the loans to colonial governments have been for railway construction, the major part of India's indebtedness to us is for railways, and a portion of the loans we have made to foreign governments has been used for a similar purpose. But beyond the money for railway construction which we have supplied to governments, we have formed a great many companies to construct and work railways in other lands.

From the capital we have supplied to railway companies working in the colonies, notably in Canada, we receive an income of 7,600,000*l.* a year, from those working in India we derive nearly 4,800,000*l.* per annum. The railways of Argentina, Brazil, Uruguay, Mexico, Chili and other foreign countries yield over 13,000,000*l.* a year to us in the aggregate, and from the railways of the United States our investors receive no less than 27,000,000*l.* a year.

The aggregate of these totals which I have compiled from the companies' reports and as far as possible from independent investigations amounts to 82,777,000*l.*, and slightly exceeds the sum of 79,560,000*l.* returned by the Commissioners of Inland Revenue.

This brings me to the great income we derive from the vast number of miscellaneous companies for which we have provided capital and which largely contribute to the production of the world's supplies of natural wealth. I have taken out the income of 2,172 of the miscellaneous companies the capital of which has been supplied by our investors and I have ascertained the great income that comes to this country for interest and profit upon this capital. The income we derive from capital invested in colonial and foreign banking companies is over 7,000,000*l.* The major portion of this comes from banks doing business in India and the colonies, but a substantial income comes from banks operating in Egypt, China, South America and Mexico.

Breweries and distilleries yield an annual income of only 732,000*l.* a year—an insignificant sum having regard to the amount of capital invested. Our investors appear to have burnt their fingers rather badly in the prices they paid for foreign breweries.

In consequence mainly of the Treasury investment in the shares of the Suez Canal Company, the income from canals and docks situated abroad reaches 1,174,000*l.* a year.

Commercial and industrial companies yield an income of nearly 5,000,000*l.* a year. It must not be supposed that this income is derived from manufacturing firms competing with British traders. One of the most noteworthy characteristics of the British investor is his objection to place capital in any enterprise, or in any country for the matter of that, the development of which appears to be against the interests of the Motherland.

From electric lighting and power companies we derive an income of 321,000*l.*

The income received from financial, land and investment companies amounts to over 6,000,000*l.* a year, and will probably show great expansion in future. A large sum of money has been expended upon the acquisition and development of land in various parts of the world which at present gives no return, and the income from this capital has yet to be received. The income from this source is derived as to two-thirds from the colonies, and as to one-third from foreign countries.

Gas companies bring to us an income of nearly 1,200,000*l.*

Colliery and iron ore undertakings yield 500,000*l.* a year. Having regard to the new capital placed in these undertakings in South Africa, in Australia, in India and elsewhere, this source of income should largely expand.

Gold, copper, diamond, silver, lead, tin and other mining enterprises yield an income of nearly 26,000,000*l.* a year. Of this large figure gold mining comes easily first with a return of nearly 15,000,000*l.* a year, copper second with over 5,000,000*l.* a year, diamonds and other precious stones third with 4,400,000*l.* a year, while silver, lead, zinc, tin, &c., produce an income of 1,100,000*l.* In consequence of the new capital embarked in mining companies and which has not yet become productive a large expansion in our income from mining may be looked for.

Nitrate companies yield an income of 1,600,000*l.*

Oil companies produce profits of 642,000*l.* per annum notwithstanding the misfortunes of the Russian oil companies in which a relatively large sum is placed.

Rubber companies give 446,000*l.* a year, a return which will largely increase as the new plantations mature.

Tea and coffee plantation companies, mainly tea, situated in India and Ceylon, yield a profit of 1,794,000*l.* per annum.

Transmarine cable companies and colonial and foreign telephones yield upwards of 2,000,000*l.* a year.

Tramways give an income of 1,809,000*l.*, and waterworks over 400,000*l.* a year.

In the aggregate, British investors receive an income of nearly 58,000,000*l.* from the miscellaneous companies the accounts of which I have analysed. This income is referred to, but is not disclosed by the report of the Commissioners of Inland Revenue.

Thus, if the Commissioners were to bring together all the income of companies trading abroad and distributing interest and profits in this country, the total would be about 140,000,000*l.*

This great sum does not include the interest upon money deposited in Indian, colonial and foreign banks by persons residing in this country, or the large amount of income derived from capital privately placed abroad, amounting to several hundred millions of pounds.

On the other hand, it is essential to recollect that foreign investors draw a good deal of income from capital placed in British companies of one kind and another, and in balancing the account it is essential not to omit this important offset.

I have taken no account of the profit on the capital invested in our mercantile marine. The country's income from shipping is an inquiry of great magnitude and of great importance and one which could not be advantageously dealt with in this paper.

The capital invested.

This brings me to the second stage of my inquiry. How much capital have the British people placed in other lands to yield them their great income of 140,000,000*l.* a year? Two considerations have to be heeded in this matter. The first is that capital, other than that placed in loans, rarely becomes fully productive until several years after it is expended. Indeed, only in recent years has the capital invested in the eighties and nineties yielded its full harvest of interest and profit.

The income received in 1907-08 did not correspond to the capital expended at that time. Probably the corresponding income will not be realised until some time during the decade ending with 1920. By that time the new lines of railway will become self-supporting, new mines will be fully opened up, new rubber plantations will be yielding their harvest, and so on.

The second is that the capital we have sent abroad does not necessarily correspond to the capital possessed by this country in other lands. On the one hand, we sometimes make bad investments, but on the other we more often find very good ones, and on balance the securities purchased ultimately possess a greater value than the price paid for them. A noteworthy instance of this is the nation's purchase of Suez Canal shares. The sum paid for these shares was 4,076,565*l.*, and their current value is 33,730,000*l.* Doubtless many other instances will occur to you. There can be no doubt that in spite of our losses the value of the capital in other lands which the country now possesses is much greater than the capital actually remitted by our investors.

To obtain an income from abroad of nearly 140,000,000*l.* per annum we have invested a sum of about 2,700,000,000*l.*, and this capital is yielding an all round return of 5·2 per cent.

I have no doubt that as soon as the large amount of capital sent out in recent years bears more fruit the annual income from our foreign investments will reach a much greater figure. Indeed, having regard to the investment of capital in Canada, in Argentina, in India, in the United States, and in other lands in the last few years and the additional sums likely to be sent out in the next few years, I look forward to a very rapid growth in our income from interest and profits on capital invested abroad.

The nature of our investments, the capital placed in each group, the income obtained and the yield returned are shown in the statement on p. 475.

Of this total of about 2,700,000,000*l.* nearly 1,700,000,000*l.* has been expended upon railway construction either by companies or by governments which have raised loans in this country for that purpose.

The capital has been supplied in about equal portions to the countries beyond the seas within the British Empire and to foreign lands. The totals are 1,312,000,000*l.* to India and the colonies, and 1,381,000,000*l.* to foreign states, mainly to the United States, to Central and South America, to Japan and to China. The sums invested (1) in India and the colonies, and (2) in foreign countries are shown in the statement on p. 476.

The capital and income contained in the following statements are compiled from reports covering the year 1907, and in some cases the early portion of 1908. Before the close of the current year (1909) the total will probably reach 3,000,000,000*l.*

In the twelve months to June, 1908, the new capital subscribed in this country for India, for the colonies and for foreign countries amounted to 110,000,000*l.* and in the period from 1st July, 1908, to 30th June, 1909, the additional capital subscribed has reached no less than 175,600,000*l.*[1] This makes a total of no less than 286,000,000*l.* subscribed in the last two years.

For a period of enterprise similar to that through which we are now passing, we have to go back to the later eighties, when we were investing vast sums in the Australasian Colonies, in the United States, in Argentina, in India, in Canada, and in other lands. At that time the country was not nearly as wealthy, nor were its annual savings available for investment in securities nearly as great. Nevertheless, in the seven years from 1884 to 1890, inclusive, we placed abroad over 400,000,000*l.* of capital. In the seven years from 1898 to 1904—a period of extravagance and war expenditures in this country—our investments in other lands were not much over 100,000,000*l.* Since 1904 we have been endeavouring to make up for lost time, and in four and a half years we have placed no less than 400,000,000*l.* of new savings in profitable Indian, colonial and foreign securities. There are good prospects that in the seven years from 1905 to 1911 inclusive we shall place new capital in other lands to the extent of at least 700,000,000*l.*, or an average of about 100,000,000*l.* a

[1] Since the Paper was read, the author has brought the amounts of capital raised in 1908-09 up to the end of June, 1909. At the time the Paper was read they were up to 14th June only.

British capital invested in Indian, colonial, and foreign loans and companies, and the income derived therefrom in 1907-08.

	Capital.	Income.	Rate of Interest.
	£	£	Per cent.
Indian government loans, including rupee loans held in England	156,369,000	5,017,000	3·21
Colonial and provincial government loans	375,190,000	13,933,000	3·71
Foreign government loans	167,000,000	8,338,000	4·75
Colonial and foreign municipal stocks	58,901,000	2,650,000	4·5
Indian railways	123,341,000	4,774,000	3·87
Colonial railways	188,950,000	7,598,000	4·0
American railways	600,000,000	27,000,000	4·5
Foreign railways	286,700,000	13,467,000	4·7
Banks	54,101,000	7,353,000	13·6
Breweries and distilleries	17,205,000	732,000	4·2
Canals and docks	5,974,000	1,174,000	19·6
Commercial, industrial, &c.	77,610,000	4,863,000	6·3
Electric lighting and power	7,686,000	321,000	4·2
Financial, land and investment	187,027,000	6,233,000	3 3
Gas	16,419,000	1,194,000	7·3
Mines—			
Coal and iron ore	12,956,000	505,000	3·9
Copper	38,525,000	5,074,000	13·2
Diamonds and other stones	14,646,000	4,468,000	30·5
Gold	161,178,000	14,947,000	9·3
Silver, lead, and zinc	10,513,000	843,000	8·0
Tin and miscellaneous	5,568,000	308,000	5·5
Nitrate	10,903,000	1,637,000	15·0
Oil	14,268,000	642,000	4·5
Rubber	5,433,000	446,000	8·2
Tea and coffee	21,399,000	1,794,000	8·4
Telegraphs and telephones	34,235.000	2,233,000	6·5
Tramways	35,289,000	1,809,000	5·1
Waterworks	6,352,000	438,000	6·9
Total	2,693,738,000	139,791,000	5·2

Great Britain's investments of capital in India and the colonies and in foreign countries. (*End* 1907.)

	India and the Colonies.	Foreign countries.	Total.
	£	£	£
Government loans	531,559,000	167,000,000	698,559,000
Municipal stocks	34,387,000	24,514,000	58,901,000
Railways	312,291,000	886,700,000	1,198,991,000
Banks	33,621,000	20,480,000	54,101,000
Breweries and distilleries	3,955,000	13,250,000	17,205,000
Canals and docks	100,000	5,874,000	5,974,000
Commercial, industrial, &c.	27,526,000	50,084,000	77,610,000
Electric lighting and power	6,461,000	1,225,000	7,686,000
Financial, land, and investment	126,040,000	60,987,000	187,027,000
Gas	3,234,000	13,185,000	16,419,000
Mines—			
Coal and iron ore	8,532,000	4,424,000	12,956,000
Copper	10,781,000	27,744,000	38,525,000
Diamonds and other stones	14,026,000	620,000	14,646,000
Gold	144,008,000	17,170,000	161,178,000
Silver, lead, and zinc	5,081,000	5,432,000	10,513,000
Tin, &c.	2,334,000	3,234,000	5,568,000
Nitrate	—	10,903,000	10,903,000
Oil	3,704,000	10,564,000	14,268,000
Rubber	3,104,000	2,329,000	5,433,000
Tea and coffee	20,765,000	634,000	21,399,000
Telegraphs and telephones	7,371,000	26,864,000	34,235,000
Tramways	11,780,000	23,509,000	35,289,000
Waterworks	1,492,000	4,860,000	6,352,000
Total	1,312,152,000	1,381,586,000	2,693,738,000

year. This amount is rather above the average we can hope to maintain. The great investment of capital now taking place is needed to restore the average which was unfortunately permitted to decline in the ten years which came to an end in 1904.

For the purpose of showing the nature and extent of our colonial and foreign investments since 1st July, 1906, I append the following statement:—

Great Britain's capital investments in other lands since 1st July, 1906.*

	1908-09.†	1907-08.	1906-07.
Government loans—	£	£	£
Indian	7,275,000	4,950,000	3,525,000
Colonial	27,072,615	12,031,269	9,593,383
Foreign	30,492,844	10,638,937	4,860,767
Total	**64,840,459**	**27,620,206**	**17,979,150**
Municipal loans—			
Indian	1,178,500	985,000	Nil
Colonial	4,455,551	3,878,306	745,293
Foreign	8,167,353	4,241,812	1,813,830
Total	**13,801,404**	**9,105,118**	**2,559,123**
Railway companies—			
Indian	5,303,875	6,674,250	400,000
Colonial	7,446,776	10,665,000	4,721,125
Foreign	40,033,278	34,213,311	29,428,120
Total	**52,783,929**	**51,552,561**	**34,549,245**
Miscellaneous—			
Banks	1,220,000	1,602,500	7,194,927
Breweries and distilleries	Nil	167,120	44,800
Canals and docks	450,000	Nil	400,250
Commercial, industrial, &c.	9,343,862	2,639,852	2,468,111
Electric lighting and power	2,403,490	1,629,440	770,000
Financial, land, investment and trust	8,326,204	5,163,144	4,445,671
Gas and water	1,218,822	519,500	280,000
Insurance	Nil	Nil	Nil
Iron, coal and steel	1,521,840	736,050	387,547
Mines	7,951,887	3,634,764	6,752,705
Motor traction and manufacturing	80,000	145,000	502,000
Nitrate	164,700	566,750	790,000
Shipping	405,000	976,000	Nil
Tea, coffee and rubber	1,824,300	1,158,048	1,030,220
Telegraphs and telephones	Nil	150,900	8,286,250
Tramways	9,330,270	2,778,400	972,402
Total	**44,240,375**	**21,866,578**	**34,234,383**
Grand total	**175,666,167**	**110,144,453**	**89,321,901**

* Amount calculated at the price of issue, and exclusive of loans raised to repay former loans.

† Period from 1st July, 1908, to 30th June, 1909.

The members of this Society may also wish to discover the countries in which we are for the moment investing a large portion of our annual savings. To reveal this I have analysed the new issues of capital for other lands placed in the United Kingdom from 1st July, 1908, to 30th June, 1909. I append the statement :—

The countries in which Great Britain has invested capital in the year from 1st July, 1908, to 30th June, 1909.

	Governments.	Municipalities.	Railways.	Other securities.	Total all securities.
India and the colonies.	£	£	£	£	£
Australasia—					
New South Wales	4,417,500	—	—	266,908	**4,684,408**
New Zealand	—	—	—	70,000	**70,000**
Queensland	1,940,000	—	—	145,500	**2,085,500**
South Australia	—	—	—	—	—
Tasmania	197,000	—	—	—	**197,000**
Victoria	1,470,000	—	—	193,000	**1,663,000**
Western Australia	1,394,425	1,222,552	—	127,833	**2,744,810**
Unenumerated Australasia	—	—	—	800,000	**800,000**
Total Australasia	**9,418,925**	**1,222,552**	—	**1,603,241**	**12,244,718**
British East Africa	—	—	—	20,000	**20,000**
British Guinea	—	—	—	—	—
British North Borneo	—	—	—	865,259	**865,259**
Canada	10,846,190	2,506,949	7,446,776	7,661,486	**28,461,401**
Gold Coast	990,000	—	—	317,286	**1,307,286**
India	7,275,000	1,178,500	5,303,875	556,970	**14,314,345**
Jamaica	—	—	—	124,144	**124,144**
Malta	—	—	—	125,000	**125,000**
South Africa—					
Cape Colony	1,500,000	372,550	—	—	**1,872,550**
Natal	477,500	185,000	—	—	**662,500**
Orange River Colony	—	73,500	—	—	**73,500**
Rhodesia	—	—	—	1,580,853	**1,580,853**
Transvaal	3,840,000	95,000	—	4,640,859	**8,575,859**
Unenumerated, South Africa	—	—	—	827,500	**827,500**
Total, South Africa	**5,817,500**	**726,050**	—	**7,049,212**	**13,592,762**
Southern Nigeria	—	—	—	113,040	**113,040**
Straits Settlements	—	—	—	1,126,907	**1,126,907**
Unenumerated colonies	—	—	—	250,000	**250,000**
Total India and the colonies	**34,347,615**	**5,634,051**	**12,750,651**	**19,812,545**	**72,544,862**

The countries in which Great Britain has invested capital—Contd.

	Governments.	Municipalities.	Railways.	Other securities.	Total all securities.
Foreign countries.	£	£	£	£	£
Argentina	3,560,800	—	14,917,090	5,044,926	23,522,816
Belgium	—	—	—	80,000	80,000
Brazil	9,267,138	1,724,700	1,029,380	2,773,479	14,794,697
Bolivia	—	—	—	10,000	10,000
Chili	2,895,000	—	846,000	398,200	4,139,200
China	3,190,000	—	—	—	3,190,000
Colombia	—	—	332,480	739,375	1,071,855
Cuba	—	—	100,000	—	100,000
Denmark	—	487,500	—	43,750	531,250
Dutch East Indies	—	—	—	177,004	177,004
,, West ,,	—	—	—	50,000	50,000
Ecuador	—	—	416,070	—	416,070
Egypt	—	—	—	769,570	769,570
Finland	1,665,000	598,400	—	—	2,263,400
France	—	—	—	335,067	335,067
Germany	—	—	—	47,000	47,000
Japan	—	3,756,353	1,950,000	970,000	6,676,353
Mexico	—	—	7,301,444	5,572,810	12,874,254
Netherlands	—	—	—	125,000	125,000
Nicaragua	460,000	—	—	—	460,000
Norway	—	381,150	—	155,000	536,150
Panama	—	—	—	111,000	111,000
Paraguay	—	—	182,000	—	182,000
Persia	—	—	—	1,200,000	1,200,000
Peru	—	—	—	130,000	130,000
Philippines	—	—	1,819,393	—	1,819,393
Portugal	—	—	—	20,000	20,000
Russia	8,475,525	—	—	1,065,250	9,540,775
Salvador	—	—	36,000	—	36,000
Spain	—	—	—	59,993	59,993
Sweden	—	881,000	—	—	881,000
Turkey	979,381	—	204,800	—	1,184,181
United States	—	338,250	10,358,621	2,937,784	13,634,655
Uruguay	—	—	540,000	158,384	698,384
Venezuela	—	—	—	25,000	25,000
Unenumerated, foreign countries	—	—	—	1,429,238	1,429,238
Total, foreign countries	30,492,844	8,167,353	40,033,278	24,427,830	103,121,305
Grand total	64,840,459	13,801,404	52,783,929	44,240,375	175,666,167

To show at a glance the countries in which we are investing our capital most freely at the present time, I give the following supplementary statement of the amount of capital supplied to our principal borrowers in the year from 1st July, 1908, to 30th June, 1909:—

	£		£
Canada	28,461,401	Mexico	12,874,254
Argentina	23,522,816	Australasia	12,244,718
Brazil	14,794,697	Russia	9,540,775
India	14,314,345	Japan	6,676,353
United States	13,634,655	Chili	4,139,200
South Africa	13,592,762	China	3,190,000

In conclusion, I would direct your attention for one moment to the immense advantages to this country of its investments in other lands. The investment in the last sixty years of about 2,500,000,000*l*. of British capital has occurred simultaneously with a vast growth of British trade and prosperity, and in my opinion this growth of our trade and prosperity is largely the result of our investment of capital in other countries. By building railways for the world, and especially for the young countries, we have enabled the world to increase its production of wealth at a rate never previously witnessed and to produce those things which this country is specially desirous of purchasing—foodstuffs and raw materials. Moreover, by assisting other countries to increase their output of the commodities they were specially fitted to produce, our investors have helped those countries to secure the means of purchasing the goods that Great Britain manufactures. Thus by the investment of capital in other lands we have, first, provided the borrowing countries with the credit which gave them the power to purchase the goods needed for their development, and secondly, enabled them to increase their own productions so largely that they have been able to pay us the interest and profits upon our capital and also to purchase greatly increased quantities of British goods.

The large sums of capital which Great Britain is now supplying to other lands will ensure greatly increased incomes to her own people of all ranks and classes, will widen the Indian, colonial and foreign markets for the goods she manufactures and will greatly assist in providing her dense and constantly growing populations with plentiful supplies of foodstuffs and of raw materials.

DISCUSSION *on* MR. G. PAISH'S PAPER.

MR. EDGAR CRAMMOND said that, working on different lines, but using largely the same data as Mr. Paish, he arrived some three years ago at conclusions almost identical with those now expressed. Mr. Paish stated that he had not allowed for any capital used in the shipping business; and he mentioned also that he had not included the private investments of mercantile and banking houses, which would amount to several hundred millions. If allowance were made for these two items he thought it would be found that he was quite in agreement with Mr. Paish as to the total amount of capital invested abroad and also as to the income therefrom; but there were one or two points upon which he should like to dwell; and the first was the important part investments of capital abroad played in the adjustment of the trade balance of this country. If they took the figures of imports and exports for 1908, they would find that the value of imports, including specie, was 649,600,000*l.*, and the value of exports, including re-exports and specie, was 520,000,000*l.*; showing an excess of imports of 129,500,000*l.* But in considering this question of the trade balance, they would have to take into consideration what had been termed their invisible imports and exports; and to that debit of 129,500,000*l.*, *i.e.*, the excess of imports of commodities and specie over the exports of commodities and specie, they must add the amount of capital invested abroad. Mr. Paish apparently estimated the total capital invested abroad during the past twelve months at 170,000,000*l.*; this seemed to him to be an excessive estimate, and he presumed it must represent the gross total of the nominal amount of capital offered for subscription, and not the actual amount subscribed by British investors.

Mr. PAISH said he did not suggest that that was all sent this year. In many of the loans, the calls were spread over several months.

Mr. CRAMMOND said he thought that about 120,000,000*l.* was an approximate figure for the year 1908, and that sum must be added to the excess of imports of commodities. Two other debit items must be included, namely, the earnings of the foreign banking houses carrying on business in the United Kingdom, and the interest on foreign investments in British, Colonial and Anglo-foreign enterprises, such as railways, mines and so on, which he believed amounted to a very large sum, and consisted of mainly French and German capital. He estimated the total income due to foreigners in respect of the last-named items at 14,000,000*l.* Adding those three items together, namely (*a*) the excess of imports over exports, (*b*) the investment of capital abroad, and (*c*) the earnings of foreign banking and mercantile houses, &c., there was a total debit of 263,500,000*l.* Against that they had to set the income earned by their investments abroad.

Mr. Paish put the income received on a total capital of 2,700,000,000*l.* at 140,000,000*l.*, but it must be borne in mind that this total was exclusive of the money invested through banks, &c., and also of the private investments of individual British subjects abroad. He should venture to estimate the total income from investments abroad at 160,000,000*l.*, and that was the first item to be set off against the debits he had mentioned. Then they must take into account the earnings of the shipping industry, which seven years ago were estimated by Sir Robert Giffen at 80,000,000*l.* Shipping had recently passed through a period of depression; and last year he had assumed the figure to be about 70,000,000*l.* Then they had to add the earnings of their mercantile houses, insurance companies, banks and commission houses carrying on business abroad. There again it was a question of estimate; and he submitted one of 35,000,000*l.* as the annual income accruing to this country in respect of such services. Sir Robert Giffen put it at 25,000,000*l.* in a paper which he wrote seven years ago, but since then the international financial operations transacted through London had increased enormously. Of course this was a very rough attempt at a balance-sheet; but he believed it represented the approximate figures. As a matter of fact, a large part of the income earned by British capital invested abroad was never brought home, but was re-invested in the country from which it was derived; in fact it could not be brought home, or it would starve the undertakings in which it was invested. One of the most important effects of the investment of capital abroad was the purchasing power it gave to foreign countries and the colonies in our markets; and unless they created credits for their colonial and foreign customers in this way, he did not see how they were going to augment their purchasing power in British markets from any other source. If the colonies and foreign countries borrowed from other countries, they must, of necessity, purchase their commodities from those countries in which they borrowed money; and if British capitalists suspended the investment of capital abroad, he believed they would inevitably reduce their export trade to a corresponding extent—namely, by one-fourth. It was however practically certain that this country must go on investing capital abroad, and probably at an accelerated rate, because the enterprises taken up must be extended and adapted to meet the growth of foreign trade, and if they did not provide for such expansion, other countries—Germany and France—would do so. Amongst the advantages of the investment of capital abroad they got stability of income, because, if one part of the world was depressed another was flourishing; and they not only got a more even income but a larger one. The investment of capital abroad provided a field for the employment of the sons of the middle classes as managers of railways, mines, and a great variety of other enterprises; and moreover it gave a great amount of employment in the city of London and other cities for directors, managers, clerks, solicitors and accountants, &c. There was no doubt that on the whole the investment of capital abroad had been beneficial to the trade of this country. But it was desirable that the money sent abroad should continue to be controlled by British companies; that was to say, that it should be under the direct control of companies, the head offices of which were situated in this country. Germany had built up her great export trade, largely by investing capital abroad—he believed the total amount of German capital invested abroad amounted to upwards of 1,500,000,000*l.*; and France also had appreciated the benefits to be derived from the investment of a portion of her capital in foreign countries, and had invested about 1,600,000,000*l.* in this manner.

Mr. HENRY BEAUMONT said this was a question in which for some years he had taken a very deep interest, and he felt very grateful to Mr. Paish for such an elaborate paper with such excellent statistics, the circulation of which would do a great deal of good, set people thinking on this question, and put a great many right who hitherto had been very wrong. He thought Mr. Paish had rather underestimated the amount of foreign investments, and that they might be safely put at 3,500,000,000*l.*, not including shipping. The very fact that these investments abroad brought in a total of 140,000,000*l.* of income to this country proved that contention, because they had a vast amount of money invested which was not bringing in any interest at all. He had taken an interest in this question owing to the teaching of a certain school of politicians who had made some very alarming statements with regard to the tremendous increase which had been going on in the last few years in capital investment abroad, and arrived at the conclusion that because the Government return had gone up about six to eight millions in two or three years, that amount, capitalised at 5 per cent., showed the increase in such investments. Sir Joseph Lawrence wrote a long letter to *The Times* in March trying to prove that conclusion. He (Mr. Beaumont) had tried to show that this tremendous increase in income was due to other reasons; not only to the increase in investments abroad, but also to a better collection of the tax and to the much larger dividends received from foreign investments. Going into this rather carefully, he found one or two remarkable instances of this increase. In 1896 they were receiving from investments in the Transvaal an income of 1,600,000*l.*, whereas last year the income had risen to 8,753,000*l.*, and very likely this year it would reach 10,000,000*l.* It would not be right to capitalise the difference on the 5 per cent. basis. The chief reason for the difference was the increasing profit to investors, and in this instance had nothing whatever to do with further capital outlay. Again there had been an enormous increase in the income derived from American investments in the last ten years. In 1896 the Canadian Pacific paid 3 per cent.; in 1908, 7 per cent.; the Grand Trunk of Canada, first and second preference, nil; last year, 5 per cent.; and many other instances could be given to a similar effect. That had not only happened in America, but also very largely in Argentina. It was quite likely that this increasing investment abroad was having a different effect on the trade of this country from what it had many years ago. In the case of a new country, if they lent it money, the whole of the money would have to go out to that country in commodities for building railways, or whatever they were doing, and the effect on the trade of the country lending that money was very great. Take the case of Argentina, which had to remit to this country every year about 15,000,000*l.* for interest on money lent to her. Argentina was continually in the market borrowing; hardly a month passed that she was not borrowing money for railways and other purposes. The result was that the loan acted as a set-off to the interest due, and nothing happened. The money was left by the investor here, but it remained here against the remittances which Argentina would otherwise have to send. There was a marked difference, therefore, between the effect of money invested abroad at the present day and ten or fifteen years ago, when that and other countries were not in such conditions of prosperity. He hoped the figures Mr. Paish had given would be published, and that some of the foolish ideas which had gathered round the question would be dissipated. After all, it was a grand thing for the country, for capitalists, and for everybody concerned, to have largely increasing investments in foreign countries.

Mr. C. ROZENRAAD (President of the Federation of Foreign Chambers of Commerce), said that the author had done good work in bringing forward this question. It was of the highest importance for every country to possess a large amount of foreign securities, and especially for England, so as to make up the difference between the imports and exports by freights, commissions, insurance premiums, and also by the interest on foreign securities. But when the author gave the amount of 2,700,000,000*l.* of British capital invested in Indian, Colonial and foreign loans, he surely made a mistake. What were the facts? Many of these loans were issued not only here, but at the same time in Paris, Amsterdam, Berlin, &c. Besides, as soon as any loan of importance is issued here, thousands of banks, bankers' brokers and other intermediaries, send the prospectus abroad, recommending the loan to their clients, who send in their subscriptions or ask their correspondents in London to subscribe to the loan for their account, and it may safely be said that a considerable amount of the different Colonial and foreign loans introduced on the London market have found their way to the Continent. When, for instance, it was said that England had invested 600,000,000*l.* in American railways, he thought that was a mistake. They were only issued here, America being in constant relations with the English money market, having sent in subscriptions here. As to France, in view of the internal situation in that country (he had just returned from Paris, where some people think that the situation is not altogether *couleur de rose*) the French rentiers invest their money in foreign securities, and Paris, where money is generally cheaper than in London, is now the principal market for international securities. According to the *Journal Officiel* of 25th September, 1902, France had already invested at that date 1,190,000,000*l.* in foreign securities, and since then this amount has been increased, at least by another 500,000,000*l.*, of

Central and South American securities, bought principally on the London market. He must question also the statement that England had invested 161,000,000*l.* in gold mines. That amount had been issued here, but had to a great extent been taken up by the French public; also by South Germany. He did not deny that the investing power of Great Britain was very great, but he did not think that the figures given by Mr. Paish could be given as representing only Great Britain's investments. It had been said that Argentina was borrowing constantly, which is true. At the end of January, 1909, 716,000,000*l.* of British capital was invested in the various Republics of South and Central America, as quoted on the London Stock Exchange, but how many millions of this amount, how many shares in Argentine, Brazilian, Peruvian and other companies, which have their head offices in London, are now in the hands of foreigners? Great Britain acts only for these loans as intermediary, as honest broker working in all parts of the world, taking over—to a great extent with the money of her customers—the loans of other nations, and is thus able to make handsome profits in the way of commissions on the loans themselves and on the payment of the coupons, rate of exchange, &c., and to give large orders to British industry, when the proceeds of these loans serve to construct railways, harbours, canals, &c., abroad, or to build ships for foreign account. As stated before, Paris is now the principal market for international securities. Formerly England used to hold considerable amounts of European government bonds. Now every broker on the Stock Exchange will tell you that she holds only relatively small amounts of Italian, Spanish, German, Austrian, Dutch and other European stocks, so that she would eventually not even be able to procure a large sum of gold by sales on the continent of European securities. Formerly England was the principal holder of American railway shares and railway bonds. Now France, Germany, Holland, Switzerland, &c., are largely interested in these shares and bonds, as well as in Japanese and Chinese securities which they bought in London or which they took over, direct, without the intervention of England. In a word, although the investment power of Great Britain is very great, London is the principal intermediary between Europe and other parts of the world for the placing abroad of foreign securities issued here.

Sir Richard B. Martin said he did not quite understand what the author meant by the statement on page 470 as to the large amount of income derived from "capital privately placed abroad." Did it mean mills built, and things of that kind?

The President said one instance would be the case of landowners who had land in Argentina not through a company, but who managed it themselves, the interest being remitted to this country.

Mr. Paish: And money invested through mercantile and banking houses.

Sir R. B. MARTIN said he should not have thought the capital derived from those sources of income amounted to the very considerable sum mentioned. The tendency lately with regard to enterprises abroad had been to turn them into companies. He had a case himself of a property in the West Indies which some years ago was made into a company for the sake of convenience. He was rather surprised that on page 466 France did not appear as a country in which investments were made. Probably not very much French stock was now held in this country, but there was a certain amount held, as also were French railway bonds. At one time his bank held a considerable amount both of French rentes and also railway bonds. In fact, originally the French railways were subscribed for in England. Only the other day he accidentally turned up the original prospectus of the "Western of France," for which subscriptions were invited in England. Again, why was not the United States included among the capital lent to "Indian, Colonial, and foreign securities." The whole paper was extremely interesting, but required a great deal of careful consideration before it was possible to criticise it usefully.

The PRESIDENT said he should like to say a word or two, although he had no original sources of information on the subject except those which came to him acting in connection with the Income Tax Committee. Since the sitting of that Committee he had read everything which had been written on the subject, and made as careful a consideration of the different estimates as he could, and checked Mr. Crammond's and Mr. Beaumont's papers and those in the *Economist* and *Statist* by asking questions of the people most likely to know in the various departments of various countries, and also as regards the colonies, through colonial houses and Agents-General. Trying to put the various estimates together, it was very striking to find that though there were great apparent discrepancies at first sight between the details, the total estimates generally came very close to one another. Even before he had the advantage of reading this paper, which was fuller than any other single source of information, he had already derived from these almost conflicting sources of information the figure of 3¼ thousand millions, excluding shipping, and that figure was really absolutely confirmed as the figure of the present day by Mr. Paish's 3 thousand millions at which he ultimately arrived. The details varied in the most singular way. For example, Canada varied the most, and he had totally failed to explain the great discrepancies there were in that case, the estimates varying far more both absolutely and proportionally than in any other case. He imagined it was what they also saw in the case of Argentina. The men in Argentina—engineers, and so on—had made their money in Argentina, but they went to Paraguay and Uruguay, next door, to invest it. They knew more about these newer countries than we did. Also in the case of Canada there was an enormous amount of practical investment on a small scale by citizens of the United States. The largest immigration into Canada last year was American, and it was accompanied by capital, and probably by a great deal of investment.

besides the capital actually brought in by the 42,000 Americans who went there to farm. But while the details differed in this way, there was the great fact that there was an enormous income in this country, far larger than the returns at first sight disclosed, drawn from foreign investments, and the greater portion of which paid taxes in this country. The portion about which there was doubt was the income of businesses which had operations in all parts of the world, where it was very difficult to say what portion was receivable in this country, and therefore liable to taxation. There were also private investments, one form of which was through companies or agents, but not as the money of companies having the income-tax deducted at the source. There were many colonial companies who acted as agents for private owners of land, and therefore that money did not come through the company and the income-tax was not deducted. There were details of this kind of great interest which might throw light on this subject if pursued. He imagined that stockbrokers must have a great deal of knowledge, outside anything which could be obtained from the returns, from what was placed before them as regards sales, for instance between English and French holders of various classes of securities. Again, taking a case like investments in tea, the figures in the paper did not look as if they were right. The author would probably feel that the dates and additions did not seem to quite correspond with the facts. Notoriously the Java tea trade, which was increasing very much, was run by British capital, not Dutch; and, notoriously, the Siberian butter companies, which were doing an enormous trade, were financed by Anglo-Danish capital—he presumed, English capital passing through Denmark. The deductions drawn from this paper got so near to the edge of what might be called a political discussion that he had listened to every speaker with a certain doubt whether he ought not to interfere; but he hoped he did right in not interfering, because everything said had been defensible from the point of view of the Society, though it had all rather tended in one direction. He was anxious that the other side, if it could be kept to statistics, should be put, but he feared that here he might be trenching on dangerous ground. There was an extraordinary agreement of view, which confirmed his own impression, as to the beneficial effect on trade of large foreign investments. But he did not think that was universally the case; it was impossible to contest the view put forward by other writers that there were cases in different directions which told both ways. For instance, how far had France benefited by her 500 millions of investment in Russia? It had not been a successful class of investment on the whole; it was 500 millions some years ago, and it had remained stationary, though now tending to increase, and the beneficial result had not been discernable. France, in proportion to her wealth, had probably a larger amount of foreign investments than we had. At all events she invested more largely in Continental securities in Spain, Portugal, Italy, Russia, Austria-Hungary and the southern Slavonic countries and Turkey. They had had no light thrown to-day on German foreign investment in countries where it existed, but Mr. Rozenraad got on to the edge of the subject, and he understood him to suggest that German capital was going largely to South America. If they watched the exact accord between the increase in recent investment in South American countries and trade, they would find that our trade had kept pace, and had been proportional to the increase in our investments. The great increase in our foreign investments of late had been in Mexico, Argentina and Brazil, and if they watched the trade figures there, they would find that those were the countries in which our trade had either grown very rapidly as against that of our rivals, as in Mexico, or in which it had remained stationary in proportion as against that of the United States and Germany. In the case of Brazil and Mexico the figures were most encouraging to our trade, and in Argentina the proportion had been fairly kept, in the last few years. The cases were all different, because in Mexico the Americans owned the railways and great numbers of concerns, yet England had the most trade. The Americans had rather lost their trade in Mexico, although they were next door. In the case of Argentina we owned nearly all the railways, yet our position there was more stationary. Still we had continuously kept such an enormous bulk of trade that substantially no one else existed. He was not going to venture on the dangerous ground of the banks, which were alluded to in the paper, and which he did not understand. There were great corporations in the position of the Credit Lyonnais which did business in all parts of the world, but it was beyond his competence to deal with them. The shipping profits had been very variously estimated, and no doubt they varied from time to time; but the amount of capital invested in shipping was much more accurately ascertainable, though it was outside the present paper. In conclusion, he must express his warm thanks to Mr. Paish for the light he had thrown on the subject. The main fact which came out—though there was a great deal of guess-work in all figures of this sort—was that the flow of investment in the case of a rich country was naturally fairly steady; that the large increase in foreign investment in the last few years had not been altogether abnormal, as there had been one period of greater investment proportionately at an earlier time; and that there was no reason why they should regard it as anything but the natural flow of capital where they got on the whole the best return, and it did not present any dangerous features or prevent the subscription of capital for home industries. This was the main doctrine, and that it led to the large purchases of our goods he did not think anybody would doubt who looked at the recent statistics concerning Mexico and Brazil. Without wishing to stop the discussion, he would propose a hearty vote of thanks to Mr. Paish.

Sir J. ATHELSTANE BAINES seconded the vote of thanks.

Sir NATHANIEL NATHAN, K.C., asked how Mr. Paish discriminated, with regard to the holdings in companies or other undertakings which he described as a means of investment of British capital abroad, between those shares and interests which were held in this country, and those which were held either directly by or on behalf of investors in other countries? How was he able to say that so much British capital, bringing in its interest or dividends here, was invested, as distinguished from, say, capital either in British or in other companies held by foreigners? Again, there was the counter question, to what extent was it possible to estimate the British holdings in undertakings and companies not subscribed here, or launched on the market here, especially such as the coupon obligations of the great American companies, the extent of the holding of which here must be very great indeed, but which there was surely no sufficient means of identifying? It was familiar to them all that with regard to a vast class of investments it varied from day to day, and almost from hour to hour. There was an enormous fluctuating world-wide capital provided by all the civilised nations which at one moment might be held by British subjects; while at another moment the same evidences of indebtedness would have passed into the hands of people abroad, and *vice versâ*. No doubt it was primarily that particular part of capital which played so important a part in the balancing of accounts and the remitting of sums which had to go into the hands of those who were, on balance, our creditors in trade. How far any of those could accurately be classed specifically as permanently British capital, and how much as only casually and momentarily British, was an important question, and one which nothing Mr. Paish had told them enabled anyone to come to a conclusion about.

Mr. George Paish said they would appreciate that this was a fundamental question as to the method of compilation; and he should like to reply at once to the point Sir Nathaniel Nathan had raised. With regard to our holdings in foreign government securities, he had not taken the amount quoted on the Stock Exchange, but merely the income upon which income tax was paid in this country. The whole of the calculation was for the purpose of ascertaining what sum would the Commissioners of Inland Revenue arrive at if they took out from the income tax returns as far as coupons were concerned, and from the reports of publicly issued companies as to dividends, the amount of income assessed to income tax in this country. In the Report of the Commissioners of Inland Revenue the amount ascertained was only 79,560,000*l.* By analysing the reports of a great many additional companies which paid income tax in this country, he arrived at the figure of about 140,000,000*l.*; and he believed that was the figure the Commissioners would reach if they went further into the matter. He thought that every figure in the paper was based on documentary evidence. Coming, then, to the question of obligations or coupons on American bonds, that was the most difficult of all calculations. His figure was arrived at in this way: the Inland Revenue Commissioners obtained from their agents in this country the whole of the income which came through coupons. The coupon buyers had to make a return to Somerset House, and they got a commission for so doing. He thought at first that foreign government coupons payable abroad were included in the item of "coupons," but on subsequent examination he found that was not so. The foreign government coupons payable abroad were taken out separately, and in this way the Commissioners arrived at the total amount of income derived from foreign government loans assessed to income tax. The interest on Austro-Hungarian debt, for instance, was payable by coupon, and as there was no agent in this country the figure of 74,000*l.* could only be known from the coupons cashed by coupon buyers. Hence the coupons shown in the Commissioners' returns were mainly American railway coupons. The second thing he did was this: there was an item for "other securities." They all knew that the dividends on American railway shares were largely received by big firms; the shares were put in the names of these firms, and those who wanted their dividends went to a big house who stamped the share certificate and handed over the dividend to the owner of the certificate. These firms also made returns to Somerset House of the income tax deducted from dividends upon these bearer shares; and they got a commission for collecting the tax. He had endeavoured to get from the United States the amounts of American shares held here, and the calculations of dividends on these shares tallied with the amount of income derived from "other securities." With regard to colonial and foreign railways, he had taken the figures from the reports of the companies as ascertained definitely. The income from companies in which foreign investors held the bulk of the shares or bonds was entirely excluded. Sir R. Martin had referred to our income from French railways; that income he had excluded entirely, as practically the whole of the securities had been repurchased by French investors. There was no doubt that, after making every possible exclusion he could think of, there was still a residue belonging to foreigners; and he had called attention to that in the paper; nevertheless, it did not affect the figure which the Commissioners of Inland Revenue would arrive at, because the income of the foreigner coming from British companies was also taxed. Against the income derived by foreigners from some of the securities included, they had to place the large amount of income obtained by private investments of British capital abroad. Most of those present, he thought, had read an excellent paper written by Mr. Huth Jackson, who contended that London had over 100,000,000*l.* of capital employed in discounting foreign bills—not bills created for the purpose of paying for goods bought, but bills created in order to finance trade between foreign countries. He made inquiry as to the proportion of the income from foreign investments assessed to income-tax in England received by foreigners, and he thought that on the average about 10 per cent. of it belonged to foreigners. That would mean that 270,000,000*l.* of capital belonged to foreigners out of the total sum calculated of 2,700,000,000*l.* But against this sum had to be placed the capital privately invested abroad by this country, and he thought the amount of income derived from that source greatly exceeded the amount of income paid over to foreign investors. He had come to the conclusion that they derived an income from something like 500,000,000*l.* of capital privately invested in other countries. He thought the figure of

2,700,000,000*l.* of British capital invested abroad was, if anything, an under-statement, but he only wished to place before the members a figure for which he had documentary evidence.

The PRESIDENT said there had been no answer given to the question with regard to the main lines of investment of German capital. They knew all about the French investments, but very little about the German. In the last number of the *Revue de Paris* there was an article about the launching of a new French iron firm, but the capital appeared to be German; and he would be interested to know whether Germany was investing very largely in industrial undertakings on the continent as France did.

Mr. ROZENRAAD said there were about 1,600,000,000*l.* of German capital invested abroad.

Mr. PERCY ASHLEY remarked that the German Government had made some elaborate attempts to estimate the extent of German investments of capital abroad; and he thought that these would to some extent answer the President's question. A report on "German Capital Investments beyond the Seas" was presented to the Budget Commission of the Reichstag by the German Admiralty in 1900; and a revised and enlarged memorandum on the same subject was included in the volume entitled *Die Entwicklung der deutschen Seeinteressen im letzten Jahrzehnt*, prepared by the economic staff of the Admiralty and published by that Department in 1905.

Mr. A. W. FLUX said he should like to ask the author to go one step further in the way of explanation. If he understood the explanation given by Mr. Paish in determining what holdings of capital in various countries were to be classed as British, he (Mr. Paish) rejected all countries in which the British holdings were not very significant; while his estimate of foreign holdings in the remaining companies accounted for, perhaps, 10 per cent. of the total. Was there any figure in this aggregate, representing British holdings in those cases, rejected on the ground that the capital was mainly held by foreigners, or were the British holdings in these cases regarded as off-setting the foreign holdings covered by the 10 per cent. estimate? The question of the basis on which to estimate the British share of capital held in various companies was one of the most interesting, and certainly one of the most difficult, points; and he knew that Mr. Paish had given it a great deal of attention; but he felt that, much as they were indebted to him, if they could get a further peep behind the scenes they would profit still more than they had done. At the same time, he might suggest that it would be exceedingly helpful if an appendix could be given with a few more tables in which the distribution of the holdings in the principal countries of the world according to main classes were given; such as Government loans, railways, municipal stocks, industrials, and so on. Then, one would have material for a comparison of some of those groups with the estimates given by other speakers and writers. There were some remarkable differences in the detail of the different calculations; and one of the most remarkable things was the way in which they gravitated to the same aggregate, however the details varied. One could not help wondering whether it was wholly accidental or whether at the back of their minds there was a certain rough figure, and whether that did not influence the way in which they set to work. No doubt they had all done their best to remove any conscious bias of that kind; still sometimes one was unconsciously led in a particular direction.

The PRESIDENT said it was notorious that the opposite was the case with regard to the Board of Trade and the Government, because they maintained 2,000,000,000*l.* sterling for a long time as the official figure.

Mr. FLUX said the various recent estimates seemed to approximate to 3,000,000,000*l.* with marvellous precision. That made it all the more desirable that they should know as much as possible of the method by which the estimates were made. Mr. Paish said that the present capital value of a good many investments represented a good deal more than was put into them; but, if he correctly understood him, the table in which he gave the 2,700,000,000*l.* did not take that into account.

The PRESIDENT said he did not think it took into account the extinction of companies. There were a lot of land companies in new countries which disappeared; in New Zealand, for instance, there were notorious cases.

Mr. FLUX asked what would happen if they were to make a deduction for the capital which had depreciated in value, and an addition for that which had appreciated? Would they get the current market value, and would that give as a result an average return of a little over 5 per cent.? Or, if the revenue was really 140,000,000*l.*, should that be capitalised at, say, 4½ per cent. or some lower rate? A very substantial addition would have to be made to the figure of the capital if they were to aim, not at the amount put into these various enterprises, but at the value that they represented to-day, based on the average rate of yield which intelligent people might expect them to give over a series of years. He felt immensely indebted to Mr. Paish for his paper; and there were a number of interesting points which, if time permitted, he should like to call attention to. One was found in the tables setting forth the average yield of different classes of investments. It was not unimportant to compare the average yield in the case of Government loans between foreign, colonial, and Indian investments; and the same in the case of railways. In each of those two cases, where discrimination was made between different classes of investments, the rate on foreign investments was substantially higher than that on colonial; and that on colonial was higher than on investments in India. The precise reason for the latter difference he did not like to guess at; but the difference between the rate secured on investments outside the British Empire and inside it, whether in Government loans or in railways, was rather a remarkable feature. Something had already been said about the shifting of investments, European investments particularly; those which were formerly largely held here being now largely held by neighbouring countries; and the table at the bottom of page 467 seemed to illustrate that. There were only two columns which showed a substantial increase during recent years, namely, those relating to colonial and Asiatic investments. The European column showed a decrease from the third year to the last year shown of about one-eighth; it appeared to be roughly a transfer from European to colonial and South American investments. He had, unfortunately, wholly failed to follow the explanation when Mr. Paish said he had adopted that method of computing which would lead to the result that the Inland Revenue Commissioners ought to get. Perhaps it was too long a matter to be explained then; but he hoped he might have the opportunity of getting a fuller explanation.

Mr. W. R. LAWSON said they seemed to be making a heroic effort to solve an insolvable problem. Nobody could appreciate better than he did the labour and ability Mr. Paish had bestowed on these calculations; and nobody would more readily admit than Mr. Paish that there was not a table among them which could be accepted as scientific statistics. Without going into the technical part of the subject, he would ask him in his reply to say whether he had not used a few ambiguous terms. Toward the close of the paper he spoke about these creations of credit, which they principally were, as "investments," which many of them were not, and as "savings," which they were still less. To give an illustration, in to-day's *Times* 9 prospectuses were published, calling for nearly 4,000,000*l.* of money. According to Mr. Paish, if those companies got the 4,000,000*l.*, it would be so much British savings invested abroad. As a matter of fact, not one penny of it needed to be British savings at all. The applications for that 4,000,000*l.* of new securities would go through the banks, and at the end of the day the application money would stand at the debit of one set of people and at the credit of another set. The bank balances which represent international credits would have been re-shuffled to a greater or less extent. The borrowing operations might be carried through, not only without any gold, but with very little real capital. They did go through that way every day. Mr. Beaumont, he thought, would bear him out in this. They had overlooked entirely the fact that these new securities were in a large and growing degree creations of credit effected through international banks. The securities themselves were for the most part international; in London to-day, in Paris to-morrow, and in New York the next day. The Chairman had referred to Canada as being a puzzling problem. Of course it was, if they viewed it from the standpoint of new securities being the investment of savings. Canada asked that day for 1,200,000*l.*

for one of its railways—the Canadian Northern, and would get the money without doubt, but possibly not a dollar of it would leave London, certainly not in the shape of rails or commodities. How could that be called an investment of our annual savings? And what influence did it necessarily have on our exports? When the railway was built it might add thousands of tons of wheat to our imports, but that would diminish rather than increase our savings, as it would mean so much more food to pay for.

The PRESIDENT said the question whether it was an investment depended on whether it was going to pay interest.

Mr. LAWSON: Whether it paid interest or not would of course depend on the success or otherwise of the railway. In any case the interest would more frequently be on a creation of credit than on savings. Subscribers to new securities seldom lent their own money, and many of them had little money to lend. That was one of the paradoxes of modern credit operations. If any of us applied for 5,000*l.* of a new issue he would most likely borrow it from a bank, and the bank would off-set the loan by a credit to some other customer or some other bank. All the evening they had been talking about Mr. Paish's figures as if they represented capital and savings, but he hoped Mr. Paish would now qualify that too flattering theory. The highest estimate ever made of our annual savings would not go far towards paying for the new securities being manufactured at the present time.

Mr. PAISH said in his opinion the money they were putting into these companies and loans were savings. They could not provide other countries with money to build railways and for other purposes which required savings, or accumulated capital, without having it; and the only way they could find the capital for another country for capital purposes was by savings.

The PRESIDENT here suggested that the nature of savings was rather a side issue.

Mr. PAISH said Mr. Beaumont had said that he had underestimated the total capital. He put forward no figure for which there was not documentary evidence, and he really believed that the total figure, after deducting the amount held by foreigners in this country, not only in these companies, but in private enterprises, was close to 3,000,000,000*l.* He compiled these figures in order that everyone might have the facts as far as he could get them. They had been guessing for a number of years, and he desired to bring together all the data it was possible to get, and which they could obtain from the reports of the numerous companies trading abroad which issued reports and balance sheets showing the paid-up capital and the profits which they were earning upon it. He had endeavoured to make the figure as accurate as possible, and if he had erred it had been on the side of conservatism. He had excluded everything he was not sure about. With regard to the income from United States Government bonds, he thought the amount was so small it was not worth putting in. The United States Government bonds were the security for the note issue of the National Banks, which gave them a special value and left no interest worth having upon them. The President's point with regard to German savings had already been answered. It was calculated that about 1,600,000,000*l*. of German capital is invested abroad. He thought everybody would bear him out that in the last ten years, and especially during the period in which we were practically a closed market for capital, the Germans were exceedingly active in placing capital abroad. They formed banks in all parts of the world, and financed foreign companies of all kinds while we were at war. The result was a wonderful growth in German trade. They took a leaf out of the book we had been reading for a number of years, and they were getting similar fruit to that we had gathered. There was room in the world for all the capital that Germany could supply, as well as for all the capital which we could find. If anything, we were supplying a little too much capital all at once to certain countries at the present time.

Sir J. A. BAINES said the formal vote of thanks to the outgoing President had been already proposed on behalf of the Society as a whole, but before the meeting closed he would like to express on behalf of the Council and officers their gratitude to Sir Charles Dilke for the assiduity with which he had entered into the work of the Society throughout his term of office as President, and especially for the stimulus he had so often given to the discussion at the ordinary meetings.

The PRESIDENT said that his only excuse, as an amateur, for interfering with the business of a scientific society was the great interest he felt in the application of statistics. Almost every subject under discussion in Parliament during the last few years appeared under a statistical aspect, and the one feature they all had in common was that there never were the statistics there ought to have been with regard to any one of them.

The PRESIDENT announced that as the result of the ballot M. Gustav Sundbärg, of Stockholm, had been elected an Honorary Fellow.

The following candidates were elected Fellows of the Society:—

Devendra Nath Ghosh, B.A.	James Walker.

GREAT BRITAIN'S CAPITAL INVESTMENTS
IN
INDIVIDUAL COLONIAL AND FOREIGN COUNTRIES

George Paish

Vol. LXXIV.] [Part II.

JOURNAL

OF THE ROYAL STATISTICAL SOCIETY.

JANUARY, 1911.

GREAT BRITAIN'S CAPITAL INVESTMENTS *in* INDIVIDUAL COLONIAL *and* FOREIGN COUNTRIES.

By GEORGE PAISH.

[Read before the Royal Statistical Society, December 20, 1910, the President, the Right Hon. LORD GEORGE HAMILTON, G.C.S.I., in the Chair.]

THIS is the second portion of the paper I had the honour of reading before the Fellows of the Royal Statistical Society in June, 1909. In the first portion I gave the results of my investigation as to the amount of capital which the United Kingdom up to the end of 1907 had invested in other lands, according to the available documentary evidence, and as to the amount of income which in 1907 this country derived from that capital. I have now brought up to the end of 1910 the approximate amount of visible capital which we have supplied to other lands in the aggregate, and I have also ascertained the amount of capital which the United Kingdom has had to place with individual countries, in order to discover the geographical distribution of our colonial and foreign investments.

I pointed out in my last paper that the Inland Revenue Commissioners do not ascertain the amount of income derived by the investors of the United Kingdom from the many miscellaneous enterprises in which they are interested other than Government and Municipal loans, and Indian, Colonial, American and other Foreign Railways, and that to ascertain the large amount of capital which we have supplied to other countries for miscellaneous purposes, such as mining, mortgages, banking, tramways, telegraphs, telephones, tea cultivation, oil, rubber, and nitrate production, and for industrial ventures generally, I examined the reports, balance-sheets and income statements of several thousand companies; in fact, I examined the reports of all British companies working abroad about which official information could be obtained. My investigations showed that according to the available documentary evidence the

British capital invested in Indian, colonial and foreign loans and companies, and the income derived therefrom in 1907–08.

	Capital.	Income.	Rate of Interest.
	£	£	Per cent.
Indian Government loans, including rupee loans held in England	156,369,000	5,017,000	3·21
Colonial and provincial Government loans	375,190,000	13,933,000	3·71
Foreign Government loans	167,000,000	8,338,000	4·75
Colonial and foreign municipal stocks	58,901,000	2,650,000	4·5
Indian railways	123,341,000	4,774,000	3·87
Colonial railways	188,950,000	7,598,000	4·0
American railways	600,000,000	27,000,000	4·5
Foreign railways	286,700,000	13,467,000	4·7
Banks	54,101,000	7,353,000	13·6
Breweries and distilleries	17,205,000	732,000	4·2
Canals and docks	5,974,000	1,174,000	19·9
Commercial, industrial, &c.	77,610,000	4,863,000	6·3
Electric lighting and power	7,686,000	321,000	4·2
Financial, land and investment	187,027,000	6,233,000	3·3
Gas	16,419 000	1,194,000	7·3
Mines—			
Coal and iron ore	12,956,000	505,000	3·9
Copper	38,525,000	5,074,000	13·2
Diamonds and other stones	14,646,000	4,468,000	30·5
Gold	161,178,000	14,947,000	9·3
Silver, lead, and zinc	10,513,000	843,000	8·0
Tin and miscellaneous	5,568,000	308,000	5·5
Nitrate	10,903,000	1,637,000	15·0
Oil	14,268,000	642,000	4·5
Rubber	5,433,000	446,000	8·2
Tea and coffee	21,399,000	1,794,000	8·4
Telegraphs and telephones	34,235,000	2,233,000	6·5
Tramways	35,289,000	1,809,000	5·1
Waterworks	6,352,000	438,000	6·9
Total	2,693,738,000	139,791,000	5·2

amount of capital invested by Great Britain in India, the colonies and foreign countries up to the end of 1907 was 2,693,738,000*l.*, of which 1,312,000,000*l.* was invested in the colonies and India and 1,381,000,000*l.* in foreign countries, and that this capital was bringing to the country an income of 139,791,000*l.* per annum, equal to a return of 5·2 per cent. It may assist the understanding of the matter if I reproduce (see page 168) the statement which I gave in my previous paper of the amount of British capital invested up to the end of 1907, the purposes for which it was supplied and the income derived therefrom in 1907.

In the three years since 1907 Great Britain has supplied other lands with a large amount of additional capital. In 1908 the amount of the new capital issues in London on behalf of Colonial and foreign Governments, municipalities, railways, banks, mining and other joint stock industrial companies was 146,000,000*l.* In 1909 it was 182,000,000*l.* And in 1910, to date, the amount is no less than 189,000,000*l.* The following statement shows the countries to which we have supplied capital so freely in the past three years and the amounts obtained by each. These amounts are calculated at the price of issue, not at the nominal value of the securities:—

New issues of capital in London for Colonial and foreign countries in the past three years.

	1910.	1909.	1908.	Total three years.
The Colonies and India.	£	£	£	£
America—				
Canada	32,359,158	37,687,464	31,309,558	**101,356,180**
British Guiana	367,000	176,500	—	**543,500**
British Honduras	50,000	—	—	**50,000**
Newfoundland	1,410,000	—	—	**1,410,000**
West Indies	340,000	390,600	124,144	**854,744**
Total America	34,526,158	38,254,564	31,433,702	**104,214,424**
Australasia—				
New South Wales	829,000	4,730,559	1,766,908	**7,326,467**
New Zealand	5,258,717	849,135	645,717	**6,753,569**
Queensland	75,000	1,990,000	—	**2,065,000**
South Australia	897,294	117,600	—	**1,014,894**
Tasmania	6,249	295,500	247,000	**548,749**
Victoria	5,000	1,663,000	135,500	**1,803,500**
Western Australia	2,884,686	1,618,925	1,047,833	**5,551,444**
Fiji	30,000	—	—	**30,000**
Unenumerated Australia	194,485	750,000	50,000	**994,485**
Total Australasia	10,180,431	12,014,719	3,892,958	**26,088,108**

New issues of capital in London for Colonial and foreign countries—Contd.

	1910.	1909.	1908.	Total three years.
	£	£	£	£
Africa—				
British Central Africa	77,500	—	—	**77,500**
British East Africa	293,019	10,000	10,000	**313,019**
British West Africa	2,490,906	1,899,003	3,382,992	**7,747,901**
Seychelles	68,000	—	—	**68,000**
South Africa—				
Cape Colony	5,693	278,550	2,598,354	**2,882,597**
Natal	405,000	285,000	802,500	**1,492,500**
Orange River Colony	66,100	—	73,500	**139,600**
Rhodesia	6,686,176	2,422,050	1,526,323	**10,634,549**
Transvaal	2,767,828	8,858,093	2,487,435	**14,113,356**
Unenumerated South Africa	90,000	587,600	349,500	**1,027,100**
Total South Africa	10,020,797	12,431,293	7,837,612	**30,289,702**
Total Africa	12,950,322	14,340,296	11,230,604	**38,521,122**
Asia—				
India and Ceylon	14,720,503	15,884,581	13,469,787	**44,074,871**
Straits Settlements	9,286,337	3,092,513	233,502	**12,612,352**
British North Borneo	848,948	1,159,126	164,000	**2,172,074**
Total Asia	24,855,788	20,136,220	13,867,289	**58,859,297**
Europe—				
Malta	—	—	125,000	**125,000**
Unenumerated Colonies	300,000	250,000	46,000	**596,000**
Total the Colonies and India	**82,812,599**	**84,995,799**	**60,595,553**	**228,403,951**
Foreign Countries.				
Algeria	320,000	—	—	**320,000**
Argentina	16,595,020	23,987,070	15,905,706	**56,487,796**
Austria	2,368,000	130,000	—	**2,498,000**
Belgium	—	80,000	—	**80,000**
Bolivia	611,500	10,000	—	**621,500**
Brazil	10,988,686	7,497,928	10,945,280	**29,431,894**
Bulgaria	3,603,600	—	—	**3,603,600**
Chili	4,684,661	4,158,750	1,379,985	**10,223,396**
China	1,610,100	740,000	5,031,125	**7,381,225**
Colombia	171,500	567,480	906,070	**1,645,050**
Costa Rica	—	—	14,625	**14,625**
Cuba	1,916,153	1,226,000	—	**3,142,153**
Denmark	1,089,000	487,500	2,343,200	**3,919,700**
Dutch Indies	6,328,916	1,195,690	145,300	**7,669,906**
Ecuador	300,000	416,070	—	**716,070**
Egypt	1,002,407	796,670	1,755,400	**3,554,477**
Finland	143,050	2,328,400	—	**2,471,450**
France	755,000	456,667	424,400	**1,636,067**
French Ivory Coast	—	50,000	—	**50,000**
Germany	202,500	47,000	—	**249,500**
German Africa	483,500	60,000	—	**543,500**

New issues of capital in London for Colonial and foreign countries—Contd.

	1910.	1909.	1908.	Total three years.
Foreign Countries—contd.	£	£	£	£
Greece	2,345,834	—	194,000	**2,539,834**
Hungary	1,950,000	—	—	**1,950,000**
Italy	55,000	—	160,000	**215,000**
Japan	31,950	4,230,523	4,880,000	**9,142,473**
Liberia	9,993	20,000	101,000	**130,993**
Madagascar	50,000	—	—	**50,000**
Mexico	4,946,139	9,109,694	7,250,528	**21,306,361**
Montenegro	—	242,500	—	**242,500**
Netherlands	82,500	534,000	125,000	**741,500**
Nicaragua	35,000	460,000	—	**495,000**
Norway	—	381,150	155,000	**536,150**
Panama	130,000	200,000	11,000	**341,000**
Paraguay	—	182,000	186,900	**368,900**
Persia	—	1,200,000	—	**1,200,000**
Peru	2,465,770	—	2,037,000	**4,502,770**
Philippines	403,890	—	1,819,393	**2,223,283**
Portugal	100,000	80,000	35,000	**215,000**
Portuguese Africa	275,000	5,000	—	**280,000**
Roumania	1,202,000	—	—	**1,202,000**
Russia	3,936,655	9,672,485	3,810,496	**17,419,636**
Salvador	—	36,000	860,000	**896,000**
Samoa	33,539	—	—	**33,539**
Siberia	257,500	—	—	**257,500**
Spain	158,500	60,000	297,493	**515,993**
Sweden	—	881,000	2,940,000	**3,821,000**
Turkey	1,431,688	2,759,381	204,800	**4,395,869**
United States	32,237,294	21,778,159	19,949,174	**73,964,627**
Uruguay	337,693	234,980	648,384	**1,221,057**
Venezuela	10,000	25,000	—	**35,000**
Unenumerated	679,000	508,750	766,488	**1,954,238**
Total Foreign Countries	**106,338,538**	**96,835,847**	**85,282,747**	**288,457,132**
Grand Total	**189,151,137**	**181,831,646**	**145,878,300**	**516,861,083**

Usually the Continent participates in the new issues of foreign Government loans and American railway securities, and, to a moderate extent, in other issues, and it is necessary to make allowance for the share of the other lending countries in these issues. After making every allowance it is evident that the actual amount of new capital supplied by Great Britain to other lands in 1908 was 130,000,000*l.*; in 1909, 160,000,000*l.*; and in 1910, 165,000,000*l.*, a total in three years of no less than 455,000,000*l.*

To give a clear notion of the purposes for which capital is now being raised so freely I set out the nature of the new issues of capital in London in the three years 1908, 1909, and 1910:—

Great Britain's capital investments in other lands*, 1908, 1909 *and* 1910.

	1910.	1909.	1908.
Government loans—	£	£	£
India and Ceylon	7,237,500	8,752,500	4,950,000
Colonies	13,495,775	24,273,124	14,912,614
Foreign countries	17,275,856	17,749,880	18,251,925
Total	**38,009,131**	**50,775,504**	**38,143,739**
Municipal loans—			
India and Ceylon	487,500	2,048,950	985,000
Colonies	3,964,200	3,487,159	4,652,905
Foreign countries	6,809,514	10,234,011	4,485,512
Total	**11,261,214**	**15,770,120**	**10,123,417**
Railway companies—			
India and Ceylon	3,100,000	3,183,875	6,894,250
Colonies	10,972,497	19,378,402	14,851,476
Foreign countries	42,670,148	39,400,633	43,457,446
Total	**56,742,645**	**61,962,910**	**65,203,172**
Miscellaneous—			
Banks	1,681,039	625,000	2,822,500
Breweries and distilleries	—	—	120,000
Canals and docks	182,000	450,000	—
Commercial, industrial, &c.	10,504,424	8,368,397	5,808,647
Electric lighting and power	3,102,726	2,413,490	1,220,271
Financial, land and investment	13,473,333	4,896,369	8,892,643
Gas and water	102,500	1,578,000	1,339,322
Insurance	246,000	—	—
Iron, coal and steel	4,396,195	2,444,034	1,027,180
Mines	10,802,352	8,300,688	5,084,376
Motor traction and manufacturing	276,149	595,000	58,000
Nitrate	—	145,500	215,700
Oil	10,508,086	2,428,250	795,540
Rubber	20,859,155	5,774,870	810,012
Shipping	—	1,187,500	200,000
Tea and Coffee	104,500	40,000	10,000
Telegraphs and Telephones	2,637,500	3,363,000	150,000
Tramways	4,262,188	10,713,014	3,853,781
Total	**83,138,147**	**53,323,112**	**32,407,972**
Grand Total	**189,151,137**	**181,831,646**	**145,878,300**

* Amount calculated at the price of issue, and exclusive of loans raised to repay former loans and all shares issued to vendors.

A very large portion of the new capital has been raised for railway construction. In the three years the amount of capital raised by railway companies has reached 184,000,000*l.*, but to this must be added a large portion of the money raised by Government loans. About 275,000,000*l.* of the 515,000,000*l.* of new issues has been directly or indirectly for the construction, improvement and equipment of Colonial and foreign railways. The nature of the borrowings in the current year, whether Government, municipal, railway or company is disclosed by the next tabular statement:—

The purposes for which each country has required capital in 1910.

	Governments.	Municipalities.	Railways.	Other securities.	Total all securities.
The Colonies and India.	£	£	£	£	£
America—					
Canada	3,647,451	3,413,983	10,402,497	14,865,227	**32,359,158**
British Guiana	—	—	—	367,000	**367,000**
British Honduras	—	—	—	50,000	**50,000**
Newfoundland	780,000	—	—	630,000	**1,410,000**
West Indies	—	—	—	340,000	**340,000**
Total America	4,427,451	3,413,983	10,402,497	16,252,227	**34,526,158**
Australasia:—					
New South Wales	—	—	—	829,000	**829,000**
New Zealand	4,349,750	520,217	—	388,750	**5,258,717**
Queensland	—	—	—	75,000	**75,000**
South Australia	797,294	—	—	100,000	**897,294**
Tasmania	—	—	—	6,249	**6,249**
Victoria	—	—	—	5,000	**5,000**
Western Australia	1,295,030	—	570,000	1,019,656	**2,884,686**
Fiji	—	—	—	30,000	**30,000**
Unenumerated Australasia	—	—	—	194,485	**194,485**
Total Australasia	6,442,074	520,217	570,000	2,648,140	**10,180,431**
Africa—					
British Central Africa	—	—	—	77,500	**77,500**
British East Africa	—	—	—	293,019	**293,019**
British West Africa	—	—	—	2,490,906	**2,490,906**
Seychelles	—	—	—	68,000	**68,000**
South Africa—					
Cape Colony	—	—	—	5,693	**5,693**
Natal	—	—	—	405,000	**405,000**
Orange River Colony	—	—	—	66,100	**66,100**
Rhodesia	—	—	—	6,686,176	**6,686,176**
Transvaal	—	—	—	2,767,828	**2,767,828**
Unenumerated South Africa	—	—	—	90,000	**90,000**
Total South Africa	—	—	—	10,020,797	**10,020,797**
Total Africa	—	—	—	12,950,222	**12,950,222**
Asia—					
India and Ceylon	7,237,500	487,500	3,100,000	3,895,503	**14,720,503**
Straits Settlements	2,626,250	—	—	6,660,087	**9,286,337**
British North Borneo	—		—	848,948	**848,948**
Total Asia	9,863,750	487,500	3,100,000	11,404,538	**24,855,788**
Unenumerated Colonies	—	—	—	300,000	**300,000**
Total India and the Colonies	**20,733,275**	**4,451,700**	**14,072,497**	**43,555,127**	**82,812,599**

The purposes for which each country has required capital in 1910—*Contd.*

	Governments.	Municipalities.	Railways.	Other securities.	Total all securities.
Foreign Countries.	£	£	£	£	£
Algeria	—	—	—	320,000	**320,000**
Argentina	2,425,520	—	11,344,000	2,824,500	**16,595,020**
Austria	—	—	—	2,368,000	**2,368,000**
Bolivia	—	—	—	611,500	**611,500**
Brazil	4,400,000	1,343,000	2,661,180	2,584,506	**10,988,686**
Bulgaria	3,603,600	—	—	—	**3,603,600**
Chili	2,574,000	—	2,090,661	20,000	**4,684,661**
China	1,601,550	—	—	8,550	**1,610,100**
Colombia	—	—	—	171,500	**171,500**
Cuba	1,099,066	—	—	817,087	**1,916,153**
Denmark	—	1,089,000	—	—	**1,089,000**
Dutch Indies	—	—	—	6,328,916	**6,328,916**
Ecuador	—	—	—	300,000	**300,000**
Egypt	—	—	—	1,002,407	**1,002,407**
Finland	—	113,050	—	30,000	**143,050**
France	—	—	—	755,000	**755,000**
Germany	—	—	—	202,500	**202,500**
German Africa	—	—	—	483,500	**483,500**
Greece	1,572,120	—	—	773,714	**2,345,834**
Hungary	—	1,910,000	—	40,000	**1,950,000**
Italy	—	—	—	55,000	**55,000**
Japan	—	—	—	31,950	**31,950**
Liberia	—	—	—	9,993	**9,993**
Madagascar	—	—	—	50,000	**50,000**
Mexico	—	178,189	792,000	3,975,950	**4,946,139**
Netherlands	—	—	—	82,500	**82,500**
Nicaragua	—	—	—	35,000	**35,000**
Panama	—	—	—	130,000	**130,300**
Peru	—	—	946,770	1,519,000	**2,465,770**
Philippines	—	—	353,890	50,000	**403,890**
Portugal	—	—	—	100,000	**100,000**
Portuguese Africa	—	—	—	275,000	**275,000**
Roumania	—	760,000	—	442,000	**1,202,000**
Russia	—	—	1,135,039	2,801,616	**3,936,655**
Samoa	—	—	—	33,539	**33,539**
Siberia	—	—	—	257,500	**257,500**
Spain	—	—	—	158,500	**158,500**
Turkey	—	995,000	293,250	143,438	**1,431,688**
United States	—	421,275	22,737,358	9,078,661	**32,237,294**
Uruguay	—	—	315,000	22,693	**337,693**
Venezuela	—	—	—	10,000	**10,000**
Unenumerated	—	—	—	679,000	**679,000**
Total foreign countries	**17,275,856**	**6,809,514**	**42,670,148**	**39,583,020**	**106,338,538**
Grand Total	**38,009,131**	**11,261,214**	**56,742,645**	**83,138,147**	**189,151,137**

The great income which British investors are deriving from their investments in other lands is small in comparison with the total income they may ultimately derive from the investment. A great deal of the capital that has been invested in the past is not yet fully productive, and will probably not become so for many years.

In recent years the income of the British people from foreign investments has grown very rapidly, not merely because of the large amounts of new savings they have placed in other lands, but because of the much higher returns they have derived from the capital formerly invested. It will be recollected that during the nineties many American railways were unable to meet their interest charges, and that others did not pay any dividends on their stocks; in recent years the railways of the United States have met their interest obligations in full, have given considerable dividends upon their stocks which previously received no distribution, and have made higher distributions upon the stocks which continued to receive dividends during the period of depression. The experience of our investors in Argentina and in other countries has been of a similar character. During the nineties dividends were low, and in recent years have been much higher.

In ascertaining the large amounts of capital that Great Britain has supplied to individual colonial and foreign countries, one is compelled to recognise the powerful influence which Great Britain has exerted in developing the world's natural resources by supplying other countries freely with the funds for railway construction, for mining, and for the production of every kind of natural wealth. It is no exaggeration to state that Great Britain's enterprise in placing her supplies of new capital wherever it could be profitably employed has been one of the great forces which have made for the increased prosperity of the human race in modern times. In the seventeenth and eighteenth centuries Great Britain supplied money for the development of the sugar, tobacco, and other plantations of the Indies and of America; but it was not until the invention of railways that the investments of British capital abroad assumed large proportions. A statement of the existing amounts of capital employed abroad by Great Britain gives practically no indication of the valuable assistance rendered by Great Britain to the Continent in the construction of railways in France, Austria, Italy, Spain and in other countries, as Continental countries have now repaid the greater portion of the sums with which Great Britain supplied them for railway construction. Nevertheless even Continental countries owe the increase in their prosperity in no small degree to the enterprise of Great Britain in building railways for them when their own supplies of capital were inadequate for the purpose.

The country which has received the largest amount of British capital is the United States, where we have been placing capital from the days of Queen Elizabeth. The War of Independence and the war of 1812–1814 caused but a temporary halt in the flow of British capital to America, but the amounts that were invested in that country prior to the days of railways were insignificant in comparison with the great sums which have been provided by investors since they began to find a large portion of the capital needed for the construction of railways in the young countries. There have, of course, been periods in which the States have been in a position to repay some of the capital obtained from this country, but these periods have been short and from decade to decade the amount of our investments in the United States has shown large expansion until at the present time it reaches the great sum of about 688,000,000*l.* It should, of course, be recognised that a part of this sum, and no inconsiderable part either, has resulted from increment or from the employment of profits by the undertakings in which the capital was placed to such good purpose, and that the value of the original sums invested has immensely increased. Of this great sum nearly 600,000,000*l.* is in railway securities. The purposes for which the investors of this country have found capital for the States are shown by the following statement:—

	United States.	Cuba.	Philippines.
	£	£	£
Government	—	2,282,000	—
Municipal	7,896,000	—	—
Railways	586,227,000	17,387,000	7,902,000
Banks	930,000	—	—
Breweries and distilleries	11,505,000	—	—
Commercial, industrial, &c.	15,715,000	1,712,000	—
Finance, land, and investment	31,437,000	182,000	—
Gas and water	1,137,000	—	—
Iron, coal, and steel	346,000	—	—
Mines	21,621,000	—	—
Motor traction and manufacturing	395,000	—	—
Oil	3,575,000	171,000	—
Rubber	—	—	50,000
Telegraphs and telephones	4,347,000	966,000	—
Tramways	2,947,000	—	250,000
Total	**688,078,000**	**22,700,000**	**8,202,000**

Inasmuch as the United States is now directly responsible for the government of the Philippines, and is indirectly responsible for the good government of Cuba, I have appended our investments in these islands.

With the exception of the United States, our greatest investments are in the daughter States of the Empire and in our great Indian possessions. Excluding the United States—to which, however, we are also attached by ties of blood and of language—Great Britain has provided more capital to Canada than to any other country, and the rate at which the British people are now increasing their investments in Canada is so rapid as to be phenomenal. The amount of visible capital our investors have placed in Canada now amounts to the great sum of 373,000,000*l.*, and new supplies of visible capital are flowing to Canada at the rate of over 30,000,000*l.* a year. Including the invisible capital, that is, the capital privately supplied for loans on mortgage, the purchase of land for the conduct of private businesses, &c., the amount is probably nearly 40,000,000*l.* a year. The amount of visible capital we have sent to Canada in the last three years has reached 100,000,000*l.* Canada still needs a large sum of money for the completion of the railways now under construction, and inasmuch as the Mother Country is proud of the great progress of her daughter, and is willing to supply her with all the capital she needs to develop her resources, it is evident that our capital investment in Canada will reach a much greater total in a few years. Practically the whole of the capital which has been spent upon railway construction in Canada has been provided by the investors of Great Britain. In the 'nineties, when our investors were suffering from a feeling of distrust of other nations, including the Colonies, the progress of Canada was very slow, and the increase in her population relatively unimportant; but in recent years the ability of Canada to obtain all the capital she needs for the development of her natural riches has stimulated the growth of her population in a wonderful manner.

The British people have provided their kinsmen in the Australasian Colonies with nearly as much capital as they have supplied to Canada, the visible amount reaching the great sum of 380,000,000*l.* Of this total, 301,500,000*l.* has been supplied to the Commonwealth, and 78,500,000*l.* to New Zealand. A few years ago the amount of capital supplied to the Australian colonies was much greater than that invested in Canada, but the rapidity with which Canada is developing, and the relatively slow progress of the Australian colonies have materially changed the situation. In the 'eighties there was a great flow of British capital to Australasia for railway construction, and population increased at a rapid rate; but in the 'nineties the country fell upon misfortune, first because British investors were not willing to find much new capital in consequence of their distrust of Colonial and foreign investments at that time, and, secondly, because Australia was visited by a series of droughts which seriously checked her progress. In recent years the credit of Australia has been fully restored, and the measures that are now being taken to increase the productive power of the country and to develop its natural resources will doubtless bring about the influx of a greatly increased amount of capital from this country, and thus stimulate the growth of population and of wealth. Last year the amount of new capital raised in London for Australasia was about 10,000,000*l*. In the statement herewith of the amount of capital invested by the British people in Australasia it will be noted that about two-thirds of it has been provided by loans to the various governments. The object of these loans was railway construction and other public works. The circumstances of Australasia were such that it was more desirable for the country to use its own credit in order to secure the necessary capital for railway construction than to leave railway extension to private enterprise. In Canada the circumstances are different, and the Canadian people have been able to get all the capital they require for railway construction by means of companies and by private enterprise; but although the methods of obtaining the capital have differed, the railways both of Canada and of Australasia have been almost entirely constructed by means of the capital supplied by the Mother Country.

The investment of the British people in South Africa is also of vast extent. The amount reaches the great sum of 351,000,000*l*. Of this total, 125,000,000*l*. is the capital of mining companies, 97,000,000*l*. loans to the various Governments of South Africa, and 73,000,000*l*. is the capital of land and investment companies. There is a certain amount of duplication in these totals, as the investment companies hold large amounts of mining shares. Although I have excluded the purely trust companies, a certain amount of duplication is unavoidable. Nevertheless the greater portion of the 73,000,000*l*. of capital which we have found for land and investment companies is not duplication, but represents the actual investments of those companies in land and property. This total includes the capital of the British South Africa Company, amounting to 8,250,000*l*. The loans to the Governments have been mainly spent on railway construction, as well as the 9,000,000*l*. of capital which we have supplied to railway companies.

The amount of visible capital we have found for our great Indian Empire is no less than 365,000,000*l*., the larger portion of which has been for the construction of railways. The capital of the railway companies is 137,000,000*l*., and the Government loans of 179,000,000*l*. have been mainly for railway purposes. The capital of tea companies provided by our investors is nearly 20,000,000*l*. No one can doubt the beneficent effect upon the prosperity of India of this expenditure of British capital for the development of the natural resources of the country, and the linking up of district with district, which has so powerfully helped to diminish the severity of famines. This great sum has been lent to India at an exceptionally low rate of interest, and having regard to the immense increase in the wealth of the Indian people which has resulted, and is resulting, from the construction of railways, the burden of the low interest charge is quite negligible. Probably the improvement in the condition of the people resulting from railway construction has been one of the most potent factors in maintaining the loyalty of the vast populations of India to the British Empire.

The investments of the British people in the minor Colonies are also of a large amount. For West Africa, where the rate of development has recently been rapid owing to the discovery of gold, the British people have found over 29,000,000*l.* of capital, of which 12,000,000*l.* has been for mines and 8,000,000*l.* for Government loans, mainly for railways. The recent development of the motor car industry in this and in other countries, which has so greatly increased the demand for rubber, has induced our investors to place considerable amounts of capital in the Straits Settlements and Federated Malay States. The total visible amount of capital we have provided for these Colonies is about 22,000,000*l.*, of which over 10,000,000*l.* is for rubber and 8,000,000*l.* for Government loans. The increase in the prosperity of our Malay Possessions, in consequence of the investment of British capital in the development of rubber plantations, has been striking. I set out in the table on page 180 the amounts of capital the British people have provided for each of the daughter States, for India and Ceylon, and for the minor Colonies.

The aggregate amount of capital which the Mother Country has provided for the British Dominions beyond the seas is the great sum of 1,554,000,000*l.* Beyond this she has found a great deal of invisible capital for mercantile and other purposes. Other nations have participated in these investments of capital in the colonies and possessions of Great Britain to only a very small extent. Probably the greatest participation has been in the mines of South Africa, but even here the total amount of shares held on the Continent is inconsiderable in comparison with the quantity held in Great Britain. If it were possible to make allowance for the holdings of other countries in British enterprises on the one hand and the amount of British capital privately placed in the colonies and in India on the other, the total would, I am convinced, be greater than 1,554,000,000*l.* Of this total we have supplied about 83,000,000*l.* in the current year, and a sum of no less than 227,000,000*l.* in the past three years. The capital invested in the Colonies alone, excluding India, is nearly 1,200,000,000*l.* To realise the magnitude of this sum it is necessary to recollect that

	Canada and Newfoundland.	Common-wealth.	New Zealand.	Total of Australasia.	South Africa.	West Africa.	India and Ceylon.	Straits Settlements and Malay States.	Miscellaneous British Possessions.
	£	£	£	£	£	£	£	£	£
Government	74,621,000	190,615,000	57,825,000	248,440,000	97,379,000	8,541,000	178,995,000	7,943,000	6,969,000
Municipal	18,327,000	7,750,000	6,896,000	14,646,000	17,701,000	—	3,522,000	—	—
Railways	223,740,000	2,951,000	761,000	3,712,000	9,354,000	—	136,519,000	—	—
Banks	4,180,000	16,784,000	2,563,000	19 347,000	4,558,000	257,000	3,100,000	—	1,717,000
Breweries and distilleries	—	725,000	—	725,000	3,065,000	—	—	—	—
Canals and docks	—	—	—	—	—	—	—	—	100,000
Commercial and industrial, &c.	14,357,000	11,900,000	400,000	12,300,000	7,024,000	1,547,000	2,647,000	—	7,112,000
Electric lighting and power	3,272,000	1,579,000	—	1,579,000	3,667,000	—	1,763,000	—	40,000
Financial, land and investment	12,613,000	21,701,000	6,256,000	27,957,000	73,363,000	5,242,000	1,853,000	1,485,000	5,255,000
Gas and water	743,000	1,997,000	250,000	2,247,000	1,339,000	—	659,000	—	245,000
Insurance	246,000	—	—	—	—	—	—	—	—
Iron, coal and steel	7,331,000	1,202,000	55,000	1,257,000	6,392,000	—	803,000	—	75,000
Mines	7,396,000	40,296,000	2,798,000	43,094,000	125,065,000	12,437,000	3,531,000	1,912,000	587,000
Motor traction and manufacturing	—	94,000	100,000	194,000	—	—	90,000	—	—
Nitrate	—	—	—	—	—	—	—	—	—
Oil	907,000	1,064,000	—	1,064,000	165,000	428,000	3,184,000	—	300,000
Rubber	—	—	—	—	495,000	1,046,000	4,610,000	10,697,000	2,843,000
Shipping	200,000	—	—	—	—	—	—	—	—
Tea and coffee	—	—	—	—	—	—	19,644,000	—	—
Telegraphs and telephones	—	—	—	—	—	—	43,000	—	7,371,000
Tramways	5,808,000	2,863,000	625,000	3,488,000	1,801,000	—	4,136,000	—	645,000
Total	**373,541,000**	**301,521,000**	**78,529,000**	**380,050,000**	**351,368,000**	**29,498,000**	**365,399,000**	**22,037,000**	**33,259,000**

the populations of the Colonies where this great amount is invested are relatively small. To Canada, Australasia, and South Africa, which possess a combined population of about 20,000,000 persons, Great Britain has supplied 1,100,000,000*l*. of capital. In so far as the prosperity of the British Empire is governed by the amount of capital which the mother country is able to supply to the colonies and to India, its future expansion in population and in prosperity is assured. Never has Great Britain had so much new capital available for investment in the colonies and in India, and never has she supplied money so freely to the other nations of the Empire as she has done in the past few years. The rapid progress of Canada, the recovery in Australia, the improvement in South Africa and the prosperity of India at the present time clearly show how potent are the influences upon the progress and development of the Empire of the large amounts of capital with which the British people are now so freely supplying to those lands.

Outside the British Empire and the United States our investments are largely confined to the young nations of America. It is true that during the Russo-Japanese War we did supply a large amount of capital to Japan, but this was an exceptional transaction, and it is probable that in twenty or thirty years Japan will repay the whole of the large sum of money borrowed for war purposes. We also have a fairly substantial investment in China, and probably the amount of our investment in China will show rapid expansion now that the Chinese people are awakening to the advantages of modern civilisation and modern science, are educating themselves on the Western plan and are favourable to the construction of a great system of railways to open up their vast country. Of the young countries not connected with Great Britain by ties of empire or of race, we have supplied the largest amount of capital to Argentina. In that fertile and progressive State we have embarked no less than 269,000,000*l*. of capital, of which by far the greater portion has been for railway and tramway construction. The capital of British companies owning railways in Argentina amounts to the great sum of 186,000,000*l*. and the capital in the tramways owned by British companies is nearly 19,000,000*l*. The extension of railways in Argentina has recently been rapid and the greater portion of the necessary capital has been supplied from London. In the last three years as much as 56,000,000*l*. of capital has been subscribed by British investors for Argentina, of which 16,500,000*l*. has been provided in the current year. Our next greatest investment is in Mexico, to whom we have supplied 87,000,000*l*. of capital, about 62 per cent. of which has been for railway purposes and over 7,000,000*l*. for the development of the mineral wealth of the

	Argentina.	Mexico.	Brazil.	Chili.	Uruguay.	Peru.	Miscellaneous American countries.
	£	£	£	£	£	£	£
Government	33,768,000	6,653,000	28,938,000	16,962,000	8,779,000	80,600	3,838,000
Municipal	4,571,000	1,623,900	11,283,000	109,000	1,081,000	—	—
Railways	186,126,000	54,306,000	29,961,000	12,646,000	21,194,000	6,476,000	11,681,000
Banks	1,850,000	1,576,000	1,000,000	1,250,000	—	—	—
Breweries and distilleries	993,000	—	—	—	—	254,000	—
Canals and docks	1,941,000	—	800,000	—	—	—	—
Commercial and industrial, &c.	6,922,000	1,875,000	4,403,000	953,000	1,562,000	321,000	250,000
Electric lighting and power	889,000	937,000	—	—	—	1,164,000	309,000
Financial, land, and investment	8,060,000	7,416,000	3,542,000	225,000	116,000	22,139,000	303,000
Gas and water	3,854,000	—	639,000	400,000	1,078,000	—	100,000
Mines	832,000	7,440,000	1,560,000	721,000	—	711,000	4,445,000
Nitrate	—	—	—	11,264,000	—	—	—
Oil	—	998,000	—	—	—	335,000	300,000
Rubber	—	1,683,000	1,318,000	—	—	506,000	622,000
Tea and coffee	—	—	1,584,000	—	—	—	113,000
Telegraphs and telephones	1,390,000	—	550,000	220,000	159,000	—	—
Tramways	18,612,000	2,827,000	8,862,000	1,625,000	1,286,000	—	556,000
Total	269,808,000	87,334,900	94,440,000	46,375,000	35,255,000	31,986,600	22,517,000

country. To Brazil our investors have lent as much as 94,000,000*l.*, also mainly for railways and public works. To Chili we have sent 46,000,000*l.*, largely for railways, but inasmuch as Chili possesses rich deposits of nitrate we have found 11,000,000*l.* of capital for the production of this valuable fertiliser. In Uruguay our investments reach 35,000,000*l.* mainly in railways. In Peru we have 32,000,000*l.*, chiefly in railways. It will be recollected that the chief asset of the Peruvian Corporation is its railway system

To other South and Central American countries we have supplied 23,000,000*l.* of capital mainly for railways and for mining. The extent of our visible investments of capital in the American countries, exclusive of Canada and the United States, are set out in the table on page 182.

I have already referred to our investments in Japan and China. The sum in Japan amounts to about 54,000,000*l.*, of which 36,000,000*l.* was supplied to the Government for war purposes, 7,000,000*l.* to municipalities, and nearly 9,000,000*l.* to railway companies. I would point out that the amount of Japanese Government loans held in this country is ascertained from the particulars of the amount of interest on the loans assessed to Income Tax as supplied to the Inland Revenue Commissioners. We hold a considerable amount of Japanese Internal Debt, of which the interest is payable in Japan, and of which consequently there is no record. It is probable that the total amount of Japanese Debt held in this country appreciably exceeds 36,000,000*l.* The visible amounts of capital we have supplied to Japan and China are as follows:—

	Japan.	China.	Miscellaneous foreign countries.
	£	£	£
Government	35,941,000	22,477,000	818,000
Municipal	6,843,000	—	—
Railways	8,910,000	—	4,521,000
Banks	1,299,000	—	2,759,000
Commercial, industrial, &c.	32,000	1,401,000	4,805,000
Electric lighting and power	—	9,000	80,000
Financial, land and investment	202,000	1,879,000	5,489,000
Gas and water	478,000	373,000	5,414,000
Iron, coal and steel	—	—	60,000
Mines	—	350,000	2,582,000
Oil	—	—	3,326,000
Rubber	—	—	8,669,000
Tea and coffee	—	—	25,000
Telegraphs and telephones	—	—	23,359,000
Tramways	—	320,000	—
Total	**53,705,000**	**26,809,000**	**61,907,000**

	Russia.	Turkey.	Egypt.	Spain.	Italy.	Portugal.	France.	Germany.	Other European Countries.
	£	£	£	£	£	£	£	£	£
Government	16,033,000	8,650,000	13,539,000	1,885,000	4,164,000	1,336,000	—	1,351,000	14,751,000
Municipal	3,076,000	1,000,000	505,000	—	—	—	—	—	8,119,000
Railways	2,013,000	6,146,000	1,916,000	5,473,000	3,284,000	4,432,000	—	—	495,000
Banks	—	2,000,000	14,413,000	—	10,000	—	—	—	299,000
Breweries and distilleries	—	—	—	—	—	—	—	564,000	564,000
Canals and docks	—	—	3,529,000	—	—	—	—	—	51,000
Commercial, industrial, &c.	—	75,000	2,091,000	180,000	997,000	203,000	5,669,000	3,489,000	5,081,000
Electric lighting and power	—	—	—	486,000	—	—	—	—	—
Financial, land and investment	946,000	93,000	5,796,000	107,000	12,000	100,000	158,000	175,000	390,000
Gas and water	130,000	91,000	1,216,000	490,000	1,622,000	37,000	840,000	—	1,401,000
Iron, coal and steel	2,813,000	—	—	952,000	—	—	—	—	100,000
Mines †	5,265,000	223,000	508,000	9,076,000	1,258,000	486,000	404,000	482,000	2,353,000
Motor traction and manufacturing	—	—	—	—	—	—	—	—	210,000
Nitrate	—	—	—	—	—	—	—	—	—
Oil	8,112,000	40,000	14,000	55,000	—	20,000	—	—	1,745,000
Rubber	—	—	—	104,000	—	—	—	—	—
Telegraphs and telephones	—	—	226,000	—	—	—	—	—	—
Tramways	—	28,000	—	—	166,000	1,520,000	—	—	760,000
Total	**38,388,000**	**18,320,000**	**43,753,000**	**18,808,000**	**11,513,000**	**8,134,000**	**7,071,000**	**6,061,000**	**36,319,000**

In Europe our greatest investment is in Russia, where the amount placed is 38,000,000*l.*, of which 8,000,000*l.* represents the capital of Russian oil companies, 5,000,000*l.* the capital of mining companies, and 16,000,000*l.* Government loans. The Government debt owned here has been raised for railway construction. In Turkey our investments total 18,000,000*l.*, of which nearly 9,000,000*l.* are loans to the Government and 6,000,000*l.* are the capital of railways owned by British companies. Inasmuch as Egypt is a portion of the Turkish Empire, I include Egypt in the same statement as Turkey. We have found about 44,000,000*l.* of capital for Egypt, of which 14,000,000*l*, is in banking companies, over 14,000,000*l.* is in loans to the Government, nearly 6,000,000*l.* is the capital of land and investment companies, and 3,529,000*l.* is the nominal value of the Suez Canal shares held by the British Government. The market value of the Suez Canal shares is now 38,000,000*l.* Our investments in Spain total 19,000,000*l.*, of which 9,000,000*l.* is in mining companies and 5,000,000*l.* in railways. In Italy the aggregate is 11,500,000*l.*, mainly in Government loans and railways. To Portugal we have supplied 8,000,000*l.*, chiefly for railways. In France, Germany, and in other European countries, our investments are of very small amount, although in the aggregate they reach the substantial sum of nearly 50,000,000*l.* The extent of our investments in the more important borrowing countries of Europe and in Egypt, as well as in France and Germany, is shown in the statement given on page 184.

The aggregate of our investments in foreign countries is 1,638,000,000*l.*, of which 42 per cent. is in the United States. Over 60 per cent. of our foreign investments has been employed in the construction of railways, either directly by British companies, or indirectly by means of the loans with which we have provided the Governments of the various countries. Most of the remaining 40 per cent. has been directly employed in developing the world's supplies of natural wealth. It will, of course, be realised that railways are the instrument mainly needed to develop the natural agricultural wealth of the young countries, and that if the capital provided for railway construction be regarded as a part of the total capital we have found for developing the riches which nature has bestowed upon the world, it is evident that almost the whole of the capital provided by Great Britain for other countries has been used for increasing the world's productions of food, minerals, lumber, oil, nitrate, rubber and other natural products. To show the amounts of capital we have supplied to the various countries of the world I give the following statement:—

The Colonies and India.

	£
North America—	
Canada and Newfoundland	372,541,000
Australasia—	
Australian Commonwealth	301,521,000
New Zealand	78,529,000
Africa—	
South Africa	351,368,000
West Africa	29,498,000
Asia—	
India and Ceylon	365,399,000
Straits Settlements	22,037,000
Hong Kong	3,104,000
British North Borneo	5,131,000
Other British Possessions	25,024,000
Total British Colonies and India	**1,554,152,000**

Foreign countries.

United States	688,078,000
Cuba	22,700,000
Philippines	8,202,000
Argentina	269,808,000
Mexico	87,334,000
Brazil	94,440,000
Chili	46,375,000
Uruguay	35,255,000
Peru	31,986,000
Miscellaneous American countries	22,517,000
Russia	38,388,000
Turkey	18,320,000
Egypt	43,753,000
Spain	18,808,000
Italy	11,513,000
Portugal	8,134,000
France	7,071,000
Germany	6,061,000
Miscellaneous European countries	36,319,000
Japan	53,705,000
China	26,809,000
Miscellaneous foreign countries	61,907,000
Total Foreign countries	**1,637,684,000**
Grand total, all countries	**3,191,836,000**

Of our total Colonial and foreign investments 53 per cent. is in the Americas, 16 per cent. is in Asia, 11 per cent. is in Africa, 12 per cent. is in Australasia, and 5 per cent. is in Europe. The geographical distribution of our investments over the various continents is shown by the following statement ;—

		Per cent. of total.
	£	
Americas	1,700,000,000	53
Asia	500,000,000	16
Africa	455,000,000	14
Australasia	387,000,000	12
Europe	150,000,000	5
Total	**3,192,000,000**	**100**

In conclusion, I would ask you to note that this great sum of 3,192,000,000*l.* of capital which Great Britain has supplied to the nations, is not the total sum her people are employing in other lands. I have taken no account of the great sum of what is termed private capital employed abroad by the British people in a variety of ways, such as the purchase of land, loans on mortgage, deposits in banks, branch manufacturing, mercantile, and trade undertakings, &c., &c. If allowance be made, on the one hand, for the foreign capital employed in British companies both at home and abroad and in British loans, and, on the other, for the vast amount of private capital which the British people have placed abroad, I think the net total of our investments in other lands would be not much short of 3,500,000,000*l.* But inasmuch as the amount of the private capital employed abroad cannot be ascertained I have ignored it, and have confined myself to that portion of our capital investments in other lands for which there is documentary evidence.

Discussion *on* Mr. Paish's Paper.

Sir Richard Martin, in proposing a vote of thanks to the author, said he had not had the Paper long enough in his hands to be able to examine it with the detail it deserved, for it was full of interesting matter. He did not quite understand whether Mr. Paish in his totals had eliminated loans granted in order to repay securities issued at a higher rate of interest. It often happened, in America especially, as well as in Japan, that money was borrowed at, say, 5 per cent., but, as the credit of the borrowers improved, they were able to borrow at, say, 4 per cent., and they did so in order to repay the previous loan. That would, of course, make a certain amount of difference. He concluded that the net sum realised was taken, and not the nominal amount of capital, for the reason that in some instances, especially a few years ago, this would show a very considerable difference. In speaking of America, Mr. Paish had said nothing about the defaulting States, and he did not know whether he had taken them into account. He must, however, be aware that certain States had absolutely repudiated their engagements, *e.g.*, Louisiana, Mississippi, West Virginia, and other States which were almost hopelessly and fraudulently bankrupt. Costa Rica and Guatemala had also repudiated. These repudiations amounted in all to about 15,000,000*l.*, and they had to be considered. Mr. Paish was quite right in saying that a very large amount of undisclosed capital was advanced, especially in Canada; and it was surprising to find the amount of money which went out of this country to support farmers and traders. This was a very healthy sign at a time when people were taken in by prospectuses and would not advance to private people unless they were thoroughly established and likely to succeed. He looked upon the money that went out of the country privately as representing some of the best investments made by the British public. One or two points were not quite clear. Did "Colonial and foreign municipal stocks" in the first table include Colonial municipal stocks or only foreign municipal and Colonial and provincial Government stocks? Just above, there was the heading "Colonial and provincial Government loans"; did that refer to the provincial Governments of the Colonies or only the provincial Governments of other countries not included in the Colonies? In the list on page 170, Algeria, Bulgaria, and several States were included; yet only a small proportion of the advances made to the South-eastern States of Europe came from this country; and, as they were nearly all contracted in Paris or Berlin, some of the loans, if held here at the beginning, very rapidly went abroad. He supposed that the total at which Mr. Paish had arrived might be considered to be absolutely up-to-date, and included loans running from remote times. He must confess that he thought the figures came out at an amazing total, and were higher perhaps than those not fully acquainted with the subject would have guessed. He would have liked to have had the opportunity of analysing one or two of the tables; and he suggested to Mr. Paish that he should, in one or two instances, give full details to show exactly how they were produced. That would be both valuable and interesting.

Mr. Paish said he would at once explain how these tables were compiled. As regards the new subscriptions in the last three years all conversions were carefully excluded, so that there was no duplication of capital issued; secondly, the new securities were taken at the price of issue; and, thirdly, vendors' shares were omitted in order to arrive as nearly as possible at the exact amount of money subscribed in the aggregate. Then, as regards the net sum subscribed by British investors, he had taken credit for only those portions of international loans, including American Railway issues, that had been subscribed for in this country. "Colonial provincial" meant loans for Colonial provinces such as Saskatchewan. With regard to the other particulars of the capital provided by our investors up to the end of 1907, they were arrived at by capitalising the income which actually paid income tax to the British Exchequer and by examination of the reports of British companies trading abroad. No credit had been taken for money lent to defaulting States, as in these instances there was of course no income tax paid in respect of coupons. If no coupons were cashed there was no capital against them. The capital sum invested in foreign loans was arrived at by capitalising the coupons that had been encashed. The return of the Inland Revenue Commissioners showed the amount of income received each year as interest from the various Governments; and, having got that, and having ascertained the credit of the Governments, he had capitalised the interest at the years purchase indicated by the interest on the bonds. So far as possible, he had excluded everything which ought to be excluded.

Mr. A. W. FLUX said he rose with great pleasure to second the vote of thanks. Everyone who had attempted to make calculations on this line must be aware of the difficulties the author had had to face, and had faced so well. The amount of instruction contained in such statistics as he had placed before them could hardly be realised on a first hearing. As had been said, they required more close study and more minute analysis than it was possible to give on such an occasion as the reading of the Paper. It struck him as a little remarkable to find, in comparing the totals which Mr. Paish gave when he read his last Paper with those given that day, divided between two great groups—the British Empire outside the United Kingdom and foreign countries—that the rate of increase of capital did not substantially differ in those two groups. He confessed to being a little surprised to find that the British Empire was not attracting an amount of new investments larger relatively to the previously existing aggregate. Comparing the figures of the first page with the summary of the totals on the last page, one found that to the 1,312,000,000*l.* invested in the British Empire three years ago there had been added 242,000,000*l.*; and to the 1,381,000,000*l.* invested in foreign countries there had been added 256,000,000*l.* The relative rate of progress was thus nearly the same. It might be that having regard to the undisclosed investments, to which reference had been made, and which constituted so serious a difficulty in making any satisfactory estimate of the total invested abroad, the unexpected nature of this conclusion might be modified a little. As to how far this was the case Mr. Paish might have formed some opinion, though he would perhaps not care to express it; but, if he did, it would be distinctly interesting. On another point he was inclined to echo the words of Sir Richard Martin, and to ask for a little more light. When one compared the new figures with the old to see what aggregate changes were indicated in different directions, the summaries which Mr. Paish had made enabled one to attempt to grasp the general significance of the Paper. If one compared the total for foreign Government loans on the first page with those shown later, grouped together, there appeared to be a difference not fully accounted for by the new investments, after making allowance for foreign participations. He would be grateful for any further explanation on that point. In view of the impossibility of analysing at short notice such a mass of material, he was tempted to give expression to one little speculation which was suggested by certain remarks in the Paper. The author pointed out that investments formerly made in European countries had been, to a large extent, redeemed as those countries had grown in wealth, in industry, and in capacity to provide for themselves the capital needed for their development. One was tempted to cast one's thoughts forward, and to wonder to what extent that same process might develop in other parts of the world, and in what kind of position our great-grandchildren might find themselves when the growth of civilisation and the development of industry in those countries which, up to the present time, had had to depend on Great Britain, France, Germany and other great capital-owning nations for the funds with which to carry on their development, had brought them to that stage of progress at which they would be able to pay off the greater part of the amounts which they had borrowed at an earlier stage. Then it would appear that the great capital-owning nations must either consume their capital unprofitably or develop within their own territories new means to find a placement for these great sums of capital. One might, of course, imagine that there were revolutionary changes ahead, but one hardly liked to make very definite the thoughts which presented themselves; while to throw out a vague suggestion was almost more unprofitable than to leave it alone. He hoped he would be pardoned for this suggestion, which arose out of some of the reflections to which Mr. Paish had given expression, and which somewhat tempted those who were speculatively inclined.

Mr. ALFRED AKERS said he must associate himself with what previous speakers had said as to the value of the Paper and the great amount of labour obviously involved in its preparation. If he might venture to offer one criticism he would suggest that although these figures dealing with the visible foreign investments might be of extreme value, the private capital employed abroad and in the Colonies could not be ascertained; and, as Mr. Paish's tables were drawn up, he understood, from figures supplied by prospectuses of companies and Government loans, one was liable to fall into grave error as to what the whole amount of capital invested abroad might be, on the ground that private capital was ignored. In the last paragraph, although Mr. Paish said that the amount of private capital could not be ascertained, he had ventured to assume that the total amount of investments abroad, including private capital, would not be much short of 3,500,000,000*l*. Now, as the ascertained visible capital abroad, according to Mr. Paish's calculations, amounted to 3,192,000,000*l*., that left a sum of 308,000,000*l*. estimated for private capital; and when one considered that this unknown private capital included a great amount found here for the purchase of land, &c., abroad, especially in Canada, not by companies but by private persons, and the large amount invested abroad by companies ostensibly working in England, whose capital was not necessarily known to be employed abroad, he asked whether

Mr. Paish could give any ground whatever for his assumption of the probable amount of invisible capital sent abroad. He might be quite right in his view that the sum privately subscribed for foreign investment was only about 308,000,000*l.*, or one-tenth of the sum which he found was known to have been publicly subscribed. He must, however, have had some reason for arriving at that figure; and if he could explain why he thought that relatively small sum was sufficient, it would be helpful. One might well surmise, he thought, that a sum similar to that subscribed openly might possibly be invested privately. Could Mr. Paish set out grounds for fixing, within limits, the amount likely to have been privately subscribed? Failing that, they were so much in the dark that they might fall into serious error in drawing deductions from the Paper.

Mr. W. R. LAWSON said the greatest compliment they could pay Mr. Paish was to recognise the fact that he had undertaken a great work, and that, so far as he had gone, he had done it with very great ability and success. At the same time, they must recognise that this work was far from being completed. As Sir Richard Martin had pointed out, much more analysis was required, and also more deduction as well as addition. After that had been done, the most important part of all had to come, namely, to find out the actual economic significance and value of these huge figures. So far, the author did not pretend to have tackled that part of the problem. He had thrown out suggestions here and there which indicated clearly enough his own opinions on the subject, but he had come to no precise scientific conclusions with regard to the meaning of these figures. For instance, the title of the paper might be objected to. With all respect for Mr. Paish, he thought the term "capital investments" was misleading and inapplicable, and that the proper term would be "financial operations." Mr. Paish was naturally aware that in every one of these transactions there was a great deal of finance; generally, there was quite as much credit as actual cash. Consequently, it was a misnomer to speak about "capital investments," and a still worse misnomer to speak of these so-called "investments" as being entirely savings. They were not wholly savings, perhaps not even the major part of them. Everything was a mixture of financial operations. He did not think Mr. Paish had made anything like sufficient allowance for what he might call the decay of our foreign investments—not merely by depreciation or actual loss, but by passing into other hands. To give an illustration of that, in connection with our foreign and Colonial railway investments, we had been the largest railway builders in the world. If anybody could challenge us on that point it was the Americans, but their railway building was confined to their own country, whereas we had built railways all over the world, and we had financed them. But we were not by any means the greatest railway owners at the present day; for thousands of miles of the railways which were built in the early days—by Brassey, for instance—had entirely passed out of our hands. Brassey built nearly the whole of the Roumanian railways; but now we did not own a mile of them.

Again, in the case of Germany, when he first knew the late Mr. Staats-Forbes, he was Chairman of several important railway companies in Rhenish Germany; but those had been all taken back by the Germans. Nearly all our Brazilian railways had been taken back by the Government. If we were going to have an exact estimate of our investments in foreign and Colonial railways we should have to make very large allowance for investments which had passed out of our hands, though in one form or another they still figured among our foreign investments. Turning to Canada, the undertaking of the Canadian Pacific Railway, when it had a stock capital of about $65,000,000, was very largely owned in this country; but now that its capital was $200,000,000 we held a comparatively small portion of it. If we imagined we possessed $200,000,000 of the Canadian Pacific capital we should be making a great mistake. Then, taking as an opposite example the Grand Trunk Railway, we put into that railway many millions of hard cash; but the hard cash had in the course of time dwindled down to a small part of what our people put into it. As he understood, the author made no deduction for that kind of loss, the wear and tear of investments. On the other hand, he made no allowance for the immense appreciation in some classes of foreign investments. Taking the rubber group as an example, he valued that at 10,000,000*l*. sterling; but most of the rubber shares stood at high premiums, some of them at 2,000 or 3,000 per cent. It would take years of labour to arrive at a really correct figure on this subject. Without presuming to say that Mr. Paish's figures were wrong, he would simply point out that they were not and could not possibly be scientific figures. His chief exception to them was that they seemed to favour the curious fallacy that our capital abroad was always going and coming—going out in the shape of exports and coming back in the shape of imports. The bulk of it does not come back at all, nor even the bulk of the interest. Both capital and interest accumulate abroad, and are moved from one country to another without ever coming home. In order to refute the savings fallacy he had made out a list of the new issues made during the eleven years beginning with 1900. The total was 1,548,000,000*l*.; but if they concluded from that that they had actually saved 1,548,000,000*l*., and put it into foreign investments, they would be living in a fool's paradise. A great part of those investments had gone into other hands, a good deal was lost, and much of it had been financed without money either going out or coming in. He hoped Mr. Paish would appreciate the friendly nature of the criticism he had ventured to make. He was simply endeavouring to point out some of the work still requiring to be done. It would be presumption for him to find fault with work which was a speciality of Mr. Paish, and unique of its kind He was only suggesting points for further elucidation.

Mr. T. A. WELTON said he would like to ask Mr. Paish, with regard to the mines in South Africa, which he had put down at 150,000,000*l*., whether that was a representation of the capitalised dividends, or whether it represented the total amount of mining capital in that part of the world; and, if the total amount issued was much greater than that, it would be of interest to know how he had got rid of the odd millions. With regard to private capital, no doubt in former years a very great deal of the business of America and also of Russia was done with English capital provided in enormous quantities. Factors who collected produce in Russia were provided with money from England. Some years ago an individual factor failed for about 200,000*l.*, nearly all of which was due to English people. As far as the United States went, he believed the position of things was altogether altered, and that the Americans were now better able to provide us with money than we were able to supply them. At the same time, no doubt, an enormous amount of English capital which could not by any possibility come within the four corners of the Paper was used for carrying on the commerce of other countries.

Mr. HENRY BEAUMONT said that, as a visitor, he wished to express how deeply grateful he felt to Mr. Paish for his very useful Paper on a subject which was paramount in the minds of many people to-day, and was often used, he was sorry to say, for very unworthy purposes. But they should dismiss all that from their minds in looking at this subject. He thought the totals arrived at were quite within the mark, but he did not agree with the totals given for the last three years. He could not bring himself to realise that in three years we had subscribed as much as 450,000,000*l.* of new capital to foreign countries and our Colonies, and he did not think sufficient allowance had been made for the large participation of foreign houses in a great many of these issues. It was very rare nowadays to get entirely to ourselves a loan of any importance; a large portion was always reserved for some foreign countries, and he did not think sufficient allowance had been made for the enormous transfer of securities from London to other European countries. For instance, there had been an enormous shifting of Mexican securities from London to other great centres in Europe. Apart from this, he thought the figures were substantially accurate; but there were two points to which he would like to invite attention. On page 181 Mr. Paish said "Never has Great Britain had so much new available capital for investment in the Colonies and in India, and never has she supplied money so freely to the other nations of the Empire as she has done in the past few years." There was a great reason for that. The total amount of foreign and Colonial investments in the last five years came to very nearly the amount of interest due from those countries, so that practically we had sent out little fresh capital. What it came to was that we had simply left in our debtor countries the amount of money due to us for interest on the moneys invested, so that fresh capital had not been found to the extent people thought. That had an important bearing on several questions. We had passed the pioneer days, and had arrived at a state of things with regard to foreign and Colonial investments which we had never touched before. We were lending every year about the amount, taking the average of five years, which was due to us from those countries. He did not think we could make better investments, as we were simply providing money for the extension of railways and other undertakings. Mr. Lawson had said something about the great economic questions underlying this Paper, to which the author had not referred, and he would refer to one of them. Something had been said about the small amount of capital which had gone to Australia; our large insurance companies had had to withdraw capital from there. Four or five years ago those companies had millions of money invested in that Continent, but they were no longer able to employ it there, for the simple reason that there was sufficient money in Australia to supply the demand at the present time and there was no room for any large outlay of new capital. The greater part of our money had gone in the construction of railways—in Australia, about 100,000,000*l.*; in Canada, about 150,000,000*l.*; in Argentina, about 170,000,000*l.*; and in India, about 150,000,000*l.* The position then was that we had lent money to Australia at a low rate of interest; she had made her railways, and she had made them at a very considerable profit—as much, taking it altogether, as half to threequarters per cent. on a total of over 100,000,000*l.* All the interest we had in that was to supply Australia with locomotives, for which, he believed, she was our best customer. The case of Canada was totally different. We had supplied 150,000,000*l.* to 160,000,000*l.*, and that investment was in most cases returning us a considerable rate of interest—in the case of the Canadian Pacific a very high rate—and therefore one could look on them, as a whole, as very profitable. But from the point of view of trade our interest ceased; we sold nothing to Canada—we did not supply even steel rails or locomotives. In Argentina there were from 16,000 to 18,000 miles of railway, all built by British firms. We had supplied them with 170,000,000*l.* of capital, 70,000,000*l.* of which brought in 7 per cent. interest and the rest a very high rate. There had been an enormous stimulus to the industries of this country, since we supplied the whole of those railways with rails, locomotives, cars, and all the necessary material. These large investments were therefore of considerable importance to this country. In the case of India we reaped a benefit all round. Next to Australia, India was the largest customer we had had for locomotives; we had supplied all the material and all the equipment, and built the railways, and we reaped the profit very largely. All those things pointed to the fact that under our present system capital flowed in the directions where it was wanted and where it could be most remuneratively employed, and that showed that our system was right. That point seemed of considerable importance, and one which should be borne in mind. Another point not mentioned in the Paper was the creation of enormous trusts. Every boom was followed by the creation of a trust, and in that form all the premier securities became exceedingly safe. We had, perhaps, 100,000,000*l.* of money invested all over the world in companies which the ordinary investor would never think of touching, and these trusts had been the means of creating an enormous amount of securities which might be considered of a premier character, and which had very largely come into competition with our own securities.

Sir EDGAR SPEYER expressed his great pleasure at listening to so interesting and important a Paper, and his admiration for the thoroughness with which the author had prepared it. He had carefully listened to the criticisms which had been offered, but he had not heard anything which invalidated the conclusions at which the author had arrived; in fact, he thought the figures given were compiled in the most careful and conservative way. Mr. Lawson had suggested that the author had not taken into account depreciation and waste, but that was, in his opinion, more than balanced by the great appreciation. On the whole, he thought the depreciation was insignificant compared with the appreciation of the investments of this country. Mr. Beaumont had brought in a good many points which seemed to go rather beyond the scope of the Paper. The author had not dealt with the economic aspect of this matter; he was simply concerned in proving what the investments were. There were a variety of magnificent results which sprang from those investments, but to deal with these results was not the nature of the Paper. He had some doubt as to whether the average rate of interest at which Mr. Paish had arrived was not a little misleading; because he thought account should be taken of the amortisation of capital. Had Mr. Paish done this? The average of 5·2 per cent. would include revenue from diamond and other mining companies *given* at 30 per cent. That might be the income to-day; but amongst investments of that character a great deal of amortisation should be allowed, and it did not seem quite fair to take such a high yield and then to conclude that the average yield was 5 per cent.

Mr. J. M. KEYNES suggested that the Paper should more properly have been entitled "Estimated Amount of Capital Subscribed in London" rather than "Estimated Foreign Investments." If they were to take it as an estimate of foreign investments, it was subject to two opposing errors, both large and both of an unknown amount; but because the errors were in opposite directions it did not follow that the estimate could be regarded as a good estimate of foreign investments proper. On the one hand, the author made no pretence of including the amount invested otherwise than by subscription in London; on the other, he could not allow fully for the capital originally subscribed in London but which had found its way abroad subsequently; and several speakers had shown that both these errors were likely to be large. They were not justified in assuming that because these two errors were in opposite directions, they therefore cancelled out. Mr. Paish had given them extremely valuable material towards making an estimate, and had calculated the most important single item which must be taken into account in estimating the amount of capital invested abroad, but he (the speaker) did not think it ought to be regarded as supplying even a temporary estimate of foreign investments proper. It had been pointed out that when Mr. Paish moved from his original estimate to his final estimate of 3,500,000,000*l.*, the addition of 300,000,000*l.* odd was perfectly arbitrary, and that no adequate reason for that had been given. He would like to ask the author whether there was any detailed evidence to support the statement that the total amount of shares held on the Continent in certain companies was inconsiderable. A good many statements made that evening had seemed to controvert it, and had suggested that the amount might be very large. He was astonished that we should have now anything like 600,000,000*l*. in American railways; but he was not in the least astonished that that amount had been subscribed originally. Again, it would be extremely useful if, in a later investigation, the author would separate Ceylon from India. In investigations concerning Indian currency and the level of prices it would be useful to have some sort of estimate of the capital invested in India; but, so long as Ceylon was included in India, the value for these purposes of Mr. Paish's calculations was much diminished. There would probably be no difficulty in separating them, as for different parts of Australasia that division had been made.

The PRESIDENT said that, before putting the vote of thanks, he might be permitted to express his personal appreciation of the Paper. What seemed to him to be perhaps the pleasantest feature of it was that when one analysed the purposes to which this enormous amount of capital was applied, one found that in almost every case it was for reproductive and beneficent purposes. It seemed to be one of the great changes which had taken place during the last forty years that Governments, when they applied for a loan of capital, had changed the application of the capital so obtained. When he was first in the House of Commons, some forty years back, in the days of austere finance, any Government that borrowed was looked upon somewhat askance, and it was assumed that the loan was required for the purpose of balancing the deficiency between the expenditure and the revenue, or for the purpose of increasing armaments or the warlike establishments of the borrowing country. This change had, in one sense, given foreign Governments a better position in the borrowing market than they had before. Assuming that the figures on page 168 were correct, the total amount of British capital invested in foreign Government loans was estimated at 167,000,000*l*.; and on page 169 there was an estimate of the amount of capital supplied to foreign countries during the last three years which amounted to no less than 54,000,000*l*. Assuming those two sets of figures to be correct, they got the astonishing fact that the British capital supplied during the last three years was equivalent to one-third of the total capital supplied during all previous years. If that was so it must be because the investor felt that he had now not only the benefit of the security of the borrower, but also the satisfaction of knowing that the money supplied would be put to a good purpose. He recollected that many years ago the Indian Government was supposed to be in a very bad way because it was constantly borrowing, but the whole of the sums so borrowed were applied to public works and railroads; and he believed the result of that policy of judicious borrowing was that the Indian Government had now as good or a better balance-sheet than any Government in the world—their assets more than covered their liabilities. Perhaps that was wandering a little from the subject, but he thought that if one wanted to test the solvency or the credit of a foreign Government one ought to take the amount of its indebtedness by itself, divide it, and see what was the total amount chargeable on its revenues, and the dead weight of expenditure in order to meet the sums borrowed. If one did that one often found there was a very wide discrepancy between the total amount of indebtedness of a country and the actual amount of dead weight which it imposed on its revenue. Mr. Paish's Paper had passed through criticism most successfully. No doubt there must be a number of difficulties in getting an absolutely accurate actuarial calculation of our foreign investments. He thought it was impossible, but Mr. Paish had placed before them a clear view of the situation, and they were much indebted to him for having taken so much trouble and for having dealt so satisfactorily with perhaps one of the most important subjects which could occupy their attention.

Mr. Paish, in returning thanks, said he thought he could answer almost every point which had been raised. He would first refer to Mr. Flux's remarks, and make an explanation with regard to foreign Government loans. In his previous Paper, in order not to overstate the amount of capital placed abroad, he had calculated our investments in Government bonds on the basis of the market prices of those bonds which paid interest. With regard to everything else but Government loans, he was obliged to take the nominal amount of capital. When he got the balance sheet, he had to take the capital raised by the company. Whether the market value of that capital had fallen in value or risen in value was immaterial; the documentary evidence was the figure contained in the balance sheet. In the aggregate, he believed that the market value of the companies' capitals was largely in excess of the sum subscribed. Indeed, it would be found that on the whole this country derived a large income from the increment in the value of securities. To take American railways as an example, about eleven years ago Atchison shares stood at 18, to-day they were at over par. Many people bought them at the low price. He also remembered that only a few years ago the shares of the United Steel Corporation stood at under 30, and many people bought at this price, and to-day they were between 70 and 80. As to foreign Government loans, one was in this position—one either had to take the market prices all round, and get away from the principle one applied to all the miscellaneous companies, or else to take the nominal amounts all round as shown by the balance sheets and the amounts of the outstanding loans. He had, therefore, taken the nominal amount of the loans of those Governments which paid interest, and had excluded the loans of Governments upon which no interest was received. That accounted for the difference of about 25,000,000*l.* between the two figures. With regard to private foreign capital, it was very difficult to make any estimate of the amount. With regard to gold mines, they had great houses here which knew where the shares were held. He had the good fortune of ascertaining, through a mutual friend, from the chairman of one of the greatest houses, what proportion of the South African gold mining shares were held on the Continent and in London, and he was surprised at the relative smallness of the percentage held on the Continent. He could not give the figure, because it had been told him in confidence; but it was comparatively small. He had made as thorough an inquiry as he could. Sir Edgar Speyer was good enough to give him the actual amount of capital put by our investors into the National Railways of Mexico, and it came to 23,000,000*l*. Last year, when he was in Canada, he had been informed by Sir Thomas Shaughnessy, the President of the Canadian Pacific Railway, that the English people held practically all the debentures, all the preference stock, and about 65 per cent. of the common stock of that great company. With regard to the depreciation and ebbing away of capital in foreign loans, he had entirely excluded all foreign loan capital upon which we were not now receiving interest. The income-tax returns showed the amount of interest which paid income tax. People would not pay income tax unless they received income, and as foreigners could not now get income tax back again, they might rest assured that the Government loans on which income tax was paid was British capital. In recent years that ebbing away of foreign Government loans, which was not an unusual feature a few years ago, had stopped. It was not correct to say that he had taken the new issues in London. He had taken the capital income received on our foreign investments as far as the Inland Revenue Commissioners took it out, and that figure applied to Government loans, and municipal and railway stocks and bonds; with regard to the remainder, the miscellaneous companies, he had taken only English reports, excluding all foreign reports. That was an actual figure as nearly as it could be arrived at, as far as the visible capital was concerned. It was only with regard to the last three years that he had to take new issues. It was obvious that it would have been quite impossible to go through the reports for the two years later than those of 1907; the work of going through between 3,000 and 4,000 companies' reports was enormous, and therefore he had to take the new issues of capital as indicating the amount subscribed in the last three years. To come, however, to a more important point, was there any confirmatory evidence that our income from foreign investments was anything like 5 per cent. on 3,500,000,000*l*.? Were we getting an income of something like 175,000,000*l*. from the interest on capital invested abroad? First of all, we had our trade balance; we knew how much our imports exceeded our exports. For the current year it would be only about 140,000,000*l*. sterling. In 1903 it was 183,000,000*l*. Then they had a rough notion of what shipping brought in. Sir Robert Giffen calculated that it brought in 90,000,000*l*. a year, and if that calculation was anything like correct, we should be certainly receiving over 100,000,000*l*. a year now.

Mr. LAWSON said Sir Thomas Sutherland had pointed out that that was gross income; and that Sir Robert Giffen did not allow anything for expenses.

Mr. PAISH said the amount spent abroad relatively to the total was comparatively small. He had already started an investigation as to the amount of income we derived from shipping, but it was a very arduous task; it necessitated going to individual companies and asking them to analyse their books, which was not an easy thing to do. We were receiving a very large income from shipping. In the first place, as far as depreciation went, a big item must come to this country; secondly, coal went from this country; some of the coal was bought abroad, but a large quantity was shipped at home. Then came provisions; a good many provisions were bought here. As to wages, a considerable part of the wages and salaries paid came to this country. Then the profits all came home. When one came to the total result, it would be found that the greater portion of the gross earnings of the ships came back to England, and the amount was certainly very large—whether 90,000,000*l.* or 100,000,000*l.* he did not know. Since Sir Robert Giffen made his statement there had been a very large increase in shipping, and he doubted if our income from shipping was now much less than 100,000,000*l.* Thus, first of all there was interest—about 175,000,000*l.*; secondly, shipping; and thirdly, services. The services performed by the British people for other countries were very valuable; a large part of the business of buying and selling securities for the whole of Europe was done on the London Stock Exchange. People found it more convenient and cheaper to do this through London rather than in Berlin or Paris; and that brought us a great deal of business. Then, to take produce, a considerable income came to brokers in this country engaged in the purchase and sale of produce for foreign clients. For instance, a ship coming into the Channel laden with wheat was probably sold to the Continent through English brokers. Then there were the tourists. It was true the English people spent much money abroad, but numbers of Americans spent large sums in this country; and Colonial friends and foreigners who came to England spent money very freely. The tourist business was very large and profitable. Beyond that, there was a certain amount of remittances to Ireland and to this country, by way of gifts, from America. He had the honour of making an investigation for the Monetary Commission into the Trade Balance of the United States; and he came to the conclusion that the American people gave away each year to Europe 30,000,000*l.* sterling, of which no small share came to these islands. He thought there was no doubt that we in England, Ireland and Scotland received something like 5,000,000*l.* from the United States and Canada in the form of gifts to friends. There was also the income we received upon the return of Civil Servants and others from other lands with considerable savings. Then, insurance was a considerable item, and education fees for children here whose parents lived abroad. When one totalled up all these items, the amount of income which came to this country was very large indeed. He had not got to the end of the investigation, but he thought it reached at least 300,000,000*l.* a year. We were entitled to receive goods from other countries to the extent of over 300,000,000*l.* a year, and not to have to export a single pound's worth of goods against it. If that were true, and as far as he could see, it was true, it was evident that if we had a trade balance of only 140,000,000*l.* a year, we had a balance representing investments of capital abroad of something like 160,000,000*l.* to account for the difference. This was the figure he had arrived at. Mr. Beaumont said we did not receive interest from other countries, but left it there. In a sense, that was true. If people owed you money and you did not draw it, it meant that you were lending it back to them. But, as a matter of fact, it did come to this country. If Mr. Beaumont would look at the trade figures he would find that whenever we exported very little capital the exports were very small. If Mr. Beaumont would go back to 1890, when we were exporting a large amount of capital, he would recollect that our export trade reached to 263,000,000*l.*; the next three years it showed great decline, as Great Britain was investing very little capital abroad. Indeed, we did not invest much until 1904; but in 1904 we lent money to Japan for war purposes. From that time we began to lend freely again and our export trade began to expand quickly. In 1904 the export trade was only about 290,000,000*l.*; by 1907, the period of great expansion, it had grown to 426,000,000*l.*—or 136,000,000*l.* in four years—and the bulk of that increase was due to our increased loans of money to other countries. We were selling our produce, and taking payment in securities. Had it been otherwise, our exports would not have gone up, but would have remained relatively stationary. So also would the imports. But it was not so. When exports went up imports also went up in some degree. It was quite evident that when we exported capital it created a great demand for British goods. Our exports expanded and the imports too; it was essential that they should. When we were doing well we consumed freely, and in order to consume freely we must buy from other countries the foodstuffs, the additional foodstuffs, and the raw materials we needed. Again, if our manufactures increased, as they always did when we invested capital freely in other lands, we must buy increased quantities of raw materials to manufacture. Anyone who looked through the trade figures of the last sixty years would find that the exports went up and down in almost exact proportion to our willingness or unwillingness to invest capital. In the fifties, sixties, and early seventies we lent freely, and our exports expanded. In the later seventies we would lend to no one, and the exports fell severely, while our imports expanded. The amount of our investments in Ceylon was not very large, and, in proportion to our investments in India, was insignificant. With regard to the gold mines, in every case where the companies allowed for depreciation, and many of them did allow either for depreciation or development, the sums allowed were deducted from the profit received.

The following candidates were elected Fellows of the Society:—

Edward Alan Christian.
Hugh Dalton.
Walter Lee-Nash.
N. J. Malachowski.
Alexander M. C. Saunders.
Johannes Viereck.

THE EXPORT OF CAPITAL AND THE COST OF LIVING

George Paish

THE EXPORT OF CAPITAL AND THE COST OF LIVING.

READ BEFORE THE

MANCHESTER STATISTICAL SOCIETY

BY

SIR GEORGE PAISH.

The advance in the cost of living in recent years has not merely created much discussion of a theoretical character, it has had far-reaching political and economic consequences. In the United States it largely contributed to the defeat of the Republican Party at the last Presidential election, and has since enabled legislation to be passed through Congress having for its objects a great reduction of the tariff, and the reform of the banking system, by means of which more banking accommodation will be made available for the farming districts. Moreover, it has caused the American people to demand the abolition of the Trust system, and the restoration of effective competition both in production and in distribution. In Germany it has compelled the Government to impose heavy taxes upon the wealthy classes in order to provide for additional expenditures under the new army law, whereas previously, when the cost of living was lower, taxation was mainly placed upon the masses. Furthermore, the high cost of living has created much discontent among the German people with the existing tariff, as the latter has greatly accentuated the effect upon retail prices in Germany of the rise in world prices. In France also it has caused a serious effort to be made to raise new taxation by means of a tax upon incomes instead of by taxes upon imports, in consequence of the urgent need of the French Government to obtain revenue without further adding to the cost of living. In this country the rise in prices has drawn attention to the desirableness of increasing the productivity of the soil by various means, including the creation of a large number of small holdings, the cultivation and improvement of derelict lands, the erection of cottages, and an advance in the rate of agricultural wages. Speaking broadly, the rise in prices has brought about reductions, or has prevented further increases, in Customs tariffs, notwithstanding the rapidly growing expenditures upon armaments; has created political unrest, has strengthened the power of the working classes, and has caused heavier taxation to be imposed upon the wealthy.

The economic consequences of the high cost of living have been equally noteworthy. The burden of higher prices has fallen mainly on the manufacturing countries, districts, and classes of the world; and everywhere there has been agitation for compensatory advances in wages—in factories, in mines, and upon railways. On the other hand, the rise in prices has brought immense advantage to the agricultural districts and classes, which have enjoyed a degree of prosperity greater than for many years. The change in the condition of the agricultural countries and districts in the last 15 or 16 years has, indeed, been remarkable, and whereas during the 'nineties, when the cost of living was so very low, farmers, pastoralists, and planters had great difficulty in making ends meet, in the last ten, and especially in the last seven, years they have enjoyed great good fortune. The agricultural industry got back to a profitable basis in 1900, and has enjoyed really good times since 1906.

To show the great fall in the wholesale prices of vegetable and animal food and of raw textiles in the 'nineties, and the substantial recovery since then, I give the respective index numbers of vegetable and animal foods and raw textiles, compiled mainly from English quotations:—

Year	Vegetable Food* (Corn, &c.)	Animal Food.† (Meat, &c.)	Raw Textiles‡
1883	**82**	**103**	**70**
1884	71	97	68
1885	68	88	65
1886	65	87	63
1887	64	79	65
1888	67	82	64
1889	65	86	**70**
1890	65	82	66
1891	75	81	59
1892	65	84	57
1893	59	85	59
1894	55	80	53
1895	54	78	52
1896	**53**	**73**	54
1897	60	79	**51**
1898	67	77	**51**
1899	60	79	**58**
1900	62	85	66
1901	62	85	60
1902	63	87	61
1903	62	84	66
1904	63	83	71
1905	63	87	72
1906	62	89	80
1907	69	88	77
1908	70	89	62
1909	71	89	64
1910	65	96	73
1911	70	90	76
1912	**78**	96	76
1913	69	**99**	**84**

* Seven vegetable foods. † Five animal foods. ‡ Six raw textiles.

There was an advance in the price of vegetable food from 1896 to 1912 of nearly 50 per cent., a rise of nearly 36 per cent. in animal food between 1896 and 1913, and of 64 per cent. in raw textiles between 1898 and 1913.

This advance, or rather, recovery, in prices has worked a revolution in the well-being of the agricultural communities of the world since 1896. To give some indication of the enormous expansion in the incomes of farmers, due both to their increased productions and the higher prices realised, I give the following statement of the world's cereal crops on the average in the three years' period 1911 to 1913 in comparison with the average of the three years 1893 to 1895:—

World's Crops.

AVERAGE ANNUAL PRODUCTION.

	1911–1913	1893–1895	Increase	
	Bushels	Bushels	Bushels	%
Wheat ..	3,929,248,000	2,514,839,000	+1,414,409,000	+56
Maize ..	3,542,384,000	2,116,000,000	+1,426,384,000	+67
Oats ..	3,842,629,000	2,486,666,000	+1,355,963,000	+54
Rye ..	1,698,504,000	1,363,467,000	+ 335,037,000	+24
Barley ..	1,571,256,000	865,333,000	+ 705,923,000	+81
Total	14,584,021,000	9,346,305,000	+5,237,716,000	+56

The average crops of 1911-13 have been worked from data contained in Dornbusch's "Floating Cargoes List," and those of 1893-5 from the "Corn Trade Year Book."

These greatly increased crops have been sold at prices nearly 54 per cent. higher than the quotations current 18 years previously. This will be seen from the following comparison of the average farm prices in the United States, which are those at which the crops of the United States are valued by the American Agricultural Department. The comparison is as follows:—

American Farm Prices, December 1.

	Average Price per Bushel 1911–13	1893–95	Increase	
	d.	d.	d.	%
Wheat	39.50	24.96	+14.54	+58.2
Maize	28.98	17.45	+11.53	+66.0
Oats	18.85	13.26	+ 5.59	+42.1
Rye	34.58	23.60	+10.98	+46.5
Barley	31.02	19.32	+11.70	+60.5
Average	29.88	19.42	+10.46	+53.8

The following comparison will give some indication of the enormous increase in the income of farmers in all the agricultural countries and districts of the world since 1893-5:—

Values of World's Cereal Crops.

	Annual Average 1911–13	1893–1895	Increase	
	£	£	£	%
Wheat ..	638,400,000	261,500,000	+ 376,900,000	+144
Maize ..	427,700,000	153,800,000	+ 273,900,000	+178
Oats ..	301,800,000	137,700,000	+ 164,100,000	+119
Rye ..	244,700,000	133,700,000	+ 111,000,000	+ 83
Barley ..	203,100,000	69,700,000	+ 133,400,000	+191
Total ..	1,815,700,000	756,400,000	+1,059,300,000	+140

Had the prices of cereals in 1911-13 been as low as in 1893-5, the incomes of farmers from the five cereal crops would have been £1,169,000,000 instead of £1,816,000,000. The advantage to farmers of the recovery in prices was thus £647,000,000.

To give some idea of the effect of the rise in the prices of textiles upon the income of the world's agricultural industry, I set out below a statement of the world's cotton production, the quantity of jute produced in India, as well as the quantities of wool exported by the chief exporting countries:—

Supply of Cotton, Wool, and Jute.

	1911-12-13	1893-4-5	Increase	
	Lb.	Lb.	Lb.	%
Cotton (a)	9,418,500,000	5,466,500,000	+3,952,000,000	+72
Wool (b)	1,336,500,000	1,118,100,000	+ 218,400,000	+20
Jute (c)	3,880,000,000	2,343,000,000	+1,537,000,000	+65
Total	14,635,000,000	8,927,600,000	+5,707,400,000	+64

(a) World's crops according to the *New York Chronicle*.
(b) Exports of Australasia, South Africa, and Argentina, according to Messrs. Helmuth, Schwartze and Co. and the Government return.
(c) Indian crop.

The prices at which these textiles were sold were approximately as follows:—

Prices of Cotton, Wool, and Jute.

	Prices per Lb. 1911-12-13	1893-4-5	Advances	
	d.	d.	d.	%
Cotton .. .. (a)	5.34	3.12	+2.22	+71
Wool .. .. (b)	10.04	6.63	+3.41	+52
Jute .. .. (c)	2.44	1.29	+1.15	+89
Average ..	4.99	3.08	+1.91	+62

(a) Farm prices, United States, December 1 (Government return).
(b) Approximate average compiled mainly from prices given by Messrs. Helmuth, Schwartze and Co.
(c) English price.

This increase of 64 per cent. in production of three textiles has been attended by a rise of 62 per cent. in prices, and has brought 166 per cent. more income to growers. How great the expansion has been is shown by the following statement:—

*Values of Cotton and Jute Crops and Wool Shipments.**

	1911-12-13	1893-4-5	Increase	
	£	£	£	%
Cotton ..	209,600,000	71,100,000	+138,500,000	+195
Wool ..	55,600,000	30,900,000	+ 24,700,000	+ 80
Jute ..	39,400,000	12,600,000	+ 26,800,000	+213
Total ..	304,600,000	114,600,000	+190,000,000	+166

* Wool shipments from Australasia, South Africa, and Argentina.

Had prices in 1911-13 been as low as in 1893-5, the income of planters and farmers from these three cereals would have been £180,000,000 instead of £304,000,000. The rise in prices has thus given them £126,000,000 of additional income. If the wool crop of the whole world were included the advantage would be still greater.

Roughly speaking, the income of the agricultural countries has increased on the average by nearly 60 per cent. owing to the rise in prices, without any additional work on their part having been necessary.

To make a comparison between the income of farmers and that of other persons is exceedingly difficult, but some idea can be formed from data compiled by the American Census Bureau, which ascertains the number of persons engaged in agriculture and the value of their products, as well as the number of wage-earners engaged in manufactures, with the aggregate wages paid to them. This shows that whereas the average income of all persons engaged in agriculture, including the farmers and planters, between 1900 and 1910 rose from £91 to £148 per head, the average wages paid to persons engaged in manufacture rose only from £86 to £104 per head.

Here are the calculations:—

Income of Persons Engaged in Agriculture.

	Persons in U.S. Engaged in Agriculture	Value of Products	Annual Income per Person
		$	$
1910	11,500,000a	8,498,000,000b	739
1900	10,382,000	4,717,000,000	454

(a) Based on the average number of persons engaged per farm.
(b) In 1912 the value of the products had grown to $9,299,000,000, equal to an income of about $750 per head of the persons engaged.

Income of Wage-earners Engaged in Manufacture.

	Wage-earners in U.S. Engaged in Manufacture Number	Wages Paid	Average per Person
		$	$
1910	6,615,000	3,427,000,000	518
1900	4,712,000	2,008,000,000	426

The American Agricultural Department makes a valuation of farm property in the United States at the end of each decade. The following comparison shows that between 1890 and 1900, when the depression in agriculture was so severe, the average value per acre of agricultural land and buildings in the United States actually declined.

Value of Farm Property and Products in United States, Census Years 1900 and 1890.

(000's omitted.)

	1900 $	1890 $	Increase $	%
Land and buildings	16,615,000	13,279,000	+ 3,335,000	+ 25
Implements and machinery	750,000	494,000	+ 256,000	+ 52
Live stock	3,075,000	2,309,000	+ 767,000	+ 33
Total	20,440,000	16,082,000	+ 4,358,000	+ 27
Acreage	838,592	623,219	+ 215,373	+ 34
Average value of land and buildings per acre	$19.81	$21.30	− $1.49	− 7

The decline of 7 per cent. in the average value of land and buildings per acre was notwithstanding the recovery in prices and in the value of property between 1896 and 1900. The following statement affords some idea of the really wonderful prosperity of farmers since 1900:—

Value of Farm Property and Products in United States, Census Years 1910 and 1900.

(000's omitted.)

	1910 $	1900 $	Increase $	%
Farm land	28,476,000	13,058,000	+ 15,418,000	+ 118
Farm buildings	6,325,000	3,557,000	+ 2,769,000	+ 78
Implements and machinery	1,265,000	750,000	+ 515,000	+ 69
Live stock	4,925,000	3,075,000	+ 1,850,000	+ 60
Total	40,991,000	20,440,000	+ 20,551,000	+ 100
Acreage	878,798	838,592	+ 40,206,000	+ 5
Average value of land per acre	$32.40	$15.57	+ $16.83	+ 108
Buildings	7.20	4.24	+ 2.96	+ 70
Average value of land and buildings per acre	$39.60	$19.81	+ $19.79	+ 100

Thus, whereas in 1900 the average value of land and of buildings per acre in the United States was under £4, in 1910 it was nearly £8, an advance of no less than 100 per cent. Since 1910 the prosperity of the farming industry has been fully maintained.

The farm prices of the principal cereal crops of the United States on December 1 of each year since 1880 are given below:—

Farm Values of Principal Crops of United States.

December 1	Wheat per Bushel Cents	Maize per Bushel Cents	Oats per Bushel Cents	Rye per Bushel Cents	Barley per Bushel Cents
1880	95.1	39.6	36.0	75.6	66.6
1881	**119.2**	**63.6**	**46.4**	**93.3**	**82.3**
1882	88.4	48.5	37.5	61.5	62.9
1883	91.1	42.4	32.7	58.1	58.7
1884	64.5	35.7	27.7	51.9	48.7
1885	77.1	32.8	28.5	57.9	56.3
1886	68.7	36.6	29.8	53.8	53.6
1887	68.1	44.4	30.4	54.5	51.9
1888	92.6	34.1	27.8	58.8	59.0
1889	69.8	28.3	22.9	42.3	41.6
1890	83.8	50.6	42.4	62.9	62.7
1891	83.9	40.6	31.5	77.4	52.4
1892	62.4	39.4	31.7	54.2	47.5
1893	53.8	36.5	29.4	51.3	41.1
1894	**49.1**	45.7	32.4	50.1	44.2
1895	50.9	25.3	19.9	44.0	33.7
1896	72.6	**21.5**	**18.7**	**40.9**	**32.3**
1897	80.8	26.3	21.2	44.7	37.7
1898	58.2	28.7	25.5	46.3	41.3
1899	58.4	30.3	24.9	51.0	40.3
1900	61.9	35.7	25.8	51.2	40.9
1901	62.4	60.5	39.9	55.7	45.2
1902	63.0	40.3	30.7	50.5	45.9
1903	69.5	42.5	34.1	54.5	45.6
1904	92.4	44.1	31.3	68.8	42.0
1905	74.8	41.2	29.1	61.1	40.5
1906	66.7	39.9	31.7	58.9	41.5
1907	87.4	51.6	44.3	73.1	66.6
1908	92.8	60.6	**47.2**	73.6	55.4
1909	**99.0**	59.6	40.5	73.9	55.2
1910	88.3	48.0	34.4	71.5	57.8
1911	87.4	61.8	45.0	**83.2**	**86.9**
1912	76.0	48.7	31.9	66.3	50.5
1913	79.9	**69.1**	39.2	63.4	53.7

These calculations agree with the general experience of persons engaged in manufacture and in agriculture respectively. Not for a long time past have the farmers of the world been as prosperous as they are at the present time, even after allowance is made for the higher prices they have to pay for the manufactured goods they consume. Moreover, the condition of unrest among the wage-earners of all countries reveals the fact that their incomes since the 'nineties have not increased as rapidly as the rise in the cost of living.

This brings me to the consideration of the question of whether the existing high cost of living is likely to be maintained. To answer this question, it is essential to note the causes first that brought about the abnormally low prices of food and raw material in the 'nineties, and, second, that have contributed to the subsequent great advance in prices. You will recollect that during the 'eighties of the last century enterprise was active and confidence was strong, and that in that decade great sums of capital were embarked in the development of the young countries. In Canada the Canadian Pacific Railway was constructed; in the United States railway construction was carried on with a speed never witnessed before or since; enormous sums of money were also poured into Australia and into Argentina for the same purpose. But the enterprise of the 'eighties was followed in the 'nineties by a period of great distrust and anxiety, and the lending countries were willing to supply relatively little to the young and agricultural countries, but confined their activities largely to exploring for gold and developing the gold mines. This nervousness resulted from the revolutions in Brazil and Argentina, from the Baring trouble, from unsound currency legislation in the United States, from a great fall in the price of silver, and from a collapse in land speculation in Australia. Countries which had previously borrowed very freely were not only unable to obtain any appreciable sums of new capital, but had to pay interest on the large amounts previously obtained from abroad, and in order to meet interest obligations had to sell their produce at any price. Indeed, their incomes became so attenuated that default was made in interest payments on a really vast amount of capital. The lowness of prices, however, stimulated consumption in the lands where credit was maintained, notably in England, France, and Germany, and the extravagant expenditures upon all kinds of objects in these countries, coupled with the maintenance of the gold standard in the United States and the outbreak of the Spanish-American War, brought general recovery in consumption and in prices, which was further accentuated by the Boer War, and later on by the Russo-Japanese War. All these events brought about a great increase in consumption, while they still prevented the investment of any large amount of capital in the borrowing countries for productive purposes. In fact, from the early 'nineties until 1905 the amount of capital provided for the extension of agriculture was extremely small, with the result that the world's supplies of food and raw material fell short of the demand. After the close of the Japanese War, however, the situation completely changed. The profitable prices to which food and raw material had then recovered, and the relative depression in trade in the older lands, attracted capital in great quantities into the new countries, and once again the construction of railways in all the great agricultural countries of the world was undertaken on a great scale. In the ten years from 1905 to 1915 the railway mileage of Canada will be nearly doubled, and vast tracts of new land will be opened up to cultivation. In Argentina there has been great activity, and in a single decade, to 1915, the railway mileage of that country will be nearly, if not quite, doubled. The great demand for food, and especially for meat, has caused a search to be made for fresh districts suitable for the raising of crops and of live stock, and a considerable number of railways have been constructed in Brazil. The United States, Russia, and Australasia have also borrowed large sums of money for the construction of railways into new agricultural districts. In fact, the profitableness of agriculture in the last ten years has attracted, as one would expect it to do, great quantities of capital and of labour into the countries which grow food and raw material. It will be understood, however, that the process of largely increasing the world's supply of primary products is a slow one. The amount of capital required for the purpose in these days is enormous, as the new districts capable of growing surplus supplies of food and raw material are getting farther and farther away from the sea-coast, and vast systems of new railways are part of the machinery which must be supplied to enable the world largely to expand its production of these essentials.

In Canada the two new systems of railways are each about 3,000 miles in length, and the additional land which these railways will bring into cultivation are situated from 1,500 to 2,500 miles away from the Atlantic seaboard. In Argentina the new grain-growing districts are many hundreds of miles inland. In the United States the districts now being developed are from 1,500 to 2,000 miles from the sea-coast. In Russia similar conditions prevail, the railways to-day being constructed far into the interior. Therefore, the initial cost of largely increasing supplies is a very heavy one. But inasmuch as the world must have food and raw material, and must pay whatever prices are necessary to obtain them, the needs of the situation have caused unprecedented amounts of capital to be raised in the last seven years for the construction of railways in all the young countries of the world. To show the great amount of railway mileage built in the 'seventies and 'eighties in the food-producing countries in which British capital is mainly invested, the small amount of new mileage constructed in the 'nineties, when British investors suffered so acutely from distrust and refused to lend freely, and the great quantity of railway mileage constructed since 1900 in consequence mainly of the return of confidence to the investor, I give the following statement:—

Miles of Railway in the United States, Canada, India, Argentina, and Australasia.

	Miles of Railway.	Miles Constructed per Decade.
1915*	385,000	+ 41,000 (5 years)
1910	344,000	+ 82,000
1900	262,000	+ 49,000
1890	213,000	+ 98,000
1880	115,000	+ 53,000
1870	62,000	+ 28,000
1860	34,000	+ 25,000
1850	9,000	—

* At the end of 1913 the aggregate was about 369,000 miles.

You may be interested in discovering the miles of new railways constructed in the countries in which British capital is largely invested, and accordingly I set out below the number of miles of railway in the United States, Canada, India, Argentina, and Australasia at the end of each decade since 1850, and give estimates based on the available information of the extent of the mileage at the end of last year, and of the extent of the mileage likely to be completed by the end of 1915. To make the statement more complete, I add the railway mileage in Russia, a country in which, until the last two or three years, we have not been disposed to embark any great amount of capital. With the opening of the British as well as the French Money markets to Russia's requirements for capital, railway extension in that country is likely to become more rapid.

Miles of Railway in Countries which Chiefly Supply Great Britain with Food.

	Est'mtd. 1915 Miles.	Partly Est'mtd. 1913 Miles.	1912 Miles.	1910 Miles.	1905 Miles.	1900 Miles.	1895 Miles.	1890 Miles.	1880 Miles.	1870 Miles.	1860 Miles.	1850 Miles.
United States ..	266,000	260,800	257,729	249,992	225,196	194,334	184,628	166,654	93,262	52,922	30,626	9,021
Canada	36,000	29,000	26,727	24,731	20,487	17,657	15,977	13,256	6,891	2,617	2,065	66
India	36,000	34,300	33,484	32,099	28,295	24,633	19,531	16,345	9,300	4,775	839	—
Argentina	24,000	22,500	21,000	17,381	12,223	10,412	8,832	5,434	1,536	637	58	—
Australia and New Zealand	23,000	22,200	21,527	20,222	17;313	15,531	13,782	11,480	4,919	999	215	—
Total	385,000	368,800	360,467	344,425	303,514	262,567	242,750	213,169	115,908	61,950	33,803	9,087
Russia	53,000	50,700	49,733	47,815	41,503	35,623	21,948	18,059	14,026	7,198	988	310
Total, including Russia	438,000	419,500	410,200	392,240	345,017	298,190	264,698	231,228	129,934	69,148	34,791	9,387

Great Britain alone has supplied colonial and foreign States with upwards of eleven hundred millions sterling (£1,100,000,000) of new capital since 1906. The statement herewith shows that almost the whole of this money has been placed in the countries which for the most part supply us with the food and raw material we need to maintain the growing population of these islands. Of course, any large increase in the world's production of primary products brings advantage to all countries, and not merely to Great Britain, and in providing capital for increasing the productions of those commodities—food and raw material—which we ourselves need, we assist in largely increasing the supplies of the whole world. The statement on the following page shows the countries to which we have supplied capital so freely in the last seven years.

The greater part of these enormous sums has been devoted to railway building. In seven years we have provided colonial and foreign railway companies with nearly £400,000,000 of capital for railway construction. Beyond this our investors have subscribed about £264,000,000 for Government loans, a large part of which has also been devoted to the construction of railways. In the aggregate Great Britain has supplied the world outside these islands with nearly £600,000,000 for the construction of railways in the last seven years, and all of the money has been placed in countries upon which we depend for our supplies of food and raw material, the increasing production of which is so essential to our welfare. The purposes for which capital has been provided to colonial and foreign countries by Great Britain since 1907 are shown on page 6.

I need scarcely point out to you that the work of providing capital for increasing the world's supplies of food and raw material has been carried on by the British people for several centuries. In the old days this and other countries provided themselves from their own lands with the food they needed and with the raw material they required for their clothing, which in those days was made from wool, flax, or leather. But the creation of the cotton industry of Lancashire in competition with the woollen and linen trades brought with it an ever-increasing demand for this new raw textile, and money was invested in the Southern States for the development of the plant. It was also sent out to Virginia for the pro-

Countries to which Great Britain has Supplied Capital (a) and Amounts Subscribed last Seven Years.

	1913 £	1912 £	1911 £	1910 £	1909 £	1908 £	1907 £	Total, Seven Years £
lia & Colonies.								
la&Newfoundland	66,255,540	37,400,488	36,793,419	33.039,566	37,687.464	31,309.558	7,601,550	250,087,585
American ...	186,600	30.000	263,958	2,167,000	567.100	124.144	100.000	3,438,802
South Wales ...	4,757.500	5,778,000	375,000	829,000	4,730,559	1,766 908	432.00)	18,668,967
Zealand	3,658,900	1,969,405	176,742	5,258.717	849 135	645,717	252,000	12,810,616
sland	2,216,500	2,490,485	2,064,000	75,000	1,990,000	—	266,000	9,101,985
Australia ...	970,000	50,000	100,000	897,294	117.600	—	—	2,134,894
ania	251,250	277,750	—	6,249	295.500	247 000	21,500	1,099,249
ria	2,056,900	12,549	109,206	5,000	1,663,000	135,500	252,144	4,234,299
Australia ...	3,460.000	2,866,678	757.343	2 884,686	1,618,925	1,047.833	1,090,000	13,725,565
Australasian ...	1,936,000	—	60,000	224,485	750,000	50,000	—	3,020,485
h West Africa ...	1,073,412	1,166,262	5,568,352	2,490,906	1,899,003	3,382,992	50,500	15,631,427
esia	175,000	1,158.421	1,339,697	6,686,176	2,422,050	1,526,323	61,850	13,369,517
vaal	1,284 630	4 008,368	3,503,003	2,767,828	8,858,093	2,487,435	332,100	23,241,457
African ...	5,138,450	220,005	1,997,661	1,005,312	1,161.150	3,833,854	5 285,213	18,641,645
and Ceylon ...	3,752 909	4,391,320	5,278,488	14,675,503	15.884,581	13,469,787	7.260 387	64,712,975
s Settlements ...	1,136,070	1,972,638	2,186,598	9,246,237	3,092,513	233.502	5,268,000	23,135,538
h N. Borneo ...	Nil	490,000	198,927	848,948	1,159,126	164,000	208,000	3,069,021
umerated ...	400,000	125,000	160,000	300,000	250,000	171,000	—	1,406,000
tal India & Colonies ...	**98,709,661**	**64,407,369**	**60,932,394**	**83,407,907**	**84,995,799**	**60,595,553**	**28,481,244**	**481,529,927**
reign Countries.								
tina	18,641,366	15.664,159	15,451,892	16,595,020	23,987,070	15,905,706	12 094,372	118,339,585
... ...	20,870,449	13 342,872	19,313,821	10,988.686	7,497,928	10,945,280	5,268,000	88,227,036
... ...	2 584,487	3,911,995	8 270.712	4,684,661	4,158,750	1,379,985	2 572 750	27,563,340
... ...	2,114,496	842,500	6,331,632	1,916.153	2,312,404	—	1,046,200	14 563,385
o	5,562,483	2,818,475	3,303 923	4,946.139	9,109,694	7,250,528	831,080	33,822 322
... ...	90,000	100,000	1,996,921	2,465,770	—	2,037,000	300,000	6,989,691
d States... ...	22,752,318	23,004,803	20,781,665	31,544,554	21,778,159	19,949,174	24,391,177	164,201,850
American ..	1,439,200	1,201,666	1,249,288	1,595,693	2,131,530	2,626,979	883,832	11 128,188
a	820,500	935,753	1,993,643	2,368,000	130,000	—	—	6,247,896
ria	Nil	—	215,899	3,603,600	—	—	—	3,819,499
ark	Nil	2,925,000	—	1,089,000	487,500	2,343,200	—	6,844,700
... ...	250,000	708,750	200.900	1,002,407	796,670	1,755,400	1,713,450	6,427,577
nd	Nil	—	970,000	143,050	2,328,400	—	—	3,441,450
e...	Nil	35,000	686,810	2,345,834	—	194,000	40,000	3,301,644
ary	57,240	—	70,000	1,950,000	—	—	—	2,077 240
y	1,286,250	482.500	3,008,500	—	—	—	56,000	4,833 250
ania	2,113,800	260,500	270,125	1,202,000	381,150	155,000	47,300	4,429,875
... ...	9,476,071	12,681,243	6,082.123	3,936,655	9,672,485	3 810,496	555,833	46,214,906
n	485,000	50,000	200,000	—	881,000	2,940,000	—	4 556,000
y...	Nil	—	350,000	1,431,688	2,759,381	204,800	—	4,745,869
European ...	105,750	3,321,035	962,064	1,353,500	990,167	1,041,893	1,505,767	9 280,176
... ...	6,675,012	8,845,000	1,554,500	1.610,100	740,000	5,031,125	3,350 000	27,805,737
Indies	1,885,528	657,987	1,573,750	6,328,916	1,195,690	145,300	449.800	12,236,971
... ...	Nil	3,230,937	5,880,000	31,950	4,230,523	4,880,000	4,193,830	22,447,240
... ...	Nil	—	1,506,250	—	1,200,000	—	—	2,706,250
pines	15,000	—	—	403,890	—	1,819,393	—	2,238,283
... ...	Nil	—	—	—	—	—	1,102,500	1,102,500
... ...	Nil	—	497,493	257,500	—	—	240,000	994,993
Asian	100,000	75,000	—	—	—	—	—	175,000
... .	506,460	240,000	318,150	1,138,493	135,000	101,000	263,500	2,702,603
merated ...	127,535	300,000	—	712,539	508,750	766,488	20,834	2,436,146
al Foreign ...	**97,958,945**	**96,635,175**	**103,040,061**	**105,645,798**	**97,412,251**	**85,282,747**	**60,926,225**	**645,901,202**
al Indian, Colnial & Foreign	**196,668,606**	**160,042,544**	**163,972,455**	**189,053,705**	**182,408,050**	**145,878,300**	**89,407,469**	**1,127,431,129**

(a) Calculated at prices of issue, and excluding all conversion loans and shares issued to vendors.

production of tobacco, and to the West Indies for sugar and rum, as well as to other places for the mining of gold and silver. From that time to this England has been increasingly engaged in supplying the world with the capital needed to produce raw material and food of all kinds and descriptions; and since the United Kingdom definitely became a manufacturing country, as it did when it decided to introduce the policy of Free Trade and to admit food (other than luxuries) and raw material without taxation, the amount of capital supplied by her investors to other lands has reached a colossal sum. A few years ago, in a paper read before the Royal Statistical Society, I calculated that at the end of 1907 British investments in Colonial and foreign lands by means of publicly issued securities amounted to two thousand seven hundred millions (£2,700,000,000). Since 1907 the enormous amount of capital which this country has provided, indeed, has been compelled to supply in its own interest for increasing the world's supply of food and raw material has been over £1,000,000,000, and this great investment in the last six years has now brought the sum of capital supplied by Great Britain to other lands to the great total of £3,700,000,000. Inclusive of capital invested privately the total is not less than £4,000,000,000.

Of this sum nearly one-half has been supplied to our overseas Dominions, while the other half has been sent mainly to the United States, to the young countries of North and South America, and to other lands which produce our food and raw material. The countries in which this great sum of £3,700,000,000 of British capital has been publicly invested are set out below:—

Capital Publicly Invested by Great Britain in Other Lands, December 1913.

India and Colonies.	£
North America—	
Canada and Newfoundland	514,870,000
Australasia—	
Australia	332,112,000
New Zealand	84,334,000
Africa—	
South	370,192,000
West	37,305,000
Asia—	
India and Ceylon	378,776,000
Straits Settlements	27,293,000
Hong Kong	3,104,000
British North Borneo	5,820,000
Other Colonies	26,189,000
Total India and Colonies	**1,779,995,000**

Purposes for which Capital has been Subscribed for Colonial and Foreign Countries by Great Britain during the last Seven Years.

Class of Security	1913 £	1912 £	1911 £	1910 £	1909 £	1908 £	1907 £	Total Seven Years £
Government—								
Indian	Nil	2,790,000	3,360,000	7,237,500	8,752,500	4,950,000	3,447,500	30,537,500
Colonial	26,888,924	12,106,534	7,430,000	13,495,775	24,273,124	14,942,614	11,973,383	111,110,354
Foreign	28,027,165	11,114,495	21,587,209	17,275,856	18,836,284	18,251,125	7,330,767	122,422,901
Total	54,916,089	26,011,029	32,377,209	38,009,131	51,861,908	38,143,739	22,751,650	264,070,755
Municipalities—								
Indian	Nil	Nil	Nil	487,500	2,048,950	985,000	Nil	3,521,450
Colonial	14,810,371	6,290,386	4,414,278	3,929,200	3,487,159	4,652,905	1,436,732	39,021,031
Foreign	8,536,570	10,643,495	2,584,000	6,809,514	10,234,011	4,485,512	313,830	43,606,932
Total	23,346,941	16,933,881	6,998,278	11,226,214	15,770,120	10,123,417	1,750,562	86,149,413
Railways—								
Indian	3,010,000	495,000	772,000	3,100,000	3,183,875	6,894,250	2,200,000	19,655,125
Colonial	34,434,522	19,012,057	15,492,766	11,687,905	19,378,402	14,851,476	3,766,648	118,623,776
Foreign	30,815,846	25,685,298	46,160,863	41,977,408	39,400,633	43,457,446	30,959,555	258,457,049
Total	68,260,368	45,192,355	62,425,629	56,765,313	61,962,910	65,203,172	36,926,203	396,735,950
Banks	2,823,750	5,888,337	3,352,000	1,681,039	625,000	2,822,500	5,459,333	22,651,959
Breweries	Nil	834,240	40,000	Nil	Nil	120,000	47,120	1,041,360
Canals and Docks ..	689,500	Nil	Nil	182,000	450,000	Nil	Nil	1,321,500
Commercial, Industrial, &c.	16,535,492	10,777,011	15,296,976	10,504,424	8,368,397	5,808,647	1,549,161	68,840,108
Electric Light and Power	2,969,061	5,360,720	4,784,479	3,102,726	2,413,490	1,220,271	959,169	20,809,916
Financial, Land, Investment and Trust ..	5,261,269	11,146,208	11,245,217	13,473,333	4,896,369	8,892,643	2,645,780	57,560,819
Gas and Water	1,133,910	1,847,887	1,700,820	102,500	1,578,000	1,339,322	435,000	8,137,239
Insurance	Nil	Nil	Nil	246,000	Nil	Nil	Nil	246,000
Iron, Coal, Steel and Engineering	2,484,222	6,536,505	1,384,580	4,396,195	2,444,034	1,027,180	514,597	18,787,313
Mines	3,841,257	5,728,390	8,881,281	10,802,352	8,300,688	5,084,376	3,390,772	46,029,116
Motor Traction	Nil	Nil	170,000	276,149	595,000	58,000	337,000	1,436,149
Nitrate	359,300	Nil	Nil	Nil	145,500	215,700	370,250	1,090,750
Oil	5,683,700	6,384,742	3,771,375	10,508,086	2,428,250	795,540	1,105,000	30,676,693
Rubber	1,387,945	2,720,195	4,316,186	20,774,055	5,774,870	810,012	1,367,520	37,150,783
Shipping	594,000	Nil	Nil	Nil	677,500	200,000	Nil	1,471,500
Tea and Coffee	255,342	239,400	582,500	104,500	40,000	10,000	118,950	1,350,692
Telegraphs and Telephones	1,642,710	2,385,625	1,031,919	2,637,500	3,363,000	150,000	7,940,000	19,150,754
Tramways	4,483,750	12,056,219	5,614,000	4,262,188	10,713,014	3,853,781	1,739,402	42,722,354
Grand Total ..	**196,668,606**	**160,042,544**	**163,972,455**	**189,053,705**	**182,408,050**	**145,878,300**	**89,407,469**	**1,127,431,129**

Foreign Countries.	£
United States	754,617,000
Cuba	33,075,000
Philippines	8,217,000
Argentina	319,565,000
Brazil	147,967,000
Mexico	99,019,000
Chili	61,143,000
Uruguay	36,124,000
Peru	34,173,000
Misc. American	25,538,000
Russia	66,627,000
Egypt	44,912,000
Spain	19,057,000
Turkey	18,696,000
Italy	12,440,000
Portugal	8,136,000
France	8,020,000
Germany	6,364,000
Misc. European	54,580,000
Japan	62,816,000
China	43,883,000
Misc. Foreign	69,697,000
Total Foreign	1,934,666,000
Grand Total	3,714,661,000

The purposes for which this great sum of capital has been raised are shown by the statement below:—

Purposes for which Capital has been supplied by Great Britain to Other Lands.

	£
Governments:	
Colonial	675,464,000
Foreign	284,059,000
Total Government Loans	959,523,000
Municipal	147,547,000
Railways:	
Colonial	306,460,000
Indian	140,796,000
American	616,581,000
Foreign	457,177,000
Total Railways	1,521,014,000
Banks	72,909,000
Breweries	17,980,000
Canals and Docks	7,111,000
Commercial, Industrial	145,332,000
Electric Lighting and Power	27,310,000
Financial, Land and Investment	244,187,000
Gas and Water	29,216,000
Insurance	246,000
Iron, Coal and Steel	30,535,000
Mines	272,789,000
Motor Traction, &c.	1,059,000
Nitrate	11,623,000
Oil	40,579,000
Rubber	40,982,000
Shipping	794,000
Tea and Coffee	22,443,000
Telegraphs and Telephones	43,692,000
Tramways	77,790,000
Total	3,714,661,000

The unprecedented quantity of capital invested by Great Britain and by other countries in recent years in constructing railways in the lands producing food and raw material has already rendered possible a vast extension of acreage, and a great increase of production. But the greater part of the advantages arising from this constructive work has yet to be realised, and in the early future a much greater increase in supplies should be shown without much additional expenditure of capital. For instance, it is obvious that Canada's production will show immense expansion in the next few years in consequence of the great amount of new railway mileage that will shortly be completed, and of the great sums of capital devoted to construction work of all kinds. In the last seven years the new investments of this country in Canada have been £250,000,000 by means of publicly issued securities, and including private capital about £300,000,000. A similar state of affairs exists in Argentina, where great tracts of virgin land have been opened up to settlement through the investment by this country of £118,000,000 of new capital largely in railway construction in the last seven years. In Brazil also the production of agricultural wealth and of raw material in the next few years is likely to show great expansion in consequence of the investment of £88,000,000 of British capital since 1906, and of large additional sums by France and by the Continent. I am also distinctly hopeful that agricultural production in the United States will now expand more rapidly. The reduction in the tariff means, for one thing, that the special stimulus given by the Dingley tariff of 1897 to the investment of capital in manufacturing industries will be removed, and that population will be less tempted to leave the country for the towns. Furthermore, the new banking legislation recently adopted in the United States will provide farmers and others with much more banking accommodation than they have hitherto enjoyed. Lastly, the efforts which the American people are making to create additional competition between the Trusts in order to reduce retail prices should also be of advantage to American farmers whose produce for the most part enjoys no protection, its value being regulated almost entirely by prices in the international markets, where there are no pools to regulate and keep up agricultural prices. In brief, everything possible is being done in the United States to stimulate the output of agricultural produce, not only by legislation, but by more scientific methods. Hence a greatly increased production may reasonably be expected.

But in considering the course of prices one has to take into account not merely the extent of the probable increase of supply, but also the volume of demand. In former days, when the mass of the people of nearly every country were sunk in ignorance and in poverty, the consumption of food and raw material per head of population was very small, and the volume of demand relatively insignificant. In this respect the situation has wonderfully changed for the better in the last two generations, thanks mainly to the progress of science, the extension of railways, and the growth of shipping, for which this country is so largely responsible. With greater intercommunication education comes, new wants arise, and people are not content to go on living in poverty and distress. The effect of education is progressive, and is increasingly powerful as enlightenment grows both deeper and more widespread. Railways and steamships have been carrying out their beneficent work of educating and enlightening the world now for over two generations until, at the present time, all the world is bound together not only by bands of steel, but by ideas and by aspirations common to all peoples. Hence from one end of the world to the other the masses of the people are demanding better conditions of life, and the request for a more plentiful supply of food and clothing, for better houses, and for opportunity of enjoyment is more insistent than it has ever been. In looking into the future it is very essential to take into account this demand of the whole world for a higher standard of comfort, which seems to foreshadow not merely the maintenance of consumption at its present relatively high level, but its ultimate advance to a much higher level.

Thus we have the prospect that production will be largely increased, and at the same time consumption maintained at a high level. But at any given moment the course of prices is regulated by very small margins either way. If consumption has a tendency to increase somewhat faster than production, prices advance, as buyers are compelled to place orders in anticipation of their needs. On the other hand, if production has a tendency to increase faster than consumption prices decline; buyers are then disposed to purchase from hand to mouth, and in consequence of the reduction of invisible stocks visible supplies largely increase, and the competition among sellers brings about an important reaction in prices. Not infrequently rises or falls in prices are brought about by pure sentiment. A general feeling arises that demand is likely to increase, and buyers rush in to purchase in anticipation of the expected advance in prices, thereby bringing about the advance, or, on the other hand, a diminished demand is anticipated, and prices fall because everyone refrains from placing orders until compelled to do so by the exhaustion of private stocks.

At the present moment there are indications that prices will probably decline for a time. For one thing, some of the great works, the construction of which has caused a great demand for capital and for labour, are now nearly completed. I refer more particularly to the Panama Canal and to railway construction in Canada, in Argentina, and in Brazil. The completion of these works will displace a good deal of labour, and for a time appreciably reduce the consuming power of these countries. Then again, the expenditures and consumption on the Continent in connection with the recent wars and mobilisations are now over, and in place of spending large amounts of borrowed money upon objects which have not added to the incomes of the various countries, Austria, Italy, Bulgaria, Servia, Greece, Turkey, and Montenegro have to make interest payments on the large sums of money they have spent. Therefore economy has become essential, and consumption may for a time be curtailed. The Mexican situation, too, is causing some uncertainty, especially in the United States, and many people in that country are disposed to spend money cautiously until matters are adjusted.

Therefore, at the present moment, indeed for some months past, prices have shown a tendency to decline. At the end of March last the index number of 45 commodities was 86.7, and at the end of January it was 83.5, a decline of nearly 4 per cent. There are, I think, no grounds for anticipating any severe set-back in prices in the current year. The world has still a great deal of construction work to get through before the work in hand is completed, and the prosecution of this work will cause the demand for labour to be fairly well maintained, and the rate of consumption kept up to a high level for a time. But when all the factors are taken into account there appear to be grounds for the expectation that production is now likely to increase faster than consumption, and that a gradual fall in prices will probably be witnessed, bringing with it, for a time, a reduction in the cost of living. Probably the fall in prices will be more pronounced next winter than it has been this. Notwithstanding the recent stringency of the Money market the amount of capital available for construction work of one kind and another has so far shown no appreciable decline, thanks to the fact that the bankers have been willing to supply funds when investors were indisposed to do so. Consequently there has been no serious curtailment of consumption, and the decline that has occurred has been largely neutralised by a contraction in production in consequence of unfavourable weather conditions. The serious decline in the quantity of cereals available for consumption in the current crop season, in comparison with the previous season, will be evident from the following:—

World's Crops, 1913 *and* 1912 (*a*).

	1913 Quarters	1912 Quarters	Total Quarters
Wheat ..	515,372,000	498,527,000	+16,845,000
Maize ..	414,288,000	509,879,000	−95,591,000
Oats ..	509,654,000	509,557,000	+ 97,000
Rye ..	211,698,000	231,371,000	−19,673,000
Barley ..	206,427,000	197,515,000	+ 8,912,000
Total ..	1,857,439,000	1,946,849,000	−89,410,000 −4·5 per cent.

(*a*) According to Dornbusch.

But for the serious shortage in the American maize crop of last year the fall in prices would have been much more serious. As it is, however, the index number of the five cereals has fallen during the past twelve months from 72.6 to 66.5, or by 9 per cent.

I would point out that the influence of crop failures on the price of food in the current year is much greater than indicated by the above statement. In India the monsoon, unfortunately, stopped too early in the north-west, and the prospect that India will have very little wheat for export in the current season is supporting prices. If next season the weather is not unfavourable the supply of food may show marked increase, in consequence of the rapidly-expanding acreage now placed under crop, as well as of weather conditions.

However, the curtailment of consumption in proportion to prduction is not likely to last long. It is true that Canada, Argentina, and Brazil have been provided with nearly all the railways they will need, and can usefully employ for some time to come; but other countries, which have not made any great progress in recent years, and which desire to increase their productions, will need to spend capital freely as soon as the urgent demands of Canada, Argentina, and Brazil are satisfied. In the past year, out of £196,000,000 of capital provided by this country for other lands, no less than £104,000,000 was supplied to these three countries alone, and in the past three years, out of £520,000,000 of capital supplied by Great Britain to Colonial and foreign countries, these three States have obtained no less than £242,000,000. As soon as Canada, Argentina, and Brazil have obtained nearly all the capital they require for the time being, the demands of other countries for capital will undoubtedly become more prominent. It is obvious that Australia will call for a great deal of capital in the next few years if it is to carry out the policy of expansion it has mapped out. As the world needs a greatly increased supply of wool and meat, there is every probability that Australia will obtain all the money she requires. India, too, has had to be content with very small amounts of capital in recent years in consequence of her unwillingness to pay the higher rate of interest which has prevailed, and it is obvious that India can profitably expend many millions of additional money upon railway extensions and upon expanding her productions, having regard to the smallness of her existing railway system, the greatness of her country, and the vastness of her population. The United States also has recently spent capital sparingly, and will need to spend great sums to provide for the extension of her agricultural industry, especially in the matter of railway facilities. The soundness of financial and economic conditions in the United States warrants the expectation that the American people will be able to maintain, indeed, to increase their consumption at the time it may be necessary for other countries which have gone ahead much more rapidly, to become more economical in their expenditures. Then again, it is obvious that the credit of Russia, which is higher now than it has ever been, will enable that country to secure all the capital it needs for the extension of its railway system throughout its vast territories. The knowledge now possessed that Siberia is, after all, a wealthy State, capable of producing almost unlimited quantities of foodstuffs, is a factor in the outlook of which due note should be taken. The extension of railways and the opening up of Asiatic Russia to settlement will doubtless cause great sums of capital to flow into that country from France, England, and Germany in the coming years, and will powerfully assist in maintaining and in increasing the world's consuming power. In taking a survey of the future, one cannot leave out of account the re-awakening of China, and the desire of the Chinese people to build railways and roads, both to increase their general prosperity and to prevent the dreadful famines which periodically visit them. Inasmuch as railway construction in China is now being taken in hand in earnest and the new railways become profitable from the day they are opened, there appear to be good grounds for the expectation that greater sums of foreign capital will be employed in China than hitherto, and that the consuming power of the Chinese people will substantially expand.

Nor can one leave out of account the very satisfactory condition of things in this country. Inasmuch as the wealth and income of the British people have grown in recent years more rapidly than ever before, they will be able to consume goods even more freely than hitherto. Moreover, the great income of over £200,000,000 a year which they now enjoy from interest on their Colonial and foreign investments, will probably come to them in lower-priced commodities, thus further increasing their consuming power.

In brief, the cost of living has already begun to decline, and will probably fall farther in the next year or two in consequence of the strong efforts now being put forth all over the world to produce increased supplies of food and raw material by the aid of the great amounts of capital which the lending countries in general, and Great Britain in particular, have supplied for the purpose. I scarcely need to state, however, that there is no prospect of prices falling back to the unprofitable level of the nineties—that condition of affairs was greatly to be regretted from every point of view, arising, as it did, from a condition of intense discredit. Such an abnormal depression in credit is unlikely to recur for many years. There are no grounds for apprehending any severe check to credit at the present time, especially having regard to the world's great output of gold, though there are reasons for expecting the three countries which have imported capital so freely in recent years to slow down in their expenditures of borrowed money, and for a moderate reduction in consumption in proportion to production for a time to bring lower prices of commodities and a reduced cost of living.

A NEW STUDY OF BRITISH FOREIGN INVESTMENTS

Robert M. Kindersley

A NEW STUDY OF BRITISH FOREIGN INVESTMENTS

Part I

My close association with the National Savings Movement is a sufficient explanation of my keen desire to arrive at some reliable statistics regarding any subject connected with the real savings of the nation. I have made many attempts in this connection to investigate the savings put into new loans, but have always been balked by the fact that, though there were available certain statistics of the amount of capital which this country lends abroad each year, there appeared to be no reliable figures of the amounts which were repaid to investors by the operation of sinking funds and on maturity of loans either at home or abroad. It is clear that sinking funds and maturity payments of our overseas investments must be deducted when attempting to estimate our yearly investment in this form of security. In regard to domestic issues the situation differs in that we ourselves provide the funds required for these purposes.

I therefore set out a year ago to try to make good what seemed to me to be a bad gap in our national statistics. This necessitated an inquiry into the amount of repayment in any one year of capital formerly lent both abroad and at home, in order to ascertain the receipts from the operation of sinking funds and maturity repayments of foreign and domestic loans. Owing to the very generous manner in which some sixty banks and several hundreds of companies have placed material at my disposal, I have been able to obtain what I believe to be, within the limits of the data available, statistics regarding these receipts. Apart from the effort of Sir G. Paish before the war to investigate our income from overseas investments, an attempt of this nature does not seem to have been made before. There were, therefore, no rules or preconceived procedure for carrying out the inquiry, and the present results are in the nature of pioneer results, and as such are to be regarded as a first approximation to the facts. It is hoped, if co-operation can be secured, to continue the investigation periodically, and to arrive at more accurate figures as better methods of conducting the inquiry are devised with experience gained.

It was only natural that when once the inquiry was started it led to a rather wider consideration of the problem than was originally intended, and the figures which follow and the deductions which are made from them cover this rather wider field, and will probably not escape criticism.

In the first instance, I had intended all material that is included in the following pages for my own personal use and that of the bankers and others who had so kindly helped me in my work, but since I spoke at the meeting of the City Savings Association, at the Mansion House in May 1928, where I referred to the provisional results of my investigations, I have received so many requests for complete details that I have decided to put the final figures in print, so that they should be available for the general public.

In collating these statistics I have had the advantage of the services of Mr. P. Holmes, B.Sc. (Econ.), a former student of the London School of Economics.

No doubt readers will find this report somewhat lengthy owing to the inclusion of the accumulation of additional material already mentioned. It seemed to me, however, that the full results of the work should be published, since they include in ready and collected form much which has up to now been scattered and much which is new.

Scope of the Inquiry

The inquiry undertaken covered the receipts in England from the operation of sinking funds and maturity payments of foreign Government, State and Municipal loans, and the capital arrangements of British companies operating abroad and at home for specified years, but did not include certain "private" receipts, *inter alia* those from private English companies operating abroad and from private or individual investment by inhabitants of the British Isles in foreign stocks and bonds. In brief, the statistics cover all the investments dealt with in the *Stock Exchange Official Intelligence* for 1926 with the following exceptions:

American Railway Stocks and Bonds.—These are excluded because the bulk of the holdings of British nationals were requisitioned by the British Treasury during the war to provide funds in America, and investigation has failed to disclose any appreciable post-war investment by British nationals in these securities. Total war-time requisitions were estimated at £623,000,000, which can be compared with an estimate made by Sir George Paish in

1907, that British nationals' investments in the American railway group totalled £600,000,000.

Financial Trust Stocks, etc.—These are excluded because their inclusion would lead to a double reckoning, as the operations of these companies usually take the form of investments either in the stocks and shares of British registered companies or in Government State or Municipal loans listed on the London Stock Exchange, and the income and capital repayment from both these sources are calculated separately for the borrowers concerned in this report.

Of course this exclusion also means that the income derived by such companies from what has already been characterised as "Private" investment abroad is not counted. In the case of financial trusts this may be appreciable, but owing to the impossibility of calculating separately the income from investments made in securities not listed on the Stock Exchange, exclusion was the only course open. It may also be noted that although subscriptions to the issues of such companies appear as new issues for home investment, in fact a considerable proportion is probably used for investment abroad. No reliable estimate of the sums so used is, however, available, and all that can be done is to bear this tendency in mind. Estimates tend to show that investment trusts invest practically two-thirds of their funds in overseas investments.

Additional Purposes of Inquiry

It rapidly became evident that while information on sinking fund and maturity repayments was the primary purpose of the inquiry, it would have to be accompanied by inquiries on other aspects of the subject, as, for example, the percentage of the various investments listed in the Stock Exchange Official Intelligence owned by British nationals so as to determine the British, and from the view-point of this inquiry the most important share in repayments by sinking funds or otherwise. Certain additional information has thus been obtained, the results of which have been included in the article.

Method

The method employed in collating the statistics was to request—

1. The London banking agents of foreign Governments, States, Municipalities, etc. to supply the following information :

(*a*) The total amount outstanding of each loan for which they were the agent.
(*b*) The total sinking fund or redemption payment made on each loan for the year 1926.
(*c*) The total interest paid on each loan during 1926, and
(*d*) The proportion of the total interest paid tax free in respect of holdings by foreign nationals.

The British and the foreign shares in redemption repayments either by the operation of sinking funds or by maturity repayments were taken to be in the same proportion as the interest payments.

2. British companies operating abroad to give the following information:

(*a*) The amount paid out by the company in capital redemption during 1926, and
(*b*) The proportion of this sum paid to persons resident in the United Kingdom.

British and Foreign Holdings of Securities Listed on the London Stock Exchange

Dividing the securities examined into groups, as is done in the *Official Intelligence*, and applying the information obtained by these methods for 1926, the following table is obtained showing the proportion of the British holdings in the various groups of overseas investments:

Table I

Proportion in 1926 of British Holdings of Total Outstanding Loans or Redeemable Capital in the Undermentioned Groups of Securities listed on the London Stock Exchange.

Group	%	Group	%
Colonial and Prov. Govts.	82%	Financial and Land	76%
Indian and Col. Corptns.	80	Gas	99
Foreign Corporations	83	Iron, Coal and Steel	48
Foreign Governments	75	Mines	82
Indian Railways	83	Nitrate	99
Foreign Railways	86	Oil	96
Rlys. in Brit. Possns.	84	Rubber	93
Banks and Discount Coys.	41	Shipping	99
Canals and Docks	96	Tea and Coffee	97
Comm. and Industrial (For.)	68	Telegraphs and Telephones	86
Ditto (Br.)	99	Tramways and Omnibus	98
Electric Light	94	Waterworks	99

The results show an average British holding in all the securities examined of 79 per cent. for 1926.

Part II

Results

Sinking Fund Receipts.—The results of the investigations into receipts from repayments, taking the term to include payments resulting from the operating of sinking funds and from maturities, are shown in the following tables, which give the actual receipts for 1926 from sinking funds and maturities, of securities listed on the London Stock Exchange, with a division of the sums into the amount received by British and by foreign holders of the securities. In the following tables "British Sinking Fund" means remittances to this country which go to swell the income of persons resident here, while the term "Foreign

Table II

Receipts from Sinking Fund and Maturity payments on Securities of Foreign Governments and Companies operating abroad, listed on the London Stock Exchange.

(£1,000.)
1926.

Group.	British.			Foreign Sinking Funds and Maturity Repayments.
	Sinking Fund and Maturity Repayments.	Redeemable Capital.	Rate of Repayment, %.	
Colonial and Prov. Govts.	6,221	594,248	1·0	1,365
Indian and Col. Corptns.	630	82,262	·8	157
Foreign Corporations	815	32,816	2·5	166
Foreign Governments	6,287	359,161	1·8	2,095
Indian Railways	1,890	91,745	2·1	387
Foreign Railways	1,970	230,409	·9	320
Rlys. in Brit. Possns.	906	159,565	·6	172
Banks and Discount Coys.	26	4,669	·6	37
Canals and Docks	130	6,342	2·0	5
Comm. and Industrial (Br.)	501	22,044	2·3	4
Ditto (For.)	823	74,122	1·1	388
Electric Light and Power	307	8,974	3·4	20
Financial and Land	892	22,943	3·9	288
Gas	157	2,188	7·2	1
Iron, Coal and Steel	229	30,570	·7	249
Mines	1,909	7,486	25·5	414
Nitrate	641	8,044	8·0	—
Oil	1,378	7,789	17·7	62
Rubber	559	6,120	9·1	40
Shipping	40	4,247	·9	—
Tea and Coffee	115	2,152	5·3	4
Telegraphs and Telephones	121	23,334	·5	20
Tramways and Omnibuses	410	40,550	1·0	9
Waterworks	53	7,805	·7	—
Total	27,010	1,829,585		6,203

Sinking Fund" covers remittances to this country which may swell the income from Overseas if re-invested here but is remitted on account of securities listed here, but owned by persons resident abroad and therefore liable to be withdrawn. "Redeemable Capital" consists of the bonds of Governments and Municipalities, etc., the debentures and redeemable preference shares of companies.

TABLE III

Receipts from Sinking Fund and Maturity Payments on Securities of Foreign Governments and Companies operating abroad, listed on the London Stock Exchange.

(£1,000.)

1927.

Group.	British.			Foreign Sinking Funds and Maturity Repayments.
	Sinking Fund and Maturity Repayments.	Redeemable Capital.	Rate of Repayment, %.	
Colonial and Prov. Govts.	16,105	620,445	2·6	3,383
Indian and Col. Corptns.	647	82,855	·8	156
Foreign Corporations	630	39,476	1·6	164
Foreign Governments	6,816	367,161	1·9	2,182
Indian Railways	1,446	89,352	1·6	289
Foreign Railways	1,120	229,830	·5	168
Rlys. in Brit. Possns.	21	156,971	·01	4
Banks and Discount Coys.	26	4,643	·6	37
Canals and Docks	130	4,839	2·7	5
Comm. and Industrial (Br.)	879	22,532	3·9	9
Ditto (For.)	859	71,319	1·2	393
Electric Light and Power	398	8,988	4·4	32
Financial and Land	940	23,745	4·0	273
Gas	94	1,988	4·7	1
Iron, Coal and Steel	176	28,731	6·1	192
Mines	707	8,030	8·8	149
Nitrate	651	7,273	9·0	—
Oil	1,361	8,168	16·7	69
Rubber	114	6,643	1·7	8
Shipping	98	4,082	2·4	—
Tea and Coffee	31	2,709	1·1	1
Telegraphs and Telephones	296	23,235	1·3	48
Tramways and Omnibuses	410	39,105	1·0	9
Waterworks	53	7,942	·7	—
Total	34,008	1,860,062		7,572

The 1927 figures of sinking fund receipts are adjusted from those of 1926, the year of investigation, and are added for purposes of comparison.

Taking the amounts of sinking fund and maturity receipts on account of persons resident here in 1926 for each group, it will be noticed that receipts from the first four groups or Governments, Municipalities, etc. contributed nearly one-half of the whole, Colonial and Provincial Governments alone giving nearly one-quarter. In 1927, Governmental institutions provided about two-thirds and Colonial and Provincial Governments nearly one-half of the total. Most of the other groups, both in 1926 and 1927, show very little change in absolute amounts, so that the chief variable factor seems to be that of Colonial and Provincial Government receipts. The reason for this is that the principal part of the receipts from this group is composed of maturities of securities falling due for payment. As such maturities are naturally haphazard, compared with the operations of sinking funds, the total receipts from the groups are thus bound to be rather irregular from year to year.

The annual rate of repayment in 1926 shows considerable variation between 0·5 per cent. in Telegraphs and Telephones and 25·5 per cent. in Mines. The higher rate in the Mining group is due to maturities in this group. In 1926, of total receipts on British account of £1,909,000 for Mines, £1,423,000 was paid as redemption at maturity; and if this sum is deducted from the total receipts in that year, the rate of repayment falls to 6·5 per cent. Maturities seem usually to form a large part of the repayments in this group.

The Financial and Land, Gas, and Rubber Company groups also exhibit the same tendency.

The group of Foreign Stocks and Bonds may be taken as an example of a group where the bulk of the receipts consist principally of annual sinking fund payments, as the following table shows:

TABLE IV

Receipts for British Account from Sinking Fund payments and Maturity Redemptions of Foreign Stocks and Bonds only.

(£1,000.)

	1926.	1927.	1928.
Maturities . . .	—	73	—
Sinking Fund Repayments	6,287	6,743	7,124
Total . . .	6,290	6,816	7,124

Thus in this group maturities are very small, as can be seen, and the bulk of receipts comes from the operation of sinking funds in contrast to the position of receipts from all the groups combined. In the latter case, in the 1926 total of receipts for British account, maturities at £11,010,000 accounted for 40·8 per cent. of the total, and in 1927 at £17,227,000 for 50·7 per cent.

Sinking Fund Receipts in Future.—By making an estimate of the future British share of receipts from the operation of sinking funds on recent overseas issues and adding to this the receipts from maturities on all existing loans, it is possible to construct a table which by including the annual repayments by the operation of sinking funds already calculated for 1927 will show an estimate of the future British receipts on account of repayment of overseas investments. This is done in Table V. There are certain limitations to the resultant estimate, since it cannot take account of any future loans issued between 1929 and 1931. On this point, however, it may be said that—

(*a*) Any such loans will not mature before 1931, and so will not add to the heading "Maturities."

(*b*) Annual receipts from such loans by the operation of cumulative sinking funds will be small in the first years of the loans.

Finally, it should be noted that the sum allocated under "Annual Repayments already calculated" is the estimate carried forward for 1927, and does not allow for falling off in the amount due to loans being finally redeemed between 1928 and 1931, nor for the automatic increase in sinking fund receipts where an accumulative Sinking Fund is in operation due to interest savings. To some extent, however, these two factors tend to neutralise one another.

TABLE V

(£1,000.)

	1928.	1929.	1930.	1931.
Maturities	5,208	36,369	8,221	19,373
New Annual Repayments	1,470	2,054	2,176	2,233
Annual Repayments already calculated	16,781	16,781	16,781	16,781
Total	23,459	55,204	27,178	38,387

The large amount due in 1929 comes mainly from Colonial Government maturities, and in 1931 from Government maturities.

Home Sinking Fund Receipts.—The figures so far examined relate to the capital operations of foreign Governments, etc., and companies operating abroad. It is now necessary to obtain similar results for companies operating at home. Below are given statistics based on information provided by British companies operating at home. From the point of view of the National Income these receipts are, of course, not in the same category as receipts on overseas investments, but they do constitute, as do allocations to reserves, moneys which tend to be reinvested and can thus be considered as a specialised source of savings.

TABLE VI

Receipts from the Operation of Sinking Funds and Maturities of Domestic Issues and of British Companies operating at Home.

(£1,000.)
1926.

Group.	British.			Foreign Sinking Funds and Maturity Repayments.
	Sinking Fund and Maturity Repayments.	Redeemable Capital.	Rate of Repayment, %.	
Corporation and County	3,247	318,125	1·0	114
Public Boards	595	103,618	·6	21
Railways	116	284,159	·04	4
Breweries	912	63,718	1·4	32
Canals and Docks	16	1,877	·9	—
Commercial and Industrial	4,080	137,114	3·0	115
Electric Light and Power	632	29,537	2·1	22
Gas	101	5,523	1·8	3
Insurance	122	10,385	1·2	4
Iron, Coal and Steel	763	64,701	1·2	19
Shipping	266	48,570	·5	9
Tramways and Omnibus	163	11,414	1·4	6
Waterworks	3	2,904	·1	—
Total	11,016	1,081,645		349

TABLE VII

Receipts from the Operation of Sinking Funds and Maturities of Domestic Issues and of British Companies operating at Home.

(£1,000.)
1927.

Group.	British			Foreign Sinking Funds and Maturity Repayments.
	Sinking Fund and Maturity Repayments.	Redeemable Capital.	Rate of Repayment, %.	
Corporation and County	5,044	345,676	1·5	156
Public Boards	377	113,289	·3	11
Railways	—	285,039	—	—
Breweries	579	62,906	·9	18
Canals and Docks	16	2,789	·6	—
Commercial and Industrial	1,732	151,454	1·1	48
Electric Light and Power	442	32,746	1·3	12
Gas	242	6,052	4·0	6
Insurance	122	11,263	1·1	3
Iron, Coal and Steel	763	67,007	1·1	24
Shipping	473	48,970	1·0	15
Tramways and Omnibus	173	12,036	1·4	6
Waterworks	—	2,900	—	—
Total	9,963	1,142,127		299

To these receipts there must be added the sinking fund applied annually to the redemption of British funds, etc. Owing to abnormal conditions in 1926 the figures to be added for that year would not give a fair result. In 1927 £65,000,000 was budgeted for sinking fund, so that the total repayment receipts on account of British-owned capital invested at home may be put around £75,000,000, to which falls to be added the items given in the Finance Accounts of the United Kingdom 1927–28 for reduction of National Debt such as "Suez Canal Drawn Bonds," "War Advances Repayments," etc., making a total figure around £80,000,000 less £5,000,000 paid to U.S.A. in reduction of our debt.

The figures given below show how much the sinking fund receipts on British account from domestic investment may be expected to amount to during 1928 to 1931, leaving out receipts on account of British funds, etc.

TABLE VIII

(£1,000.)

	1928.	1929.	1930.	1931.
Maturities	3,350	12,830	4,756	5,336
Annual Repayments	341	852	1,189	1,474
Annual Repayments from 1927 [1]	5,848	5,848	5,848	5,848
Total	9,539	19,530	11,793	12,658

[1] Subject to same qualifications as for estima e of future receipts from overseas loans, etc. (*q.v.*).

Total Overseas Capital Investments and Interest Receipts thereon.—The results obtained regarding interest receipts in 1926 from overseas investments are tabulated below. They are, of course, not repayments of capital as are sinking fund and maturity receipts, but the position in regard to them is that they do increase *cæteris paribus* the yearly national income and thus enhance the possibilities of savings. From the main point of investigation they are not of first importance, but are added merely for information.

Tables IX and X given below show the nominal British-owned portion of loans and paid-up capital invested abroad, and the amount paid as interest thereon for the years 1926 and 1927.

Net Income.—The figures of income in Tables IX and X are all gross figures, and corrections must be made for the various intergovernmental payments on account of interest on loans, reparations, etc., together with the interest payable on foreign-owned investments in the United Kingdom.

From a study of the Finance Accounts of the United Kingdom

TABLE IX

Gross Income from British-owned Capital Invested Abroad.

(£1,000.)

1926.

Group.	Income.	Nominal Amount of Loan & Share Capital.	Rate %.
Colonial and Prov. Govts.	31,561	594,248	5·3
Indian and Col. Corptns.	4,793	82,262	5·8
Foreign Corporations	1,539	32,816	4·7
Foreign Stocks and Bonds.	15,998	359,161	4·4
Indian Railways	7,271	116,444	6·2
Rlys. in Brit. Possns.	15,103	276,201	5·5
Foreign Railways	24,320	483,999	5·0
Banks and Discount Cos.	15,796	143,609	11·0
Canals and Docks	651	20,160	3·2
Commercial and Industrial (For.)	30,328	340,118	8·9
Ditto. (Br.)	6,343	92,971	6·8
Electric Lighting and Power	21,572	294,934	7·3
Financial and Land	8,359	110,108	7·6
Gas	776	25,015	3·1
Iron, Coal and Steel	7,845	134,427	5·8
Mines	12,985	118,517	11·0
Nitrate	1,696	18,171	9·3
Oil	36,619	222,386	16·5
Rubber	31,988	156,827	20·4
Shipping	692	21,288	3·3
Tea and Coffee	7,601	36,162	21·0
Telegraphs and Telephones	7,147	91,844	7·8
Tramways and Omnibus	5,800	105,964	5·6
Waterworks	1,408	18,525	7·6
Total	298,191	3,896,157	

for 1927–28 it appears that on the first item there would be a credit balance, including reparations of about £5,000,000 for 1927. An estimate of interest on foreign-owned investments in the United Kingdom for 1927, made by applying the percentages of foreign holdings already obtained to the figures concerned, would put this item at about £14,000,000.

On balance, therefore, there is a net debit to be taken from the gross income figures of between £8,000,000 and £10,000,000, leaving a result for net income from this category of overseas investment of between £289,000,000 and £291,000,000 for 1927.

This figure, of course, is even then not final, since it cannot allow for such factors, not susceptible to estimate, as *inter alia* the earnings of foreign balances in the London market, the profits of foreign companies operating factories in England, and balances held by British banks abroad, together with their short loans abroad. Moreover, it does not, of course, represent the net income of the country, for a calculation of which banking commissions and earnings of our shipping would have to be taken into account among other items.

Table X

Gross Income from British-owned Capital Invested Abroad.

(£1,000.)

1927.

Group.	Income.	Nominal Amount of Loan & Share Capital.	Rate %.
Colonial and Prov. Govts.	32,883	620,445	5·3
Indian and Col. Corptns.	4,805	82,855	5·8
Foreign Corporations	1,885	39,476	4·8
Foreign Stocks and Bonds.	16,155	367,161	4·4
Indian Railways	7,102	114,554	6·2
Rlys. in Brit. Possns.	14,871	275,389	5·4
Foreign Railways	23,992	489,642	4·9
Banks and Discount Cos.	15,785	143,583	11·0
Canals and Docks	644	16,130	4·0
Commercial and Industrial (For.)	30,195	339,617	8·9
Ditto (Br.)	7,253	97,968	7·4
Electric Lighting and Power	23,994	299,627	8·0
Financial and Land	8,970	118,727	7·6
Gas	745	24,858	3·0
Iron, Coal and Steel	6,595	130,598	5·0
Mines	11,932	127,471	9·4
Nitrate	1,262	16,530	7·6
Oil	35,739	233,374	15·3
Rubber	30,960	170,353	18·2
Shipping	752	21,488	3·5
Tea and Coffee	9,642	45,918	21·0
Telegraphs and Telephone	7,156	92,943	7·7
Tramways and Omnibus	4,424	102,909	4·3
Waterworks	1,420	18,472	7·7
Total	299,161	3,990,088	

Distribution of Overseas Capital Investments.—From Tables IX and X it appears that over one-quarter of our capital invested abroad is in the form of loans to Governments and Corporations as distinguished from shareholdings in and loans to industrial undertakings. Only about one-sixth of our total income, however, is derived from this quarter. Of this proportion roughly 63 per cent. is invested in the Dominions and Colonies, which is a reflection of the influence of the Trustee Act. Loans to Colonial Governments of course are used mainly for reproductive purposes and augment the demand for capital goods from this country, while it is certain that even without the Trustee Act there would have been large investments in the Colonies. The results shown, however, raise the question whether the Trustee Act has not given an undue impetus to the export of capital, thus making it dearer for home industries to borrow.

Rate of Remuneration of Overseas Capital Investments.—From Tables IX and X it is seen that Government, Municipal and Railway investments account for roughly one-half of our capital and yield about one-third of our income.

TABLE XI

British Capital invested in Indian, Colonial and Foreign Loans and Companies and the Income derived therefrom in 1907–8.

(£1,000.)

	Income.	Capital.	Rate of Interest, %.
Indian Government Loans	5,017	156,369	3·21
Colonial and Prov. Govts.	13,933	375,190	3·71
Foreign Govt. Loans	8,338	167,000	4·75
Colonial and Foreign Municipalities	2,650	58,901	4·5
Indian Railways	4,774	123,341	3·87
Colonial Railways	7,598	188,950	4·0
American Railways	27,000	600,000	4·5
Foreign Railways	13,467	286,700	4·7
Banks	7,353	54,101	13·6
Breweries	732	17,205	4·2
Canals and Docks	1,174	5,974	19·6
Commercial and Industrial	4,863	77,610	6·3
Electric Light	321	7,686	4·2
Financial and Land	6,233	187,027	3·3
Gas	1,194	16,419	7·3
Mines: Iron and Coal	505	12,956	3·9
Copper	5,074	38,525	13·2
Diamonds	4,468	14,646	30·5
Gold	14,947	161,178	9·3
Silver	843	10,513	8·0
Tin	308	5,568	5·5
Nitrate	1,637	10,903	15·0
Oil	642	14,268	4·5
Rubber	446	5,433	8·2
Tea and Coffee	1,794	21,399	8·4
Telegraphs and Telephones	2,233	34,235	6·5
Tramways	1,809	35,289	5·1
Waterworks	438	6,352	6·9
Total	139,791	2,693,738	5·2

Comparing 1926 with 1927, it will be noticed that our capital invested overseas increased by about £94 million, whilst the income from the investments only increased by approximately £1 million. This was due to a falling off in the income from the Oil and Rubber groups of investments, and in part probably to the fact that the new capital invested had not become fully productive.

Sir G. Paish's Estimate of Overseas Investment and Income therefrom.—Table XI reproduces an estimate made by Sir George Paish in 1907 of our Overseas Investments. A later estimate was made in 1911, in which the capital invested overseas was placed at £3,500 million, and the income therefrom between £175 and £190 million, but since the figures are not in a convenient form, the earlier estimate has been used.

This and the present estimates are not on comparable bases owing to differences in methods employed, but, bearing this in mind and allowing for changes in the value of money according to the *Statist* Index of Wholesale Prices, the 1927 figure of capital invested overseas is less than that of 1907 at 1927 values by roughly £118,000,000, and is still smaller when compared with the 1914 figure, which was estimated in the *Board of Trade Journal* in March 1923 at £4,000 million at 1914 prices. The 1927 figure of gross income received is, however, larger than that of 1907 in terms of 1927 values by roughly £86,000,000.

Changes in Direction of Overseas Investment.—In the 1907 estimate the capital invested in Governments and Municipalities is nearer one-quarter than one-third of the whole, and the income is a little less than one-quarter. The Government, Municipality and Railway groups provided in 1907 about three-quarters of the whole of our capital and nearly two-thirds of our income, as compared with one-half of the capital and one-third of the income in 1927. Overseas investments since 1907, therefore, have apparently changed their constitution and have a larger proportion of industrial investments.

The figures of the two estimates show changes in the earnings of our investments during the last twenty years. The Oil and Rubber groups, for example, show an increased earning on their capital from 4·5 per cent. and 8·2 per cent. respectively to 15·3 per cent. and 18·2 per cent., although 1927 was an exceptional year for oil companies. Electric Light capital earnings rose from 4·2 per cent. to 8 per cent., but, on the other hand, capital in Canals and Docks shows a decline in earnings from 19·6 per cent. to 4·0 per cent., and in Nitrate companies from 15 per cent. to 7·6 per cent., due probably to the rise of the synthetic industry.

Conclusions

It now becomes necessary to attempt to arrive at some conclusion regarding the adequacy of that part of the nation's new annual savings expressed in the figures of new capital issues for each year.

For this purpose the receipts from the operation of sinking funds and maturity repayments on our overseas investments may be regarded as repayments of capital assisting subscription to such issues without effort on our part, or in other words may be looked upon as "automatic" savings. The corresponding position of domestic receipts of a similar character is that they are a definite form of collective savings, and the excess of new issues over both such figures can alone be regarded in this part of the nation's savings as the result of *individual* desire to save.

One method of judging the adequacy of this branch of saving is to compare the individual saving, as already defined, in the years investigated with the corresponding figure before the war. Owing to the absence of the necessary data regarding repayments before the war, certain assumptions are necessary for such a comparison. These are:

1. That the rate of repayment of capital invested overseas was the same before the war as it has been ascertained to be by the present investigation for 1926 and 1927.
2. That foreign subscriptions to new issues before the war may be taken to be in the same proportion to total subscriptions as the present-day figures. The present percentage of foreign subscriptions has been ascertained from issuing houses and leaves out of account applications made by residents here on behalf of foreign clients which cannot be estimated. The omission, however, does not affect the general argument.

On these assumptions a figure of receipts from the operations of sinking funds in 1913 is obtained, showing that such payments from overseas on British account may be taken at about £11,000,000, while the foreign subscriptions to new capital issues for overseas may be put at £3,000,000 for 1913 and £2,300,000 for 1927.

The individual saving in this branch of savings may then be calculated, in accordance with the definition already given, as follows:

(£1,000.)

		1913.		1927.
Total capital issues [1]: Home		£50,709		£164,321
Overseas		197,528		152,991
		248,237		317,312
Deduct money "automatically" available for subscription:				
1. Foreign subscriptions to new overseas issues	£3,000		£2,300	
2. Sinking Funds:				
(a) Government [2]	7,600		65,000	
(b) Domestic	3,500		5,850	
(c) Overseas Capital (British portion)	11,000		17,000	
		25,100		90,150
"New" money subscribed		£223,137		£227,162

[1] Taken from *Statist* Jubilee No. 1928, where comparable figures for both years are given which exclude refunding operations, etc.

[2] Included and considered as a collective saving from taxation as distinct from individual saving. It is recognised that not necessarily all these sums went to British nationals as there was probably some foreign holding. There are no data available regarding this percentage, however, and the only course is to work on the figures taken.

These figures take no account of British subscriptions to foreign issues owing to the impossibility of obtaining a reliable estimate of such investment.

The resultant figures of " new " money invested are not comparable owing to changes in the price level. Adjusting according to the *Statist* index-number of wholesale prices the revised figures at 1927 values are:

1913	£320,270,000
1927	227,162,000

We were thus saving about £93 millions less in 1927 at 1927 values than in 1913 in this particular individual part of our saving. It is not my purpose to comment here on the reasons for this result, but merely to point out the fact that we are individually making available for investment at 1927 values only slightly over two-thirds of the amount we should to maintain the 1913 rate.

Moreover, if the overseas investment position alone is taken after deducting sinking fund receipts from the figures of new issues, excluding refunding operations, the figures work out as follows:

1913 (at 1927 values)	£263,400,000
1927	133,700,000

In other words, on the overseas investment position in terms of 1927 values we are individually providing only about half of what we did in 1913. More accurate comparison than this is not possible owing to the fact that the various figures are not on exactly comparable bases and could not be so established without inordinate difficulty, but the general result is sufficient and errors in the estimates would not upset it.

It is realised, of course, that other forms of savings at home, such as housing, roads, savings certificates, etc., have increased since before the war, but, as the Colwyn Committee pointed out, on balance there has been a decided falling off in the volume of savings, while the possible effects of the falling off of the amount of new money invested overseas on our trade will be evident to anyone.

Finally, one has to allow for changes in population and national income in relation to savings. The *per capita* figures of " new " money for investment in the securities dealt with in this article at home and abroad in terms of 1927 values are:

1913	£7·5
1927	5·0

while Professor Bowley and Sir Josiah Stamp have estimated that even in 1924 there had been no diminution in our national income. These considerations enforce still further the moral to be drawn from the figures and facts just quoted.

I wish to reiterate that this article attempts to deal with a particular type of saving and investment only, and is limited to those stocks and shares which are dealt with in the *Stock Exchange Official Intelligence*.

ROBERT KINDERSLEY

BRITISH FOREIGN INVESTMENTS IN 1928

Robert M. Kindersley

THE ECONOMIC JOURNAL

JUNE, 1930

BRITISH FOREIGN INVESTMENTS IN 1928

In 1929 I published the results of my first inquiry into the amount of British capital invested overseas and the volume of annual repayments to this country.

At the time it was emphasised that the results were in the nature of pioneer attempts, subject to revision with the invention of better methods of pursuing the inquiry in future years. During the past year I have been endeavouring to obtain more accurate results and to perfect the machinery of the inquiry.

Scope of the Inquiry

In the course of this work certain difficulties have become evident with the closer examination and more detailed knowledge now available of the subject. In view of this, it has been thought best to publish only those results where a fair degree of accuracy by statistical measurement has been ensured, leaving other parts of the problem subject to a degree of estimate to be dealt with subsequently, if the efforts which I am still making to find better methods of measurement are successful.

For these reasons it is not possible to indicate any broad changes which have taken place in the nature of our investments overseas since the first investigation, but this should be possible in future years as the methods of inquiry are put on a comparable basis.

The figures which I have examined relate to capital invested in those overseas loans to Foreign and Dominion Governments, States and Municipalities which are included in the Stock Exchange Official Intelligence and service of which is in any degree effected in London. Results relating to other forms of overseas investments and domestic and overseas capital repayment have been omitted from my inquiry because—

1. In the case of figures relating to redeemable capital invested at home it has not been possible to separate satisfactorily inter-company holdings.
2. Figures relating to the investment of British capital in companies *registered abroad* cannot accurately be determined. Apart from this difficulty there is also the further problem of taking account of the considerable investment by our nationals in companies operating abroad not mentioned in the Stock Exchange Official Intelligence and in foreign bonds and stocks not quoted here. For example, although it is seldom the practice of residents of the United States to subscribe to the sterling portion of a loan issued both in London and New York, on the other hand, British nationals frequently subscribe for or purchase large quantities of the dollar portion of such an issue. There is also a large and increasing investment by our nationals in United States securities issued and quoted only in New York. This investment has been greatly stimulated by the activities of the agencies of United States banks and of bondselling houses in London, which have largely increased in number during recent years.
3. Statistics relating to capital invested in British companies registered at home but operating abroad have this year been the subject of a separate inquiry by the *Economist*, of which I received notice. I have in consequence taken their results this year, instead of carrying out a separate investigation on this part of the problem, which would have meant duplication of inquiries from company secretaries.

I should like at this point to acknowledge the courtesy of the *Economist* in this respect, and also to express my appreciation of the generous manner in which some sixty banks have again placed material at my disposal for the inquiry.

In addition to the difficulty mentioned above of ascertaining the considerable British holding of dollar bonds, any attempt at an estimate of the net income and net capital investment of the United Kingdom from foreign loans or from British companies operating abroad encounters the further and increasingly important problem of taking account of the acquisition by American finance and other companies of substantial or controlling interests in British companies operating at home or abroad. The growing encroachment of American interests in British industry, commerce and finance is giving rise to a problem which needs the more to be stressed since there is this prevailing ignorance of the dimensions it has reached.

For example, according to Standard Statistics Service, the General Electric Co. of New York acquired in 1928 a substantial interest in the Associated Electrical Industries, a British company, which in its turn controls the British Thomson Houston Co., Metropolitan Vickers Electrical Products, Edison Swan Electric Co. and Ferguson Pailin Ltd. These companies form the largest combination for the manufacture and distribution of electrical equipment in Great Britain.

Another typical example is found in the activities of the International Telegraph and Telephone Co. In addition to its control of various British companies operating in South America, such as the Chile Telephone Co., the Montevideo Co. and the United River Plate Co., it also owns factories in England, and acquired in 1928 controlling interests in Creed & Co. Ltd., Croydon, manufacturers and world-wide distributors of telegraph equipment.

Again, during 1928 and 1929 the Electric Bond and Share Co. of America, through its subsidiary the American and Foreign Power Co., not only acquired the Mexican and Chile interests of the Whitehall Electric Investments Ltd. and the Argentine interests of the Atlas Light and Power Co., but also obtained a 50 per cent. interest in Tata and Sons Ltd., a company controlling the electric power supply in Bombay. In addition, it was largely responsible for the formation early this year of the European Electric Corporation Ltd., the main purpose of which is the control of important sources of power supply throughout Europe.

These examples should serve not only to illustrate the difficulties in the way of an accurate estimate of net British income and capital investment, but also to emphasise the growing American influence in public utility companies throughout the world. This influence is serious from the point of view of our overseas trade, since the change from British to American ownership must obviously lead in many cases to changes in the source of supply of equipment and credit, etc., with a consequent loss to our trade, shipping and finance. The possibility of an unchecked development of this tendency, unless counteracted by reinvestment of the monies received in similar British enterprises abroad, constitutes a grave menace to our economic prosperity, and justifies the need for drawing attention to the importance of maintaining our overseas investments.

Method of Inquiry

The method used is as follows :

The stocks that have been analysed are, as already mentioned, those classified in the Stock Exchange Official Intelligence under the titles of Dominion, Provincial and Colonial Government Securities; Dominion, Indian and Colonial Corporation Stocks; Foreign Corporation Stocks and Foreign Government Stocks.

Figures relating to capital invested overseas on which neither interest nor sinking fund payments were made in 1928 have been excluded.

The London banking agents of Foreign Governments, etc. were asked to give for this analysis :

(1) The total sinking fund or redemption payment made in the U.K. on each loan for the year 1928.

(2) The total interest paid in the U.K. on each loan during 1928.

(3) The proportion of such interest paid tax free.

Information supplied in answer to the last question gave the amounts of interest paid to persons resident in the United Kingdom and to persons resident overseas, since interest is payable tax free to the latter class. The British and the foreign shares in the repayment of capital either by operation of sinking funds or at maturity were taken to be in the same proportion as the interest payments.

It may be noted that this division does not give a strictly accurate apportionment as between British and foreign owners, since the use of the method of division on the basis of tax-free or tax-deducted interest means that foreigners resident here (and in consequence subject to income tax here) are included among the tax-deducted section, while British nationals resident overseas (and exempt from income tax here) are included among the tax-free section. Throughout the remainder of the article the term " British " must be read in this connection.

Where loans were originally issued entirely here and interest and redemptions take place in this country alone, no difficulty in compiling results of our overseas investments and repayments of capital from them occurs. But difficulties become apparent in more complex cases. Among these may be mentioned the case where the loan was originally issued in more than one centre and interest and/or repayment takes place at the option of the holder in any of these centres. In such cases the method applied this year to determine the British holding has been to take interest paid in London, tax deducted, and from this figure to calculate the British holding. The British and foreign shares of the redemption made in London were again taken to be in the same proportion as the interest payments made in London.

This method appears to be the only one available, although it is open to some errors on special occasions. For example, during the three months October, November, December 1928, the sterling-dollar exchange stood below \$4·85. Holders of many foreign stocks having the option of payment in New York or in London at fixed rates of exchange consequently secured a more profitable payment of their coupons at New York during this period, so that in such circumstances the interest paid in London tax deducted was not representative of the total interest due on holdings of persons resident in the United Kingdom.

In addition, payments made in London include payments on the foreign portions of many international issues, the coupons of which are payable here if desired by their holder. This fact in part accounts for the high percentage, shown later, of tax-free interest payments on foreign Government stocks. A further factor in this connection is that in some cases foreign Governments, although unable, under the terms of their loan contracts, to redeem by drawing a portion of their borrowings at present are known to be buying up for their own account portions of the issue.

For these reasons the figures of British-owned capital and repayments are conservative estimates. A method of overcoming these difficulties in the investigation has been devised, and if it can be perfected it is hoped to use it in the next investigation.

The results I have obtained are summarised in the following tables :

Table I

Proportion in 1928 of Interest paid in London tax free and tax deducted on certain classes of Investments.

Nature of Investments.	Tax free, %.	Tax deducted, %.
Dominion and Provincial Government Securities .	9·8	90·2
Dominion, Indian and Colonial Corporation Stocks	8·9	91·1
Foreign Corporation Stocks	23·7	76·3
Foreign Government Stocks	45·2	54·8

Table II

Amount of Capital invested Overseas owned by residents in the United Kingdom on December 31, 1928, *and the Repayments made thereon during* 1928.

(£000's.)

Nature of Investments.	Capital owned.	Amount of repayment by Sinking Fund and at Maturity.
Dominion, Provincial and Colonial Government Securities	944,497	4,410
Dominion, Indian and Colonial Corporation Stocks	91,453	860
Foreign Corporation Stocks	40,491	2,029
Foreign Government Stocks	324,008	8,277
	1,400,449	15,576

The figures of repayment exclude all amounts repaid out of refunding operations conducted in this country.

The results shown in Table II may be amplified by analysing the nature of the amount repaid in 1928. This is done in Table III below :

Table III

Analysis of Repayments during 1928 *to persons resident in the United Kingdom of Capital invested Overseas.*

(£000's.)

Nature of Investments.	Maturities.	Optional Redemption.	Sinking Fund Repayments.	Rate of Repayment by Sinking Fund.
Dominion and Provincial Government	525	—	3,885	0·41
Dominion, Indian and Colonial Corporation Stocks . .	308	—	552	0·60
Foreign Corporation Stocks .	—	1,438	591	1·43
Foreign Government Stocks .	—	—	8,277	2·55
	833	1,438	13,305	—

These tables, as mentioned earlier, do not include capital where the service is in default, but include the amount of loans issued in 1928.

The figures of overseas capital investment in these tables include our investments in Indian Government Stocks, whereas in the Stock Exchange Official Intelligence these are grouped under the title of "British Funds."

The income received in the United Kingdom during 1928 is shown by the following table. This income includes interest payments made on loans issued in 1928.

Table IV

Income received in the United Kingdom during 1928 *from Capital invested Overseas*

(£000's.)

Nature of Investments.	Tax deducted.	Tax free.
Dominion, Provincial and Colonial Government Securities	39,770	4,315
Dominion, Indian and Colonial Corporation Stocks	4,050	392
Foreign Corporation Stocks	2,028	630
Foreign Government Stocks	16,048	13,193
	61,896	18,530

Table II brings out clearly the large proportion of this Government class of our investments in the British Colonies and Overseas possessions. Of a total amount of investment outstanding of £1,400,449,000, as much as £1,035,950,000 is in Colonial securities, or 74 per cent. The effect of the Colonial Stock Act of 1900 is thus very evident, and the figures are interesting in the light of present discussions on the direction of our overseas investments.

The extent of repayment indicated at £15,576,000 compares with figures for 1926 and 1927 of £13,953,000 and £24,198,000 respectively. The large amount during 1927 was due to heavy maturity payments in the Colonial Government group—a factor largely absent in 1928, as indicated in Table II.

Table IV must, of course, be read in conjunction with what has already been said regarding the constitution of the tax-free payments made, but even making allowance for those factors it emphasises the fact that foreign nationals do own a considerable portion of loans to foreign countries originally issued here. In respect of Colonial loans (where the foreign portion would be mainly held by Colonials) the proportion is not so high. One factor accounting for this difference is probably that Colonial loans on the whole have not been outstanding so long as loans to foreign Governments. Moreover, foreign nationals have a greater incentive to purchase their Government stocks than Colonials have to purchase Colonial securities, since the Colonial Stock Act has the effect of reducing the yield on Colonial securities, while no such factor is present in the case of foreign Government bonds.

The rate of interest on the nominal value of our overseas investments in the groups analysed is approximately 4·4 per cent.

It is interesting to analyse as far as possible the geographical distribution of our overseas investments in the groups taken. The following table does this.

TABLE V

Table showing the nominal value of Overseas Investments in the groups analysed, by persons resident in the United Kingdom, in the countries indicated, and the Income derived therefrom during the year 1928.

(£000's.)

Area of Investment.	Capital.	Income.
Europe	113,000	6,050
America (excluding Canada)	149,000	7,014
Asia (excluding India)	93,000	4,677
Australia and New Zealand	521,000	23,744
Canada	102,000	3,872
Africa (including Egypt)	163,000	6,811
India	219,000	8,189
Other Colonies	40,000	1,539
	1,400,000	61,896

N.B.—Egyptian Income and Capital of £335,000 and £9,000,000 respectively included in Table IV under Foreign Government and Corporation Stocks.

It will be seen that the amount of British capital to which this year I have confined my examination, namely, the bonds and stocks of foreign and Colonial Governments and Municipalities, is £1,400 million. The figure obtained by the *Economist* for the amount of loan and share capital invested in British companies operating abroad but registered here is £1,053 million, making a total of £2,453 million for these two classes of investment. It must be remembered that this figure, for which a degree of accuracy may be claimed, covers only a part of the field of British overseas investment. It excludes from consideration :

(1) The large amount of capital invested by residents here in companies both registered and operating abroad, whether included in the Stock Exchange Official Intelligence or not.

(2) The sums, which I think are fairly considerable, invested privately either in loans to Governments, etc. entirely

dealt with abroad (*e.g.* investments in recent American foreign loans), or in private companies and ventures whose seat of operation is abroad.

No accurate estimate of these items has been possible, so that, as I have already indicated, they have been omitted pending the possibility of accurate methods of measurement being discovered. Nevertheless, from comparison with my previous experimental but wider investigation, and with the results obtained by the Inland Revenue authorities from their estimates of our overseas capital investment, I consider that the figure of £4,000 million for our total overseas investments is a first approximation to the facts.

In regard to repayment of investments, the sum repaid by sinking or maturity repayments and by redemption of capital in 1928 in the categories covered by my investigation and that of the *Economist* amounted to £22 million. To this, again, would fall to be added the amount due from investments of the type I have indicated as not included.

In 1928 the total of new issues, according to the figures of the Midland Bank, was £143 million, which excludes all refunding issues. Against this the present investigation shows that we had automatically available for new issues at least £22 million received from abroad. We therefore invested in new money abroad a sum in the neighbourhood of £121 million, compared with an amount in 1913 of £253 million at 1928 values. Of course such a comparison takes no account of home savings, but it is safe to say that these also are probably smaller, and that in total therefore we are saving much less than before the war on this basis of estimate.

I wish to express my regret to readers that the information contained in this article does not cover the whole field of our overseas investments. For the reasons given, however, the difficulties are very apparent and will take time to overcome. I am hopeful of devising methods of doing this in certain cases, and if these are perfectible I hope shortly to undertake a much wider investigation of the problem, the results of which I shall hurry forward as much as possible.

R. M. KINDERSLEY

BRITISH FOREIGN INVESTMENTS IN 1929

Robert M. Kindersley

BRITISH FOREIGN INVESTMENTS IN 1929

In March 1929 I published the results of a first inquiry into the amount of British capital invested abroad and the volume of annual repayments to this country. This inquiry was a pioneer attempt of a tentative nature, and it was realised at the time that as the problem became subject to closer examination in later investigations, more systematic methods would have to be used and the field of inquiry more clearly defined in order to ensure a fair degree of accuracy. Consequently, in my second inquiry, the results of which were published last year in the June issue of the ECONOMIC JOURNAL, pending the elaboration of a systematic method I decided to confine myself to one class of security only, namely, the bonds and stocks of Foreign and Colonial Governments, the British holdings of which could be determined with some degree of accuracy.

The present essay, however, attempts to survey the main field of British investment overseas. The results now published have been obtained by methods which have been devised to ensure their ready application to all the classes of securities examined, and will probably be applied with but little change in further inquiries of the same nature. It will therefore be possible in the future to compare results from year to year, and so to indicate periodically the changes that take place in the nature of our investments overseas. Thus a comparison is made later on in this article of our investments in Foreign and Colonial Government and Corporation Stocks for the years 1928 and 1929, estimated on comparable bases. It is hoped in later investigations to make comparisons which will cover the main field of investment.

OBJECTS OF THE INQUIRY

These investigations were originally inspired by a desire to arrive at an estimate of the volume of repayments coming into this country through the operation of sinking funds and maturities, so as to make it possible to separate the automatic portion from the real savings of the nation. In order to do this, however, it became necessary to collect information which also threw light upon other important aspects of our foreign investments. The results published in this essay, therefore, include as regards the securities examined: (*a*) the total nominal amount of British capital overseas outstanding in 1929; (*b*) the income derived therefrom; (*c*) the volume of repayments in 1929; and finally, (*d*) the "new money" saved for overseas investment in 1929, this being regarded as the British subscription to new issues less the sum repaid during that year.

FIELD OF INQUIRY

The investigations undertaken cover British investments in the bonds and stocks of Foreign and Colonial Governments and Corporations, interest payments on which are made in London, and in the securities dealt in on the London Stock Exchange of companies, both British and foreign, operating abroad. The whole field of British foreign investments is therefore covered, with the exception of (1) individual private investments, (2) companies operating abroad whose securities are not officially dealt in here, (3) the bonds and stocks of foreign Governments not quoted here. For example, although it is seldom the practice of residents in the United States to subscribe to the sterling portion of a loan issued both in London and New York, British nationals frequently subscribe for or purchase large quantities of the dollar portion of such an issue. There is also a large and increasing investment by our nationals in United States securities issued and quoted only in New York, largely owing to the increasing activities of the agencies of United States banks and bond-selling houses in London. In addition to this omission, the securities of insurance companies and many financial trusts deriving a major portion of their income from abroad have also been omitted, since the operations of these companies usually take the form of investments in the securities of British registered companies or in Government and Corporation stocks already included in these investigations. It is recognised, however, that owing to the increasing interest in dollar securities displayed by financial trusts, this omission may give rise to an appreciable error.

METHOD

The securities examined fall naturally into three broad categories, each requiring separate analysis. They are:

1. Securities of Foreign and Colonial Governments and Corporations.

2. Securities of British Companies operating abroad and registered in the United Kingdom.
3. Securities of Companies both operating and registered abroad, but dealt in here.

This analysis was only made possible by the information supplied to me by some seventy banks and issuing houses and well over a thousand companies, and I should like at this point to express my appreciation of the very helpful spirit in which these banks and companies have assisted me.

GROUP 1.

Foreign and Colonial Government and Corporation Stocks

The method applied to this group of securities was explained in some detail in the ECONOMIC JOURNAL of June 1930. Particulars were obtained from banks and issuing houses in respect of each foreign or colonial loan, interest on which was paid in London, regarding the total sinking fund payment made in the United Kingdom in 1929; the total interest paid in the U.K. during 1929, and the proportion of such interest paid free of British income tax.

For further information the reader should refer to the abovementioned article.

The results obtained for 1929 are summarised in the following tables and compared with the corresponding results obtained for 1928:

TABLE I

Proportion in 1929 of total Interest paid in London, tax deducted, on certain classes of Investments, and comparison with 1928.

	1929.	1928.
Dominion and Provincial Government Securities .	90·2%	90·2%
Dominion and Colonial Corporation Stocks . .	91·4	91·1
Foreign Government Stocks	53·6 [1]	54·8
Foreign Corporation Stocks	76·6	76·3

[1] As explained in my article of last year, the high foreign percentage in this group is due largely to payments made in London in respect of the foreign tranches of international issues.

Table I reveals little change in the proportions of British and foreign holdings for the two years under consideration, except in foreign Government bonds and stocks. Indeed, it is quite clear from other information obtained for previous years that foreign nationals are gradually buying back the bonds issued in this country on behalf of their Governments. In addition to this continuous repurchase of bonds, Table II shows that the repayments in this group are becoming increasingly heavy pending the extinction of old loans, mainly of the Argentine, Brazil, Chile and China, as the cumulative arrangements of sinking funds through which these repayments are annually made take effect. For these reasons the figure for British capital shows a decline in this group from £324,008,000 in 1928 to £312,792,000 in 1929, and it is certain that failing substantial new investment in this class of security, this figure will continue to decline more rapidly from year to year. The decline in 1929, however, was more than made up by increasing investment in the securities of Colonial Governments. Thus, in this group, in spite of a heavy repayment of £17,782,000 in 1929, the figure for British capital increased from £944,497,000 in 1928 to £970,551,000 in 1929, entirely as a result of the Colonial issues made in London during 1929.

TABLE II

Table showing the nominal amount of British Capital outstanding invested in 1929 *in certain classes of Securities, the Income derived therefrom, the volume of Repayment, and comparison with similar results for* 1928.

(£000's.)

	Capital.[1]		Interest.		Repayment.[2]	
	1929.	1928.	1929.	1928.	1929.	1928.
Colonial Govts. .	970,551	944,497	41,994	39,770	17,782	4,410
Colonial Corpns.	90,887	91,453	4,422	4,050	2,502	860
Foreign Govts. .	312,792	324,008	16,205	16,048	9,404	8,277
Foreign Corpns.	38,195	40,491	2,040	2,028	737	2,029
Total .	1,412,425	1,400,449	64,661	61,896	30,425	15,576

[1] The figures for capital include British subscriptions to issues floated in the year under consideration, but on which a full year's interest would not be due until the succeeding year.

[2] The figures for repayment exclude stock converted during the years under consideration.

It will be observed that despite the fact that the figures for British capital invested in the securities of Colonial Corporations and Foreign Governments and Corporations were less in 1929 than in 1928, yet the corresponding income showed an increase for each group. It should be remembered, however, that the interest in the year 1929 is more affected by the repayments in 1928 than by those in the same year. Table II shows that these were only £15,576,000 in 1928, as compared with £30,425,000 in 1929. Again, a full year's interest was not payable until 1929 on most of the loans issued in 1928, a year of heavier investment. These facts, in conjunction with the further fact that the rate of interest is higher on the recently issued loans than on matured or expiring loans, account for the apparent paradox of an increased income accruing from decreased capital investments in three of the above groups of securities. Table III gives a more detailed comparison of the repayments in 1928 and 1929.

TABLE III

Analysis and Comparison of Repayments for the years 1928 *and* 1929.

(£000's.)

Group.	Sinking Fund.		Maturity.		Optional Redemptions.[1]		Total.	
	1928.	1929.	1928.	1929.	1928.	1929.	1928.	1929.
Colonial Govts.	3,885	3,995	525	13,787	—	—	4,410	17,782
Colonial Corpns.	552	744	308	1,758	—	—	860	2,502
Foreign Govts.	8,277	8,907	—	—	—	497	8,277	9,404
Foreign Corpns.	591	737	—	—	1,438	—	2,029	737
Total	13,305	14,383	833	15,545	1,438	497	15,576	30,425

[1] The figures given as Optional Redemptions represent loans redeemed by Governments and Corporations prior to the final date of maturity.

It will be seen that the large increase in repayments in 1929 over that calculated for 1928 was, in the main, due to the heavy maturities of loans of Colonial Governments in 1929. These amounted to £13,787,000, for which the maturities of the loans of Australian States were largely responsible. It should, however, be borne in mind that a substantial proportion of this sum was derived from funds raised by new Australian issues in 1929, and thus does not constitute an effective repayment to Britain as a whole, as distinct from individual British stock-holders.

Companies operating abroad.

This investigation analyses the securities officially marketable here, of about 3,000 companies operating abroad. The capital of each of these companies was set down separately for British registered and foreign registered companies, classified in accordance with the divisions made in the Stock Exchange Official Intelligence (*e.g.* Foreign Rails, Mines, Rubber, to name only a few), and was further divided into two main categories representing the share and loan capital respectively. This latter division is essential, since the proportion of British holding is generally higher and of a different character in the debenture group than in the share group, and also because a larger sample of information is obtainable regarding the loan capital of companies registered abroad. In any case this division is necessary for the calculation of the income derived from British investments in these securities, since, unlike fixed interest bearing securities, dividends on share capital fluctuate widely from company to company, group to group, and year to year.

For these reasons a sample which did not differentiate between the two kinds of capital would yield altogether misleading results.

Information was obtained from companies relating to the amount spent on the redemption of capital in 1929; the proportion of registered share capital held by residents of the United Kingdom at the end of 1929, and the proportion of loan capital so held.

This information made possible the calculation, among other things, of the British holdings of the total capital examined, and the British portion of total repayment. Information regarding dividends and interest during 1929 was derived from the Stock Exchange Official Intelligence and Official List.

It is important to note some of the limitations of the above method of procedure.

Little information is obtainable regarding the proportions of *bearer* securities held by British residents, except in a few instances, such as the Canadian and Mexican Eagle Companies and the bearer securities of a few Swedish companies, coupons of which are payable to some extent in London. Consequently there is no alternative but to apply the British percentage obtained from a sample of the registered capital in any group to the bearer capital of the same group. In view of the greater popularity of the bearer security on the Continent and in the U.S.A. than in Britain, it is probable that the foreign holding of bearer securities is somewhat higher than the foreign holding of the corresponding registered security. This has more particular reference to the securities of companies registered abroad, since in this group the bearer security figures more prominently.

The practice of holding securities through nominees is another obstacle to accurate calculation. It is certain, for example, that there is a substantial foreign holding of securities registered in the names of English banks and other nominees, and it is equally certain that there is a still more considerable British holding of dollar securities in the names of American banks and other companies. There is a distinct danger that this practice, gradually becoming more widespread, will render it difficult for decisive conclusions to be drawn from future investigations of this nature.

It has already been noted that Insurance Companies and many Financial Trusts have been omitted from the scope of these investigations, since their operations usually take the form of investments in other companies already considered. Double counting has to a large extent also been avoided by excluding the share capital of companies more or less completely controlled by others. There is, however, a considerable amount of cross-holding between companies (for example, in the Mining group) with which it has not been possible to deal in this way, and which clearly leads to an over-estimate, particularly in the case of interholding between British registered companies.

GROUP 2.

British Companies operating abroad.

A company is taken to be operating abroad if its main plant and equipment are abroad. Holding companies investing their funds in the securities of companies not already examined also come within this category. A number of large companies, however, particularly in the group covered by Commercial, Industrial, etc., do extensive business both at home and abroad. Owing to the difficulty of separating out the portion of the capital of these companies that can be considered to be invested abroad, not all of these companies have been included in the investigation. A difficulty of the same kind occurs with regard to the main body of shipping companies whose vessels travel to and from Great Britain. In this case again account has been taken of those shipping companies only whose vessels voyage almost entirely in foreign waters.

It is recognised that these inevitable omissions are serious, since these companies do derive a considerable part of their income from abroad.[1] On the other hand, almost every British company operating abroad maintains an expensive London head office or agency, which absorbs part of the company's capital. This discrepancy, for which no reliable adjustment can be readily made, tends to neutralise the former source of error. The table

[1] As regards the annual balance of payments, a calculation of the net income from abroad derived by British shipping companies is unnecessary, since it is included in the annual estimate of the gross receipts of these companies made by the Board of Trade.

given below should therefore be studied with these limitations in mind:

Table IV

Table showing the nominal amount of British Capital invested in Companies operating abroad and registered in the U.K., the Income derived therefrom, and the volume of Repayments in the year 1929.

(£000's.)

Type of Company.	Share Capital.	Dividends.	Loan Capital.	Interest.	Repayment.		
					Sinking Fund.	Rate %.	Maturities.
Dom. & Col. Rails	1,645	20	22,636	1,157	28	0·1	794
Indian Rails	23,088	1,980	48,150	1,828	83	0·2	876
Ind. Rly. Annuities	—	—	26,187	1,296	1,114	4·3	—
American Rails	800	37	800	32	—	—	—
Foreign Rails	212,226	11,450	166,518	7,841	593	0·4	—
Banks & Disct. Coys.	30,368	3,248	—	—	—	—	—
Breweries	4,992	395	911	32	—	—	—
Canals & Docks	776	?	1,000	60	—	—	467
Commercial & Industrial	55,868	4,025	21,037	1,163	437	2·1	52
Elec. Lighting & Power	8,886	888	7,542	480	21	0·3	—
Fin., Land & Investment	94,392	7,333	29,363	1,201	855	2·9	711
Gas	8,565	716	2,339	95	89	3·4	—
Iron, Coal & Steel	6,108	266	1,580	107	38	2·4	—
Mines	74,354	6,950	3,393	225	104	3·1	132
Nitrates	6,449	266	2,497	179	210	8·4	—
Oil	99,626	14,600	13,224	647	508	3·8	290
Rubber	82,223	6,549	5,712	370	12	0·2	47
Shipping	11,880	782	4,593	240	294	6·4	—
Tea & Coffee	37,904	4,662	2,668	161	22	0·8	—
Telegraphs & Telephones	23,626	2,726	4,540	270	158	3·5	—
Tramways & Omnibus	14,382	488	19,070	850	153	0·8	398
Waterworks	3,447	293	1,446	75	2	0·1	—
Total	801,605	67,674	385,206	18,309	4,721		3,767

Total Loan and Share Capital	1,186,811
Total Income	85,983
Total Repayment	8,488

The results shown in the above table have been arrived at with the aid of returns from companies covering about 65 per cent. of the total capital analysed. This percentage of course varies from group to group, fluctuating from nearly 100 per cent. for the Tramways and Omnibus Group to about 30 per cent. in the case of Banks and Discount Companies. In every group, however, the size of the sample has been sufficiently large to ensure a tolerable degree of accuracy, subject to the limitations mentioned, both in the method and scope of the inquiry.

Total British loan capital outstanding in 1929 was £385,206,000 and repayments amounted to £8,488,000 during that year. The percentage of repayment is affected in a haphazard manner by maturities from year to year. If, however, we consider the regular repayment through the operation of sinking funds, the average percentage repaid is 1·23 per cent. This percentage varies from group to group, being 8·4 per cent. in the case of Nitrates and 0·1 per cent. in the case of Colonial Railways in 1929. Indian Railway Annuities have been split up into two portions, representing interest and repayment of principal respectively, the figures for loan capital being based upon the former.

The income derived from a total British loan and share capital of £1,186,811,000 was £85,983,000 in 1929, or, roughly 7¼ per cent. Interest was slightly under 5 per cent. of the total loan capital in these groups, and dividends distributed amounted to 8·4 per cent. of the total share capital. The latter vary in important groups from 14·65 per cent. in the Oil group and 9·35 in the Mining group, to 7·96 per cent. for Rubber and 5·4 per cent. for Foreign Rails.

About one-half of the loan and share capital examined in the above table is absorbed by railways and other public utility undertakings, whilst British railway enterprises in foreign countries alone account for nearly one-half of the loan capital and more than one-quarter of the share capital. This, of course, represents almost entirely old investment of the nineteenth century, during which period the British company was the favourite medium for the investment of British capital overseas. The high rate of income tax now payable by British registered companies as compared with companies registered abroad, and the rapid industrialisation of foreign countries has now left but little scope for the further development of this method of investment, and it will be observed that comparatively little headway has been made by the British company even in the newer public utility enterprises abroad, such as Electric Lighting and Power, Telegraphs and Telephones, despite the fact that these utilities absorb an enormous amount of capital in South America.

We therefore turn to the avenue of investment now offering a wider scope to the British investor, namely, the company registered and operating abroad.

GROUP 3.

Companies registered abroad.

Analysis of British investments in this group is more difficult than in either of the two preceding groups investigated. The mass of securities examined is of an extremely miscellaneous character, and the type of company to which they belong varies from the company which is virtually British owned and controlled (*e.g.* many of the mining companies registered in South Africa) to the company in which British interests are insignificant. Thus many American securities, despite the fact that only a very small percentage is held by British residents, are given a quotation on the London Stock Exchange simply because of their volume and market activity; these are consequently included in the analysis. On the other hand, many foreign companies have also made sterling issues. Consequently it is extremely difficult to collect a sample which is really representative of the mixture of securities analysed.

Wherever possible, separate samples of sterling and non-sterling issues have been used in arriving at the results. This is important, since naturally the British holding will be higher amongst sterling than foreign issues. Unfortunately, owing to the difficulty of obtaining information about the latter (in which bearer securities figure so prominently), many gaps were inevitable.

Wherever possible, the shares of no par value have been included at the figure given in the latest balance sheet of the company.

These comments should be borne in mind in a perusal of the table on p. 380.

Of a total nominal share capital examined of £2,623,374,000 for companies registered abroad, samples have been collected relating to £2,148,271,000. British holdings in this latter amount were calculated at 16·62 per cent. This general percentage was also applied, in arriving at the figure for British share capital, to the total capital in those groups in which sufficient information was lacking. The same percentage, of course, must not be taken as applying to each of the blank groups (*e.g.* to Foreign Rails, where the percentage British held is appreciably higher).

Total repayments amount to £9,593,000, of which £5,606,000 was repaid by the operation of sinking funds. The rate of repayment by sinking fund varied in important groups from 5·5 per cent. for Mines to 0·4 per cent. in the case of Dominion and Colonial Railways. The figure of £202,000 repaid in the Oil group was due entirely to the redemption by sinking fund of Preference share capital of the Mexican and Canadian Eagle Companies. The largest maturities occur in the Mining, Tramways and Omnibus, and Iron, Coal and Steel groups.

TABLE V

Table showing the nominal amount of British Capital outstanding invested in Companies registered and operating abroad, the Income derived therefrom, and the volume of Repayments in 1929.

(£000's.)

Type of Company.	Share Capital.	Divi-dends.	Loan Capital.	Inter-est.	Repayment.		
					Sink-ing Fund.	Rate of Repay-ment by S.F. %.	Matu-rity.
Domn. & Col. Rails.	55,287	5,501	161,127	6,491	626	0·4	—
American Rails	9,671	796	18,519	615	—	—	430
Foreign Rails [1]	?	?	75,709	4,078	888	1·2	—
Banks & Disct. Coys.	29,982	2,532	12,999	807	216	1·7	—
Breweries [1]	?	?	40	2	—	—	—
Canals & Docks [1]	1,742	1,175	2,436	52	—	—	—
Commercial & Industrial	70,648	7,348	21,464	1,646	723	3·4	592
Elec. Lighting & Power	11,820	600	31,002	1,724	650	3·1	494
Fin., Land & Investment	24,416	1,067	29,965	1,603	1,011	3·4	165
Gas [1]	?	?	392	23	—	Share Capital repaid	66
Iron, Coal & Steel	31,905	1,669	8,893	635	268	3·0	638
Mines	82,937	13,523	4,085	246	223	5·5	825
Nitrates	—	—	3,195	223	137	4·3	—
Oil	23,321	634	—	—	202	Pref. Capital repaid	—
Shipping	4,183	228	2,445	155	51	2·1	—
Telegraphs & Telephones [1]	?	?	17,768	840	387	2·2	—
Tramways & Omnibus	10,108	657	10,794	533	224	2·1	777
Waterworks [1]	?	?	1,953	51	—	—	—
Total [1]	436,002	41,997	402,786	19,724	5,606	1·4	3,987

[1] General average percentage applied where sample information insufficient in blank groups. The totals include estimates for the blank groups of £79,982,000 share capital, £6,267,000 dividends.

Total Share and Loan Capital	838,788
Total Income	61,721
Total Repayment	9,593

The average rate of interest on loan capital was 4·90 per cent. as compared with an average rate of dividends on share capital of 9·63 per cent. This latter rate varied in important groups from 16·3 per cent. for Mines, 10·4 per cent. for Commercial and

Industrial, 9·9 per cent. for Railways in British Possessions to 5·2 per cent. for Iron, Coal and Steel, 4·4 per cent. for Financial, Land and Investment and 2·7 per cent. for Oil.

Railways in British Possessions account for £216 millions, or over one-quarter of the total loan and share capital analysed in the above table. This is almost entirely due to the heavy British investments in the Canadian National and Canadian Pacific Railway companies.

The total British loan and share capital in the Electric Lighting and Power group is £43 million, contrasted with only £16 million in the case of British companies operating abroad. In the case of the loan capital in the Telegraphs and Telephones group. the corresponding figures are nearly £18 million for companies registered abroad and £4½ million for British companies (see Table IV). These comparisons relating to British investment in the younger industries bear out the view that the British company operating abroad is no longer so favourable a medium for the investment of capital. It is true that among the securities analysed, the British company accounts for £1,187 million as compared with £839 million for the company registered abroad. But it must be remembered that there is a considerable amount of British money invested in foreign securities not quoted here; and the inclusion of these would probably increase the latter to a larger figure than the former. It would therefore appear that with the growth in our foreign investments the proportion British controlled is tending to diminish.

It is now possible to summarise the results obtained for the three groups of securities analysed.

Table VI

Table showing the nominal amount of British Capital invested Overseas in the classes of Securities analysed, the Income derived therefrom, and the volume of Repayments in 1929.

(£000's.)

Group.	Capital.	Income.	Repayment.
1. Foreign and Colonial Government and Corporation Stocks	1,412,425	64,661	30,425
2. Companies registered in the U.K. and operating abroad	1,186,811	85,983	8,488
3. Companies registered and operating abroad	838,788	61,721	9,593
Total	3,438,024	212,365	48,506

The above table shows that in the field of investment examined, British capital aggregated £3,438 million. As already explained, this omits the important body of British holdings of securities not quoted on the London Stock Exchange, and a certain amount of bearer securities of Foreign and Colonial Governments and Corporations, the coupons of which were cashed abroad by British investors. Taking this in conjunction with the substantial British holding through foreign nominees of securities under Group 3, and individual private holdings and investment in real estate abroad, we consider that this total should be written up by at least £300 million to £3,738 million, covering the whole field of British investment overseas.

The income derived from the capital dealt with in the above table was over £212 million, and the rate of income 6·17 per cent. in 1929. In order to make this figure comprehensive, this again would have to be written up by at least £19 million to £231 million. The table given below throws some light upon the possible fluctuations of this figure in good and bad times.

TABLE VII

Table showing the division of British Capital invested abroad as between Loan and Share capital, and the Income derived from each class in 1929.

(£000's.)

Group.	Share Capital.	Dividends.	Loan Capital.	Interest.
1. Foreign and Colonial Governments and Corporations .	—	—	1,412,425	64,661
2. Companies registered in U.K. and operating abroad .	801,605	67,674	385,206	18,309
3. Companies registered and operating abroad . .	436,002	41,997	402,786	19,724
Total . . .	1,237,607	109,671	2,200,417	102,694

These figures reveal that in spite of the fact that debentures and other forms of loan capital constitute nearly two-thirds of British capital overseas, yet dividends on share capital averaging 8·86 per cent. amounted to more than half of the total income from these investments in 1929. If in a bad year average dividends decline, say, to 3 per cent., then, assuming no default in debentures, it is clearly possible for our income from overseas investments to fall to as low a figure as £140 million, thus illustrating the extent to which world depression may affect our balance of payments through this item. Conversely, in a good year this figure may rise to as much as £300 million.

Overseas Investments in 1929.

According to the Midland Bank figures, money subscribed for overseas issues in London in 1929 was £94,347,000, excluding issues made for conversion or redemption. The figures for repayment given in Table II include, however, certain sums repaid by the Australian and New Zealand Governments from funds raised by new issues in 1929. The inclusion of these funds brings the Midland Bank total to £105,567,000. It appears from the interest payments made on certain of these new issues that as great a proportion as 9·56 per cent. was paid tax free to foreigners. Applying this percentage to the total new money subscribed, the British subscription to sterling issues in 1929 was £95,475,000. If then we deduct the sum of £48,452,000 representing capital repayment, and therefore automatically available for reinvestment, the new money invested in this class of security amounted to £47,026,000 for 1929. The following table facilitates comparison with previous years:

	(£000,000's.)
1929	47
1928	108
1927	134
1913	243 [1]

These figures disclose the striking decline that has taken place in our annual new overseas investments, not only since 1913, but also since 1927. It is important, however, to remember that they do not give an accurate picture, but rather an indication of the position of our annual investment overseas, since they exclude the money absorbed annually in the net purchase of existing securities, or invested in new issues made entirely abroad. With regard to the bonds of Foreign and Colonial Governments and Corporations, apart from a gradual repurchase of securities by foreign nationals, very little change in ownership during 1928 and 1929 is noticeable, but, as has already been stated, the practice of investment in securities not quoted here is growing, and the new capital invested in this way is not easily ascertainable. But it is certain that the diminished attractiveness of overseas investment in 1929 as revealed by the above figures, and the heavy

[1] The figure for 1913 is adjusted in accordance with the index-number of wholesale prices for 1929.

liquidation of American securities accompanying the Wall Street crash, were reflected in a like decline in investment in this form of security during that year. This general decline in overseas investment is particularly serious at the present moment, when Britain is struggling to maintain her export trade, since her income from this item is becoming increasingly important as a means of paying for imports, which tend to grow steadily with the growth in population. This income, calculated at £231 million for 1929, in view of the subsequent world depression will almost certainly fall by something like £70 million to about £161 million for 1931, thus still further emphasising the great need for building up these investments as a bulwark against bad times.

It has not been possible in this analysis to throw much light upon the changes that have taken place in the nature of our investments overseas during 1928 and 1929, except in the case of the securities of Foreign and Colonial Governments and Corporations, where the results for 1929 were obtained by the same methods as those used for 1928. Further inquiries which I hope to undertake will render possible a more complete survey of these changes. Meanwhile, in response to many requests, it is hoped in a later article to analyse the results contained here on a geographical basis, so as to obtain an indication of the volume of British investments in particular colonies and foreign countries.

ROBERT KINDERSLEY

BRITISH FOREIGN INVESTMENTS IN 1930

Robert M. Kindersley

THE ECONOMIC JOURNAL

JUNE, 1932

BRITISH FOREIGN INVESTMENTS IN 1930

IN the September issue of the ECONOMIC JOURNAL of last year I published the results of a survey of British Foreign Investments in 1929. The methods then used were devised to ensure their ready application to all the classes of securities examined, and the hope was expressed that these methods would be applied with but little change to further investigations of the same nature.

The present investigation has been conducted on the same lines and the results published in this article admit of comparison with those obtained for 1929. It has therefore been possible to indicate some of the changes that have taken place in the nature of our overseas investments and the income derived from it. These changes assume a particular importance in the present survey, not only because of their relation to changes in the Balance of Payments, but also because the close of 1929 saw the beginning of a severe slump in the Stock and other markets, accompanied by the liquidation of international and other securities on a large scale.

However, not all the changes that are apparent from the figures contained in the present article can be ascribed to these factors. Owing to the increasing amount of material that is being so kindly placed at my disposal in connection with these investigations, and also to some differences that unavoidably occur in the types of samples used from year to year, some of these changes really represent a growth in our knowledge of our overseas investments, and some are the results of slight differences in classification. Nevertheless, these considerations do not seriously impair the conclusions that are to be drawn from the results obtained.

Objects and Field of Inquiry

As in the previous inquiry, the securities examined here in detail include :

1. The bonds and stocks of Foreign and Colonial Governments and Municipalities, interest payments on which are made in London.
2. Securities of all British companies, classified in the Stock Exchange Official Intelligence, operating abroad and registered in the United Kingdom.
3. Securities of companies classified in the Stock Exchange Official Intelligence, both registered and operating abroad.

In the previous inquiry, of the securities in Group 3, only those in which dealings are permitted were subject to detailed examination. The present survey has been extended to include the whole of the loan and share capital of American railways, in addition to other foreign securities known to be held in some degree by British residents. Moreover, some care has been exercised in obtaining an approximate estimate of the British holdings of securities issued and dealt in entirely abroad, and of individual private investments, although these forms of investment are not susceptible to detailed investigation.

The main results obtained as regards the securities examined are estimates for 1930 of :

(*a*) the total *nominal* amount of British capital invested overseas outstanding at December 31st, 1930;
(*b*) the income derived therefrom during that year;
(*c*) the volume of repayment and
(*d*) the "new money" saved for overseas investment, this being regarded as the British subscription to new issues less the sum repaid through sinking funds and maturities during that year.

In addition to an outline of the changes that these figures indicate, a tentative estimate is also made of the income derived from these investments during 1931, and its relation to the Balance of Payments is discussed.

The results contained here have been arrived at by the use of information supplied to me by some seventy banks and over a thousand companies, and I should like again to express my appreciation of the helpful spirit they have shown, and of their ready assistance, without which these inquiries could not be continued.

GROUP 1.

Foreign and Colonial Government and Municipality Stocks and Bonds.

The method applied to this group of securities was discussed in some detail in the ECONOMIC JOURNAL of June 1930. Particulars are obtained from banks and issuing houses in respect of all foreign and colonial loans, interest on which is paid in London, regarding (*a*) the total interest paid; (*b*) the proportion of this interest paid free of British income tax, and (*c*) the sinking fund payment made in the United Kingdom. For further information as to the manner in which these particulars were used in arriving at the figures below, reference should be made to the above-mentioned article. The results obtained for 1930 are summarised in the following tables and compared with the corresponding results for 1928 and 1929.

TABLE I

Showing the proportion in 1930 *of the total Interest paid in London, tax deducted, on certain classes of Investments, and a comparison with the position for* 1928 *and* 1929.

Type of Security.	1928.	1929.	1930.
Dominion and Provincial Government Securities	90·2%	90·2%	90·4%
Dominion and Colonial Municipality Stocks	91·1	91·4	91·9
Foreign Government Bonds and Stocks .	54·8	53·6	55·0
Foreign Municipality Stocks . . .	76·3	76·6	74·6

As explained in previous articles, the high percentage of interest paid tax free on Foreign Government Bonds is in large measure due to payments made in London in respect of the foreign *tranches* of international issues, as well as of sterling issues placed abroad. In the case of most of these securities coupons are cashable not only in London, but also abroad at the option of the holder, and hence the total interest paid in London on Foreign Government Bonds, as well as the proportions paid tax free and tax deducted, are liable to fluctuations from year to year that are not necessarily to be explained by the transfer of securities from British to foreign ownership or vice versa.

TABLE II

Showing the nominal amount of British Capital outstanding invested in 1930 *in certain classes of Securities, the Income derived therefrom, and comparison with similar results for* 1928 *and* 1929.

(£000's.)

A. CAPITAL.[1]

Type of Security.	1928.	1929.	1930.
Colonial Governments . . .	944,497	970,551	985,532
Colonial Municipalities . . .	91,453	90,887	94,965
Foreign Governments . . .	324,008	312,792	320,112
Foreign Municipalities . . .	40,491	38,195	36,730
Total . . .	1,400,449	1,412,425	1,437,339

B. INCOME.

	1928.	1929.	1930.
Colonial Governments . . .	39,770	41,994	42,490
Colonial Municipalities . . .	4,050	4,422	4,388
Foreign Governments . . .	16,048	16,205	15,793
Foreign Municipalities . . .	2,028	2,040	1,995
Total . . .	61,896	64,661	64,666

C. REPAYMENT.[2]

	1928.	1929.	1930.
Colonial Governments . . .	4,410	17,782	8,288
Colonial Municipalities . . .	860	2,502	1,531
Foreign Governments . . .	8,277	9,404	9,032
Foreign Municipalities . . .	2,029	737	830
Total . . .	15,576	30,425	19,681

[1] The figures for Capital include British subscription to issues floated in the year under consideration, but on which a full year's interest would not be due until the succeeding year.

[2] Repayment as used in the above table excludes stock converted.

The British subscription to new issues of this class floated in 1930, *less* repayment through the operation of sinking funds and maturities amounted to £58 million. Nevertheless, Table A shows that British capital increased from £1,412 million at December 1929 to £1,437 million at December 1930, a net addition of only £25 million. To some extent this is explained by the comparative weakness of sterling during 1930, resulting in an encashment abroad of a greater number of coupons during that year. But in the main the repurchase by foreign nationals of the bonds and stocks of their Governments is responsible for this difference.

During the three-year period covered by the above table, British investments have substantially increased only in the securities of Colonial Governments, the actual increase being some £41 million between December 1928 and December 1930. This is in line with the noticeable tendency of British investors to show a stronger desire to invest their funds in the Colonies than in the bonds of Foreign Governments. Indeed, whereas the latter on the whole are not being renewed as they mature, repayments of Colonial loans are in the main effected by conversion or by the issue of further loans, which find a ready market in the United Kingdom.

It will be observed that in spite of an increase of £25 million in 1930 of British capital invested in the group of securities considered above, the interest paid in London during 1930 remained at practically the same figure as that for 1929. The explanation is that the issues responsible for this increase in capital in 1930 were almost in every case made late in the year, and consequently bore little interest during that year. In addition, repayments in 1929 were exceptionally heavy, viz. £30 million as compared with £16 million in 1928 and £20 million in 1930. These repayments are obviously responsible for a greater decline of interest in the succeeding year than in the year in which they are made. For these reasons no appreciable increase in income was recorded in 1930.

The securities examined above, covering well over one-third of all British overseas investments, constitute the most stable form of these investments. Apart from the evidence of a gradual repurchase by foreign nationals of the bonds of their Governments, economic depression and weakness in the Stock Markets had but little effect on the amount of British capital invested in this form or on the income derived from it during 1930. It is true that during 1931 some defaults did occur in payments due in respect of the service of these loans, but, as figures given later on will show, the reduction in income during 1931 from this cause was inconsiderable, and not to be compared with the heavy reductions that occurred in other forms of investment.

British Commercial Capital Abroad.

The method used in the analysis of this important body of British overseas investments was explained in some detail in the ECONOMIC JOURNAL of September last. The field covered comprises the securities of roughly 3,000 companies operating abroad, and the results obtained are based on sample information of considerable magnitude. As stated at the outset, however, these samples are not identical in all respects with those used in the previous inquiry, and in addition, as regards dollar and other foreign securities, considerably more information has been available for 1930. Consequently, the changes disclosed by comparison between the two years are approximate, and do not strictly reflect actual movements.[1]

GROUP 2.

British Companies Operating Abroad.

For the purpose of this inquiry a company is taken to be operating abroad if its main plant and equipment are situated abroad. A number of companies, however, particularly in the group classed as "Commercial and Industrial," do extensive business both at home and abroad and larger companies that come under this category have been covered by the present investigations. In the case of shipping, however, account has been taken only of companies whose trading is almost entirely between ports in foreign waters. It is, of course, true that of the earnings of the vast body of British capital sunk in the shipping trade between the U.K. and the rest of the world, a considerable proportion is derived from abroad. Since, however, no part of the capital employed by these companies is actually spent abroad, the services they render can be more conveniently regarded as an export. Consequently it is preferable not to regard this capital as a foreign investment.

From the figures on pp. 183–4 no substantial change is apparent in the *total* nominal amount of British capital invested in the securities of the companies covered by the Tables on pp. 183–4 at the close of 1930, although the total does show a small increase of about £18 million. There are, however, substantial changes, particularly in the holdings of share capital, in some of the groups set out in these tables.

In the Commercial and Industrial Group, British capital increased by over £6 million to £62 million in 1930, due largely to new issues made in 1930, mainly in connection with the flotation of new companies. In the Financial, Land and Invest-

[1] For a full discussion of the field covered, of the method used and its limitations, the above-mentioned article may be consulted.

ment Group the decline from £94 million to £86 million is largely the result of the transference of a number of investment trusts to other groups in the more recent classification adopted in the Stock Exchange Official Intelligence. In the Mining Group the decline in holdings by £8 to £66 million in 1930 arose from the liquidation of a large number of unprofitable enterprises in that group. In the Oil Group an increase in the capitalisation of some of the companies combined with a decline in the percentage held by foreigners was responsible for an increase of £12 million in British holdings.

The most significant feature of the table dealing with Share Capital is, of course, the general reduction in earnings reflected in the reduced dividends paid in almost every section. The average rate of dividend paid on the whole of the Share

TABLE III

A.

Showing the nominal amount of British Capital invested in 1929 *and* 1930 *in Companies operating abroad and registered in the U.K., the Income derived from it, and the volume of Repayments.*

(£000's.)

Type of Company.	1929.		1930.	
	Share Capital.	Dividends.	Share Capital.	Dividends.
Dominion and Colonial Rails	1,645	20	1,381	27
Indian Rails	23,088	1,980	20,991	2,052
American Rails	800	37	800	37
Foreign Rails	212,226	11,450	220,202	10,257
Banks and Discount Companies	30,368	3,248	26,591	3,431
Breweries	4,992	395	4,755	329
Canals and Docks	776	—	1,377	—
Commercial and Industrial	55,868	4,025	62,249	3,699
Electric Lighting and Power	8,886	888	7,905	569
Financial, Land and Investment	94,392	7,333	85,604	4,230
Gas	8,565	716	8,812	1,017
Iron, Coal and Steel	6,108	266	8,018	474
Mines	74,354	6,950	66,023	4,731
Nitrates	6,449	266	5,969	262
Oil	99,626	14,600	112,010	16,997
Rubber	82,223	6,549	84,245	4,465
Shipping	11,880	782	15,154	720
Tea and Coffee	37,904	4,662	39,542	2,907
Telegraphs and Telephones	23,626	2,726	23,940	2,041
Tramways and Omnibus	14,382	488	14,948	382
Waterworks	3,447	293	4,606	339
Total	801,605	67,674	815,122	58,966

TABLE III—*continued*

B.

Type of Company.	1929. Loan Capital.	1929. Interest.	1929. Repayment.	1930. Loan Capital.	1930. Interest.	1930. Repayment.
Dom. and Col. Rails	22,636	1,157	822	26,927	1,416	52
Indian Rails	48,150	1,828	959	42,867	1,612	5,050
Indian Rail Annuities	26,187	1,296	1,114	25,816	1,284	1,126
American Rails [1]	800	32	—	800	32	—
Foreign Rails	166,518	7,841	593	170,589	7,152	447
Breweries	911	32	—	835	40	—
Canals and Docks	1,000	60	467	2,237	103	7
Commercial and Industrial	21,037	1,163	489	20,638	1,049	627
Electric Light and Power	7,542	480	21	6,112	393	55
Financial, Land and Investment	29,363	1,201	1,566	25,162	1,056	386
Gas	2,339	95	89	2,150	89	236
Iron, Coal and Steel	1,580	107	38	2,284	105	40
Mines	3,393	225	236	5,731	257	53
Nitrates	2,497	179	210	2,440	122	308
Oil	13,224	647	798	14,347	707	505
Rubber	5,712	370	59	5,849	368	73
Shipping	4,593	240	294	6,856	372	188
Tea and Coffee	2,668	161	22	2,561	135	24
Telegraphs and Telephones	4,540	270	158	4,560	265	38
Tramways and Omnibus	19,070	850	551	18,860	836	225
Waterworks	1,446	75	2	2,021	107	115
Total	385,206	18,309	8,488	389,642	17,500	9,555

	1929.	1930.
Share Capital	801,605	815,122
Loan Capital	385,206	389,642
Total	1,186,811	1,204,764

[1] The bulk of British capital invested in American Rails appears in Tables IV and V. The figures appearing above represent the capital of Atlantic Leased Lines, Ltd., a company registered in London owning the shares of a United States railway.

Capital declined from 8·4 per cent. in 1929 to 7·1 per cent. in 1930. This decline reflects only a part of the decrease in earnings during that year, for the reason that dividends distributed in 1930 were, of course, largely based upon the earnings of 1929, a comparatively good year. The full effect on dividends was experienced during 1931, and an estimate is made later on of the income accruing from these investments during that year.

In important sections of the above table, rates of dividends declined between 1929 and 1930 from 5·4 per cent. to 4·7 per cent. in Foreign Rails, 7·2 per cent. to 5·9 per cent. in the Commercial and Industrial Group, 7·8 per cent. to 4·9 per cent. in Financial, Land and Investment, 9·3 per cent. to 7·7 per cent. in Mining, and from 8·0 per cent. to 5·3 per cent. in Rubber. A striking contrast, however, was made by the results for Oil shares, dividend rates increasing from 14·7 per cent. to 15·2 per cent. Elsewhere the decline was general, except for Indian Rails and Banks and Discount Companies.

Table III, B, dealing with Loan Capital, shows that British holdings remained substantially unchanged at the close of 1930. Among Indian Rails, British Loan Capital declined by over £5 million as a result of the sale of H.E.H. the Nizam's Guaranteed State Railways and the repayment of the company's stockholders. New loans raised in 1930 increased British holdings of Mining debentures by £3 million, and among Foreign Rails new issues raised holdings of debenture stock by £10 million. The actual increase for Foreign Rails shown in the table is only £4 million, some £6 million of income stock having been reclassified as Share Capital in the figures for 1930.

The average rate of interest paid on British capital invested in these debentures declined from 4·8 per cent. in 1929 to 4·5 per cent. in 1930, a decline caused mainly by the default in the payment of certain Foreign Railway debenture stock. The result was a decline in total interest paid in 1930 of about £800,000.

Repayment of capital amounted in 1930 to £9½ million, as compared with £8½ in the previous year. The heavy repayment appearing under Indian Rails was partly due to the repayment of a large amount of Share Capital.

	(£000's.) 1929.	1930.
Dividends on Share Capital .	67,674	58,966
Interest on Loan Capital .	18,309	17,500
	85,983	76,466
Repayment of Capital . .	8,488	9,555

These figures show that the total income derived from British investments in the securities examined in Group 2 was reduced from £85,983,000 in 1929 to £76,466,000 in 1930, a reduction of over £9 million, whilst the rate of income declined from 7·25 per cent. to 6·35 per cent.

The securities examined in Group 2 constitute the main body of commercial capital directly under British control. In view of their greater knowledge of these companies, and the greater confidence reposed in enterprises controlled by British management, it is only natural that in a period of general liquidation, British investors would be less likely to dispose of holdings in these securities than in the more speculative shares of foreign companies. This observation derives support from the circumstance that owing to the heavy rate of income tax payable by British companies, the foreigner has little inducement to acquire large holdings of shares of these companies. Thus, in spite of economic depression accompanied by large reductions in dividends, no decline is apparent in the nominal British holdings of capital in this group of securities.

Group 3.

Companies Registered Abroad.

The securities examined under this heading are extremely miscellaneous in character, and the type of company to which they belong varies from the company which is virtually British owned and controlled, to the company in which British interests are insignificant. Owing to the prominence of bearer securities in this group, it has not been possible to obtain very precise results for a few sections, notably Foreign Rails, but the larger amount of material available this year has improved our knowledge of British investments in these sections, and thus the results for 1930 have attained a still greater degree of accuracy.

The field of investment covered comprises all securities of companies registered abroad in which dealings are allowed in the United Kingdom. An exception to this rule was made for 1930 in the case of American Railway securities, respecting which, owing to the data now available, it has been possible to obtain results for the whole of the loan and share capital of the American Railways. For information regarding the technique adopted in dealing with the variety of securities examined below, the article of September 1931 may be referred to.

Between the end of 1929 and the end of 1930, British nominal capital in this class of investment apparently declined by £45 million, accompanied by a reduction of income of over £10 million. Part of the difference between the two results, however, is explained by the smaller estimate of British holdings in the groups left blank for 1930, justified by the additional material available for that year, but the larger part of these declines does correspond to the actual conditions of 1930.

In individual sections of the table the most important decline took place in Mining shares. This decline, which was roughly

Table IV

Showing the nominal amount of British Share Capital of Companies registered abroad at December 1930, the Income derived therefrom and a comparison with the position for the previous year.

(£000's.)

Type of Company.	1929.		1930.	
	Share Capital.	Dividends.	Share Capital.	Dividends.
Dominion and Colonial Rails	55,287	5,501	57,024	4,926
American Rails	9,671	796	14,599	1,092
Foreign Rails [1]	?	?	?	?
Banks & Discount Companies	29,982	2,532	25,999	2,115
Breweries [1]	?	?	1,266	—
Canals and Docks	1,742	1,175	1,616	1,471
Commercial and Industrial	70,648	7,348	73,788	7,003
Electric Lighting and Power	11,820	600	11,042	750
Financial, Land and Investment	24,416	1,067	24,005	952
Gas [1]	?	?	?	?
Iron, Coal and Steel	31,905	1,669	28,237	1,425
Mines	82,937	13,523	70,558	7,339
Oil	23,321	634	24,520	999
Shipping	4,183	228	4,183	231
Telegraphs and Telephones [1]	?	?	4,761	342
Tramways and Omnibus	10,108	657	9,500	501
Waterworks [1]	?	?	?	?
Total	356,020	35,730	351,098	29,146

[1] In the groups for which precise results are not obtainable, estimates were based on the average percentage of the securities owned in the U.K. For five of such groups the 1929 estimates were £79,982,000 capital and £6,267,000 dividends, increasing the totals obtained for 1929 to £436,002,000 capital and £41,997,000 dividends. The corresponding estimates for the three groups in 1930 are £39,965,000 capital and £2,547,000 dividends, increasing the totals obtained for that year to £391,063,000 capital and £31,693,000 dividends.

£12 million, represents in the main sales to foreigners, affording striking evidence of the growing popularity in recent years of these shares abroad, particularly in France. Other important changes were declines in British holdings by £4 million in Banks and Discount Companies and £3 million in Iron, Coal and Steel, while British holdings increased by £4 million in the miscellaneous group of securities in the Commercial and Industrial section. It will also be noted that in the new estimates covering the whole of the share capital of American Railways, British holdings at December 1930 amounted to over £14½ million, although substantial sales were known to have taken place.

The most important feature of the above table, as in the

previous table dealing with British companies, is the conspicuous decline in dividends distributed in 1930. The average rate of dividend declined from 9·6 per cent. to 8·1 per cent., as compared with a decline in the case of British companies operating abroad from 8·4 per cent. to 7·1 per cent., a decrease of roughly the same dimensions. In important sections of this table, dividends decreased from 16·3 per cent. to 10·5 per cent. in Mines, 9·9 per cent. to 8·6 per cent. in Colonial Rails, 8·5 per cent. to 8·1 per cent. in Banks and Discount Companies and from 10·4 per cent. to 9·6 per cent. in Commercial and Industrial. Elsewhere income was fairly well maintained, the decline being less general than in the case of Group 2, whilst there were actual increases in dividend rates among Oils, Electric Light and Power Companies, and Canals and Docks.

TABLE V

Showing the nominal amount of British Capital outstanding at December 1930, *invested in the debentures of Companies registered and operating abroad, the Income derived therefrom, the volume of Repayments and a comparison with the position in the preceding year.*

(£000's.)

Type of Company.	1929. Loan Capital.	1929. Interest.	1929. Repayment.	1930. Loan Capital.	1930. Interest.	1930. Repayment.
Colonial Rails	161,127	6,491	626	160,516	6,531	3,344
American Rails	18,519	615	430	12,037	511	150
Foreign Rails	75,709	4,078	888	69,389	3,508	935
Banks and Discount Companies	12,999	807	216	18,631	1,175	313
Breweries	40	2	—	28	1	—
Canals and Docks	2,436	52	—	2,473	21	1
Commercial and Industrial	21,464	1,646	1,315	24,807	1,875	789
Electric Light and Power	31,002	1,724	1,144	31,483	1,754	915
Finance, Land and Investment	29,965	1,603	1,176	27,962	1,536	760
Gas	392	23	66	—	—	—
Iron, Coal and Steel	8,893	635	906	8,748	536	182
Mines	4,085	246	1,048	3,561	202	223
Nitrates	3,195	223	137	3,125	219	144
Oil	—	—	202	—	—	207
Shipping	2,445	155	51	1,037	145	1,305
Telegraphs and Telephones	17,768	840	387	14,039	650	304
Tramways and Omnibus	10,794	533	1,001	11,831	598	125
Waterworks	1,953	51	—	1,804	88	—
Total	402,786	19,724	9,593	391,471	19,350	9,697

Little net change is observable as between the two years examined in the bonds and debenture stocks of companies registered abroad, either in British holdings, interest received or the volume of repayments. In individual sections of the table, the sale of at least £6½ million American Railway Bonds is traceable, whilst new loans raised in 1930 increased British holdings among the debentures of Banks and Discount Companies by some £6 million. The decline in Foreign Railway Bonds was due to the exchange of certain Railway securities into shares of a financial company.

Interest on these securities remained practically unchanged at £19½ million in 1930, default being negligible during that year. This is rather surprising in view of the measure of default previously noted in interest payment among certain British companies in 1930. Repayments, which were also unchanged at £9½ million, include repayment of Preference capital in the Oil Group.

	1929.	1930.
	£	£
Share Capital	436,002,000	391,063,000
Loan Capital	402,786,000	391,471,000
	£838,788,000	£782,534,000

	1929.	1930.
Income from Share Capital .	41,997,000	31,693,000
Income from Loan Capital .	19,724,000	19,350,000
	£61,721,000	£51,043,000

The above figures disclose declines of £56 million in British capital and £10½ million in income between the estimates for 1929 and 1930 as regards securities of companies registered and operating abroad. As has already been pointed out, this must not be taken as a strictly accurate interpretation of the actual changes that took place between 1929 and 1930, since in part the smaller figures for 1930 are due to supplementary information rendered available for 1930. But even allowing for this factor, it is evident that in 1930 the continuous growth of British investment in this class of security received a severe check.

The following tables summarise the results obtained for the three groups of securities analysed in detail.

The 1930 aggregate of British capital invested in the securities examined is £13 million less than the figure obtained for 1929. This suggests that the decline in our investments overseas through sale of securities and other sources in 1930 was not entirely offset

TABLE VI

Showing the nominal amount of British Capital invested Overseas in the classes of Securities examined, the Income derived therefrom, and the volume of Repayments in 1929 *and* 1930.

(£000's.)

A. 1929.

	Capital.	Income.	Repayment.
1. Foreign and Colonial Governments and Municipalities . .	1,412,425	64,661	30,425
2. Companies registered in the U.K. and operating abroad . .	1,186,811	85,983	8,488
3. Companies registered and operating abroad	838,788	61,721	9,593
Total . . .	3,438,024	212,365	48,506

B. 1930.

	Capital.	Income.	Repayment.
1. Foreign and Colonial Governments and Municipalities . .	1,437,339	64,666	19,681
2. Companies registered in the U.K. and operating abroad . .	1,204,764	76,466	9,555
3. Companies registered and operating abroad	782,534	51,043	9,697
Total . . .	3,424,637	192,175	38,933

by increased investments in that year through new overseas issues or purchase of existing securities. Further comment on this is made later.

Income derived from these investments showed a decline of £20 million in 1930, a small part of which is explained by the increased accuracy of the results for this year. The average rate of income on the whole of the nominal capital declined from 6·17 per cent. in 1929 to 5·61 per cent. in 1930, a decrease the smallness of which is due to the fact that almost two-thirds of these investments take the form of fixed interest securities, among which there was little default in 1930.

Repayments, which were not quite so heavy in 1930, amounted to £39 million as compared with £48½ million in 1929. This decrease was due to the absence in 1930 of the heavy maturities that occurred in Colonial Government loans in 1929.

The above results cover the main field of British investment overseas. Attention has, however, also been given to investment undertaken by individuals privately, and in the foreign securities not dealt in in the United Kingdom. Of the British holdings in securities not quoted or dealt in on the London Stock Exchange, the largest contribution is made by Investment Trusts and Insurance Companies. Inquiries relating to the investments of these bodies indicate that at the end of 1930 the amount invested by them in the dollar securities not covered in the above tables did not exceed £130 million. In the previous survey a figure of £300 million was taken to embrace British holdings in foreign securities not dealt in here and other forms of British Investment Overseas not examined in detail. It is true that since the close of 1929 some of these holdings were disposed of, but, on the other hand, substantial purchases were also known to have been made in 1930. In view of this and of other considerations, the figure of £300 million is retained for 1930.

The effect of this is to increase the nominal amount of British capital arrived at for 1930 to £3,724,000,000, yielding an income of £209,005,000, covering the whole field of British Investments abroad. The corresponding figures for 1929 were £3,738 million capital, yielding £231 million income.

Income from Foreign Investments and the Balance of Payments.

The surveys which I have made during the past few years deal entirely with investments overseas, and no attention has been given to the problem of countervailing investment by foreigners in Great Britain. Consequently, the results arrived at here are not *net* figures, either as regards the long-term creditor position of Great Britain or as regards the income arising from her long-term investments. In applying these figures in an estimate of the Balance of Payments, considerable caution must be exercised. For, apart from the deduction in respect of foreign investment in the United Kingdom, there are also other modifications to be made.

In respect of British companies abroad, the calculated income has been derived from dividend payments, a basis which does not necessarily correspond with the net earnings of these companies abroad, since (*a*) dividends distributed tend to reflect the earnings of the previous year, and (*b*) they may be considerably less than earnings in a good year, or be paid largely out of accumulated reserves in a bad year. Furthermore, an addition must be made in respect of companies maintaining expensive head offices here and paying salaries to directors resident in Great Britain. Finally, for the purpose of the Balance of Payments as estimated by the Board of Trade, the shipping income included under foreign investments must be deducted, since this is presumably already included in their estimate of the Net National Shipping Income.

The above reservations should be borne in mind in a study of the following table, dealing with the *gross* income from our foreign investments during the past three years.

Table VII

Showing the Income derived from British Investments during 1929 *and* 1930, *with a tentative estimate for* ~~1913~~.

(£000's.)

	1929.	1930.	1931.
1. Foreign and Colonial Governments and Municipalities	64,661	64,666	63,883
2. British Companies registered in the U.K. and operating abroad	85,983	76,466	52,707
3. Companies registered and operating abroad	61,721	51,043	39,339
4. Other investments not covered by the above	18,510	16,830	13,632
Total	230,875	209,005	169,561

The tentative estimate of £169½ million for 1931 is based on British holdings of investments as at December 1930, and does not take account of changes caused by Britain's abandonment of the gold standard. Changes occurring in the last quarter of the year would in any case have had little influence.

The above table shows that during 1931 income dropped by nearly £40 million from the previous year and by £61 million as compared with 1929. Among British companies, the severest declines in 1931 occurred in Foreign Rails, Mining, and Rubber, dividends being reduced by over one-half in the two former groups, whilst Rubber dividends were practically wiped out. In the case of foreign companies the declines in 1931, though heavy, were not quite so severe, shares in the Commercial and Industrial Group and again in Mining suffering the greatest loss in dividends.

The prospect for 1932 is not encouraging, since dividends paid during this year will largely reflect the conditions of 1931, a year of almost unrelieved trade depression. In addition, there is also a substantial reduction to be made in respect of default among Foreign Government and other bonds. On the other hand, these circumstances will to some extent be countered by the lower level of sterling, in reducing the foreign burden of indebtedness and increasing earnings by raising the selling prices in terms of sterling of the products of British and other companies operating abroad.

Foreign Investments and the Position of Sterling.

The heavy decline in our foreign investment income between 1929 and 1931 was, of course, a factor of the highest importance in turning the Balance of Payment against Great Britain. This balance, substantially adverse in 1931, was already becoming so in 1930, but the effect of reduced income on the exchange was partially obscured by capital movements, and in particular by the repatriation of long-term assets. It must be emphasised, however, that, contrary to a large body of opinion, the extent to which British foreign investments can be used to protect the sterling exchange is limited. The largest part of the £3,724 million arrived at for 1930 is invested in the sterling bonds of Foreign and Colonial Governments and in the securities of British companies operating abroad; securities which outside the United Kingdom have only a limited market, particularly during a period of sterling depreciation, and which therefore could not be used for the purpose of securing foreign exchange. There remain, therefore, the securities of companies registered abroad and the dollar holdings of Investment Trusts and Insurance Companies. Of the former, British investment in sterling bonds is again high, and it is a widespread practice among Insurance Companies to keep foreign assets against foreign liabilities maturing from year to year.

Careful examination goes to show that in all not more than £550 million, or less than one-sixth of the total investments abroad, could be used for this purpose, and indeed of these securities a large proportion has only a narrow market outside London. Finally, against this must be set not only the volume of British domestic securities held by foreigners, but also the substantial body of investment by foreigners in overseas sterling loans and in the securities of British companies operating abroad, as shown by Table VIII.

This block of £481 million of securities owned outside the U.K., taken in conjunction with their investment in War Loan and other domestic issues, is liable if withdrawn to constitute a drain on sterling against which the sale of foreign assets could not easily prevail. Thus the extent to which our foreign investments can be used to protect the sterling exchange is limited.

Table VIII

Foreign and Empire holdings of Overseas Sterling Loans and of Shares and Debentures of British Companies abroad in 1930.

	(£000's.)
Colonial Government and Municipalities	116,626
Foreign Government and Municipalities	276,306
Indian Rails	191
Colonial Rails	427
Foreign Rails	4,721
Banks and Discount Companies	9,901
Breweries	183
Canals and Docks	—
Commercial and Industrial	8,901
Electric Lighting and Power	4,292
Financial, Land and Investment	5,586
Gas	1,254
Iron, Coal and Steel	1,133
Mines	26,576
Nitrates	6,989
Oil	6,006
Rubber	1,554
Shipping	347
Tea and Coffee	309
Telegraphs and Telephones	1,279
Tramways and Omnibus	7,484
Waterworks	1,111
Total	481,176

New Overseas Issues in 1930.

According to the Midland Bank figures, money subscribed for overseas issues in London in 1930 was £108,804,000. The figures for repayment in Table II include certain sums repaid by new issues raised in 1930, and the inclusion of these sums brings the Midland Bank total to £114,120,000. Of this total, from information available, it appears that £97,590,000 was subscribed by U.K. investors. Deducting from this the repayment of £38,933,000 automatically available for reinvestment in 1930, the "new money" saved according to the definition given at the beginning of the article was £58,657,000 in 1930. This compares with the figures of previous years as follows:

New Money Invested Abroad (£000,000).

1927	134
1928	108
1929	47
1930	59

These figures, of course, do not take account of the money absorbed in the net purchase of existing securities, or invested in new issues made entirely abroad, and therefore do not present an adequate picture of the net investment overseas in any year.

The improvement shown in the figure for 1930 over the previous figure is apparent only. For in 1930, in spite of the £59 million "new money" raised for overseas investment, the total figure for British nominal capital abroad declined by £13 million. Thus even when allowance is made for the fact that a part of this decline is attributable to a greater knowledge of these investments in 1930, and a further part to the liquidation of unprofitable enterprises, it is difficult to resist the conclusion that during the year there was a net sale of British investments abroad of something like £35 million.

The results contained in the present article reveal that in 1930 not only did we fail to maintain the total amount of our foreign investments, probably for the first time in over fifty years, but also that the income derived from these investments declined considerably. Nor does the immediate future hold out prospects of a reversal of these downward tendencies. Defaults on foreign bonds are increasing and dividends on companies operating abroad are continually declining. In this regard, apart from the fact that there is for the time being no favourable balance from which investments could be made abroad, it has to be recognised that in the final analysis it is the public who decide where money is to be invested, and to-day the tendency is towards the employment of capital at home rather than abroad, while the further repatriation of capital is not unlikely.

On the other hand, it should be borne in mind that the decline of 26·4 per cent., as herein calculated, in our income from foreign investments between 1929 and 1931 was accompanied by and indeed was mainly the result of a fall in world prices to the extent of 23·7 per cent. in the same period. Measured, therefore, in terms of goods received, our real income has not suffered to the same degree, and it is clear that its restoration to its former level in terms of money is bound up with the recovery in world prices.

ROBERT KINDERSLEY

BRITISH OVERSEAS INVESTMENTS IN 1931

Robert M. Kindersley

THE ECONOMIC JOURNAL

JUNE, 1933

BRITISH OVERSEAS INVESTMENTS IN 1931

The aim of the following paper, the fifth of a series of annual surveys of British Overseas Investments, begun in 1928, is to set forth the results of a study of the position in 1931,[1] and to discuss such changes as have emerged in comparison with the preceding year.

As on an earlier occasion, provisional figures are submitted for 1932—in anticipation of the detailed scrutiny of the full data now becoming available—in order to bring the general conclusions arrived at into closer relation with the realities and implications of our present economic position.

In the belief that this may prove a desirable addition, an attempt has been included for the first time in the following pages to analyse and present in tabular form the geographical distribution of the main body of foreign investments which forms the subject of this study.

The procedure followed in conducting this investigation has remained substantially the same as in previous years,[2] while at the same time it has been possible to eliminate some sources of possible error and to supplement the available data in certain respects. The results obtained and the accuracy that may be claimed for them are only rendered possible, however, by the authentic information placed at my disposal by the Banks and Issuing Houses of London and by a great number of commercial and industrial Companies, both in the United Kingdom and abroad, and I am happy to have this opportunity of making due acknowledgment of their courtesy and valuable assistance.

As in previous inquiries, the securities examined include :

1. The bonds and stocks of Colonial and Foreign Governments and Municipalities, interest payments on which are made in London.

[1] The reader, if interested to compare the results for 1931 as now ascertained with the provisional estimate essayed last year, may be referred to the Economic Journal, June 1932, p. 192.

[2] See Economic Journal, June 1932 and September 1931.

2. Securities of all British companies, classified in the Stock Exchange Intelligence, operating abroad and registered in the United Kingdom.
3. Securities of Foreign and Colonial companies registered and operating abroad in which dealings are permitted on the Stock Exchanges of the United Kingdom.

This detailed analysis, although covering the main field of British investments overseas, is incomplete in so far as it omits from consideration a body of foreign securities held here but not dealt in in the British markets, other individual investments in private companies and firms and other property, and the oversea activities of a number of British companies whose main assets are situated in the United Kingdom. As on previous occasions, however, an attempt is made to include an estimate covering these forms of investment in the final totals.

Group I.

Colonial and Foreign Government and Municipal Stocks and Bonds [1]

The following table, which shows the proportion of interest paid in London, tax deducted, in respect of the bonds of foreign and Dominion Governments and Municipalities, reveals that the amount held abroad is surprisingly high.

TABLE I

Type of Security.	1930.	1931.
Dominion and Provincial Government	90·4%	88·8%
Dominion and Colonial Municipalities	91·9	89·8
Foreign Governments	55·0	54·2
Foreign Municipalities	74·6	74·7

In considering the above percentages it should be borne in mind that they relate not only to sterling issues made in London, but also to the not inconsiderable amount of sterling *tranches* placed abroad. This latter consideration does not, however, destroy the conclusion that during 1931, owing to the rapid and widespread fall in prices in the Foreign Bond market, Foreïgn and Colonial nationals repurchased some of the issues floated by their Governments on the London market.

[1] The method applied to this group of securities has been discussed in previous articles in the ECONOMIC JOURNAL and in detail in the June issue of 1930. The proportion of the interest paid in London, tax deducted, indicates the British holding in this class of investment.

TABLE II

(£000's.)

Type of Security.	Capital.		Income.		Repayment.	
	1930.	1931.	1930.	1931.	1930.	1931.
Colonial Governments . .	985,532	1,014,826	42,490	44,145	8,288	2,568
Colonial Municipalities . .	94,965	88,620	4,388	4,260	1,531	2,939
Foreign Governments . .	320,112	301,875	15,793	15,715	9,032	10,139
Foreign Municipalities . .	36,730	35,562	1,995	1,800	830	621
Total . .	1,437,339	1,440,883	64,666	65,920	19,681	16,267

British money invested in new issues of Colonial and Foreign bonds in 1931, *less* repayment to British nationals through the operation of sinking fund and maturities, amounted to nearly £10 million. Nevertheless, it will be seen that the total amount of British capital outstanding did not increase to the same extent, thus affording some confirmation of the conclusion arrived at above regarding repurchases by Foreign nationals. Among Foreign bonds only, the heavy annual repayment through the operation of sinking funds combined with the gradual repurchase by foreigners has been responsible for a further reduction of £19 million during 1931 in British capital invested in these bonds. The following figures illustrate the changes that have taken place in the British holdings of Empire and Foreign loans.

TABLE III

British Capital invested in Empire and Foreign Loans.

(£000,000's.)

	Empire.	Foreign.	Total.
1928	1,035·9	364·5	1,400·4
1929	1,061·4	351·0	1,412·4
1930	1,080·5	356·8	1,437·3
1931	1,103·5	337·4	1,440·9

Therefore between December 1928 and December 1931, British holdings of Dominion loans increased by £68 million, whilst holdings of Foreign loans declined by £27 million, and amounted to only 23 per cent. of the aggregate at December 1931.

In spite of defaults on some Foreign bonds during 1931, income from Colonial and Foreign bonds (as shown in Table II) increased during that year by £1¼ million. This is explained by the fact that during 1930 a number of important issues were floated in London on which a full year's interest was not due until the succeeding year. Further, although moratoria were declared in 1931 by several South American countries, effective default on a full year's coupons did not take place until 1932. Of a total service of £14,457,000 in default in 1932 in respect of the above loans, the loss sustained by British investors amounted to £8,140,000, of which £3,095,000 was in respect of sinking fund payments.

Service in Default in 1932.

Europe	£2,109,000
Latin America	12,212,000
China	136,000

It will be noted that, in spite of financial and economic difficulties on the Continent, the extent of European default is surprisingly small, having regard to the fact that British investments in the bonds of European Governments and Municipalities constitute well over one-third of the total British capital invested in this class of security.

Repayments in 1931 amounted only to £16·3 million as compared with £19·7 million in 1930 and £30·4 million in 1929. These wide fluctuations from year to year in this item are inevitable, however, as repayments naturally vary in accordance with the loans which happen to mature and are actually repaid in the course of any one year. These maturities were over £16 million in 1929, but were negligible in 1931. Repayments in 1932, which included two large Indian loans, may be provisionally estimated at £34 million, after deducting some £3 million in respect of suspended sinking funds.

British Commercial Capital Abroad

It is convenient for purposes of analysis to divide this body of investment into two parts, one part comprising the securities of British companies operating abroad, *i.e.* companies registered in the United Kingdom; the second part consisting of British investment in foreign and colonial companies.[1]

[1] Roughly, 3,000 companies have come under the purview of this investigation, and British holdings have been assessed by means of samples averaging 50 per cent. of the total capital involved. These samples are not identical in all respects with those used in previous inquiries, and consequently completely accurate comparisons with previous years cannot be made, particularly when changes are inconsiderable. For a full discussion of the method used and of its limitations in respect of bearer securities, nominee holdings, etc., the reader may be referred to the article on British Overseas Investments in the Economic Journal of September 1931.

Group II.

British Companies Operating Abroad.

For the purpose of this investigation a company is taken to be operating abroad if its plant and equipment are in the main situated abroad. A number of companies, however, particularly among those classed under "Commercial and Industrial," carry on extensive business both at home and abroad. The larger companies of this nature have been covered by these inquiries, but no attempt has been made to estimate in detail the oversea assets of minor British companies.[1]

It has to be borne in mind, in a study of the tables given below, that dividends distributed on account of share capital, and interest paid on debentures, may not even approximately represent the effective remittances or the total earnings abroad of British companies operating overseas. For these receipts include remittances in respect of head office expenses and directors' salaries, and net earnings must take account of sums placed to reserve out of profits or drawn from reserves to meet deficiencies. Since 1929, in which year net profits were frequently in excess of distributed dividends, the margin has shrunk considerably, and owing to losses suffered by important groups of companies, particularly Rubber companies, it may be doubted whether net earnings exceeded dividends declared for 1931. Similarly for 1932, it is probable that on balance dividend payments were somewhat in excess of net earnings.

The total nominal British capital invested in these securities tends to remain very stable in the absence of new issues or the flotation of new companies. Purchases and sales, although extensive, mainly result in transfers of securities between holders in the United Kingdom, the high rate of British income tax acting as a strong deterrent to foreigners to the purchase of shares and bonds of British properties situated in their countries.[2]

[1] In the case of shipping, account has been taken only of those companies whose trade is conducted almost wholly in foreign waters. It is, of course, true that of the earnings of the vast shipping trade between the U.K. and the rest of the world a considerable proportion is derived from abroad; this income, however, is more appropriately viewed as payment for the export of shipping services.

[2] The investment in Mines increased from £72 million to £84 million as a result of new issues floated in 1931. The decline among Nitrates from £8·4 million to £5·1 million was due to the absorption of a number of British companies by Cosach, this company being registered abroad. Commercial and Industrial increased by £3·3 million owing to new issues. Elsewhere declines among Oil. Rubber, Tea, etc., were due to the writing down of capital.

Table IV

Nominal amount of British Capital outstanding invested in British Companies operating abroad, the Income derived and the amount repaid.

(£000's.)

	Share Capital.		Loan Capital.		
	Nominal Amount.	Dividends.	Nominal Amount.	Interest.	Repayment.
			1930.		
Dominion and Colonial Rails	1,381	27	26,927	1,416	52
Indian Rails	20,991	2,052	42,867	1,612	5,050
Indian Rail Annuities	—	—	25,816	1,284	1,126
American Rails	800	37	800	32	—
Foreign Rails	220,202	10,257	170,589	7,152	447
Banks and Discount Companies	26,591	3,431	—	—	—
Breweries	4,755	329	835	40	—
Canals and Docks	1,377	—	2,237	103	7
Commercial and Industrial	62,249	3,699	20,638	1,049	627
Electric Light and Power	7,905	569	6,112	393	55
Financial, Land and Investment	85,604	4,230	25,162	1,056	386
Gas	8,812	1,017	2,150	89	236
Iron, Coal and Steel	8,018	474	2,284	105	40
Mines	66,023	4,731	5,731	257	53
Nitrates	5,969	262	2,440	122	308
Oil	112,010	16,997	14,347	707	505
Rubber	84,245	4,465	5,849	368	73
Shipping	15,154	720	6,856	372	188
Tea and Coffee	39,542	2,907	2,561	135	24
Telegraphs and Telephones	23,940	2,041	4,560	265	38
Tramways and Omnibus	14,948	382	18,860	836	225
Waterworks	4,606	339	2,021	107	115
Total	815,122	58,966	389,642	17,500	9,555
			1931.		
Dominion and Colonial Rails	1,593	54	27,312	1,448	31
Indian Rails	20,871	1,768	43,171	1,583	95
Indian Rail Annuities	—	—	25,579	1,272	1,156
American Rails	800	37	800	32	—
Foreign Rails	221,191	4,004	173,539	5,819	148
Banks and Discount Companies	26,339	3,300	—	—	—
Breweries	4,739	320	835	38	—
Canals and Docks	1,377	—	2,222	145	15
Commercial and Industrial	65,611	1,924	20,583	712	478
Electric Light and Power	7,758	608	6,841	316	153
Financial, Land and Investment	85,925	2,322	27,287	1,114	394
Gas	8,964	1,002	1,318	61	37
Iron, Coal and Steel	7,609	196	2,130	87	153
Mines	72,565	1,864	11,804	584	54
Nitrates	3,372	—	1,747	105	200
Oil	107,514	11,306	12,852	639	456
Rubber	81,951	218	5,685	157	60
Shipping	12,050	482	6,312	313	308
Tea and Coffee	38,610	1,735	2,542	122	26
Telegraphs and Telephones	23,948	1,657	4,349	190	61
Tramways and Omnibus	15,512	296	18,666	612	860
Waterworks	4,521	203	1,911	102	215
Total	812,820	33,296	397,485	15,451	4,900

SUMMARY

(£000's.)

	1930.	1931.
Dividends on Share Capital . . .	58,966	33,296
Interest on Loan Capital . . .	17,500	15,451
	76,466	48,747

The decline in dividends from £59·0 million in 1930 to £33·3 million in 1931 reflects the accentuation of the depression that took place during the year.[1] The following figures show the movement for the four-year period, 1929–32 :

	Dividends.	
	Amount (£000's).	Per cent.
1929	67,674	8·4
1930	58,966	7·1
1931	33,296	4·1
1932 (provisional estimate) . . .	27,300	3·4

It should be remembered, however, that a part of the decline in dividends remitted is due to exchange restrictions, especially in South America, where a substantial sum of service money has accumulated and would be transferred if exchange conditions permitted.

In addition to the heavy fall in dividends in 1931, interest on loan capital (as shown above) declined by £2 million, the average rate of interest on the total outstanding falling from 4·5 per cent. to 3·9 per cent. owing to default, particularly among Foreign Railways. Repayments fell from £9·6 million in 1930 to only £4·9 million in 1931 owing to the absence of maturities and to the suspension of sinking funds in some instances during the latter year.

GROUP III.

Foreign and Colonial Companies (registered abroad).

The securities examined under this heading are extremely diverse in character, and the type of company to which they belong varies from the company which is virtually British owned and controlled to the company in which British interests are

[1] In important sections of the above table dividends declined between 1930 and 1931 as follows : Foreign Rails 4·7 to 1·8 per cent.; Commercial and Industrial 5·9 to 2·9 per cent.; Mines 7·2 to 2·6 per cent.; Land and Investment 4·9 to 2·7 per cent.; Rubber 5·3 to 0·2 per cent.; Oil 15·2 to 10·5 per cent.

insignificant. They also relate to large numbers of companies whose shares and bonds are traded in internationally, as, for example, South African Mines, American Railways and Public Utilities, Canadian Power Companies, etc. Consequently purchases and sales between holders in the United Kingdom and abroad more readily affect the volume of British capital invested in these securities than in the securities of registered British companies operating overseas, which have practically no market outside the United Kingdom.

The total nominal amount of British capital invested in these securities appears to have declined from £782 million at December 1930 to £759 million at December 1931, but it does not follow that the whole of this decline was due to repatriation of capital. Other important factors were the winding up of insolvent enterprises, the writing down of capital accompanying financial reorganisation and the loss in market value of shares of no par value.[1] There is little evidence to show that repatriation in regard to these securities took place on a large scale during 1931, but it should be remembered that the body of investments examined above comprises mainly securities which are dealt in on the London Stock Exchange. There is also a large amount of investment in foreign securities not dealt in on the London market, and these investments have not been examined in detail. There is evidence to show that some of these securities were sold late in 1931, advantage being taken of the gold premium caused by Britain's abandonment of the Gold Standard. Further reference to this fact is made later on.

SUMMARY

(£000's.)

	1930.	1931.
Dividends on Share Capital . .	31,693	22,654
Interest on Loan Capital . .	19,350	18,192
	51,043	40,846

[1] In the case of securities of no par value there is no method of arriving at a figure corresponding to nominal value. These shares have consequently been included at the values in the balance sheets. The reduction in British holdings of share capital from £28 million to £13 million in the Iron, Coal and Steel section is due both to this factor and to the financial reorganisation of a group of Canadian companies in which British interests were substantial. The estimates of share capital for Foreign Rails, Gas and Waterworks show a decline from £40 million in 1930 to £32 million in 1931, due largely to the loss sustained by shares of no par value.

TABLE V

Nominal amount of British Capital invested in Foreign and Colonial Companies, the Income derived and the amount repaid.

(£000's.)

	Share Capital.		Loan Capital.		
	Nominal Amount.	Dividends.	Nominal Amount.	Interest.	Repayment.
			1930.		
Dominion and Colonial Rails	57,024	4,926	160,516	6,531	3,344
American Rails	14,599	1,092	12,037	511	150
Foreign Rails [1]	?	?	69,389	3,508	935
Banks and Discount Companies	25,999	2,115	18,631	1,175	313
Breweries	1,266	—	28	1	—
Canals and Docks	1,616	1,471	2,473	21	1
Commercial and Industrial	73,788	7,003	24,807	1,875	789
Electric Lighting and Power	11,042	750	31,483	1,754	915
Financial, Land and Investment	24,005	952	27,962	1,536	760
Gas [1]	?	?	—	—	—
Iron, Coal and Steel	28,237	1,425	8,748	536	182
Mines	70,558	7,339	3,561	202	223
Nitrates	—	—	3,125	219	144
Oil	24,520	999	—	—	207
Shipping	4,183	231	1,037	145	1,305
Telegraphs and Telephones	4,761	342	14,039	650	304
Tramways	9,500	501	11,831	598	125
Waterworks [1]	?	?	1,804	88	—
Total	351,098	29,146	391,471	19,350	9,697
			1931.		
Colonial Rails	60,050	3,543	160,848	6,559	240
American Rails	17,985	1,014	9,527	412	165
Foreign Rails [1]	?	?	65,389	3,096	974
Banks and Discount Companies	27,263	1,837	18,012	1,158	282
Breweries	1,266	—	28	1	—
Canals and Docks	1,616	1,539	2,491	22	—
Commercial and Industrial	70,235	5,115	25,250	1,600	799
Electric Lighting and Power	13,297	956	32,192	1,701	1,097
Financial, Land and Investment	24,555	656	25,080	1,370	485
Gas [1]	?	?	390	22	—
Iron, Coal and Steel	13,048	560	8,858	474	161
Mines	68,236	4,008	4,134	273	241
Nitrates	2,997	—	5,045	271	241
Oil	24,500	566	—	—	204
Shipping	5,359	298	811	51	42
Telegraphs and Telephones	5,871	422	12,406	570	496
Tramways	9,500	501	11,520	531	158
Waterworks [1]	?	?	1,773	81	—
Total	345,778	21,015	383,754	18,192	5,585

[1] In the three sections for which precise estimates are not obtainable, rough approximations for 1930 were £39,965,000 Share Capital and £2,547,000 Dividends, increasing the totals to £391,063,000 Share Capital and £31,693,000 Dividends. The corresponding figures for 1931 are £29,734,000 Share Capital and £1,639,000 Dividends, increasing the totals to £375,512,000 Share Capital and £22,654,000 Dividends.

It will be noted that the decline in dividends [1] from £31·7 million to £22·7 million is not as heavy as the decline occurring among the British companies already examined. Some relief, it is true, was afforded by the gold premium included in dividend payments made in the last quarter of 1931, but it should be observed that Rubber and Tea companies, which were responsible for large losses in dividends during 1931, do not figure in the above table, British interests in foreign Rubber and Tea companies being negligible.

The decline in dividends during the four-year period 1929–32 is shown by the following figures of dividends distributed and the rate per cent. paid on the corresponding capital.

(£000,000's.)

	Amount.	Per cent.
1929	42·0	9·6
1930	31·7	8·1
1931	22·7	6·0
1932 (provisional estimate) . .	18·5	4·9

It is interesting to note that the average rate of dividends over each of the above years is greater on these securities than on the shares of British companies operating abroad for the corresponding year (see p. 193).

To some extent this extra yield may be regarded as a recompense for the greater skill and knowledge required in the selection of securities for investment in this group. Dividend payments in 1932 are tentatively estimated at £18·5 million, a decline of only £4·2 million on the preceding year. The decline would, of course, have been much greater in the absence of the premium on gold. The gold premium has been even more effective in preventing a decline in sterling income from loan capital in this group.

	British Income from Loan Capital.
1929	£19·7 million
1930	19·4 ,,
1931	18·2 ,,
1932 (provisional estimate) . . .	19·7 ,,

Thus in spite of some degree of default it is estimated that the appreciation of gold in terms of sterling resulted in an increase of

[1] In individual sections of the above table the largest declines were Mines, £3·3 million; Commercial and Industrial, £1·9 million; Colonial Rails, £1·4 million. Dividend payments were increased in the case of Electric Lighting and Canals and Docks, the latter dividends being in respect of British Government holdings of Suez Canal shares.

£1½ million in 1932 in the income from British capital invested in the bonds of foreign and colonial companies.

We are now in a position to summarise the results so far obtained in the following table :

TABLE VI

Nominal amount of British Capital Overseas outstanding, invested in certain classes of securities, the Income derived and the amount repaid.

(£000's.)

	Capital.	Income.	Repayment.
A. 1929.			
Foreign and Colonial Governments and Municipalities	1,412,425	64,661	30,425
British Companies (registered in U.K.)	1,186,811	85,983	8,488
Foreign and Colonial Companies (registered abroad)	838,788	61,721	9,593
Total	3,438,024	212,365	48,506
B. 1930.			
Foreign and Colonial Governments and Municipalities	1,437,339	64,666	19,681
British Companies (registered in U.K.)	1,204,764	76,466	9,555
Foreign and Colonial Companies (registered abroad)	782,534	51,043	9,697
Total	3,424,637	192,175	38,933
C. 1931.			
Foreign and Colonial Governments and Municipalities	1,440,883	65,920	16,267
British Companies (registered in U.K.)	1,210,305	48,747	4,900
Foreign and Colonial Companies (registered abroad)	759,266	40,846	5,585
Total	3,410,454	155,513	26,752

As stated at the outset of this article, the above results deal with British nominal capital outstanding in Foreign and Colonial bonds, the securities of British Companies operating abroad, and the securities of foreign and colonial companies, dealings in which are permitted in the United Kingdom. The rate of income on this body of capital declined from 6·17 per cent. in 1929 to 5·61 per cent. in 1930 and to 4·56 per cent. in 1931. This decline would, of course, have been much more pronounced were it not for the fact that almost two-thirds of these oversea investments are in fixed interest-bearing securities (excluding fixed interest Preference stock). Thus in spite of some defaults during 1931, interest payments declined only slightly from £103 million in

1929 to £100 million in 1931, while dividends on ordinary and preference capital fell from £110 million in 1929 to £56 million in 1931.

In the surveys for 1929 and 1930 a figure of £300 million was taken to cover British holdings in foreign securities not dealt in in the U.K. and other forms of British investment not examined in detail. Analysis of the holdings of Investment Trusts and Insurance Companies which contribute largely to this figure indicates that in spite of some selling by such institutions late in 1931 the total volume of these securities did not suffer a considerable decline. In this respect it is worth noting that the funds available for investment by Insurance Companies, and the capital subscribed to Investment Trusts, are continually increasing notwithstanding economic depression, and that new outlets for investment were considerably restricted during 1931. Allowing for these factors, a net decline of more than £10 million in the above figure seems improbable and the figure of £290 million has been adopted to cover the balance of British Oversea Investments. The nominal amount of British capital for 1931 is thus increased to £3,700 million, yielding £169 million income.[1] The corresponding figures for 1930 were £3,724 million capital, yielding £209 million income. The next table indicates the decline in income from British overseas investments in the four-year period 1929–32, the figures for 1932 being provisional only:

TABLE VII

Income from British Overseas Investments, 1929–32.[2]

(£000's.)

	1929.	1930.	1931.	1932.
Foreign and Colonial Governments and Municipalities . . .	64,661	64,666	65,920	60,000
British Companies (registered in U.K.)	85,983	76,466	48,747	42,500
Foreign and Colonial Companies (registered abroad) . . .	61,721	51,043	40,846	38,200
Other Investments not covered by above	18,510	16,830	13,224	11,900
Total	230,875	209,005	168,737	152,600

The forecast of £152·6 million for 1932 is based on British

[1] The average rate of income derived from the £290 million British capital representing securities not quoted in the U.K. and other private investments is assumed to be the same as that accruing from the main body of investment examined in detail.

[2] The figures for 1932 are provisional.

capital outstanding at December 1931, but takes into account changes in sterling income due to abandonment of the Gold Standard. It is largely in consideration of this factor that the decline provisionally estimated for 1932 was only £16 million as compared with the £40 million decline in 1931; and an even smaller decline might have been assumed but for the impact of widespread restrictions on the remittance of funds from foreign countries during 1932.

The prospect for 1933 seems even less unfavourable. The default on Foreign bonds that occurred in 1932 has largely been checked and negotiations have been opened in many instances for the payment of interest in arrears. The beneficial effect of the premium on gold continues in the current year and has been reinforced by South Africa's abandonment of the Gold Standard late in 1932, resulting in a large increase in gold-mining profits. Finally, there are indications that the downward trend in trade and net earnings is less marked, while efforts are now being made to lessen the effect of exchange restrictions and to bring about reductions in tariffs. These considerations indicate that on balance a further substantial reduction in the current year in our income from overseas investments is unlikely.

Geographical Distribution of British Overseas Investments at December 1930

The following analysis deals with nominal British capital invested overseas amounting to £3,186 million, being confined entirely to securities in which dealings are permitted on the various stock exchanges of the United Kingdom. This constitutes 85 per cent. of the total British overseas investment at December 1930. The balance, some £540 million, not included in this analysis, consists of private investments and securities not dealt in in the United Kingdom, as well as the overseas assets of a number of British companies whose activities are spread throughout the globe. A geographical analysis of the nominal capital corresponding to these overseas assets cannot readily be attempted.[1]

The bonds of Governments and companies that have defaulted for many years and the assets of a large number of oil and other companies expropriated by Soviet Russia have been excluded.

[1] The £540 million not included in this geographical analysis are roughly distributed as follows: Dominions £200 million; United States £120 million; South America £130 million; Europe £50 million. It is hoped that a more accurate and detailed geographical analysis of this body of investment will be possible at a later period.

TABLE VIII

Geographical distribution of £3,186 *million British Capital Overseas outstanding at December* 1930.

(£000,000's.)

Dominions.	
Australasia	£494
India and Ceylon	458
Canada	446
South Africa	224
New Zealand	123
Malaya [1]	108
British W. Africa	46
West Indies	40
Other British Colonies	48
Total Dominions	£1,987
Foreign Countries.	
Europe [2]	£245
Argentine	360
Brazil	151
Chile	49
Rest of South America	83
Mexico [3] and Central America	50
United States [4]	81
Japan	63
China	40
Other Asiatic Countries	47
Non-British Africa [5]	29
Total Foreign Countries	£1,198

Although the above figures as a whole cover 85 per cent. of British capital invested abroad, the percentage covered in the case of individual countries varies considerably. For example, while the above figures for Australia and New Zealand may be assumed to cover nearly the whole of our investments in these Dominions, the ascertained percentage is only about 40 per cent. for the United States, and probably less than 80 per cent. for the Argentine [6] and Brazil. In the case of India and Canada the percentage is about 85 per cent., but total investment in India and China would have to be substantially increased if proprietary holdings by British nationals permanently resident in these

[1] Malaya is here taken to include the whole of the Malayan Archipelago, including non-British territory and the Dutch East Indies.

[2] The whole of Turkey has been included in the European figures.

[3] The total for Mexico would be considerably increased if capital long in default were included.

[4] The total amount of long-term British capital in the United States, including the subsidiaries and branches of British Companies, and securities not dealt in in the U.K., is roughly estimated at £200 million nominal value.

[5] Including Egypt.

[6] The smaller percentage in the case of the U.S. and the Argentine is due to the large amount invested in securities not quoted in the U.K.

countries are included. The following table indicates the distribution of the above body of investment according to various classes of enterprise :

TABLE IX

Distribution of £3,186 million British nominal capital in various classes of enterprise over the territories of the world.

(£000,000's.)

Area.	Governmental and Municipal.	Railways.	Public Utilities.	Mines.	Miscellaneous.	Total.
Australasia	432	2	9	9	42	494
New Zealand	110	—	—	—	13	123
Canada and Newfoundland	97	213	32	2	102	446
South Africa	118	20	3	50	33	224
India and Ceylon	261	90	12	14	81	458
Malaya [1]	4 [1]	—	4	8	92	108
Other British Territories	65	29	3	9	28	134
Total Dominions	1,087	354	63	92	391	1,987
Europe (including Turkey)	120	30	18	6	71	245
South America	134	353	54	6	96	643
U.S., Mexico and Central America	2	49	29	10	41	131
China and Japan	83	—	5	1	14	103
Other Foreign Territories	14	2	3	3	55	77
Total Foreign Territory	353	434	109	26	277	1,199
Total—the World	1,440	788	172	118	668	3,186

[1] Malaya including foreign territory as well as British. In particular, the £4 million under Governmental and Municipal represent the Bonds of the Dutch East Indies Government held in the U.K.

Although the geographical distribution shown above applies to a total of £3,186 million of capital outstanding at December 1930, such changes as have since occurred are not likely to have modified the position appreciably. About two-thirds are invested in the Dominions. The capital invested in Australia and New Zealand in the main takes the form of Government and Municipal loans. In the case of Canada less than a quarter consists of Government securities, but a substantial proportion of the £213 million invested in Canadian Railways in fact carries the Government guarantee. Miscellaneous enterprise in the Empire includes a single item of £92 million largely invested in Malayan rubber production; and about one-half of the £81 million attributed to India represents ownership of tea plantations.

In South America, Railways account for over one-half of the British capital invested there, and it is of particular interest to note that investments in Railways represent nearly a quarter of British overseas capital throughout the world. Indeed the figure would be still greater if account were taken of the large proportion of Government borrowing by China, Japan and others applied to the financing of railway construction.

Of £118 million in Mines, £92 million are invested in the Colonies, £50 million in South Africa being connected largely with the production of gold.

Balance of Payments.

In the annual survey for 1930 [1] it was pointed out that the figure obtained for total Income from British Overseas Investments should not be used as a net figure for the purpose of estimates of the Balance of Payments. For apart from the deduction that must be made on account of income accruing to foreigners from investments in the U.K., account must be taken of the net amount placed to reserve by British Companies operating abroad, and of the cost of maintaining their head offices at home (see p. 191, ECONOMIC JOURNAL, June 1932). Moreover, the substantial default on foreign Government and commercial bonds during last year raises an important consideration connected with the present method of estimating Balances of Payments. A Balance of Payments may represent the difference between the annual *cash* receipts and *cash* outgoings of a country in respect of all transactions of a revenue character. The official estimate of the Balance of Payments of the United States appears to be based on this model. On the other hand, a Balance of Payments may represent the annual net balance of all *claims* arising out of transactions or contracts of a revenue character, even though actual remittance in some cases may be deferred. Much confusion of thought has arisen as a result of no clear distinction being drawn between the two methods and many current estimates suffer from this inconsistency. The latter method, which is the one adopted by the Board of Trade in its estimate of the Balance of Payments of the United Kingdom, gives a truer account of the country's trading position. For example, in its estimate for 1932 the Board of Trade includes the value of the whole of our exports during the year, although, in fact, a part

[1] See ECONOMIC JOURNAL, June 1932.

was not paid for, owing to exchange restrictions and difficulties existing in many countries. Again, in the past, the whole of the net earnings abroad of British Companies appear to have been included, although in practice large sums may not have been remitted home. From this point of view the earnings of British Railways in the Argentine must appear in these Board of Trade returns as a credit item, although in many instances dividends were suspended owing to the impossibility of remitting funds. In so far as payment of the interest on many Foreign bonds has been made in foreign currencies or funded, as in the case of Brazil, such interest must logically be regarded in the same light and therefore included in the Balance of Payments. In essence the effect is the same as if these sums had been transferred and the funds then re-exported as capital.[1] Thus in so far as interest due is deferred or funded, the aggregate of British capital abroad on short or long term is correspondingly increased, and the net increase may conveniently be regarded as an "involuntary export" of British capital. The provisional estimates for 1932 (see Table VII) indicate a decline of nearly £6 million in the income from Foreign and Colonial Government and Municipal securities, and of another £6 million in the income from British Companies abroad, a total of £12 million in these two groups. In view, however, of the above considerations, it would seem consistent to include only a part of this decline in the Balance of Payments.

New Overseas Investments in 1931 *and* 1932.

In previous articles figures have been given showing the net amount of new long-term overseas investments in each year since 1927, exclusive of capital movements due to the purchase or sale of existing securities, and money directly subscribed to new issues in overseas countries. This net "new money" invested abroad is equal to the British subscriptions to oversea loans less repayments to British nationals through the operation of sinking funds and through loan maturities.

The figures on p. 204 do not give an adequate picture of the net overseas investments during any of the above years, since they exclude other outward capital movements. They reveal, however, the striking decline that has been taking place during the last four years, while in 1932 for the first time in many years, due to the incidence of the Treasury embargo on foreign loans, repayments actually appear to have exceeded subscription to new overseas

[1] The effect is not exactly the same since these funds are for the time being immobilised.

(£000,000's.)

	British Subscriptions to New Oversea Issues.[1]	Repayment to U.K.	"New Money"[2] Invested.
1929	96	49	+ 47
1930	98	39	+ 59
1931	41	27	+ 14
1932 (provisional estimate) .	35	42	− 7

[1] These figures exclude conversions but include issues the proceeds of which were used for redemption.

[2] The "New Money" invested in 1927 and 1928 is roughly estimated at £132 million and £108 million respectively.

issues floated in London. This decline in new overseas investments, accompanied during the last two years by a moderate repatriation of long-term capital, indicates that the total volume of these investments is declining. A similar trend in the total volume of overseas investments last occurred during the early years of the War, when American securities were sold in large quantities to provide funds for War purposes.

Although, as already noted, the position in the current year is much more favourable and the adverse tendencies in the balance of payments and oversea investment income have largely been checked, it is as yet too early to discuss the possibility of the resumption of foreign lending either by London or foreign centres. Political uncertainty, the limited operation of the Gold Standard and restrictions on foreign exchange dealings, high tariffs and other impediments to trade all tend to postpone indefinitely such a revival.

At the same time, there are indications that since the abandonment by Great Britain of the Gold Standard in September 1931, the process of readjustment of the factors responsible for persistent disequilibrium in world economy has been greatly accelerated. The adverse trade balances of many debtor countries have been noticeably reduced; labour and other industrial costs have to some extent been cut; and conversion schemes have substantially relieved the burden of indebtedness in several important countries. In spite of this, progress towards the readjustment essential to solid recovery remains slow and a resumption of foreign lending at this stage, even though accompanied by a rise in world prices, would only encourage debtor countries to postpone rather than proceed with the readjustments indispensable to genuine recovery.

ROBERT KINDERSLEY

BRITISH OVERSEAS INVESTMENTS IN 1932 AND 1933

Robert M. Kindersley

THE ECONOMIC JOURNAL

SEPTEMBER, 1934

BRITISH OVERSEAS INVESTMENTS IN 1932 AND 1933

THE following paper is the sixth of a series, begun in 1928, embodying the results of annual surveys of British Oversea Investments. The detailed results relate to the year 1932. Owing to the large increase in default in 1932 and to the exchange movements following upon the abandonment of the Gold Standard by this country towards the close of 1931, calculations have been rendered more involved, and in consequence publication of the results of this study has suffered some delay. Nevertheless, as in previous articles, an attempt has been made to bring the subject-matter up to date by including provisional estimates of the main items for 1933.

The procedure adopted has remained the same as in previous years.[1] The securities examined in detail are:

1. All bonds and stocks of Dominion, Colonial and Foreign Governments, States and Municipalities on which interest is payable in London;
2. All bonds and shares of registered British companies (as classified in the Stock Exchange Official Year Book) operating entirely or mainly abroad;
3. All bonds and shares of Dominion, Colonial and Foreign companies registered and operating abroad quoted and/or dealt in on the Stock Exchanges of the United Kingdom.

These three categories constitute the main body of British investment abroad and at the same time that part which is most readily subject to scrutiny and accurate assessment. In order, however, to cover the field as far as possible, rough estimates have also been made to include the substantial amount of foreign securities held in the U.K. but not dealt in regularly in British markets, as well as other individual investments (*e.g.* in property, mortgages, etc.) abroad and the oversea assets of British companies whose main activities are confined to the United Kingdom.

[1] See ECONOMIC JOURNAL, September 1931 and June 1932.

Estimates are again given of the *nominal* amount of British investments in the three classes of securities specified above, and some explanation is offered of the differences that emerge in comparison with previous years. No attempt, however, is made to relate these differences to the movements of capital on long-term account except for estimates of sinking fund and maturity repayments.

The year 1932 is now generally regarded as the year in which the depression was definitely checked in the United Kingdom. This view finds some support from the results in the present article, which indicate that the downward trend of income from oversea investments was less marked than in the two preceding years. On the one hand, earnings continued to reflect the substantial contraction in world trade, and bond interest was further adversely affected by budgetary and transfer difficulties resulting in increased default. On the other hand, the process of adjusting costs to prices had already made considerable headway and enabled many companies operating overseas to achieve a profit margin; at the same time, abandonment of the Gold Standard in September 1931 afforded handsome profits from gold mines and increased the sterling income derived from bonds payable in gold currencies.

Before passing on to detailed results, I should like once more to express my appreciation of the support received from Banks and Issuing Houses of London as well as from a large number of companies, both at home and abroad, whose readiness to supply the statistical information required has made it possible to renew this study and to improve year by year upon the accuracy of the results obtained.

Group I.

Dominion, Colonial and Foreign (Government and Municipal) Loans.

As explained in previous articles, interest paid in London, tax deducted, is taken to indicate United Kingdom holdings, and the amount paid free of tax, foreign holdings.[1] Table I shows the results of analysis by this method.

These percentages apply to a total which in the case of a limited number of foreign loans includes not only sterling bonds issued in London, but also sterling tranches placed abroad, so that the corresponding percentages held in the United Kingdom if taken for the former alone would be slightly higher than those

[1] For a full explanation of the use of this method see Economic Journal, June 1930.

TABLE I

United Kingdom and Foreign Holdings of Dominion, Colonial and Foreign (Government and Municipal) Loans.[1]

	U.K.	Foreign.
Dominion and Provincial Governments . .	88·9%	11·1%
Dominion and Colonial Municipalities . . .	89·0	11·0
Foreign Governments	54·9	45·1
Foreign Municipalities	74·9	25·1

in the above table. This, however, does not alter the fact that the amount of these loans held abroad is and has been for some years very substantial. In consequence (see Table II), British investors have in reality suffered less from foreign default than would appear from the total of foreign loans outstanding. Indeed, the foreign holding is conspicuously large precisely in the case of those bonds on which default has occurred.[2]

Turning now to a consideration of the actual volume of British investments in Dominion, Colonial and Foreign loans, the following table shows the nominal amounts at the end of 1931 and 1932, the income received and the sums remitted to meet sinking fund requirements and maturities.

These figures call for some comment. New Issues in 1932

TABLE II

(£000's.)

Type of Security.	1931.			1932.		
	Capital.	Income.	Repayment.	Capital.	Income.	Repayment.[3]
Dominion and Colonial Governments .	1,014,826	44,145	2,568	1,025,408	44,997	23,740
Dominion and Colonial Municipalities .	88,620	4,260	2,939	83,531	3,922	3,061
Foreign Governments . .	301,875	15,715	10,139	289,375	11,984	12,032
Foreign Municipalities .	35,562	1,800	621	33,585	1,474	853
Total .	1,440,883	65,920	16,267	1,431,899	62,377	39,686

[1] Although the percentages in the above table are taken to represent United Kingdom and foreign holdings, actually they are the proportions of interest paid in London, tax deducted and tax free respectively.

[2] It is for this reason that in the case of Foreign Municipal bonds the proportion of interest paid in London subject to tax deduction has actually risen from 74·7% in 1931 to 74·9% in 1932, in spite of net sales by U.K. investors. (See ECONOMIC JOURNAL, June 1933.)

[3] The figures for repayment include sums received in the case of loans redeemed from the proceeds of new issues.

for account of Dominion and Colonial Governments amounted to £35 million. Repayments, however, amounted to over £23 million. And the net increase shown above is even a little smaller than the difference between these two figures, indicating some net sales of Dominion and Colonial bonds by United Kingdom holders to investors outside the United Kingdom. At the same time it is worth noting that repayments by Dominion and Colonial Governments reached an unusually high figure in 1932—India alone accounting for nearly £16 million. The comparable figures for 1930 and 1931 were respectively £8,288,000 and £2,568,000. It seems fair to suggest, therefore, that repayment on this substantial scale was somewhat fortuitous, assisted, in fact, in the case of India by an unforeseen export of gold which enabled the India Government to accumulate large sterling balances in London.[1]

As regards Dominion and Colonial Municipal loans, repayments for the year (£3 million) fell short by £2 million of the reduction in United Kingdom holdings, suggesting that a net transfer had taken place from United Kingdom to outside investors.[2]

In the absence of new loans to foreign countries during 1932, the normal operation of sinking fund payments on existing loans would account for a reduction in the British holding of foreign Government and Municipal loans. Such reduction has, as the figures show, occurred. Moreover, in the case of foreign Municipal bonds, sales by United Kingdom investors to foreigners appear to have been conspicuous.

The continuous reduction over the last five years in the nominal amount of British capital invested in foreign loans, both absolutely and relatively to the amount invested in Empire loans, is shown by the following figures :

TABLE III

British Investment in Empire and Foreign Loans.

(£000,000's.)

End of	Empire Loans.	Foreign Loans.	Total.	Ratio of Foreign Loans to Total.
1928	1,036	364	1,400	26·0%
1929	1,061	351	1,412	24·9
1930	1,080	357	1,437	24·9
1931	1,104	337	1,441	23·4
1932	1,109	323	1,432	22·6

[1] Redemption operations of the Indian Government were also assisted by the funds received from a large sterling issue floated in 1932.

[2] It is the practice of Dominion authorities to invest part of the sinking fund reserves held against internal debt in Dominion sterling loans. As a result the amount of these loans held by them is gradually increasing with the steady rise in the internal debt.

Thus from 1928 to the end of 1932 the amount invested in foreign bonds declined from 26·0 to 22·4 per cent.

The decline in income resulting from foreign default in 1932 was only slight in proportion to total income owing to the predominance of Empire loans in British oversea investments. Thus total income was reduced from £65·9 million in 1931 to £62·4 million in 1932, this being entirely accounted for by the reduction in income from foreign bonds. It should be borne in mind, however, that in subsequent years some decline must also be anticipated in the rate of income from Dominion and Colonial loans following the extensive conversion operations which economic recovery in the Dominions and conditions prevailing in the London Money Market have rendered possible and which are still in progress. The average rate of income on Empire loans in 1932 was 4·4 per cent., as compared with 4·2 per cent. on foreign bonds, but of course the average rate of interest on foreign loans, if fully remitted, is considerably higher. The next table shows the sums in default on foreign loans.

TABLE IV

Service in Default since December 1930.[1]

(Government and Municipal Loans.)

(£000's.)

	Interest.	Sinking Fund.	Total.
1931	1,453	1,095	2,548
1932	9,044	5,413	14,457
1933	9,544	7,745	17,289
Total since December 1930	20,041	14,253	34,294

[1] These figures relate to total loans outstanding, irrespective of the domicile of the holder.

Thus interest and sinking fund due and unpaid to British and other investors since December 1930 amounted to £34·3 million (interest £20 million; sinking fund £14·3 million). As already explained (see p. 367), in view of the substantial foreign holdings of these loans the loss to British investors is considerably less, amounting to £19·3 million (£11·1 million interest; £8·2 million sinking fund). The increase in default in 1933 took the form chiefly of further suspension of sinking fund rather than of interest payments. Incidentally the transfer moratorium declared by Germany in July 1933 only affected coupons due in the second half of the year; while certain other countries, notably Greece, partially resumed interest payments. In view of the economic and financial adjustments that have been made in the past few years by a number of countries, and the recent substantial improvement in prices, particularly of the primary products of debtor countries, it seems possible that further default may not be incurred on a large scale, although the German situation remains full of uncertainty.

In spite of the extent of default in 1932, Table II shows that repayments to British investors in respect of all Dominion, Colonial and Foreign sterling loans actually increased from £16·3 million in 1931 to £39·7 million in 1932. There were, however, substantial maturities in 1932, particularly of India loans, while among foreign bonds the Brazilian 7½ per cent. Coffee Loan of 1922 and the Japanese 5 per cent. South Manchurian Railway Loan were called for redemption. Repayments in 1933 are provisionally estimated at £28 million.

British Commercial Capital Abroad.

For the sake of convenience this term is applied to United Kingdom funds invested abroad otherwise than in Government and Municipal loans, though including in some cases securities which carry a Government guarantee, such as, for example, certain bonds of the Canadian National Railways.

Following the method hitherto adopted the investments falling under this heading are divided into:

(*a*) bonds and shares of companies registered in the United Kingdom;

(*b*) bonds and shares of companies registered abroad.[1]

GROUP II.

British Companies operating Abroad.

The investments here dealt with consist mainly of capital employed abroad under direct British control.[2]

Table V below records the nominal amount of British capital

[1] The British holdings in individual companies, covering about 50 per cent. of the total capital of some 3,000 companies, have been ascertained, and the detailed results are arrived at by carefully selected representative samples. This method suffers, however, from certain unavoidable limitations in respect of bearer securities, nominee holdings, etc. These have been fully discussed in previous articles (see ECONOMIC JOURNAL, September 1931).

[2] A British company is considered to be operating abroad if its plant and equipment are mainly situated abroad. A number of companies, however, particularly among those classified as "Commercial, Industrial, etc.," do extensive business both at home and abroad, and possess important fixed assets in the United Kingdom and overseas. The larger companies of this nature have been covered by these investigations, but no attempt has been made to estimate in detail the oversea assets of minor companies.

Table V[1]

Nominal Capital invested in British Companies operating Abroad; Interest and Dividends received and Loan Capital repaid[2] (£000's).

	Share Capital.		Loan Capital.		
	Amount.	Dividends.	Amount.	Interest.	Repayment.
	1931.				
Dominion and Colonial Rails	1,600	54	27,300	1,448	31
Indian Rails	20,900	1,768	43,200	1,583	95
Indian Rail Annuities	—	—	25,600	1,272	1,156
American Rails	800	37	800	32	—
Foreign Rails	221,200	4,004	173,500	5,819	148
Banks	26,300	3,300	—	—	—
Breweries	4,700	320	800	38	—
Canals and Docks	1,400	—	2,200	145	15
Commercial and Industrial	65,600	1,924	20,600	712	478
Electric Light and Power	7,800	608	6,900	316	153
Financial, Land and Investmt.	85,900	2,322	27,300	1,114	394
Gas	9,000	1,002	1,300	61	37
Iron, Coal and Steel	7,600	196	2,100	87	153
Mines	72,600	1,864	11,800	584	54
Nitrates	3,400	—	1,700	105	200
Oil	107,500	11,306	12,900	639	456
Rubber	82,000	218	5,700	157	60
Shipping	12,000	482	6,300	313	308
Tea and Coffee	38,600	1,735	2,600	122	26
Telegraphs and Telephones	23,900	1,657	4,300	190	61
Tramways	15,500	296	18,700	612	860
Waterworks	4,500	203	1,900	102	215
Total	812,800	33,296	397,500	15,451	4,900
	1932.				
Dominion and Colonial Rails	1,600	—	27,300	1,415	40
Indian Rails	20,900	1,872	43,200	1,581	—
Indian Rail Annuities	—	—	24,300	1,138	1,290
American Rails	800	44	800	32	—
Foreign Rails	221,200	2,220	173,100	4,769	225
Banks	26,300	2,122	—	—	—
Breweries	4,700	377	600	38	270
Canals and Docks	1,400	—	2,300	145	—
Commercial and Industrial	65,600	2,154	19,800	545	761
Electric Light and Power	7,900	572	6,600	295	265
Financial, Land and Investmt.	86,000	1,534	26,900	1,056	433
Gas	11,700	1,263	1,300	89	341[3]
Iron, Coal and Steel	7,600	136	2,100	62	—
Mines	72,500	2,292	7,300	534	59
Nitrates	3,400	—	1,700	—	—
Oil	108,600	10,170	12,400	618	501
Rubber	81,300	200	5,600	140	54
Shipping	12,100	457	6,000	213	339
Tea and Coffee	38,600	1,226	2,600	107	26
Telegraphs and Telephones	23,900	1,744	4,300	181	7
Tramways	15,500	337	18,500	425	148
Waterworks	4,600	309	1,900	101	17
Total	816,200	29,029	388,600	13,484	4,776

[1] In this table the estimates of income represent dividends distributed and interest paid to British investors. For the purpose of calculations of the U.K. balance of payments, therefore, these figures would have to be supplemented by additional remittances effected by these companies to cover Head Office and other U.K. expenses or appropriations, or alternatively reduced by the amount of any outward remittances in cases where reserves invested in the U.K. have been drawn upon to meet expenses abroad.

[2] Repayments in this table, as also in Table VI, are the actual sums repaid as distinct from the nominal amounts.

[3] Of this, £300,000 represents repayments of Share Capital.

invested abroad in various classes of enterprise. No deduction, however, has been made for the value of certain capital assets at home such as Head Office buildings in London possessed by some of the concerns in question.

Without new issues on any noticeable scale little change is to be expected in the nominal amounts held by British investors in the above securities since foreign holdings seldom exceed 1 per cent., the high rate of British income tax being a strong deterrent to would-be foreign purchasers of these stocks and bonds. The slight decline in the amount of loan capital outstanding reflects the automatic operation of sinking fund payments and maturities in 1932 as well as a certain amount of writing down of nominal values.[1]

Dividends received in 1932 declined by a further £4·3 million, the categories chiefly affected being Foreign Rails and Banks. Declines, however, were not as general as in 1931, payments being well maintained among the miscellaneous companies included under "Commercial, Industrial, etc.," while Mining dividends in 1932 already showed the effect of the increase in the sterling price of gold.[2]

The following figures, which also include a provisional estimate for 1933, illustrate the trend of dividend payments by British companies operating overseas.

Dividend Payments of British Companies Abroad.

	Amount of Dividend.	Percentage of Capital.
1929 . . .	£67,674,000	8·4%
1930 . . .	58,966,000	7·1
1931 . . .	33,296,000	4·1
1932 . . .	29,029,000	3·6
1933 (provisional) .	27,100,000	3·3

The provisional estimate for 1933 indicates a further decline of about £1·9 million in spite of the improvement in business activity. As already pointed out, the improved earnings of 1933 should be reflected in substantially greater dividends during 1934.[3] The higher prices obtaining for Tin, Tea and Rubber

[1] In many instances drastic reorganisation was accompanied by exchange of debentures into shares of lower par value.

[2] In important sections of the above table the rate of dividend declined between 1931 and 1932 as follows: Foreign Rails from 1·8 to 1·0 per cent.; Financial, Land and Investment 2·7 to 1·8 per cent.; Oil 10·5 to 9·4 per cent.; Banks 12·5 to 8·1 per cent. On the other hand, increases occurred in the following: Mines 2·6 to 3·2 per cent.; Commercial and Industrial 2·9 to 3·3 per cent.

[3] From the point of view of the balance of payments, *net remittances* to the U.K. arising from the activities of British companies abroad were already more favourable in 1933 than in 1932, in spite of the decline in dividend payments.

during 1933 will, in many instances, make possible the resumption or increase of dividend payments.

Interest on loan capital in 1932 was severely affected by transfer difficulties. Interest on the debentures of foreign rails declined from £5·8 million in 1931 to £4·8 million in 1932. As a result of default, non-transfer and conversion, the average income from the bonds and debentures of registered British companies operating abroad has declined from 4·8 per cent. in 1929 to 3·5 per cent. in 1932, *i.e.* by about 25 per cent.

GROUP III.

Companies registered Overseas.

This section covers British investment in the shares and bonds of Dominion and foreign companies (*i.e.* companies registered overseas) dealt in on the Stock Exchanges of the United Kingdom.[1] The degree in which these companies are financed by British capital varies considerably, some being virtually British-owned and controlled, while in other instances British participation is insignificant, as, for example, in the case of American Railroad companies. Unlike those dealt with in the previous section, many of the securities classified in Table VI below are quoted in a number of foreign centres, and mostly in New York, Paris and Amsterdam.[2] It follows that in a year of active Stock Exchange dealings, a considerable change may occur in the total amount held in the United Kingdom. Unfortunately, owing to the predominance of bearer securities in the case of foreign companies, a high degree of accuracy is not attainable in estimating British holdings in securities of this class.

For this reason and also because the samples obtained are necessarily less representative than those for British companies, it would be unsafe to attempt to draw detailed conclusions as to the changes that may have taken place in British shareholdings by comparing the totals obtained from year to year.[3] The main part of the estimated decline in British holdings from £375 million in 1931 to £344 million in 1932 is, however, undoubtedly attributable to (*a*) the drastic writing down of capital and (*b*) to the considerably lower balance sheet values of shares of no par value.

[1] British holdings of "unquoted" shares and bonds are included in a rough estimate of all other forms of foreign investment given on a later page.

[2] South African mining shares and the securities of American railways and public utilities, Canadian power companies, etc., are conspicuous in this category.

[3] These considerations do not apply with equal force to changes in income since these are influenced chiefly by the reduction or increase in earnings.

TABLE VI

Nominal Capital invested in Foreign and Colonial Companies ; Interest and Dividends received and Loan Capital repaid.

(£000's.)

	Share Capital.		Loan Capital.		
	Nominal Amount.	Dividends.	Nominal Amount.	Interest.	Repayment.
1931.					
Dominion and Colonial Rails	60,000	3,543	160,800	6,559	240
American Rails	18,000	1,014	9,500	412	165
Banks	27,300	1,837	18,000	1,158	282
Breweries	1,300	—	—	1	—
Canals and Docks . .	1,600	1,539	2,500	22	—
Commercial and Industrial .	70,200	5,115	25,300	1,600	799
Electric Light and Power .	13,300	956	32,200	1,701	1,097
Financial, Land and Investmt.	24,600	656	25,100	1,370	485
Iron, Coal and Steel . .	13,000	560	8,900	474	161
Mines	68,200	4,008	4,100	273	241
Nitrates	3,000	—	5,000	271	241
Oil	24,500	566	—	—	204
Shipping	5,400	298	800	51	42
Telegraphs and Telephones .	5,900	422	12,400	570	496
Tramways	9,500	501	11,500	531	158
Foreign Rails . .	29,700[1] (Foreign Rails, Gas, Waterworks)	1,639[1] (Foreign Rails, Gas, Waterworks)	65,400	3,096	974
Gas			400	22	—
Waterworks			1,800	81	—
Total . . .	375,500	22,654	383,700	18,192	5,585
1932.					
Dominion and Colonial Rails	62,500	1,616	159,600	7,088	227
American Rails . . .	18,200	308	9,700	571	—
Banks	25,600	1,472	18,000	862	258
Breweries	1,300	24	100	5	—
Canals and Docks . . .	1,600	1,946	2,800	1	—
Commercial and Industrial, .	63,700	5,613	24,400	1,321	602
Electric Light and Power .	15,200	1,023	30,700	1,536	1,095
Financial, Land and Investmt.	26,800	626	25,000	1,013	393
Iron, Coal and Steel . .	6,800	198	10,000	506	62
Mines	56,800	6,975	6,600	462	76
Nitrates	3,000	—	5,300	226	78
Oil	20,300	140	—	—	208
Shipping	6,600	342	800	47	52
Telegraphs and Telephones .	6,000	494	10,000	558	31
Tramways	10,600	113	11,200	549	12
Foreign Rails	19,000[1] (Foreign Rails, Gas, Waterworks)	1,225[1] (Foreign Rails, Gas, Waterworks)	60,600	2,340	425
Gas			400	22	—
Waterworks			—	6	52
Total . . .	344,000	22,115	375,200	17,113	3,571

[1] Owing to great preponderance of bearer securities in the categories Foreign Rails, Gas and Waterworks, the estimates for share capital and dividends in these three sections are only approximations.

Dividends received by British investors in 1932 showed little change on balance from those of the previous year, although there were some important changes in individual categories. The slump in railway traffic receipts was reflected in a sharp decline in distributions by American and Canadian railway companies, while dividends from investments in foreign and colonial banks also showed the effects of the depression. On the other hand, American and Canadian dividends were higher in terms of sterling in consequence of the depreciation of the pound, while Mining dividends increased by £3 million as a result of the higher price of gold.[1] The following figures illustrate the trend over the last five years of dividends accruing to British investors from holdings in foreign and colonial companies.

Dividends on British Holdings in Foreign and Colonial Companies.

	Amount of Dividends received.	Percentage of Capital.
1929	£42·0 million	9·6%
1930	31·7 ,,	8·1
1931	22·7 ,,	6·0
1932	22·1 [2] ,,	6·4
1933 (provisional estimate) .	22·6 ,,	6·6

In spite of the fact that remittances in respect of Gold-mining shares are estimated to have increased by £3 million and although dividend payments were resumed on other classes of capital in 1933, the provisional estimate for that year indicates little change on balance. To a large extent this is, of course, due to the fact that dividend payments in 1933 reflect the earnings of the previous year, but a further important consideration was the loss to Britain of the benefit of sterling depreciation after the abandonment of the Gold Standard by the United States and the subsequent depreciation of the American and Canadian dollars.

The decline in the rate of dividend from 9·6 per cent. in 1929 to 6·6 per cent. in 1933 was not as great as the corresponding decline from 8·4 to 3·3 per cent. in the case of registered British companies (see p. 372). The latter, particularly Tea and Rubber producers, felt the incidence of depression rather earlier and more severely than foreign companies; but, as a result of the adjust-

[1] In individual sections of the above table, the rate of dividend declined between 1931 and 1932 as follows: Dominion and Colonial Rails from 5·9 to 2·6 per cent.; Oil 2·3 to 0·7 per cent.; Banks 6·4 to 5·7 per cent.; and Tramways 5·3 to 1·1 per cent. On the other hand, increases occurred as follows: Commercial and Industrial 7·3 to 9·0 per cent.; Mines 5·8 to 12·3 per cent.; Canals and Docks 96 to 122 per cent.

[2] The final estimate for 1932 is larger than the provisional estimate contained in a previous article, the benefit from the higher price of gold having been greater than anticipated.

ments they have been able to make, are now in a better position to take advantage of an improvement in general conditions. For this reason a more rapid recovery in dividends may be expected in the case of British companies in the near future.

As regards interest on Loan Capital, Table VI shows that the favourable effect of exchange depreciation on sterling income from abroad was insufficient to offset the extension of default in 1932; there was a decline of about £1 million in this item. In this connection it is worth noting that the benefit of exchange depreciation was smaller in the case of bonds than of shares, as the indebtedness of the companies in question consisted largely of sterling loans. The effect of default in respect of suspension of sinking fund operations and postponement of maturities was both percentually and absolutely much greater in 1932.

SUMMARY.

In the following table the complete results for 1932 are summarised and compared with those of previous years:

TABLE VII

Nominal Amount of British Oversea Investment in Quoted Securities; Interest and Dividends received and Loan Capital Repaid.

(£000's.)

	Capital.	Income.	Repayment.
1930.			
Foreign, Dominion and Colonial Governments and Municipalities	1,437,000	64,666	19,681
British Companies Abroad	1,205,000	76,466	9,555
Foreign and Colonial Companies	783,000	51,043	9,697
Total	3,425,000	192,175	38,933
1931.			
Foreign, Dominion and Colonial Governments and Municipalities	1,441,000	65,920	16,267
British Companies Abroad	1,210,000	48,747	4,900
Foreign and Colonial Companies	759,000	40,846	5,585
Total	3,410,000	155,513	26,752
1932.			
Foreign, Dominion and Colonial Governments and Municipalities	1,432,000	62,377	39,686
British Companies Abroad	1,204,000	42,513	4,776
Foreign and Colonial Companies	719,000	39,228	3,571
Total	3,355,000	144,118	48,033

Income from British Overseas Investments.

In the previous table the nominal amount of British capital invested abroad in negotiable securities at December 1932 is put at £3,355 million. The income obtained by way of interest and dividends received is estimated to have been £144 [1] million in 1932, equivalent to an average return of 4·3 per cent. To this must be added the amount derived from investments not included in the table, *i.e.* such as investments in property, mortgages, etc., and securities not dealt in on the London market. The amount of these investments in terms of nominal values was roughly estimated at £290 million in 1931, consisting largely of security holdings by Investment Trusts and Insurance Companies. An examination of the investment lists of a number of the former shows that during 1932 advantage was taken of the depreciation in sterling to effect a reduction in holdings of foreign and domestic dollar bonds; although this was to some extent offset by the acquisition of Australian dollar bonds yielding substantially more than the corresponding sterling issues. Pending a thorough examination, the amount of these investments at December 1932 is approximately estimated at £285 million.[2]

TABLE VIII

Income from British Oversea Investments 1929–33.[3]

	1929.	1930.	1931.	1932.	1933.
Foreign, Dominion and Colonial Governments and Municipalities . .	64·7	64·7	65·9	62·4	62·5
British Companies (registered in the U.K.)	86·0	76·5	48·8	42·5	40·6
Foreign and Colonial Companies (registered abroad)	61·7	51·0	40·8	39·2	39·6
Other Investments [4] (not covered by above)	18·5	16·8	13·2	12·3	12·2
Total	230·9	209·0	168·7	156·4	154·9

The forecast of £154·9 million for 1933, based on the estimate of British Oversea Investments as at December 1932, indicates

[1] This figure does not allow for remittances to meet Head Office expenses or for receipts or outgoings in connection with allocations to or drafts on reserves.

[2] No great accuracy is claimed for this figure, since it is intended to cover not only security investments but also a large number of miscellaneous oversea assets of companies and individuals to which in any case a nominal value can only be somewhat arbitrarily assigned.

[3] The figures for 1933 are provisional estimates.

[4] The average rate of income derived from these investments is assumed to be the same as that obtained from negotiable securities.

that the decline in the income from these investments during the past five years has now almost been checked and that for reasons given below it is probable that it reached its lowest level in 1933. It is remarkable that even in that year the average rate of income still appears to have been as high as 4·3 per cent., compared with an average rate of 6·17 per cent. in 1929 :—

Average Rate of Income on Long-Term Investments.

	Amount of Income.	Percentage of Capital.
1929	£230·9 million	6·17%
1930	209·0 ,,	5·61
1931	168·7 ,,	4·56
1932	156·4 ,,	4·30
1933 (provisional) . . .	154·9 ,,	4·26

This is due to the fact that of a total of £3,355 million of British capital invested in negotiable securities, £2,195 million, or very nearly two-thirds, consist of bonds and debentures, and although default has reduced the interest normally obtained on these bonds, the reduction is small compared with the decline in receipts arising from equity stocks. For 1934 the prospects of a greater income seem favourable. In spite of increasing trade restrictions, the decline in world trade has been partially checked, a greater degree of currency stability [1] has been attained and a substantial rise has occurred in the prices of important primary commodities produced by British companies abroad.[2] Thus not only has an increase in earnings been made possible, but the external indebtedness of many countries has at the same time been rendered less burdensome.

The outlook for an improved rate of income from oversea investments is undoubtedly better. On the other hand, the reduction in that part of these investments consisting of loan capital must through the operation of sinking fund and maturity repayments, together with the increasing repurchase by foreign nationals, continue until Dominion and foreign lending is resumed

[1] The extent to which *de facto* stabilisation already exists is insufficiently realised by many who persistently advocate the stabilisation of the pound. The sterling area now comprises the Crown Colonies, Egypt, India, Australia and New Zealand, South Africa, the Scandinavian countries and the Argentine. Moreover, through the operations of the Exchange Equalisation Account a close relation has also been maintained between the gold currencies and the pound during the past six months.

[2] With the increase in earnings it is becoming the general practice to place a larger proportion of net profits to reserve and consequently dividend payments will not fully reflect the improvement.

on an appropriate scale. The modification of Britain's creditor position is illustrated by the following figures :

	British Subscription to New Oversea Issues.[1]	Repayment to the United Kingdom.
1929	£96 million	£49 million
1930	98 ,,	39 ,,
1931	41 ,,	27 ,,
1932	37 ,,	48 ,,
1933 (provisional) . . .	50 ,,	55 ,,

Thus, in addition to the moderate repatriation of capital through the sale of dollar bonds, etc., during the last two years, repayments alone by way of sinking funds and maturities have actually exceeded new oversea issues.[2] To some extent, no doubt, the incidence of the Treasury ban on foreign loans has been responsible for this trend, but even in the absence of this embargo, the flotation of new foreign issues is for obvious reasons hardly practicable at the moment. Moreover, although Britain's fiscal policy and the abandonment of the Gold Standard were effective in eliminating the adverse balances of 1931 and 1932, the improvement in domestic trade has necessitated larger imports of raw materials, with the result that the balance of payments has probably resumed its adverse tendency. While for the moment this is being met by an increase of foreign and Dominion sight deposits in London, there is nevertheless a certain danger that a persistently adverse balance may create conditions favouring further repatriation of long-term capital in addition to the normal reduction in total investments through sinking fund and maturity repayments.

ROBERT KINDERSLEY

[1] The figures exclude conversions, but not new issues, the proceeds of which have been used wholly or in part to effect redemption, as such repayments are already included in Table II.

[2] Repayments in 1933 were, however, exceptionally heavy.

BRITISH OVERSEAS INVESTMENTS IN 1933 AND 1934

Robert M. Kindersley

BRITAIN'S OVERSEA INVESTMENTS IN 1933 AND 1934

THE following survey of Britain's Oversea Investments is the seventh of a series of annual studies on this subject made possible by the courtesy of the Banks and Issuing Houses in London and of a large number of companies, both at home and abroad, whose continued assistance in furnishing me with the relevant data I am again happy to acknowledge.

Former articles contain a detailed explanation of the method used in these researches and the limitations unavoidably imposed upon them by the difficulties of tracing the ownership of bearer securities, nominee holdings, etc.[1] As on earlier occasions, it has been found convenient to classify securities into three broad groups as follows :—

(1) All bonds and stocks of Dominion, Colonial and Foreign Governments, States and Municipalities, interest on which is payable in London.

(2) All bonds and shares of registered British companies operating entirely or mainly abroad.

(3) All bonds and shares of Dominion, Colonial and Foreign companies registered and operating abroad, quoted and/or dealt in on the Stock Exchanges of the United Kingdom.

In order to cover the field as far as possible, a rough estimate is also included of that part of Britain's oversea investments less readily subject to accurate assessment, viz. foreign securities held in the U.K. but not dealt in regularly in British markets; other private investments such as property, mortgages, etc. abroad; and the oversea assets of British companies whose main activities are in the United Kingdom.

The estimated aggregates of British capital invested abroad are expressed in terms of nominal values, a procedure which, although possessing certain drawbacks, is superior to, and more convenient for purposes of calculation than, the alternative methods of adopting market values or original costs.[2]

[1] See ECONOMIC JOURNAL, September 1931 and June 1932.

[2] Market values, for example, are subject to substantial and abrupt fluctuations as a result of changing economic conditions and their use would destroy the continuity essential to a series of investigations of this nature. Calculations

On the other hand, comparison of the yearly totals of the nominal amount of British Oversea Investments for the purpose of arriving at an estimate of net long-term capital movements is vitiated by fortuitous changes arising from writing-down of capital, bonus issues, conversion, etc. Consequently, except for estimates of sinking fund and maturity repayments, no elaborate attempt is made to relate the difference between the totals of successive years to the changes on capital account.

The detailed results given below relate to the year 1933 and estimates shown for 1934 are merely forecasts subject to revision. Before passing on to these results, however, a short summary of the principal economic changes that affected Britain's Oversea Investments, and more particularly the income derived from them, may be helpful.

Despite the signs of economic recovery already visible in the summer of 1932, earnings and wholesale prices reached their lowest levels in that year and in the first quarter of 1933. At the close of 1932 South Africa abandoned the Gold Standard and attached its currency to sterling. This enabled gold-mining companies to reap larger profits in terms of South African currency which were partly counter-balanced by the Excess Profits Duties imposed by the South African Government. Moreover, owing to the depreciation in South African currency brought about by its link with sterling, dividends in terms of sterling were not as yet substantially higher. The early months of 1933 witnessed the development of the banking crisis in the United States accompanied by a renewed sharp fall in wholesale prices which spread to all the principal countries and was responsible for a further contraction in foreign earnings. At the same time investment trusts and other institutions interested in dollar securities disposed of part of their holdings. Abandonment of the Gold Standard by the United States in April 1933 and the ensuing depreciation of the dollar entailed a reduction in the sterling income derived from investments in dollar bonds. For a time the depreciation of the

---

in terms of original costs would suffer a serious disadvantage in that, aside from the labour involved in the employment of this method, changes in the price level would invalidate comparison from year to year.

Inasmuch as the main emphasis in this study is on the income derived from British Oversea Investments, the employment of nominal values has the advantage that in the vast majority of cases the rate of interest and dividend is expressed in terms of the £1 share or £100 bond as the "unit of account," so that calculation of income is thereby greatly facilitated. At the same time the totals arrived at do to some extent reflect the original cost of these investments, since in most cases the issue price of debentures or shares does not greatly differ from the face value.

dollar proceeded simultaneously with a boom in American stock and commodity markets, with the result that commodity prices rose faster than the dollar depreciated. Not only was there a sharp upturn in prices in the sterling area, but even gold prices were favourably affected, the wholesale price index in France rising from 383 in May to 401 in July. The resulting improvement in earnings, however, did not persist and with the collapse of the boom in America a severe deflationary influence, arising from the gold policy of the United States in the autumn, made itself felt, particularly outside the sterling area. Meanwhile, interest on bonds was adversely affected by the German moratorium in June 1933, while increasing exchange restrictions throughout the world not only hampered remittances to this country but, together with the multiplication of tariffs and quotas, contributed actively to a further reduction in world trade. In the sterling countries, owing to the partial adjustment affected in the relation between costs and prices, trade and industry displayed a strong resistance to the deflationary factors referred to above, and on balance British investments in the Dominions yielded as large an income in 1933 as in 1932. Successful conversions and fiscal improvement raised the market value of the bonds of Dominion Governments, while interest remitted to London underwent no reduction on account of these conversions until the following year. Moreover, in addition to the handsome profits that were being made by gold mines in South Africa, the successful operation of restriction schemes in tea and tin were beginning to be reflected in an improvement in earnings of companies engaged in their production.

Group I.

Dominion, Colonial and Foreign (Government and Municipal) Loans.

Reference has been made in previous articles to the detailed method by which the proportion held abroad of the outstanding sterling loans of Empire and Foreign Governments and Municipalities has been computed.[1] It is worth repeating that these foreign holdings are roughly indicated by the amount of interest paid in London free of income tax.

Sterling *tranches* placed abroad are also included in the total of loans to which the above percentages apply, so that the proportion held abroad as appearing from the above table is somewhat higher than the corresponding percentage which would apply if loans issued in London were exclusively considered. Nevertheless,

[1] See Economic Journal, June 1930.

TABLE I.[1]

United Kingdom and Foreign Holdings of Dominion, Colonial and Foreign (Government and Municipal) Loans.

	United Kingdom.	Foreign.
Dominion and Provincial Governments . .	90·4%	9·6%
Dominion and Colonial Municipalities . . .	88·6	11·4
Foreign Governments	56·3	43·7
Foreign Municipalities	74·6	25·4

it remains true that the amount of these loans held abroad has for some years been very substantial and is continuing to increase owing to the stimulus given to repatriation by the low quotations for a large number of these foreign bonds.[2]

TABLE II.

British Capital (nominal) invested in Dominion, Colonial and Foreign Government and Municipal Loans; Income derived and Sums repaid.

(£000.)

	1933.			1932.		
	Capital.	Income.	Repayment.	Capital.	Income.	Repayment.
Dominion and Colonial Governments . .	1,061,262	45,137	37,122	1,025,408	44,997	23,740
Dominion and Colonial Municipalities . .	85,828	4,001	1,490	83,531	3,922	3,061
Foreign Governments .	298,840	10,762	10,209	289,375	11,984	12,032
Foreign Municipalities .	33,666	1,226	571	33,585	1,474	853
Total . .	1,479,596	61,126	49,392	1,431,899	62,377	39,686

Despite repayments amounting to nearly £50 million, there was an increase of £48 million in the nominal amount of British capital invested in the above loans, of which £38 million represented an increase in Empire Loans and the balance in those of foreign

[1] The figures in this table are, in fact, the proportions of interest paid in London under tax deduction and free of tax, respectively, in 1933. A number of loans are payable at the option of the holder in centres abroad as well as in London, and while this affects only slightly the total amount of interest paid in London to British holders, fortuitous variations do occur in the total amount and consequently the percentage of interest paid in London to foreign holders. Exchange rates and currency uncertainties naturally play a part in affecting these percentages.

[2] The fact that over 10 per cent. of the loans of Dominion and Colonial Governments and Municipalities is held abroad may also seem surprising. This, however, is largely explained by the substantial investment in these loans by Dominion Government and local authorities of the sinking funds held against internal and other loans.

countries. The increase in foreign loans may seem surprising in view of the substantial repayment and having regard to the virtual ban on new foreign issues. The explanation lies in the fact that the new foreign loans consisted mainly of issues for the funding of unpaid interest and frozen balances of which the outstanding example was the Argentine Government 4 per cent. loan for £13½ million, issued in exchange for balances awaiting remittance to the United Kingdom in accordance with the terms of the Anglo-Argentine Trade Convention of May 1933. New cash actually subscribed to foreign loans amounted only to £5 million, as compared with repayments of nearly £11 million. The Dominion Governments in 1933 took advantage of their improved financial status to follow Britain's example of the previous year by undertaking conversion and refunding operations not only of their internal debt but also in the London market. Consequently, the new issue market for Dominion loans was very active during the year. New issues in this market totalled £116 million, of which £79 million was subscribed for cash, the balance representing conversion. The increase by £38 million in 1933 in the amount of British capital invested in Dominion loans is therefore accounted for by the difference between the new issues for cash and the loans repaid.[1] The persistent decline in the proportion of foreign to Empire loans held by British investors is illustrated by the following table.

TABLE III.

British Investment in Empire and Foreign Loans (Government and Municipal).

(£000,000.)

End of	Empire Loans.	Foreign Loans.	Total.	Ratio of Foreign to Empire Loans.
1928 . .	1,036	364	1,490	26·0%
1929 . .	1,061	351	1,412	27·9
1930 . .	1,080	357	1,437	24·9
1931 . .	1,104	337	1,441	23·4
1932 . .	1,109	323	1,432	22·6
1933 . .	1,147	333	1,480	22·5

The virtual cessation of foreign long-term lending, except for isolated cases of loans made with the consent of the Treasury, to certain countries in the sterling area, is reflected in the

[1] Repayments in Table II include not only the sums remitted to London in respect of sinking fund drawings and purchases, but also the sums raised in London to repay existing loans. In fact the larger part of the £79 million of cash subscriptions to new issues was employed for such repayments.

above figures. Statistics compiled by the Midland Bank show that while cash subscribed in London on behalf of Governments, Municipalities and private undertakings declined in the case of the Dominions from £424 million in the six year period 1922–7 to £306 million for 1928–33, the amount for foreign countries declined from £311 million to £154 million for the comparative periods. It is perhaps no coincidence that the pronounced preference shown for Empire investments has been accompanied in recent years by a similar striking re-orientation in Britain's oversea trade, the share of trade with the sterling area having increased noticeably at the expense of trade with other foreign countries. It is not, of course, suggested that the decline in Britain's long-term investments in foreign countries has actively influenced oversea trade in this direction. The Ottawa Agreements, the subsequent Trade Agreements with other countries in the sterling area and the high industrial costs prevailing in Gold Bloc countries were obviously the more relevant factors in this connection, while at the same time the Treasury ban on foreign issues would in any case have prevented any substantial flotation of new foreign loans on the London market.[1] From the point of view of the investor the significance of increased trade with the group of sterling countries, reinforced by the stimulus given to gold production, lies in the fact that remittances between its constituents are facilitated, and the scope for investment in these countries increased. The next few years may, therefore, witness a marked accentuation of the preference shown by U.K. investors towards investment in the Empire. This conclusion is arrived at independently of a consideration of the Trustee Acts, which for many years have been largely responsible for the growth—not always prudent—of Dominion borrowing in London.

Turning now to a consideration of income derived from investments in Dominion, Colonial and Foreign Government and Municipal bonds, the following figures show the trend since 1928.

The remarkable stability of this income in spite of widespread default on foreign bonds is, of course, due to the preponderance of investments in Empire loans. Thus the decline of £6 million in income from foreign loans between 1928 and 1933 due to default and to a reduction in the total outstanding was counterbalanced by an increase during this period of over £5 million in the income from Colonial loans as a result of new Dominion loans issued in

[1] Even in the absence of the Treasury ban it is very doubtful if new foreign loans could have been successfully raised on any important scale during recent years.

London. During 1933, as a result of the German moratorium, other suspension of payments, notably by South American States and Municipalities, and intensification of restrictions in exchange, income from foreign bonds declined by nearly £1½ million from the previous year.

TABLE IV.

Income obtained from U.K. Investments in Empire and Foreign Loans (Government and Municipal).

(£000.)

	Empire Loans.	Foreign Loans.	Total.
1928	43,820	18,076	61,896
1929	46,416	18,245	64,661
1930	46,878	17,798	64,676
1931	48,405	17,515	65,920
1932	48,919	13,458	62,377
1933	49,138	11,988	61,126

A preliminary examination of remittances in 1934 indicates that on balance income from foreign bonds was maintained. Cash payments in respect of German bonds were lower and isolated instances of new defaults were recorded, but these losses were counterbalanced by the partial resumption of interest payments, the case of Brazil being worthy of mention. The total amount of interest lost to British investors in respect of foreign Government and Municipal bonds since the end of 1930, when default became noticeable, until the end of 1934 is estimated at £16 million. Referring to Table II it may be observed that the average rate of interest obtained on Colonial Government and Municipal loans was still over 4¼ per cent. in 1933. Conversions both in that year and in 1934 have slightly reduced the average rate paid on these loans in 1934, but on the other hand interest on new loans has balanced this loss. Given a continuance of cheap money in the United Kingdom and of economic and financial recovery in the Dominions, a gradual reduction in the rate of interest through conversion and refunding operations may be anticipated.

The income obtained from investment in Dominion, Colonial and foreign Government and Municipal bonds is provisionally estimated at £61·0 million for 1934.

GROUP II.

British Companies operating Abroad.

The historical origin of the British company operating abroad is closely associated with some of the earliest pioneer work in the development of overseas territories by British enterprise. Perhaps the most outstanding example of the fruits of this pioneer work is to be found in the network of important British railways in South America, and more especially the Argentine, in which a considerable amount of British capital is invested. Despite the long history of these companies the foreign participation in the share and loan capital has been and remains very small, in fact seldom exceeding 2 per cent., except in the case of certain public utilities in South America, notably Tramways and Telephones, in which controlling interests have been acquired by United States companies. The chief reason for this small foreign participation is, of course, the high rate of British income tax, which is a strong deterrent to would-be foreign purchasers of these stocks and bonds. Consequently, except for the automatic reduction in loan capital due to sinking fund and maturity repayments, and some alteration in nominal values due to capital reorganisation, the nominal amount of British capital invested in these companies has remained exceedingly stable from year to year. Indeed, of recent years this characteristic has been even more marked owing to the absence of new issues on any important scale and the partial interruption of sinking fund repayments due to exchange restrictions over a wide area. The next table records the amount invested in various enterprises and the income obtained from these investments.[1]

The only notable change in 1933 in the share capital held by British investors occurred in the case of Mines, the nominal amount of capital having risen by £8 million, partly as a result of new issues for cash and partly owing to an issue of shares in exchange for the sterling debentures of a foreign railway company.[2]

Income figures in Table V represent the dividends and interest actually paid to U.K. investors before deduction of income tax. The total of this income in any year may differ considerably from the gross receipts accruing to the United Kingdom in respect of the operations of British companies

[1] This table includes the capital of all British registered companies whose plant and equipment are entirely or mainly situated abroad. A number of companies, however, particularly among those classified as "Commercial and Industrial," do extensive business both at home and abroad and possess important fixed assets in the United Kingdom and overseas. The larger companies of this nature have been covered by these investigations, but no attempt has been made to estimate in detail the foreign assets of minor companies. For details of the method used in arriving at the above figures the reader is referred to previous articles (see ECONOMIC JOURNAL, September 1931).

[2] Apart from repayments almost all other changes are ascribable to capital reconstruction or issues in exchange for unpaid interest, the amount of new capital raised in cash during the year having been negligible.

abroad during the year. The latter include remittances for head office expenditure and remuneration of directors resident in London, as well as sums invested in the U.K. as an addition to

TABLE V.

U.K. Capital invested in British Companies operating Abroad; Interest and Dividends received and Loan Capital Repaid.

(£000.)

	Share Capital.		Loan Capital.		
	Amount.	Dividends.	Amount.	Interest.	Repayment.[1]
			1932.		
Dominion and Colonial Rails	1,600	—	27,300	1,415	40
Indian Rails	20,900	1,872	43,200	1,581	—
India Railway Annuities	—	—	24,300	1,138	1,290
American Rails	800	44	800	32	—
Foreign Rails	221,200	2,220	173,100	4,769	225
Banks	26,300	2,122	—	—	—
Breweries	4,700	377	600	38	270
Canals and Docks	1,400	—	2,300	145	—
Commercial and Industrial	65,600	2,154	19,800	545	761
Electric Light and Power	7,900	572	6,600	295	265
Financial Land and Investment	86,000	1,534	26,900	1,056	433
Gas	11,700	1,263	1,300	89	341
Iron, Coal and Steel	7,600	136	2,100	62	—
Mines	72,500	2,292	7,300	534	59
Nitrates	3,400	—	1,700	—	—
Oil	108,600	10,170	12,400	618	501
Rubber	81,300	200	5,600	140	54
Shipping	12,100	457	6,000	213	339
Tea and Coffee	38,600	1,226	2,600	107	26
Telegraphs	23,900	1,744	4,300	181	7
Tramways	15,500	337	18,500	425	148
Waterworks	4,600	309	1,900	101	17
Total	816,200	29,029	388,600	13,484	4,776
			1933.		
Dominion and Colonial Rails	1,600	—	27,100	822	919
Indian Rails	20,900	1,800	44,400	1,625	—
Indian Railway Annuities	—	—	23,100	1,225	1,203
American Rails	800	42	800	32	—
Foreign Rails	221,200	1,619	175,200	4,406	65
Banks	26,300	2,080	—	—	—
Breweries	4,700	396	800	34	—
Canals and Docks	1,400	—	2,300	128	—
Commercial and Industrial	65,400	2,220	20,600	788	3,250
Electric Light and Power	8,200	597	7,000	283	70
Financial, Land and Investment	86,200	1,268	26,600	930	327
Gas	11,800	1,275	2,000	93	46
Iron, Coal and Steel	6,700	115	2,200	66	—
Mines	80,300	2,905	6,300	305	620
Nitrates	3,400	—	1,700	—	—
Oil	108,600	11,125	12,100	638	279
Rubber	81,500	269	5,600	174	—
Shipping	11,800	540	5,600	197	697
Tea and Coffee	38,600	1,429	2,400	101	4
Telegraphs and Telephones	24,000	1,192	4,300	175	2
Tramways	15,500	349	15,300	344	310
Waterworks	4,600	229	1,900	82	3
Total	823,500	29,450	387,300	12,448	7,795

[1] Repayments in all cases are actual sums repaid as distinct from the nominal amounts. They also include, in a few instances, the sums returned to shareholders in connection with the reduction of ordinary share capital or redemption of preference shares.

reserves. In good times the former may amount to as much as £10–15 million, while the sums placed to reserve out of profits may be considerable. Conversely, in bad times substantial sums may be drawn from reserves in the United Kingdom to meet head office expenses and for payment of dividends.[1]

In spite of the intensification of world depression as a whole in 1932, the year prior to the abandonment of the Gold Standard in the United States, total dividend payments were slightly higher in 1933, although interest on loans was reduced by another £1 million as a result of increased exchange restrictions and further defaults. Oil companies recorded better results, while the earnings of Mining and Tea companies began to reflect the favourable influence of the restriction schemes in Tin and Tea.[2] On the other hand, exchange difficulties were chiefly responsible for a decline in dividends remitted in the case of railway and telegraph companies in South America. The following figures show the dividends distributed to U.K. investors since 1929 by British companies operating overseas.

Dividend Payments of British Companies operating Abroad.

	Dividends Distributed.	Percentage of Capital.
1929	£67,674,000	8·4%
1930	58,966,000	7·1
1931	33,296,000	4·1
1932	29,029,000	3·6
1933	29,450,000	3·6
1934 (provisional estimate) .	33,200,000	4·0

Dividends in 1934 are provisionally estimated to have increased by £3¾ million as a result of the noticeable recovery in the summer months of 1933 and the spring of 1934. Changes in earnings tend to follow closely changes in the world price level and for a time the depreciation of the dollar, as already stated, was successful not only in raising prices in the United States but also in the sterling area and in Gold Standard countries.[3] A more important contribution to the improvement in 1934 in the earnings of British companies abroad was made by the international restriction schemes in Tin, Tea and Rubber. Whereas during the downward course of a trade cycle restriction schemes become ineffective since they tend to accelerate the shrinkage in demand, a considerable measure of

[1] For the purposes of the calculation of the U.K. balance of payments the above estimates of income cannot, therefore, be applied unless appropriately adjusted.

[2] The improvement in the earnings of gold mines is dealt with in the next section, the South African gold-mining companies being nearly all registered in the Union of South Africa.

[3] In the autumn of 1933, however, the whole of this improvement was lost and the decline in the dollar exerted a marked deflationary effect on world prices.

success may be achieved during the period of recovery. The remarkable extent to which prices of commodities subject to restriction schemes have, in fact, responded to the curtailment in production since 1932 is shown herewith :

Average Yearly Prices.

	1934.	1933.	1932.
Tin (per ton) . .	£230 7*s.* 5*d.*	£194 11*s.* 1*d.*	£135 18*s.* 10*d.*
Tea (per lb.) . .	13·27*d.*	11·78*d.*	9·45*d.*
Rubber (per lb.) .	6·24*d.*	3·25*d.*	2·34*d.*

The importance of the rise in the prices of these commodities may be gauged from the fact that about £100 million of British capital is invested in companies producing Tin and Rubber in Malaya alone and over £40 million in Tea companies in India and Ceylon.

Group III.

Companies Registered Overseas.

The bulk of investment in the bonds and shares of Foreign and Colonial companies (*i.e.* companies registered abroad) is of more recent date than the capital examined in the previous section. In fact, it may be said that the growth of the form of investment now being considered indicated the diminished scope for the direct development of overseas territories by British skill and enterprise, and the desire of Dominion and foreign countries, after a certain stage, to proceed with further developments under their own management. The incidence of British income tax, particularly in post-war years, has been an important factor in this connection. Nevertheless, a large number of companies registered in the Dominions is substantially owned and virtually controlled by British interests.[1] Unlike those dealt with in the previous section, many of the securities classified in Table VI below are quoted in a number of foreign centres, more particularly New York, Paris and Amsterdam. It follows that in a year of active Stock Exchange dealings a considerable change may take place in the total nominal amount held in the United Kingdom. Owing to the fairly high proportion of bearer securities in the case of foreign companies, the nominal amounts

[1] The South African gold mines are the principal example of such companies, although large blocks of the shares are held in South Africa and on the Continent.

of capital shown in the next table include items which can only be approximately assessed.[1]

TABLE VI.

Nominal British Capital invested in Foreign and Colonial Companies; Interest and Dividends received and Loan Capital repaid.

(£000)

	Share Capital.		Loan Capital.		
	Nominal Amount.	Dividends.	Nominal Amount.	Interest.	Repayment.
			1932.		
Dominion and Colonial Rails	62,500	1,616	159,600	7,088	227
American Rails	18,200	308	9,700	571	—
Banks	25,600	1,472	18,000	862	258
Breweries	1,300	24	100	5	—
Canals and Docks	1,600	1,946	2,800	1	—
Commercial and Industrial	63,700	5,613	24,400	1,321	602
Electric Light and Power	15,200	1,023	30,700	1,536	1,095
Financial Land and Investment	26,800	626	25,000	1,013	393
Iron, Coal and Steel	6,800	198	10,000	506	62
Mines	56,800	6,975	6,600	462	76
Nitrates	3,000	—	5,300	226	78
Oil	20,300	140	—	—	208 [1]
Shipping	6,600	342	800	47	52
Telegraphs and Telephones	6,000	494	10,000	558	31
Tramways	10,600	113	11,200	549	12
Foreign Rails			60,600	2,340	425
Gas	19,000 [2]	1,225 [2]	400	22	—
Waterworks			—	6	52
Total	344,000	22,115	375,200	17,113	3,571
			1933.		
Dominion and Colonial Rails	63,500	123	158,200	6,531	500
American Rails	17,300	113	9,200	448	—
Banks	26,000	1,399	15,100	570	1,459
Breweries	1,300	12	100	5	3
Canals and Docks	1,600	2,064	2,800	—	—
Commercial and Industrial	70,000	5,151	21,400	1,094	870
Electric Lighting and Power	16,500	1,018	28,400	1,368	2,054
Financial Land and Investment	21,900	617	23,000	1,002	299 [1]
Iron, Coal and Steel	6,800	245	8,900	331	108
Mines	57,900	7,331	8,300	582	178 [1]
Nitrates	3,000	—	5,200	10	71
Oil	19,300	720	—	—	278 [1]
Shipping	6,600	368	700	33	42
Telegraphs and Telephones	5,700	346	9,400	510	73
Tramways	10,600	2	10,800	420	12
Foreign Rails			47,900 [3]	1,815	3,698
Gas	17,000 [2]	1,000 [2]	400	22	—
Waterworks			—	—	—
Total	345,000	20,509	349,800	14,741	9,645

[1] Repayments in certain sections, viz. Financial Land and Investments, Mines and Oil, include repayments of capital to shareholders.

[2] Owing to the great preponderance of bearer securities in the categories Foreign Rails, Gas and Waterworks, the estimates for share capital and dividends in these three sections are only approximations.

[3] The reduction in British loan capital outstanding in Foreign Rails from £60·6 million in 1932 to £47·9 million in 1933 is explained only partly by the substantial repayments. The chief reason was the exchange of sterling debentures of a foreign railway for shares of a mining company (see p. 446).

[1] The task of measuring the change in the nominal amount of share capital held in the United Kingdom from year to year is also rendered more difficult by the inclusion of shares of no par value which figure in the above table at the values assigned to them in latest available balance sheets.

The reduction in the total amount of bonds held in the United Kingdom is explained partly by conversion of debentures into shares, partly by the repurchase by foreign nationals of the sterling bonds of companies domiciled in their respective countries, and finally by exceptionally heavy repayments amounting to £9·6 million in 1933. These repayments included the sterling bonds of the Agricultural Bank of Egypt, Industrial Bank of Japan, and the Paris, Lyons and Mediterranean Railway.

Turning to a consideration of the income received from these investments, it will be observed that total dividends in 1933 showed a decline of £1·6 million, for which the complete suspension of dividend payments by the Canadian Pacific Railway was mainly responsible. Owing to their poor operating results in 1933, shares in American companies yielded a small return, and this is reflected in the diminished dividend figures for American Rails and Telegraphs and Telephones. In spite of considerably higher gross profits the increase in dividend payments by South African gold-mining companies was only of moderate dimension, owing to the imposition of Excess Profit Duties by the South African Government.

A decline of no less than £2·4 million occurred in the total amount of loan interest received in the United Kingdom. To some extent this was due to additional defaults and to the reduction in the total amount of loan capital outstanding. The chief reason for the decline, however, was the abandonment of the gold parity of the dollar, as a result of which British holders of American and Canadian bonds lost the greater part of the benefit conferred upon them in 1932 by the depreciation of sterling. The average value of the pound in terms of American and Canadian dollars was $4·22 and $4·57 respectively in 1933, as compared with $3·50 and $3·98 respectively in 1932.

Dividend payments received since 1929 in respect of British holdings in Foreign and Colonial companies are given below, together with a provisional estimate for 1934 :—

Dividends on British Holdings in Foreign and Colonial Companies.

	Amount of Dividends.	Percentage of Capital.
1929	£42·0 million	9·6%
1930	31·7	8·1
1931	22·7	6·0
1932	22·1	6·4
1933	20·5	5·9
1934 (provisional estimate) .	23·5	6·8

The increase of £3·0 million estimated for 1934 reflects the improvement in earnings in the sterling area during the year as well as the further depreciation in sterling which was responsible for another advance in the average price of gold, from £124 9*s.* per oz. in 1933 to £137 8*s.* in 1934. Dividends received in the United Kingdom on account of gold-mining shares are estimated to have increased by a further £1·5 million in 1934.

SUMMARY.

The complete results for 1933 for the three classes of securities examined in the previous pages are summarised in the following table and compared with the corresponding results for two previous years :—

TABLE VII.

Nominal Amount of British Oversea Investment in Quoted Securities; Interest and Dividends received and Loan Capital repaid.

(£000.)

	Capital.	Income.	Repayment.
		1931.	
Foreign, Dominion and Colonial Governments and Municipalities	1,441,000	65,920	16,267
British Companies abroad	1,210,000	48,747	4,900
Foreign and Colonial Companies	759,000	40,846	5,585
Total	3,410,000	155,513	26,752
		1932.	
Foreign, Dominion and Colonial Governments and Municipalities	1,432,000	62,377	39,686
British Companies abroad	1,204,000	42,513	4,776
Foreign and Colonial Companies	719,000	39,228	3,571
Total	3,355,000	144,118	48,033
		1933.	
Foreign, Dominion and Colonial Governments and Municipalities	1,480,000	61,126	49,392
British Companies abroad	1,211,000	41,898	7,795
Foreign and Colonial Companies	695,000	35,250	9,645
Total	3,386,000	138,274	66,832

The nominal amount of British capital invested abroad in *marketable* securities at the end of 1933 is estimated at £3,386 million. This total does not, of course, include the considerable amount of investment in property, mortgages, etc., and in securities not regularly dealt in on the London market. Dollar bonds and shares are an important part of this item and these are held predominantly by Insurance Companies and Investment Trusts.

Returns received from a number of American companies indicate that British participation in their share and loan capital was somewhat less at the end of 1933 than in the previous year; this is also confirmed by an examination of the change in the volume of dollar securities held by Investment Trusts in these years. The sharp decline in business activity in the United States leading up to the grave banking crisis of the spring of 1933 caused some selling of investments and, although boom conditions again prevailed on Wall Street during the summer months, uncertainty about the future of the dollar was too great to permit of any appreciable reinvestment.[1] The nominal amount of British capital investment other than in quoted securities is, therefore, approximately estimated at £280 million at December 1933 as compared with £285 million at December 1932. No great accuracy is claimed for this figure, since it is intended to cover not only security investments, but also a large number of miscellaneous assets of companies and individuals to which in any case a nominal value can only be arbitrarily assigned.

However, if this approximation is added to the statistically more reliable figure arrived at above, British capital employed in all forms of oversea investment is calculated at £3,666 million at the end of 1933, as compared with £3,640 million at the end of 1932. Although the absolute change in the nominal amount is of little significance, the reversal in 1933 of the downward trend which had been in evidence since 1930 is important.

A comparison of the sums raised on the London market for oversea issues with the amounts repaid through the operation of sinking funds and maturities may be of interest.

	British Subscription to New Overseas Issues.	Repayment to the United Kingdom.
1929	£96 million	£49 million
1930	98	39
1931	41	27
1932	37	48
1933	83	67

Repayments in 1933 amounted to an exceptionally heavy item of £67 million. The above figures, however, exclude con-

[1] It may be recalled that in 1933 almost the whole of the U.K. 5½ per cent. dollar loans due 1937, of which $136 million was outstanding, was converted into U.K. sterling bonds. The proportion of this dollar loan held by British nationals had already been high prior to conversion, but further amounts were purchased in New York before the final date for conversion.

versions, but not new issues, the proceeds of which have been used wholly or in part to effect redemption of existing loans. Such refunding operations, which were of frequent occurrence in 1933, account for the apparently large volume of repayments during that year.

Income from British Oversea Investments.

The following table illustrates the trend of the annual income obtained from Britain's oversea investments since 1929. The figures show the income accruing to investors (before deduction of British income tax), and for reasons already stated (see p. 446) should not be applied in a calculation of the balance of payments of the United Kingdom unless suitably adjusted.[1]

TABLE VIII.

Britain's Oversea Investment Income 1929–34.[2]

	1934.[2]	1933.	1932.	1931.	1930.	1929.
Dominion, Colonial and Foreign Government and Municipalities . .	61·0	61·1	62·4	65·9	64·7	64·7
British Companies (registered in the U.K.) . .	45·7	41·9	42·5	48·8	76·5	86·0
Foreign and Colonial Companies (registered abroad)	39·5	35·3 [3]	39·2	40·8	51·0	61·7
Other Investments (not covered by above) [4] .	12·1	11·4	12·3	13·2	16·8	18·5
Total . . .	158·3	149·7	156·4	168·7	209·0	230·9

The rise of £8·6 million in 1934 from the low figure of £149·7 million in the previous year does not fully reflect the improvement that occurred in the remittances to the United Kingdom in respect of capital employed abroad. During the years of depression large sums were frequently drawn from reserves to meet dividend payments and other commitments, while the usual allocations to provide for depreciation and obsolescence were well below normal. The welcome improvement in earnings in 1934 provided British companies with an opportunity to improve their

[1] Account would have to be taken not only of head office expenses and sums placed to or withdrawn from reserves, but also of the income derived by oversea nationals from their investments in the U.K.

[2] The figures for 1934 are provisional.

[3] The figure finally obtained for the income from British investments in Foreign and Colonial companies in 1933 is appreciably less than the forecast given in a previous article. The loss in sterling income due to the depreciation of the dollar and to increased default was greater than anticipated.

[4] The average rate of income derived from these investments is assumed to be the same as that obtained from negotiable securities.

financial structure, with the result that the proportion of profits placed to reserve during the year rose sharply. Thus from a large sample of reports of British companies (operating at home and abroad) the *Economist* estimated the sums placed to reserve at 19·7 per cent. of profits in 1934, as compared with 11 5 per cent. in 1933 (see *Economist*, Jan. 19, 1935, p. 112).

The factors responsible for the rise in investment income in 1934 have already been discussed in previous pages. The outlook for further improvement is undoubtedly brighter than for some time past. Income from foreign Government and Municipal bonds is unlikely to suffer further serious loss through default, while, on the other hand, there is hope for an improvement in this income as a result of negotiations for at least partial resumption of service. The proposal of the Chilean Government to allocate the proceeds of an export tax on nitrate and copper for debt service is a case in point. The increasing trade within the sterling area, the prospect of a continued high price for gold and the operation of the restriction schemes in Tea, Tin and Rubber may afford a higher level of earnings for a large number of British companies operating abroad, while the latest restriction agreement for Copper may substantially raise the earnings of copper-producing companies in the Empire. On the other hand, beyond a certain point, any further improvement would seem to depend upon an increase of trade throughout the world and a general advance in world prices. The problem of securing these is closely associated with that of stabilisation of the major currencies at appropriate levels and of a general reduction in tariffs and other trade restrictions prior to or following stabilisation. However, even if these desirable objectives could be attained, it is questionable if Britain's income from her Oversea Investment can for many years reach the high level of £300 million per annum such as prevailed in 1926 and 1927. Final settlements will result in a considerable reduction in the rate of interest payable on defaulting foreign bonds, while conversion and refunding operations will effect a gradual but substantial decline in the rate payable on Dominion loans. Restriction schemes may succeed in forcing up prices of important commodities to higher levels, but the stimulus given to production outside restricting areas and modern intensive research into the possibilities of substitute products indicate that the fantastic prices attained by certain articles in the years prior to the depression are no longer possible.

ROBERT KINDERSLEY

BRITISH OVERSEAS INVESTMENTS IN 1934 AND 1935

Robert M. Kindersley

BRITISH OVERSEAS INVESTMENTS IN 1934 AND 1935

The present article contains the detailed results of a survey of British Overseas Investments for the year 1934. At the same time provisional figures are also given for the year 1935.

I am happy to repeat my annual tribute to the valuable assistance afforded to me by the London Banks and Issuing Houses, and by the industrial and commercial companies in this country and abroad.

The year 1934 was notable for monetary and other changes which had appreciable effect both on the income obtained from oversea investments and on the character of capital movements as reflected by purchases and sales of international securities. Early in the year the return of America to the gold standard, with the dollar at 59·06 per cent. of its former gold parity, signalled the end of a policy which had for its object the raising of the price-level, and thereby reduction of the burden of debt. In consequence, the London price of gold had risen by February to 140*s.* per oz., compared with an average price of 137*s.* 6*d.* per oz. during 1933.

Wholesale Prices.

	1933.	1934.	1935.
United States	69·3	78·7	83·9
United Kingdom	75·0	77·1	77·8
India	61·7	63·1	64·5
France	63·6	60·0	54·0
Holland	63·1	63·2	61·7
Switzerland	64·5	63·6	63·6

Wholesale prices, the trend of which has a vital influence on the income from Britain's oversea investments, were affected in different ways in different countries. In the United States prices rose visibly, but not to the same extent as the dollar depreciated; in the United Kingdom, the Dominions and other countries on the "sterling standard," prices rose only slightly.

Trade between countries which had linked their currencies to sterling continued to improve, while domestic recovery, which had received a slight setback in the second half of 1933, resumed the upward trend which had already been apparent earlier in that year. The upward movement in Wall Street caused considerable foreign buying of American securities, and British holdings of such securities, which had declined appreciably in the preceding years, showed a marked rise in 1934. On the other hand, the deflationary measures taken by countries attempting to defend the gold standard—wage cuts, economy decrees, import restrictions and the like—were clearly exerting a considerable effect in impeding the progress of world recovery. Large arrears on account of exports began to accumulate, and attempts to increase payments in respect of loans in partial default were on balance counteracted by reduced payments on other loans.

Nevertheless, apart from the substantial increase in gold-mining profits and the benefit directly accruing therefrom to British investors, the rise in the price of gold resulting from the depreciation of the pound and the dollar has been a potent factor in aiding world recovery, the influence of which may in the long run prove to have been considerably under-estimated. For not only has the stimulus to gold production of the high price of gold directly aided internal recovery in countries like South Africa, Australia and Canada, but it has also helped other gold-producing countries in South America in financing their import requirements. Moreover, the rise in the price of gold has laid the basis for an expansion in credit which will permit a considerably larger measure of world recovery, and will be adequate to finance an indefinite increase in world trade.

We turn now to the main subject matter of our investigation.

Dominion, Colonial and Foreign Public Loans.

It is not often appreciated that the amount of foreign and Empire sterling loans held outside the United Kingdom is of considerable dimensions.

United Kingdom and Foreign Holdings[1] *of Dominion, Colonial and Foreign Public Sterling Loans* (*as at December* 31*st*, 1934).

	United Kingdom.	Foreign.
	(Per cent.)	(Per cent.)
Dominion and Provincial Governments	90·7	9·3
Dominion and Colonial Municipalities	87·2	12·8
Foreign Government	58·0	42·0
Foreign Municipalities	71·1	28·9

[1] The percentages in this table relate in fact to the interest paid in London, tax deducted and free of tax respectively. They may, however, be taken as an approximation to the respective proportions of these loans held in the United Kingdom and abroad.

It is known, of course, that the low prices of foreign bonds in recent years have enabled foreigners to buy back their bonds advantageously, and foreign Governments themselves have not been averse to repurchasing such bonds, in some cases even where interest payments have been in partial or complete default. This, however, is not the only reason for the high percentage of sterling loans held abroad. In pre-War years the practice of issuing large blocks of sterling foreign loans abroad, notably in Paris, Amsterdam and Berlin, was not unusual, Brazilian and Chinese bonds being good examples of issues of which the proportion held abroad is conspicuously high in consequence.[1] The oversea holding of 9·3 per cent. of Empire Government loans and 12·8 per cent. of Municipal loans is explained by the fact that these loans are a favourite medium for investment of sinking funds held against internal loans by public and local authorities in the Dominions. In view of the noticeable tendency for Dominion Governments to replace sterling by internal loans as a result of the increasing foreign exchange reserves acquired by their Central Banks, a gradual rise of the percentage of Dominion loans held overseas may be anticipated in the future.

The figures in the table below and in subsequent tables, in so far as they refer to British capital invested overseas, relate to United Kingdom holdings only.

British Capital Invested in Oversea Government and Municipal Loans : Income Derived and Sums Repaid. (000's)

	1934.			1933.		
	Nominal Capital.	Income.	Repayment.	Nominal Capital.	Income.	Repayment.
Dominion and Colonial Governments . . .	£1,078,900	£45,074	£13,222	£1,061,300	£45,137	£37,122
Dominion and Colonial Municipalities . . .	84,200	4,016	1,835	85,800	4,001	1,490
Foreign Governments . .	303,600	11,036	7,468	298,800	10,762	10,209
Foreign Municipalities . .	32,500	1,003	645	33,700	1,226	571
Total . . .	£1,499,200	£61,129	£23,170	£1,479,600	£61,126	£49,392

Total income obtained from investments in Public loans in 1934 at £61 1 million was practically unchanged from that of the previous year despite the increase in the total nominal amount held in the United Kingdom. This was due to a com-

[1] Incidentally, since the interest on such bonds is generally payable both in London and other centres abroad at the option of the holder, the proportion of interest paid in London tends to rise on currency scares abroad.

bination of causes, the chief of which was the conversion of Dominion, and particularly Australian loans, to a lower rate of interest. Foreign Government bonds produced a slightly larger income owing to increased payments and the partial resumption of interest payments on defaulting bonds, notably Brazil and Greece, but this increase would have been greater had not payments in certain other directions been reduced, as in the case of Hungary, while the reduction of cash interest on German bonds was responsible for an appreciable decline in the income obtained from foreign Municipal loans. Over the whole group of public loans the rate of interest actually received was slightly lower, at 4·08 per cent. in 1934, as against 4·13 per cent. in 1933. The stability of the income obtained from investments in foreign Public loans is noteworthy.

1929	£64·7 million
1930	64·7 ,,
1931	65·9 ,,
1932	62·4 ,,
1933	61·1 ,,
1934	61·1 ,,

Despite depression and widespread default on foreign bonds, income from this source did not decline by more than 7·3 per cent. in any subsequent year from the high level it reached in 1931. As an interesting comparison it is worth noting that income obtained from variable dividend securities was at its lowest level in 1933, and was only 45·5 per cent. of the corresponding figure in 1929. The stability of the income derived from investment in oversea Public loans arises, of course, from the fact that the preponderant part of these investments consists of loans to Dominion Governments and Municipalities.

British Investment in Empire and Foreign Loans

CAPITAL.

	Empire Loans.	Foreign Loans.	Total.	Ratio of Foreign Loans to Total.
	(£000.)	(£000.)	(£000.)	(Per cent.)
1928. .	1,036,000	364,000	1,400,000	26·0
1929. .	1,061,000	351,000	1,412,000	24·9
1930. .	1,080,000	357,000	1,437,000	24·9
1931. .	1,104,000	337,000	1,441,000	23·4
1932. .	1,109,000	323,000	1,432,000	22·6
1933. .	1,147,000	333,000	1,480,000	22·5
1934. .	1,163,000	336,000	1,499,000	22·4

INCOME.

	Empire Loans.	Foreign Loans.	Total.	Ratio of Income from Foreign Loans to Total.
	(£000.)	(£000.)	(£000.)	(Per cent.)
1928. .	43,820	18,076	61,896	29·2
1929. .	46,416	18,245	64,661	28·2
1930. .	46,878	17,798	64,676	27·5
1931. .	48,405	17,515	65,920	26·6
1932. .	48,919	13,458	62,377	21·6
1933. .	49,138	11,988	61,126	19·6
1934. .	49,090	12,039	61,129	19·7

Income from Empire loans has expanded steadily with the growth of investment in the Dominions, even through the depression years. While British investments in foreign loans declined from 26·0 per cent. in 1928 to 22·4 per cent. in 1934 of the total British capital invested in oversea Government and Municipal loans, the income obtained fell much more sharply, owing to default, from 29·2 per cent. of the total in 1928 to 19·6 per cent. of the total in 1933, although the percentage was a shade higher in 1934. Interest received on Empire loans in 1934 was 4·2 per cent. of the nominal capital, compared with 3·6 per cent. on Foreign loans.

In order to bring the subject-matter of this section up to date, the results of a preliminary examination of remittances in 1935 are here summarised. Income from Dominion loans showed a further decline during 1935, partly because of a net reduction in the capital outstanding through maturity and sinking-fund repayments, but chiefly as a result of the heavy conversions carried out by Dominion Governments in 1934 and 1935. On the other hand, partial interest payments on foreign loans, such as Brazilian and Greek loans, were increased, while there were isolated instances of resumption of interest payments on loans previously in complete default. These increased remittances were only partially offset by the suspension of cash payments on German loans (other than Dawes and Young Loans), which were effected instead in funding bonds. On balance, the total income obtained in 1935 from British investments in oversea Government and Municipal loans appears to have declined by slightly more than £0·5 million from the previous year, and the figure for 1935 may be provisionally estimated at £60·5 million.

It is highly probable that in the absence of a major cataclysm this income will remain almost stationary during the next few years. Foreign bond income seems unlikely to suffer further serious default, while the gradual improvement in the position of debtor countries is more likely to move it in an upward direction. Conversion of Dominion loans to lower rates of interest, which had an appreciable effect in reducing income during the past few years, has already proceeded to a point which renders the possibility of further substantial progress in this direction unlikely. On the other hand, as has already been pointed out, accumulations of foreign exchange by Dominion Central Banks may give an impetus to the replacement of Dominion external loans by internal loans. An expansion of income from investments in oversea Public loans depends almost entirely on the volume of new issues on the London market during the coming years. But, for the next few years, at any rate, new oversea issues on the London market cannot be expected to do more than keep pace with the annual repayment of oversea loans through sinking-fund, maturity and other forms of redemption.

We next proceed to examine how British commercial investments abroad fared during 1934 and 1935. In order to facilitate

United Kingdom Capital invested in British Companies operating abroad; Dividends and Interest received and Capital Repaid.

SHARE CAPITAL.
(£000.)

	1933.		1934.	
	Nominal Amount.	Dividends.	Nominal Amount.	Dividends.
Dominion and Colonial Rails	1,600	—	1,600	7
Indian Rails	20,900	1,800	21,700	1,618
Indian Railway Annuities	—	—	—	—
U.S. Rails	800	42	800	26
Foreign Rails	221,200	1,619	219,000	1,845
Banks	26,300	2,080	28,600	1,742
Breweries	4,700	396	5,900	340
Canals and Docks	1,400	—	500	—
Commercial and Industrial	65,400	2,220	62,100	1,500
Electric Light and Power	8,200	597	10,200	670
Financial, Land and Investment	86,200	1,268	90,500	1,662
Gas	11,800	1,275	9,200	833
Iron, Coal and Steel	6,700	115	6,100	42
Mines	80,300	2,905	99,100	4,443
Nitrates	3,400	—	7,800	—
Oil	108,600	11,125	108,900	11,400
Rubber	81,500	269	83,000	1,932
Shipping	11,800	540	7,400	159
Tea and Coffee	38,600	1,429	39,500	2,509
Telegraphs	24,000	1,192	21,000	1,093
Tramways	15,500	349	13,900	430
Waterworks	4,600	229	3,500	195
	823,500	29,450	840,300	32,446

LOAN CAPITAL.

(£000.)

	1933.			1934.		
	Nominal Amount.	Interest.	Repayment.	Nominal Amount.	Interest.	Repayment.
Dominion and Colonial Rails	27,100	822	919	27,600	1,498	106
Indian Rails	44,400	1,625	—	43,500	1,657	337
Indian Railway Annuities	23,100	1,225	1,203	23,000	1,200	1,230
U.S. Rails	800	32	—	800	32	—
Foreign Rails	175,200	4,406	65	178,000	4,626	202
Breweries	800	34	—	1,000	47	92
Canals and Docks	2,300	128	—	2,300	174	—
Commercial and Industrial	20,600	788	3,250	17,200	572	1,010
Electric Light and Power	7,000	283	70	9,000	378	514
Financial, Land and Investment	26,600	930	327	34,000	1,110	339
Gas	2,000	93	46	1,800	87	27
Iron, Coal and Steel	2,200	66	—	1,600	61	—
Mines	6,300	305	620	7,900	401	774
Nitrates	1,700	—	—	1,400	—	—
Oil	12,100	638	279	2,100	75	8,300
Rubber	5,600	174	—	4,400	209	204
Shipping	5,600	197	697	5,600	194	84
Tea and Coffee	2,400	101	4	2,200	83	31
Telegraphs	4,300	175	2	4,300	176	2
Tramways	15,300	344	310	17,900	383	18
Waterworks	1,900	82	3	2,200	105	12
Total	387,300	12,448	7,795	387,800	13,068	13,282

analysis, the procedure followed in former articles, namely of dividing these investments into two classes, viz.—(*a*) Investments in British registered companies operating abroad; (*b*) Investments in foreign registered companies—is again adopted. Naturally the income derived from these investments is more variable than that obtained from those examined in the previous section, since it depends more directly on the level of economic activity, and in particular on commodity prices. Although world trade in terms of gold registered a further decline in 1934, and only a slight increase in 1935, the increase in production and trade and the rise in commodity prices within the sterling area were responsible for an impressive recovery in the income obtained from British commercial investments overseas.

A detailed examination of the table shows that, except in the case of Mines, the additional capital absorbed by these companies was small. New capital for mining companies was, of course, attracted by the increased price of gold, by the high price of tin and for the development of the copper mines in

Rhodesia.[1] Foreign holdings in British companies operating abroad are always very small on account of high British income tax,[2] so that, apart from changes due to the employment of new or repayment of old capital, the total nominal British investment in these companies shows little change from year to year.[3] Repayment of capital in 1934 was particularly heavy, at £13·3 million as compared with £7·8 million in 1933. This was mainly due to the redemption of the outstanding debenture stocks of the Anglo-Persian and Burmah Oil companies. Such repayments do not necessarily mean that corresponding remittances were made into the United Kingdom during the year, since they were presumably effected by the use of reserve funds gradually accumulated and invested here over a number of years.[4]

Total dividends distributed in 1934 showed an increase of £3·0 million on the total of the preceding year. Among the different sections there were substantial variations. Mining dividends rose from £2·9 million to £4·4 million, but in spite of the large rise in the price of gold, the average rate of dividend paid out by these mining companies[5] was less than 4½ per cent. The explanation is, of course, that the gold mines considered here are mainly those operating in British West Africa. Most of these mines had long ceased operations before the rise in the price of gold took place, and although it enabled the mines to resume working, their profits in 1934 were naturally not as large as those of the Rand mines. Rubber dividends increased from £0·3 million to £1·9 million as a result of restriction. On the other hand, declines were registered by companies classified under Commercial and Industrial, Banks, Gas and Shipping companies. Total interest payments in 1934 increased by £0·6 million to £13·1 million, following increased earnings and the slight improvement in the exchange position of South American countries, but, as the

[1] The actual increase in the capital of mining companies in 1934 was greater than that shown in the table, since a large number of companies shown under Financial, Land and Investment are, in fact, mining companies. It will be seen that a considerable increase was shown in this section.

[2] Operating for the foreigner virtually like a coupon tax.

[3] Changes (other than in Mines and Financial, Land and Investment) that have occurred in the above table are largely due to company reorganisation, conversion of shares into debentures and vice versa, and the reclassification of companies in accordance with the *Stock Exchange Official Year Book* into different sections.

[4] To a lesser extent this applies also to the dividends and interest payments distributed by British companies operating abroad.

[5] The Mines considered in this table omit, of course, most of the South African gold mines, which, being registered in the Union of South Africa, are included in the section dealing with companies registered overseas.

next table shows, default is still heavy, and recovery must proceed a long way further before interest is transferred in full. For example, the average interest paid on nominal capital invested in Foreign Railways was still only 2·6 per cent. in 1934, as compared with 4·2 per cent. in 1929.

Investment income received in the United Kingdom through the medium of British companies operating abroad during the years 1929 to 1935 is shown below :—

British Companies Operating Abroad ; Dividend and Interest Received in the United Kingdom.

	Dividends.	Per Cent. of Capital.	Interest.	Per Cent. of Capital.	Total Dividends and Interest.
1929 .	£67·7 million	8·4	£18·3 million	4·7	£86·0 million
1930 .	59·0 ,,	7·1	17·5 ,,	4·5	76·5 ,,
1931 .	33·3 ,,	4·1	15·5 ,,	3·9	48·8 ,,
1932 .	29·0 ,,	3·6	13·5 ,,	3·5	42·5 ,,
1933 .	29·5 ,,	3·6	12·5 ,,	3·2	42·0 ,,
1934 .	32·4 ,,	3·9	13·1 ,,	3·4	45·5 ,,
1935 (estimated)	37·5 ,,	4·5	13·5 ,,	3·5	51·0 ,,

A tentative examination of 1935 results indicates that owing to improved earnings of Oil, Mines, Rubber and other companies, dividends distributed rose by £5·1 million and interest payments by £0·4 million during the year. The total received by investors at £51·0 million was the highest since 1930, though the average rate of dividend paid during 1935 was only slightly more than half that during 1929. Nevertheless, with the present trend in commodity prices and a fair prospect of enlarged world trade, dividends may continue to climb towards the 1929 figure.

We now examine British investments in companies registered abroad, confining attention to securities which are dealt in on United Kingdom Stock Exchanges.[1] British holdings in these companies differ considerably in important respects from those of the securities previously considered. The securities of British companies labelled in sterling and subject to high British income tax offer little inducement to would-be foreign purchasers, and consequently tend to remain entirely in British hands. On the other

[1] United Kingdom investments in securities not dealt in here are also considerable. The bulk of these investments are in American securities. A rough estimate is given later.

hand, the shares here examined consist largely of well-known international counters. Their prices and the amounts held by nationals in different countries are as much affected by the large and often unpredictable migrations of international funds as by their earning power. Royal Dutch, Unilever, Mexican Eagle, Brazilian Traction, International Nickel, the South African Gold Mines, are only a few examples of companies whose shares are subject to international trading on a substantial scale whenever currency fears, disturbed political situations and other international complications occur. From a national standpoint the mobility of these assets and the ease with which they are realisable give them an important advantage over the shares of British companies, since in times of national emergency they may be mobilised to provide a reservoir of foreign exchange for payment of vital foodstuffs and raw materials, while in times of economic depression they provide a means of "living on the nation's capital" and avoiding a severe reduction in the standard of living.

Foreign and Dominion Companies.

SHARE CAPITAL.
(£000.)

	1933.		1934.	
	Nominal Amount.	Dividends.	Nominal Amount.	Dividends.
Dominion and Colonial Rails	63,500	123	65,700	133
U.S. Rails	17,300	113	23,700	300
Banks	26,000	1,399	28,000	1,530
Breweries	1,300	12	1,300	75
Canals and Docks	1,600	2,064	1,700	2,424
Commercial and Industrial	70,000	5,151	67,600	4,963
Electric Lighting and Power	16,500	1,018	16,900	963
Financial, Land and Investment	21,900	617	14,900	100
Iron, Coal and Steel	6,800	245	6,000	200
Mines	57,900	7,331	64,200	13,548
Nitrates	3,000	—	3,000	—
Oil	19,300	720	18,000	105
Shipping	6,600	368	7,100	462
Telegraphs and Telephones	5,700	346	6,200	344
Tramways	10,600	2	10,700	—
Foreign Rails, Gas, Waterworks	17,000	1,000	16,600	835
	345,000	20,509	351,600	25,982

United Kingdom share holdings rose from £345 million in 1933 to £351·6 million in 1934. A rise of £6·3 million investments in Mines and a corresponding decline in Financial Land and Invest-

LOAN CAPITAL.

(£000.)

	1933.			1934.		
	Nominal Amount.	Interest.	Repayment.	Nominal Amount.	Interest.	Repayment.
Dominion and Colonial Rails	158,200	6,531	500	155,900	6,600	1,900
U.S. Rails	9,200	448	—	9,500	420	—
Banks	15,100	570	1,459	14,500	285	550
Breweries	100	5	3	100	5	10
Canals and Docks	2,800	—	—	2,800	—	—
Commercial and Industrial	21,400	1,094	870	23,300	1,390	857
Electric Lighting and Power	28,400	1,368	2,054	31,200	1,350	864
Financial, Land and Investment	23,000	1,002	299	15,700	800	90
Iron, Coal and Steel	8,900	331	108	8,500	443	75
Mines	8,300	582	178	7,700	272	250
Nitrates	5,200	10	71	5,300	105	—
Oil	—	—	278	—	—	—
Shipping	700	33	42	1,800	112	50
Telegraphs and Telephones	9,400	510	73	6,400	318	120
Tramways	10,800	420	12	10,100	440	85
Foreign Rails	47,900	1,815	3,698	41,900	1,274	695
Gas	400	22	—	400	22	—
	349,800	14,741	9,645	335,100	13,836	5,546

ment reflect reclassification of certain companies from the latter to the former category in accordance with the *Stock Exchange Official Year Book*. Actually an appreciable amount of new capital was raised by certain gold-mining companies in 1934, but this was offset by equivalent sales of South African gold-mine shares by United Kingdom holders to Continental and South African purchasers. The rise in Wall Street and the prospect of recovery in earnings in the United States attracted foreign funds both for speculative profits and for long-term investment, and British holdings in the share capital of United States Railways advanced by £6·4 million during the year.[1] This tendency was also in evidence during 1935, when foreign long-term investments in the United States rose by $765 million, according to the United States Department of Commerce. British investors were estimated by this institution to have been responsible for about 20 per cent. of the increase, the total British investment outstanding in 1935 being put at £282 million. This figure is, of course, a long way

[1] The actual sum of money exported in this connection was, of course, considerably smaller, since the prices of United States railway shares were at a considerable discount in 1934.

from the total in pre-War years, which was believed to be in the neighbourhood of £700 million sterling, but a sizeable increase in the next year or two would not be surprising, since the view is gaining ground that recovery in the United States, as evidenced by the fact that it has so far proceeded without any corresponding activity in the capital goods industries, is still in the early stages, as compared with that in the United Kingdom.

In other sections of the above table, although active dealings took place, changes in ownership as between British and foreign nationals were not on balance noteworthy.

Total dividends remitted to the United Kingdom are estimated to have been £5½ million greater in 1934 than in the preceding year, the whole of this increase resulting from the remarkable profits earned by gold-mining companies. Mining dividends, which of course include the dividends distributed by the South African gold mines in 1934, were £13·5 million, or 21 per cent. on the capital, and actually accounted for more than half the total dividends shown in the above table. Other company dividends showed little change from the figures of 1933, although Oil dividends declined exceptionally by £0·6 million, owing to the suspension of payments on the Preference shares of the Canadian and Mexican Eagle Oil Companies. The absence of an improvement in dividends in 1934 other than those of mining companies is not surprising, since dividends reflect the earnings of these companies in 1933, a year in which economic depression was still acute in most countries outside the sterling area, and contrasts with the better results shown in the previous table, in connection with the securities of companies operating largely within that area. The moderate decline in total interest received in 1934 reflects partly the smaller total nominal capital outstanding and partly the depreciation of the American and Canadian dollars, which fell from an average of \$4·22 and \$4·57 to \$5·04 and \$4·99 respectively.

Dividends and interest payments by companies registered abroad remitted to the United Kingdom since 1929 are estimated in table on p. 657.

The trend of dividend payments in 1935 was in an upward direction, despite the fact that the advance in gold-mining profits was arrested. As in the case of British companies, the rise in commodity prices played an important part in making this trend possible, while, although social legislation in the United States tended to increase industrial costs, the basis of recovery was so well set that on balance earnings tended to increase faster than costs.

Dividend and Interest Payments remitted to the United Kingdom by Companies Registered Abroad.

	Dividends.	Per Cent. of Nominal Capital.	Interest.	Per Cent. of Nominal Capital.	Total Dividends and Interest.
1929 .	£42·0 million	9·6	£19·7 million	4·9	£61·7 million
1930 .	31·7 ,,	8·1	19·3 ,,	4·9	51·0 ,,
1931 .	22·7 ,,	6·0	18·2 ,,	4·7	40·9 ,,
1932 .	22·1 ,,	6·4	17·1 ,,	4·6	39·2 ,,
1933 .	20·5 ,,	5·9	14·7 ,,	4·2	35·2 ,,
1934 .	26·0 ,,	7·4	13·8 ,,	4·1	39·8 ,,
1935 (estimated)	28·0 ,,	7·9	13·8 ,,	4·1	41·8 ,,

It seems at first sight remarkable that neither the rate of dividends on share capital nor the rate of interest on loan capital fell as low during the depression years as the corresponding receipts from British companies operating abroad (see p. 653). The explanation, of course, is that despite the heavily reduced earnings of foreign companies and a considerable amount of default on interest payments, the sterling equivalent of the sums remitted was favourably affected by reason of the depreciated level of sterling in relation to foreign currencies after the autumn of 1931. Thus the rate of interest declined only from 4·9 per cent. in 1929 to a low point of 4·1 per cent. in 1934, as compared with a fall of 4·7 per cent. in 1929 to 3·2 per cent. in 1933 in the case of British companies. Total interest and dividend payments remitted by foreign and colonial companies were, at their lowest, still 57 per cent. of the high figure for 1929, as compared with 49 per cent. for British companies.

We may now complete and summarise the results given in the preceding pages.

Total British capital invested in Dominion and Foreign Government and Municipal loans, in British companies operating abroad and in the quoted securities of Foreign and Colonial companies registered overseas, is estimated at £3414 million at the end of 1934. A considerable amount of British capital is also invested by institutions like investment trusts, insurance companies, etc., in securities not quoted in London, although a large proportion of the funds held by insurance companies have, in fact, been invested in compliance with legal requirements as cover against contingent underwriting liabilities or as legal deposits, and cannot be strictly regarded as net British investments. Moreover, individual investment in miscellaneous unquoted securities and in private property abroad constitutes a further item of British capital not included in the above table. This body of capital is by its nature not readily subject to accurate assessment. However, at the end of 1933 British investments in private property, unquoted securities, etc., were taken roughly at £280 million. The figure was undoubtedly larger at the end of 1934. The return of the United States to a *de facto* gold standard, and the encouraging view taken of business prospects in that country, attracted foreign funds for investment purposes. British capital, which had been repatriated in the depression years, began to flow back in substantial amounts. An examination of the lists of investment trusts, together with other information available, indicates that apart from further purchases of United States railroad securities,[1] United Kingdom investments in American equities and dollar bonds may have increased by £15 million nominal, while in Canada and elsewhere investment also increased. Total British investments in unquoted securities, property, etc., is therefore calculated at £300 million at the end of 1934.[2] If this approximation is added to the more reliable estimate of the capital invested overseas in Government and Municipal loans and in companies registered at home and abroad, total British capital employed abroad is estimated at £3714 million nominal value at the end of 1934, as compared with £3666 million at the end of 1933, indicating an increase of £48 million.

Some indication has already been given in the preceding pages of the movement of capital in and out of the securities examined in this article.[3]

Subscriptions to new oversea Government and Municipal loans in 1934 amounted to £30·4 million. This money went mainly into new loans for the Governments of Canada, Australia, South Africa and the Crown Colonies. According to Midland Bank figures, new oversea issues for industrial and commercial purposes totalled £32·4 million. These, too, were mainly for account of companies in British territories, principally in gold mines. On the other hand, repayment of capital in 1934 amounted to £42·0 million. The figures for new issues and repayments since 1929 are shown herewith.

[1] Investments in American Railroads, whether the securities are quoted in London or not, are included in the table dealing with companies registered overseas.

[2] No great degree of accuracy is claimed for this figure, which, until a suitable technique for its calculation has been evolved, is intended to be an indication, rather than a first-class estimate, of the amount of British capital in this class of investment.

[3] Owing to changes that have no relation to movements of capital, *i.e.* issue of bonus shares, the scaling up or down of capital, capital reorganisation, etc., it is not possible to enter into a detailed discussion of the capital movements that have affected the total British capital invested abroad.

	British Subscription to New Oversea Issues.	Repayment to the United Kingdom.
1929 . . .	£96 million	£49 million
1930 . . .	98 ,,	39 ,,
1931 . . .	41 ,,	27 ,,
1932 . . .	37 ,,	48 ,,
1933 . . .	83 ,,	67 ,,
1934 . . .	63 ,,	42 ,,

The excess of new issues over repayment of existing loans was £21 million in 1934.

An examination of long-term capital movements is not strictly relevant to the present inquiry, but since some attention has already been directed in this article to a moderate flow of funds to Wall Street during the past two years, it is also worth noting that one or two other interesting developments resulting in movements of long-term capital have been noticeable. For example, protective duties and domestic recovery have undoubtedly encouraged the establishment of branches, factories, etc., of foreign companies in this country. Against this must be put the growing tendency to repurchase large blocks of securities, occasionally amounting to controlling interests, owned by American firms in English companies. Thus the repurchase of one million American-owned shares of Boots Pure Drug Co. involved an export of about £6½ million of capital in 1933, while about £5 million was exported in 1935 in connection with the repurchase from American interests of blocks of shares of General Electric Co., Associated Electrical Industries and Electric and Musical Industries.

Our final summary is as follows :—

Income from British Oversea Investments.

(£000,000.)

	Dominion, Colonial and Foreign Governments and Municipalities.	British Companies registered in the United Kingdom.	Foreign and Colonial Companies.	Other Investments.[1]	Total.
1929 . .	64·7	86·0	61·7	18·5	230·9
1930 . .	64·7	76·5	51·0	16·8	209·0
1931 . .	65·9	48·8	40·8	13·2	168·7
1932 . .	62·4	42·5	39·2	12·3	156·4
1933 . .	61·1	41·9	35·3	11·4	149·7
1934 . .	61·1	45·5	39·8	12·8	159·2
1935 (tentative estimate).	60·5	51·0	41·8	14·6	167·9

[1] The average rate of income from these investments is assumed to be the same as that obtained from negotiable securities.

Total interest and dividends received from British Oversea Investments in 1934 are estimated at £159·2 million, an increase of £9·3 million as compared with the previous year. For 1935 income has been provisionally assessed at £167·9 million, *i.e.* £8·7 million more than the figure for 1934. Thus in 1935 oversea investment income had risen by approximately £18 million from its lowest level in 1933, but was still £63 million less than the corresponding income in 1929. As is natural, almost the whole of this increase has been provided by commercial investments, as distinct from Government and Municipal loans. Associated with it is the rise in sums placed to reserve by British companies operating abroad. These cannot strictly be regarded as income accruing in that year, since in times of depression they are frequently drawn upon to meet losses or to provide dividends which cannot be met from earnings. Nevertheless, in so far as they are remitted to the United Kingdom, they may be regarded as an additional item in a calculation of the United Kingdom's balance of payments. With the expansion in earnings since 1933, the proportion of profits placed to reserve has, of course, risen, since companies have been anxious to strengthen financial positions which were weakened by the severity and prolonged duration of the depression. Reserve allocations made by British companies are estimated at £5·9 million in 1934–35, exclusive of reserves for depreciation and obsolescence.[1] This amounts to 0·7 per cent. of the share capital, as compared with 3·9 per cent. for dividends distributed in 1934.

	Percentage of Share Capital placed to Reserves 1934–35.	Average Rate of Dividends in 1934.
	Per cent.	Per cent.
Foreign Rails	Nil	0·8
Oil	1·1	10·5
Rubber	1·1	2·3
Mines	1·2	4·5
Banks	1·0	6·1
Land and Investment	Nil	1·8

In the case of British-owned railway companies, exchange losses absorbed the increase in profits, while sums placed to reserve by companies in the category Financial, Land and Investment were about equal to sums withdrawn from reserves to meet dividends and other charges. Reserve allocation by companies paying appreciable dividends were approximately between 1·0 per cent. and 1·2 per cent. of the share capital employed.

The prospect for a further rise in oversea investment income

[1] It seems that the Board of Trade in past years has made excessive allowances for this item in its Balance of Payments estimates.

has undoubtedly been greatly improved by the recent currency changes in the former Gold Bloc. As the deflationary pressure exerted by these over-valued currencies has been removed, an expansion in trade is a reasonable expectation in the near future, while at the same time the *raison d'être* for prohibitive tariffs, quotas and other exchange restrictions will slowly disappear, and hopes for a gradual removal of these obstacles to international trade may be entertained. Moreover, it is permissible to anticipate that a gradual return to *de facto* stability in exchange rates will be accompanied by a more economic distribution of gold reserves in accordance with the requirements of various countries, and that these revalued reserves will provide an adequate basis for a greatly enlarged volume of world production and trade. Under the circumstances the fears expressed in some quarters that Britain's adverse trade balance, which has grown steadily under the influences of cheap money, domestic recovery and the rearmament programme from an average of £21·5 million per month in 1933 to an average of £26·9 million per month in 1936, is likely to increase faster than Britain's invisible exports, may, in the long run, prove to have been unwarranted. Given the absence of major international political disturbances, there is every reason to hope that oversea investment income will during the next few years rise more rapidly towards the level attained in 1929. National net shipping receipts should benefit considerably from the expansion of world trade and the higher freights accompanying rising commodity prices. These receipts, according to the Board of Trade, dropped in 1933 to £65 million, which was only half the corresponding receipts in 1929 and, although they were estimated at £75 million in 1935, it is clear that there is ample scope for an impressive recovery should the restrictions on international commerce be relaxed. Moreover, the debit item in respect of tourist expenditure, which was noticeably reduced during the past few years, is unlikely to increase substantially as a result of the depreciation of the former gold currencies, since the United Kingdom has gained considerable popularity among foreign tourists, while the growing prosperity of the Dominions is likely to cause a gradual increase in both the number and expenditure of Dominion travellers to this country. Thus, although a moderate deficit in the balance of payments in 1936 seems probable, careful examination suggests that, provided the growth in the adverse trade balance is arrested, the increase in the invisible exports in the coming years may be sufficient not only to offset it, but also to provide a moderate surplus available for capital investment abroad.

ROBERT KINDERSLEY

BRITISH OVERSEAS INVESTMENTS IN 1935 AND 1936

Robert M. Kindersley

BRITISH OVERSEA INVESTMENTS IN 1935 AND 1936

THE present study is a continuation of the series of studies on British Oversea Investments, the first of which was published in 1929. Hitherto the statistical results obtained related to a period of about two years prior to their compilation. The present survey, however, contains the final results for both 1935 and 1936. In addition, a geographical analysis of these investments for 1936 has been included. Annual surveys will in future each relate to the previous year; and it is hoped that this procedure will increase the value of these statistics to those interested in studying the trend of Great Britain's oversea investments and its bearing on the economic welfare of the country.

I should like at this juncture once again gratefully to acknowledge the courtesy of Banks and Issuing Houses of London and of several hundred commercial and industrial companies both at home and abroad [1] in providing me with the material indispensable to the completion of these yearly studies and to their presentation in up-to-date form.

Before passing on, a brief description of the economic circumstances which influenced our investments abroad during the past two years may not be out of place.

Roughly two-thirds of British oversea capital is invested in bonds and debentures, and although default has in recent years affected income in a downward direction, fluctuations in the yield from this part of our investments are small compared with variations in income from shares. Although the former constitute an important stabilising element in investment income, influences bearing on profits are reflected in variations in share income.

Prime importance in this connection attaches, of course, to the trend of commodity prices and the state of international trade.

The forces making for world recovery exerted a conspicuous influence during 1935 and 1936. A net increase in the gold value of world trade was recorded in 1935, for the first time since 1930, and towards the end of that year most commodity prices

[1] My special thanks in this connection are due to numerous American and Canadian companies who have provided me with valuable statistics of the amounts of stock registered in the names of U.K. residents.

advanced sharply. During 1936 industrial production rose rapidly, while devaluation of the currencies of the former Gold Bloc in the autumn also contributed to a strengthening of confidence and paved the way for a further substantial upward movement in prices.

Domestic booms in a number of countries necessitated an increasing volume of imports of raw materials and semi-manufactured products, while the rise in primary products gradually afforded increased purchasing power to raw-material-producing countries, thus enabling them to increase their imports of manufactured goods.

We now pass on to our principal theme of Oversea Investments.

Government and Municipal Bonds and Stocks.

At the end of 1936 the total nominal value of Dominion, Foreign Government and Municipal Loans amounted to £1,780 million, of which, it is estimated, £339 million was held by residents domiciled outside the United Kingdom. Reasons for the large amount, particularly of foreign sterling bonds held abroad, have been frequently given in previous surveys. It is not always realised, however, that since these loans are readily saleable on the London market, they constitute an important part of the money invested by foreigners in the U.K. They can be converted at will into cash balances which can be withdrawn through the foreign exchanges. Indeed, the amount of these loans owned by foreigners may well be greater than their holdings of British bonds and shares.

Dominion, Colonial and Foreign Public Sterling Loans ; Holdings in the U.K. and Abroad.[1]

(As at December 31, 1936.)

	United Kingdom.	Abroad.
	%	%
Dominion and Provincial Governments	90·1	9·9
Dominion and Colonial Municipalities	86·5	13·5
Foreign Governments	60·2	39·8
Foreign Municipalities	70·9	29·1

[1] The percentages in this table relate to the interest paid in London tax deducted and free of tax respectively. They may be taken as an approximation to the respective proportions of these loans held in the U.K. and abroad. Annual changes in these figures, however, do not necessarily indicate corresponding changes as between British and foreign holders, since the amount of foreign-owned coupons cashed in London in respect of sterling tranches issued abroad or of other loans payable abroad at the option of the holder, varies considerably in certain circumstances.

Unlike Foreign Government sterling loans, some of which are placed in financial centres abroad, in the case of Dominion Government sterling loans no effort is made to utilise foreign markets since the Trustee Act renders the London market specially favourable to Dominion and Colonial Government borrowers. The fact that approximately 10 per cent. of Dominion Government sterling loans is held outside the U.K. is due to the investment of sinking funds accumulated against these and internal Dominion loans. The percentage may be expected to rise further in the event that Dominion Governments continue to replace sterling loans by domestic issues.

TABLE I.

British Capital Invested in Oversea Government and Municipal Loans: Income Remitted and Sums Repaid.

(£'000.)

	Nominal Capital.		Income.		Repayment.	
	1935.	1936.	1935.	1936.	1935.	1936.
Dominion and Colonial Governments	1,072,300	1,016,000	44,115	42,344	44,091	74,711
Dominion and Colonial Municipalities . . .	84,800	84,200	4,046	4,020	1,611	2,438
Foreign Governments . .	316,100	312,600	11,343	11,685	8,540	8,850
Foreign Municipalities . .	29,900	28,400	1,012	868	1,965	1,547
	1,503,100	1,441,200	60,516	58,917	56,207	87,546

Income from Dominion Government loans in 1936 at £42·3 million was £1·8 million less than in the previous year. This was partly a reflection of the decline in total loans outstanding in 1936, and partly due to previous conversion operations to lower

TABLE II.

Income.

(£'000.)

Year.	Foreign Loans.	Empire Loans.	Total.	Ratio of Income from Foreign Loans to Total.
				%
1928	18,076	43,820	61,896	29·2
1929	18,245	46,416	64,661	28·2
1930	17,798	46,878	64,676	27·5
1931	17,515	48,405	65,920	26·6
1932	13,458	48,919	62,377	21·6
1933	11,988	49,138	61,126	19·6
1934	12,039	49,090	61,129	19·7
1935	12,355	48,161	60,516	20·4
1936	12,553	46,364	58,917	21·3

rates of interest. On the other hand, income from Foreign Loans has risen slightly for the third year in succession, the gain in 1936 being due mainly to increased payments on Greek and Rumanian bonds and to limited resumption of service on Chilean loans. Even so, the absence of any conspicuous improvement in respect of defaulted bonds stands out in contrast to the recovery in commercial dividends, figures for which are given later.

Thus, despite a minor rise, income from foreign loans is still more than £5 million below its 1930 figure. Although part of this decline is due to a decrease in U.K. investments in loans of this class, and to conversion operations, particularly of Argentine loans, most of the loss is still directly attributable to default.

TABLE III.

British Investment in Empire and Foreign Loans.

(£'000,000.)

Year.	Empire Loans.	Foreign Loans.	Total.	Ratio of Foreign Loans to Total.
				%
1928	1,036	364	1,400	26·0
1929	1,061	351	1,412	24·9
1930	1,080	357	1,437	24·9
1931	1,104	337	1,441	23·4
1932	1,109	323	1,432	22·6
1933	1,147	333	1,480	22·5
1934	1,163	336	1,499	22·4
1935	1,157	346	1,503	23·0
1936	1,100	341	1,441	23·7

The rise in investments in Empire loans, uninterrupted up to 1934, was reversed in 1935, which year showed a decline for the first time since these estimates were compiled, while in 1936 the fall amounted to £57 million.

Between 1930 and 1934, Canada, New Zealand, India and South Africa were the principal borrowers. But Australia, already disturbed by the magnitude of her external debt, which, as a result of the heavy fall in the prices of her principal products, was imposing an increasingly heavy burden on her exchange resources, took steps to reduce her debt by applying larger sums to the redemption of loans in London. It may perhaps seem remarkable that in view of the rapid acceleration of the pace of industrialisation in Canada, South Africa and Australia, and the consequent increased demand for capital, the total of Dominion loans outstanding in London should have fallen during the past two years. Recovery has enabled these countries to finance new projects in their domestic markets, while the growing volume of their export trade has permitted them to pay for imported capital goods from the proceeds of their exports and to redeem sterling loans from accumulated foreign exchange reserves. It is also worth noting that the Ottowa duties have been a factor in increasing direct American investments in Canada. Gross redemption of Dominion Government loans in London totalled £74·7 million in 1936. This is easily the highest figure of which we have a record. Australia was responsible for £25 million, South Africa for £23 million, India for £13 million and the Crown Colonies for £9 million.

Repayment of Dominion Government Loans.

(Excluding loans converted.)

(£'000.)

Year	£'000
1928	4,410
1929	17,782
1930	8,288
1931	2,568
1932	23,740
1933	37,122
1934	13,222
1935	44,091
1936	74,711

No doubt Imperial tariff policy has strengthened the trade balance of the Dominions with the U.K. Nevertheless the size of the export surplus is still mainly governed by the prices and yields of certain primary products.[1]

The increase of British capital, more apparent than real, invested in Foreign loans since 1932, so far from reflecting a corresponding investment of new money, may not unfairly be described as the involuntary conversion of unremitted interest into capital.

Our next principal item comprises British Commercial Investments overseas as ascertained for 1935 and 1936. As on earlier occasions, separate estimates are given in respect of the securities of companies registered in the U.K. and for those registered abroad. The companies include all those classified in the *Stock Exchange Official Year Book* whose assets are either entirely or mainly outside the United Kingdom, share and loan capital being taken at their nominal values. In the case of companies regis-

[1] The policy of drawing heavily upon foreign exchange reserves for the redemption of overseas debt may have its drawbacks. Large Dominion export surpluses depend so much on high prices of a few commodities that it may be questioned whether foreign exchange accumulations should not be regarded, to some extent at least, as a safeguard against adverse circumstances brought about either by crop failures or world depression.

tered abroad, only those whose securities are dealt in or known on the London market have been included. Shares of no par value are taken at the values assigned to them in the latest balance sheets.[1]

Total British share and loan capital invested in the above companies at the end of 1936 amounted to £1,220 million, or about one-third of total quoted security investments abroad. Since 1930, owing to depression and restrictions on oversea lending, little new money has been raised to finance either new British ventures abroad or to increase the scale of operations of existing enterprise. Thus in 1930 the corresponding figure for these investments was £1,205 million. Mining companies were, however, an exception. British share capital in this section has increased by over £40 million since 1930, such increase representing genuine new investment. This, of course, was due to the sharp rise in the price of gold and the consequent demand for new equipment for the working of lower-grade ore. Elsewhere, except for some instances of capital reorganisation and repayments of loan capital, the nominal value of securities of British companies abroad has suffered little decline through sales to foreigners, the high rate of British income tax rendering these securities unattractive to other nationals. On the other hand, nationalist tendencies and the internal politics in South American and other countries are causing Governments to turn their attention to the question of taking over important industries at present under foreign management and control. The Argentine Government have already taken the initiative in this respect. Last year the Central Railway of Chubut was sold to the State Railways, while negotiations were opened between the Argentine Government and the Cordoba Central Railway Co., Ltd., and Argentine Transandine Railway for the transfer of assets of these companies to the Government. The aggregate capital of these companies amounts roughly to £23 million. These transactions are being partly financed by the issue of Argentine Government sterling bonds, so that the resulting net change in British investments in the Argentine may be both qualitative and quantitative.

It will be observed that the expansion of dividends witnessed since 1932 has continued more rapidly throughout 1935 and 1936.

[1] The adoption of nominal values avoids fluctuations due to arbitrary movements of the stock market, and so facilitates, to some extent, a comparison of investments from year to year. Nevertheless strict comparison is not possible owing to more formal than material changes, due to writing up or down of capital, bonus issues, capital reorganisation, etc.

Table IV.

United Kingdom Capital Invested in British Companies Operating Abroad; Dividends and Interest Received and Capital Repaid.

Share Capital.
(£'000.)

	1935.		1936.	
	Nominal Amount.	Dividends.	Nominal Amount.	Dividends.
Dominion and Colonial Rails	1,500	3	1,500	3
Indian Rails	20,700	1,586	20,600	1,507
U.S. Rails	800	24	800	16
Foreign Rails	226,900	1,641	226,700	1,208
Banks	31,400	2,022	27,100	2,009
Breweries	6,000	580	6,100	665
Canals and Docks	600	—	600	12
Commercial and Industrial	58,600	1,498	57,800	2,372
Electric Light and Power	11,500	670	11,600	775
Financial, Land and Investment	90,400	1,927	87,700	2,572
Gas	8,800	790	7,800	634
Iron, Coal and Steel	6,400	52	3,600	66
Mines	103,800	7,930	108,200	9,532
Nitrates	7,800	—	2,600	—
Oil	103,500	11,516	106,800	13,795
Rubber	83,700	3,640	84,600	3,782
Shipping	7,300	179	7,200	189
Tea and Coffee	40,300	1,756	40,400	2,213
Telegraphs and Telephones	24,000	1,468	24,200	1,502
Tramways and Omnibus	10,700	297	10,600	308
Waterworks	3,900	206	3,900	203
	848,600	37,785	840,400	43,363

Loan Capital.
(£'000.)

	1935.			1936.		
	Nominal Amount.	Interest.	Repayment.	Nominal Amount.	Interest.	Repayment.
Dominion and Colonial Rails	27,600	1,706	113	27,500	1,381	149
Indian Rails	40,000	1,541	3,488	38,000	1,440	2,088
Indian Railway Annuities	26,300	1,315	1,515	25,100	1,255	1,575
U.S. Rails	800	32	—	800	32	—
Foreign Rails	179,300	5,164	491	177,800	5,465	1,410
Breweries	900	48	3	900	47	8
Canals and Docks	2,800	170	109	2,800	185	27
Commercial and Industrial	18,200	647	748	17,100	598	1,650
Electric Light and Power	4,900	250	598	4,700	250	439
Financial, Land and Investment	36,000	1,318	1,949	34,600	1,372	3,558 [1]
Gas	2,000	96	36	2,000	94	24
Iron, Coal and Steel	1,600	61	—	1,300	72	21
Mines	8,600	483	451	8,200	423	340
Nitrates	1,400	—	28	1,400	—	—
Oil	1,500	84	1,124	1,800	41	84
Rubber	4,700	233	358	4,700	223	270
Shipping	4,200	182	1,109	3,800	137	359
Tea and Coffee	2,700	101	44	2,600	93	168
Telegraphs and Telephones	4,300	179	6	4,200	176	202
Tramways and Omnibus	17,700	254	174	17,800	252	63
Waterworks	2,300	99	12	2,200	97	90
	387,800	13,963	12,356	379,300	13,633	12,525

[1] Includes £1,497,000 share capital.

TABLE V.

British Companies Operating Abroad; Dividends and Interest Received in the United Kingdom.

Year.	Dividends.	Per cent. of Capital.	Interest.	Per cent. of Capital.	Total Dividends and Interest.
1929	£67·7 mill.	8·4	£18·3 mill.	4·7	£86·0 mill.
1930	59·0 ,,	7·1	17·5 ,,	4·5	76·5 ,,
1931	33·3 ,,	4·1	15·5 ,,	3·9	48·8 ,,
1932	29·0 ,,	3·6	13·5 ,,	3·5	42·5 ,,
1933	29·5 ,,	3·6	12·5 ,,	3·2	42·0 ,,
1934	32·4 ,,	3·9	13·1 ,,	3·4	45·5 ,,
1935	37·8 ,,	4·5	14·0 ,,	3·6	51·8 ,,
1936	43·4 ,,	5·2	13·6 ,,	3·6	57·0 ,,

Mining dividends at £9·5 million for 1936 have more than doubled since 1934, and give a yield of 8·8 per cent. on the invested share capital compared with 9·3 per cent. in 1929 on a considerably smaller capital. But whereas the rise in Mining Income between 1931 and 1934 was accounted for entirely by gold-mining profits, the further progress since 1934 has been largely associated with the upward price movements in copper, lead and spelter. The latter are shown in the following table.

Gold and Non-Ferrous Metal Prices.
Yearly Average Prices.

Year.	Gold, per fine oz.		Copper, per ton.	Tin, per ton.	Lead, per ton.	Spelter, per ton.
	s.	d.	£	£	£	£
1930	85	0	54·5	142·6	18·1	16·8
1931	92	6	38·3	118·1	13·0	12·4
1932	118	1	31·7	136·1	11·0	13·6
1933	124	9	32·6	194·8	11·7	15·7
1934	137	8	30·3	230·4	10·9	13·9
1935	142	1	31·9	224·9	14·3	14·1
1936	140	3	38·5	204·6	17·6	14·9

Oil dividends rose to £13·8 million in 1936, as compared with £11·4 million in 1934 and £10·2 million in 1932, while Rubber Company dividends at £3·8 million in 1936 were twice the amount distributed in 1934. Three groups of enterprise, Mines, Oil and Rubber, were responsible for over 60 per cent. of total dividends disbursed in 1936 by British companies operating entirely or mainly abroad. Other categories also reflected the gradual improvement in world economic conditions, but up to 1936 had regained only a small part of the ground lost between 1929 and 1933. Thus the yield on shares, despite substantial company reorganisation and writing down of capital, is still only 5·2 per cent., against 8·4 per cent. in 1929. Nor has there been any notable increase in the total interest received on loan capital since 1933. It was £18·3 million in 1929; fell to £12.5 million in 1933; and has since recovered to £13·6 million. The average rate of interest has fallen from 4·7 per cent. in 1929 to 3·6 per cent. in 1936, default on South American Railway bonds playing an important part in this decline. However, even if payments on defaulted bonds were resumed, total interest remitted could no longer be expected to attain the 1929 level, as conversion operations have in recent years to some extent reduced debt charges.

Our third section relates to U.K. investments in companies registered abroad. Apart from South African mining companies, which are largely British-controlled and managed, U.K. investments in companies registered abroad are small minority holdings generally involving no participation in their management.

It is interesting to note that in recent years circumstances have become more favourable to the investment of money in existing enterprise than in new companies. For, with the advent of economic recovery, the purchase of existing low-priced shares involved less risk than the subscription of funds to new companies with uncertain prospects. Since the capital of British companies operating abroad is held almost entirely in the U.K., it is clear that Foreign and Dominion companies have offered a greater scope for the investment of new money abroad. With the growing volume of funds seeking profitable outlets, it is therefore not surprising that international counters like Royal Dutch, International Nickel, Mexican Eagle, etc., have become increasingly popular on the London market. These circumstances also explain why the yearly fluctuations in the capital shown below are greater than those of British companies operating abroad.

U.K. holdings of share capital in companies registered abroad rose by £25 million between 1934 and 1936. Investments in U.S. Rails were responsible for some £15 million of this rise, while an expansion of £10 million in Commercial and Industrial and £6 million in Iron, Coal and Steel also reflected increased investments, mainly in American companies. The rise in Wall Street and expectations of a high level of business activity in the United States encouraged a larger volume of buying of U.S. securities from London than these figures suggest, since the above table excludes securities which are not well known or dealt in on the London market. According to a report issued by the United States Treasury Department, the net purchase of dollar securities

Table VI.

United Kingdom Capital Invested in Companies Registered Abroad; Dividends and Interest Received and Capital Repaid.

Share Capital.

(£'000.)

	Nominal Amount.		Dividends.	
	1935.	1936.	1935.	1936.
Dominion and Colonial Rails	67,900	67,000	154	148
U.S. Rails	33,400	38,000	200	415
Foreign Rails	8,700	8,700	100	75
Banks	29,000	27,800	1,470	1,440
Breweries	2,100	2,100	36	36
Canals and Docks	700	700	2,430	2,440
Commercial and Industrial	76,900	77,600	7,892	9,850
Electric Light and Power	18,900	19,000	1,568	1,520
Financial, Land and Investment	14,400	14,600	353	356
Iron, Coal and Steel	10,800	12,400	280	370
Mines	60,300	63,000	14,239	16,012
Nitrates	—	—	—	—
Oil	18,500	18,000	162	1,483
Shipping	7,200	7,200	304	304
Telegraphs and Telephones	6,500	6,300	346	373
Tramways and Omnibus	10,600	10,600	—	105
Gas / Waterworks	4,000	4,000	200	195
	369,900	377,000	29,734	35,122

Loan Capital.

(£'000.)

	Nominal Amount.		Interest.		Repayment.	
	1935.	1936.	1935.	1936.	1935.	1936.
Dominion and Colonial Rails	149,100	148,000	6,466	6,415	4,320	800
U.S. Rails	9,000	10,800	410	535	—	—
Foreign Rails	38,100	37,100	1,510	1,210	1,331	492
Banks	15,900	16,500	447	522	607	953
Breweries	—	200	—	5	—	—
Canals and Docks	3,200	3,200	27	27	—	—
Commercial and Industrial	25,600	25,600	1,262	1,197	2,045	962
Electric Light and Power	33,100	32,600	1,480	1,404	2,556	1,674
Gas	400	400	21	21	—	—
Financial, Land and Investment	16,200	14,400	668	600	100	100
Iron, Coal and Steel	7,700	7,900	385	375	365	530
Mines	6,100	5,800	410	390	150	175
Oil	—	—	—	—	156	485
Nitrates	8,300	8,000	111	146	—	220
Shipping	2,200	1,900	64	105	836	51
Telegraphs and Telephones	4,600	4,300	180	114	74	67
Tramways	8,900	9,000	301	352	13	17
	328,400	325,700	13,742	13,418	12,553	6,526

traced to U.K. account during the years 1935 and 1936 was $484 million, of which $368 million was domestic securities and the rest foreign dollar securities. It is probable, however, that some part of the buying of American securities in London was in reality for account of U.S. residents, as margin requirements in practice are now less stringent on the London Stock Exchange than in New York.

Despite the flotation of new gold-mining companies in South Africa and the larger capital needed to finance development work, U.K. investment in Mines showed no increase from the 1934 total. The explanation lies in the great interest in the Kaffir market taken by the Continent, and particularly by Paris, in which centre gold-mining shares are traditional favourites. There is little doubt that during the past two years French holdings of South African gold-mining shares have risen substantially, although early in the present year fears of a reduction in the price of gold may have induced some liquidation.

The steady decrease in loan capital through the operations of sinking-fund and maturity repayments continued during the past two years, only partially offset by occasional new issues and purchases of dollar bonds. Since 1929 the total amount of bonds held has, in fact, declined by £77 million, or by nearly one-fifth. Repayments in 1935 and 1936 amounted to £19 million, of which nearly £5 million was due to the maturing of Canadian railway loans. The Canadian National Railways have in recent years adopted the practice of repaying sterling loans partly from the proceeds of new issues floated in New York.

The trend of dividend and interest payments is shown below :—

TABLE VII.

Dividends and Interest Payments Remitted to the United Kingdom by Companies Registered Abroad.

Year.	Dividends.	Per cent. of Nominal Capital.	Interest.	Per cent. of Nominal Capital.	Total Dividends and Interest.
1929 . .	£42·0 mill.	9·6	£19·7 mill.	4·9	£61·7 mill.
1930 . .	31·7 „	8·1	19·3 „	4·9	51·0 „
1931 . .	22·7 „	6·0	18·2 „	4·7	40·9 „
1932 . .	22·1 „	6·4	17·1 „	4·6	39·2 „
1933 . .	20·5 „	5·9	14·7 „	4·2	35·2 „
1934 . .	26·0 „	7·4	13·8 „	4·1	39·8 „
1935 . .	29·7 „	8·0	13·7 „	4·2	43·4 „
1936 . .	35·1 „	9·3	13·4 „	4·1	48·5 „

Somewhat surprisingly, the above table discloses that the rate of dividend is now almost as high as in 1929. It contrasts sharply with the low rate paid by British companies in 1936 (see Table V). It is noteworthy, however, that Mining dividends, which contributed £16 million of the 1936 total of £35·1 million, were at a rate of 25 per cent. on nominal capital. The Mining section here includes practically the whole of the South African gold mines; and although working costs and taxation have risen considerably, dividends paid rose both in 1935 and 1936, and were substantially in excess of those paid in 1929.

In the Commercial and Industrial group substantial rises in dividends were recorded both in 1935 and 1936, the total for the latter year being £9·8 million, compared with £5·0 million in 1934, while the rate of dividends was 12·7 per cent. in 1936. This category includes a number of companies paying extremely large dividends, like International Nickel, Imperial Tobacco Co. of Canada, British Tobacco Co. of Australia, etc.[1] Nevertheless the fact remains that a much more impressive recovery was witnessed in this section than was the case of the corresponding companies domiciled in the U.K.

Oil dividends rose from £162,000 in 1935 to £1,483,000 in 1936, mainly through resumption of Preference dividends by the Canadian and Mexican Eagle Oil Companies, which had been suspended since 1933. Most of the other categories also showed progress in consonance with the general improvement in prices, production and world trade.

On the other hand, interest received on loan capital in 1936, at £13·4 million, is the lowest since the compilation of these estimates was begun. The decline, however, has been brought about not so much by default, although this has of course been a factor, as by progressive reduction in the amount outstanding through sinking-fund and maturity repayments. The average rate of interest paid in 1936 was 4·1 per cent., as compared with 4·9 per cent. in 1929, since which year conversion and refunding operations have slightly reduced interest rates.

The final total for 1936 of the three categories of British oversea investment in quoted securities that have been examined in the preceding pages is shown in Table VIII, and compared with the corresponding total for 1935. The amounts of capital repaid in the two years are also indicated.

[1] The high rate of dividend is to some extent due to the fact that shares of no par value have been taken at the values assigned to them in the latest balance sheets; these being generally conservatively valued.

TABLE VIII.

Nominal Amount of British Oversea Investment in Quoted Securities and Loan Capital Repaid.

	Capital.	Repayment.
	(£'000,000)	(£'000,000)
	1935.	
Foreign, Dominion and Colonial Governments and Municipalities	1,503	56·2
British Companies abroad	1,236	12·4
Foreign and Colonial Companies	698	12·5
Total	3,437	81·1
	1936.	
Foreign, Dominion and Colonial Governments and Municipalities	1,441	87·5
British Companies abroad	1,220	12·5
Foreign and Colonial Companies	703	6·5
Total	3,364	106·5

The following table shows the trend of the income obtained from Britain's oversea investment in all securities dealt in or known to the London market.

TABLE IX.

Income from Britain's Investments in Oversea Securities dealt in or known to the London Market.

(£'000,000.)

Year.	Dominion, Colonial and Foreign Governments and Municipalities.	British Companies Registered in the United Kingdom.	Companies Registered Abroad.	Total.
1929	64·7	86·0	61·7	212·4
1930	64·7	76·5	51·0	192·2
1931	65·9	48·8	40·8	155·5
1932	62·4	42·5	39·2	144·1
1933	61·1	41·9	35·3	138·3
1934	61·1	45·5	39·8	146·4
1935	60·5	51·8	43·4	155·7
1936	58·9	57·0	48·5	164·4

Despite the improvement since 1933, income received by investors in 1936 was still only 77 per cent. of that obtained in 1929, and this in a year when wholesale prices and industrial production in a number of the most important countries were already equal to, or above the 1929 levels. Part of the decline, as already explained, is due to the reduction in loan capital and to conversion operations. It is clear, however, that domestic booms by themselves, unless accompanied by a substantial recovery in international trade, are unlikely to provide the conditions necessary for a restoration of investment income to the former level. Britain's Oversea Investments are widely spread and highly diversified, and the products derived from British enterprise abroad enter into the consumption of almost every country. In consequence, the yield from these investments is intimately linked with variations in world demand and the volume of international trade. It is perhaps worth observing in this connection that shipping earnings, which directly reflect the state of international trade, have risen more impressively. The Board of Trade estimated these earnings at £95 million in 1936, a figure indicating a recovery of over 45 per cent. from the low level of 1933. However, both the volume of tonnage afloat and world trade were considerably lower in 1936 than in 1929. The recent improvement in the earnings of shipping was mainly caused by the conspicuous rise in freights, the index for which has risen from 77·5 per cent. in 1933 to 96·5 per cent. in 1936.[1]

The increase of only £26·1 million since 1933 in the income from security investments is perhaps almost as unsatisfactory as are the rather ill-balanced, and sometimes even unwelcome factors which have contributed to its development. Continued default on Foreign Bonds has prevented a recovery in receipts from Government and Municipal securities, while commercial dividends have been too weighted by Mining income. For example, of the total increase of £28·3 million in income from commercial investments between 1933 and 1936, £15·2 million is accounted for by the rise in income from Mining investments due to the special factor of the increased price of gold.

Nevertheless, despite the recent setback in security markets and commodity prices, investment income in 1937 will undoubtedly show a further marked expansion. In view of the time lag between the disbursement of dividends and the earnings on which they depend, 1937 dividends should reflect the highest level of commodity prices attained since the depression. Moreover, the past eighteen months have witnessed an encouraging upturn in the volume of international trade. In some countries noteworthy progress towards a relaxation of exchange restrictions has recently been made and means have been found, although largely through the canalisation of the channels of trade, to liquidate those commercial balances which exchange restrictions had immobilised. Despite the widespread recognition of the urgency of the problem, progress towards a reduction of tariff barriers has, however, been

[1] Figures from Chamber of Shipping of the United Kingdom.

almost negligible. And until positive steps in this direction have been taken, the extent to which world trade can continue to expand must remain limited.

So far the estimates submitted have referred exclusively to quoted securities or securities well known to the London market. Their total has been assessed at £3,364 million. But although these cover the main field of British Oversea Investments, a substantial income accrues to the United Kingdom from investments in unquoted securities, from oversea plant and factories, from branches of British companies operating chiefly at home, as well as from other miscellaneous and private commercial assets abroad. During the past few years a marked increase in investments in unquoted securities, notably in U.S.A., but also in Canada and other Dominions, has taken place. As already mentioned, it has been estimated by the United States Department of Commerce that United Kingdom holdings of American securities increased during 1935 and 1936 by $484 million (see p. 652). The same source calculates total United Kingdom investments in American common and preferred Stocks and Bonds at the end of 1936 at about $1,237 million. The rise in Canadian security markets and the rapid advance in mineral production in Canada under the stimulus of the high level of non-ferrous metal prices also led to purchases of Canadian securities not quoted in London during the year under review. This is confirmed by the estimates of the Canadian Department of Commerce, which place the amount of British long-term capital invested in Canada, exclusive of Government and railway obligations, at the end of 1936 at $1,133 million, compared with $1,076 million at the end of 1933.

The substantial changes that take place in these unquoted investments, and the circumstance that the income obtained from them constitutes a not inconsiderable part of the total income from Britain's Oversea Investments, render it desirable to secure more accurate data regarding them. Some tentative steps have already been taken with this object in view. For the sake of completeness a rough approximation of these assets and the income produced by them in the years 1935 and 1936 is appended in a footnote.[1] No high degree of accuracy is claimed

[1] Rough estimates are as follows :—

	1935.	1936.
Unquoted Investments . . .	£350 mill.	£400 mill.
Income . . .	15·9 ,,	19·6 ,,

Adding these figures to the statistically more reliable estimates for quoted securities we obtain :—

	1935.	1936.
Total U.K. Overseas Investments	£3,788 mill.	£3,764 mill.
Income . . .	171·6 ,,	184·0 ,,

for these figures. They may, however, be compared with similar estimates given in previous surveys.

Geographical Distribution of British Oversea Investments in 1936.

The total nominal amount of U.K. Capital invested in Oversea Government and Municipal loans and in all securities quoted in London of companies operating abroad is estimated to have amounted to £3,364 million at the end of 1936.

A number of important British companies operating abroad possess assets widely spread in various forms throughout the world. In consequence, a territorial classification of these assets is not readily possible. Companies of this description are therefore excluded from the geographical table given below, which deals with a nominal capital of £3,240 million.

Companies registered abroad have in the main been assigned to the countries in which they are registered.

Geographical Distribution of £3,240 *million Nominal British Capital Invested Abroad at the End of* 1936.

Dominions.	(£000,000.)
Australia	505
India and Ceylon	438
Canada and Newfoundland	443
South Africa and Rhodesia	248
New Zealand	146
British Malaya	84
British East Africa	31
British West Africa	37
Other British Territories	49
	1,981
Foreign Countries.	
Europe [1]	236
Argentine	372
Brazil	160
Chile	50
Rest of South America	85
Mexico [2] and Central America	52
United States	81
Cuba	27
Japan	53
China	41
Rest of World [3]	102
	1,259

[1] Turkey as a whole has been included in the figures for Europe.
[2] The total for Mexico would be considerably increased if capital long in default were included.
[3] Rest of World comprises mainly Dutch Malaya, Iran, Egypt, Iraq and Portuguese East Africa.

The above figures cover probably about 85 per cent. of the total of all British long-term investments.[1] The percentage covered varies considerably, however, for individual countries. Thus, for instance, unquoted and private investments are small in Australia and New Zealand, but have risen in recent years in South Africa. They are substantial in Canada, India, China and South America; and the figure of £81 million covering quoted securities in the U.S.A. probably represents less than one-third of total U.K. investments in that country.

The following table provides a re-analysis of the foregoing according to various classes of enterprise.

Distribution of £3,240 *million British-owned Securities in Various Classes of Enterprise Among the Territories of the World at the End of* 1936.

(£000,000.)

	Government and Municipal.	Railways.	Public Utilities.	Mines.	Miscellaneous.	Total.
Australia	427	2	7	20	49	505
India and Ceylon	256	84	7	12	79	438
Canada and Newfoundland	118	216	26	4	79	443
South Africa and Rhodesia	103	21	6	72	46	248
New Zealand	131	—	—	1	14	146
British Malaya	6	—	4	7	67	84
Other British Territories	59	4	6	25	23	117
Total Dominions	1,100	327	56	141	357	1,981
Europe	120	23	21	9	63	236
South America	139	362	49	7	110	667
U.S.A., Mexico and Central America	1	78	20	6	28	133
China and Japan	70	—	9	1	14	94
Other Foreign Territories	11	36	4	5	73	129
Total: Foreign Countries	341	499	103	28	288	1,259
Total: The World	1,441	826	159	169	645	3,240

Of the total of £3,240 million classified above, £1,981 million, or more than 60 per cent., is invested in the Dominions. Government and Municipal loans account for 44 per cent., Railways for

[1] Pending an accurate assessment of U.K. investments in unquoted securities, direct and private investments, etc., the figure of 85 per cent. is put forward only as a very rough approximation.

25 per cent. and Mines for 5 per cent. The bulk of the capital invested in Canadian railways carries a Dominion Government guarantee, and might therefore alternatively have been classified among Government loans. Conversely, a large amount of capital borrowed by Oversea Governments has in fact been employed in the construction of railways, notably in Australia and China. Railway investments, constituting one of the most popular forms in which British capital was invested in the past, have lost their attraction in recent years, owing to the competition of other forms of transport and increasing restrictions imposed by foreign Governments on the working of British-owned railways. However, they still comprise an important part of Britain's capital abroad.

Mining enterprise is the only category in which commercial investments abroad have appreciably increased since the depression, notably in Rhodesia, which has witnessed a development of its highly important copper mines, and in South Africa where gold-mining operations have been extended. Thus, of the total of £169 million invested in Mines, £72 million, about 43 per cent., is accounted for by South Africa and Rhodesia. There is little doubt, moreoever, that given a continuance of favourable circumstances, the enormous Rhodesian ore deposits should in due course require more capital for their development.

Among other commercial categories there has been little change; for, apart from the difficulties involved in new investment abroad, restriction schemes have in many instances reduced the scale of operations and have obviated the necessity for fresh development.

A geographical distribution of Britain's Oversea Investments was last published in the June issue of the ECONOMIC JOURNAL in 1933. It related to the year 1930, but it was necessarily of a tentative nature and, except for Government and Municipal loans, was compiled on a somewhat different basis than the present one. However, as regards Government and Municipal loans, the 1930 and 1936 figures are strictly comparable. They are accordingly appended.

Net changes between 1930 and 1936 are, in fact, insignificant. Investments in Dominion public loans have increased on balance by £17 million; those in Foreign bonds have declined by £16 million. The increase in Dominion loans would have been considerably greater but for heavy repayments in the last two years by South Africa and India. As it is, Canadian loans held in the U.K. have risen by £21 million, New Zealand loans by the same amount, and those of other British Territories by £11 million. Borrowing by Mandated Territories like Palestine and Tanganyika has, in the main, been responsible for the increase in other British Territories.

Comparison of British Capital Invested in Oversea Government and Municipal Loans at the End of 1936 *and* 1930 *Respectively.*
(£000,000.)

	1936.	1930.
Australia	427	432
India and Ceylon	256	261
Canada and Newfoundland	118	97
South Africa and Rhodesia	103	118
New Zealand	131	110
British East Africa	15	18
British West Africa	20	28
Other British Territories	30	19
Total Empire	1,100	1,083
Europe	120	120
Argentine	35	33
Brazil	74	73
Chile	20	21
Rest of America [1]	10	9
China	26	26
Japan	45	57
Rest of World	11	18
	341	357

[1] Excluding Mexican Government bonds which are almost in entire default.

Apart from a net repayment of £12 million of Japanese loans, investments in Foreign Public Loans appear to have remained practically unchanged since 1930, or at any rate the changes that have occurred have cancelled one another out. For example, both in Europe and South America repurchases by foreigners of their Government sterling bonds have been counter-balanced by the issue of new bonds, either in lieu of interest on defaulted bonds, or in exchange for frozen commercial balances. In the case of China, a reduction through sinking-fund payments has been offset by the inclusion of loans whose service has been resumed after a long interval.

New Issues and Repayments.

A study of long-term capital movements to and from the United Kingdom does not fall properly within the scope of these surveys. However, fairly complete information has been available concerning two interesting types of long-term capital movements, viz. the subscription of new money on the London market to oversea issues, and the repayment of loans and share capital through the operation of sinking funds and the incidence of maturities. Repayments comprise all cash remittances to U.K. holders, whether or not these payments have been effected from the proceeds of new issues. Similarly, U.K. subscriptions to new oversea issues include all cash subscribed, although in some instances it may have been applied to the redemption of maturing loans.

Year.	British Subscription to New Overseas Issues.	Repayment to the United Kingdom.	Difference.
1929	£96 mill.	£49 mill.	+£47 mill.
1930	98 ,,	39 ,,	+ 59 ,,
1931	41 ,,	27 ,,	+ 14 ,,
1932	37 ,,	48 ,,	− 11 ,,
1933	83 ,,	67 ,,	+ 16 ,,
1934	63 ,,	42 ,,	+ 21 ,,
1935	51 ,,	81 ,,	− 30 ,,
1936	61 ,,	107 ,,	− 46 ,,

The remarkable increase in the volume of repayments during the past two years has been due to a combination of circumstances intimately associated with world recovery. Oversea loans, particularly those to Dominion Governments, are generally repayable, at the option of the borrowing Government, at any time during a period of many years prior to the final date of maturity. During 1935 and 1936 the Gilt-edged market remained steady at a high level and similar conditions prevailed in the various Dominion markets. The low yields obtaining on these bonds consequently stimulated a large number of conversion and refunding operations which might otherwise have been spread over a number of years. At the same time, the inducement to repay was increased by the abnormal volume of sterling exchange accruing to Dominion Governments as a result of their growing export trade and increased gold production. The exchange factor also explains, in part at any rate, why the volume of new oversea issues on the London market has not risen in the same proportion. A repetition of such heavy repayments need hardly be expected during the coming years, for, on the one hand, the number of loans which may be redeemed at an early date has been considerably reduced, and, on the other hand, the bond market and the exchange situation have undoubtedly become less favourable to those envisaging refunding and repayment operations in the London market.

The heavy repayments in recent years have provided us with

a further means of paying for our growing volume of imports. But the resulting decline, not only in the total, but also in the quality of our loans abroad must be viewed with concern. Apart from some repurchases by foreign nationals of their own countries' low-priced defaulted bonds, repayments since the depression have been mainly concentrated on our best-class loans. For, it is in respect of these that contractual sinking funds have been maintained or that total repayment has been effected in anticipation of maturity. Moreover, by far the greater proportion of the new Foreign Government bonds that have made their appearance on the London market since 1930 are not the result of genuine investment, but of the enforced conversion of unpaid and unremitted interest, as well as of frozen commercial and other balances. These additions cannot, of course, be regarded as constituting a desirable increment of our foreign holdings.

It is, of course, only natural that the Dominions should have taken advantage of high prices and rising exports to reduce their external indebtedness, and in view of the heavy charge which it constitutes in times of depression, this reduction is undoubtedly a healthy development. Nevertheless, from the point of view of the United Kingdom, a progressive deterioration in our position as a long-term creditor may in the long run result in a substantial and permanent decline in income from abroad. This would make it difficult to deal with the continued rise in imports without enforcing upon us a socially disturbing and detrimental reduction in the general standard, in order to lower costs and raise the volume of visible exports. For this reason the problem of maintaining Oversea Investments merits close attention.

R. M. KINDERSLEY

BRITISH OVERSEA INVESTMENTS, 1937

Robert M. Kindersley

THE ECONOMIC JOURNAL

DECEMBER, 1938

BRITISH OVERSEA INVESTMENTS, 1937

In presenting the results of my survey of Britain's oversea investments in 1937, I wish, at the outset, to renew my thanks to the banks and issuing houses in London, and to many hundreds of companies at home and abroad, who, by their continued co-operation, now extending over a period of ten years, have made it possible for me to follow the progress of these investments during a period in which world production and trade have not only passed alternately through slump and boom, but also through economic and political changes of unprecedented rapidity. I should also like to make special acknowledgment of the additional material placed this year at my disposal by a large number of banks and companies, which has enabled me to reduce the margin of error in the section dealing with investments in companies registered abroad, and to arrive at figures for which a considerable degree of reliability may now be claimed.

Before proceeding, I wish to make clear, first, that the figures relating to capital refer (wherever possible) to nominal capital, and that detailed analysis is confined to securities quoted officially or unofficially or otherwise known to the London market; secondly, that income figures comprise interest and dividends accruing to United Kingdom investors *before* deduction of British income tax; and, lastly, that repayments represent actual sums repaid and remitted to the United Kingdom, and not the nominal value of bonds and shares redeemed. Repayment figures, moreover, include sums remitted in connection with refunding operations—*i.e.*, sums which may have been raised in whole or in part by the proceeds of fresh borrowing.[1]

No direct relation subsists between income as here specified and income from oversea investments as understood in a discussion of the United Kingdom balance of payments. For the latter purpose net profits are the important consideration; and these may be considerably greater than dividend disbursements in times of good years, or substantially less in poor. Again,

[1] Conversion operations are, however, excluded.

dividends distributed are generally based on profits which are earned many months prior to the date of dividend declarations. Finally, there are one or two classes of remittances other than dividend and interest payments associated with the operations of British companies abroad, such as head-office expenses, salaries and fees of London directors, etc., which also have an important bearing on the balance of payments, but which do not come within the scope of the present study.

In some respects the 1937 results are of special significance, since it now appears that the upward movement of the trade cycle which began in 1932 reached its peak in that year. At any rate, profits, which after 1933 rose continuously and mounted very steeply in the second half of 1936 and the early part of 1937 under the influences of world rearmament and inflated commodity prices, were severely reduced in the latter part of 1937 following the collapse in the commodity markets. Over the whole year, however, profits both of companies operating at home and abroad were, on balance, still considerably higher than in 1936, and despite the sharp decline in industrial activity in the current year, for reasons which will be given later, profits are not expected to show a corresponding shrinkage in 1938. The time-lag between a change of trend in the trade cycle and its effect on dividends and interest payments is, of course, greater than in the case of profits. Total oversea investment income rose between 1933 and 1936 from 72 to 88 per cent. of its 1930 level. In 1937 it advanced still further to 94·6 per cent. of the 1930 figure, whilst it is even possible that another small increase may be registered in 1938.

Security markets, however, more immediately sensitive to changes in cyclical activity, and indeed often preceding them, fully reflected the recession in trade and industrial activity of 1937. As a result, the flow of British investment capital to Wall Street, which during the preceding years had almost restored United Kingdom investments in the United States to the 1929 level, received a sharp check, the precipitate decline in Wall Street markets causing a moderate reversal of this movement in the latter part of 1937.[1]

Oversea Government and Municipal Bonds and Stocks.

Since the depression which began in 1929, opportunities for investment abroad have been so limited that it is very doubtful,

[1] On balance, however, ignoring fluctuations in market value, a net increase was recorded in British investments in the U.S.A. in 1937.

even in the absence of Treasury restrictions on new oversea lending, whether any substantial foreign investment would have been undertaken. This applies with even greater force to investments in oversea Government and Municipal bonds. New lending for foreign Government account has been negligible, whilst if funding bonds issued in respect of unpaid interest, commercial indebtedness, etc., were excluded from consideration, the total amount outstanding in foreign Government and Municipal bonds would show a considerable reduction. For this, sinking-fund payments (where still operating) and repurchases by foreign Governments or their nationals of bonds issued on the London market have been mainly responsible. Dominion Government loans have been floated from time to time, although in the past few years these have been mainly connected with conversion and refunding operations. Here again, however, the net increase has not been appreciable. Thus, almost the most that can be said about this category is that it has remained rather stationary in quantity. Meanwhile the status of foreign bond investments has undergone progressive deterioration, a development which has become still more pronounced owing to increasingly adverse political developments in the Far East, and the general worsening of the political situation in Europe during the past year.

Dominion, Colonial and Foreign Public Sterling Loans; Holdings in the United Kingdom and abroad (*as at December* 31, 1937).

	United Kingdom, %.	Abroad, %.
Dominion and Colonial Governments	88·7	11·3
Dominion and Colonial Municipalities	85·8	14·2
Foreign Governments	58·2	41·8
Foreign Municipalities	72·6	27·4

The percentages in the above table relate to interest paid in London, tax-deducted and tax-free respectively. Subject to qualifications mentioned in previous articles, they may be taken as indicating roughly the respective proportions of these loans held in the United Kingdom and abroad. Difficulty sometimes arises regarding sterling *tranches* issued abroad and other loans payable either in London or abroad at the option of the holder; but since sterling exchange displayed general strength almost throughout 1937, there is no reason to believe that British holders [1] cashed many coupons abroad last year.

[1] The term "British holder" is taken to mean a resident or institution domiciled in the United Kingdom.

The fact that a substantial amount of foreign Government sterling bonds (exceeding 50 per cent. for some countries) is held abroad is now a matter of common knowledge, owing to the prominence given in recent years to the re-purchases by foreign nationals of the low-priced, defaulted bonds of their own countries. It is not equally well known that over 11 per cent. of Dominion Government loans and over 14 per cent. of Dominion Municipal loans are held abroad. There is reason to believe, however, that the amounts in the possession of individual oversea holders are relatively small, and that most of the Dominion loans held abroad are owned by public bodies in the Dominions either in the shape of sinking funds for internal loans or as invested reserve funds. The proportion of 11·3 per cent. of Dominion Government loans held abroad compares with 9·9 per cent. at the end of 1936, from which it may be inferred that a part of the increase in the London balances of the Dominions last year was invested in these loans. A growing reluctance on the part of some Dominion authorities to make use of oversea capital markets is observable, due partly to a natural anxiety to avoid a further enlargement of an already burdensome external debt, partly to increased savings enabling them to make better use of their own capital markets. Should this tendency continue, the accumulation of sinking funds, whether invested on account of internal loans or against sterling loans, may gradually cause a further rise in the proportion of sterling loans held overseas.

TABLE I.

British Nominal Capital Invested in Oversea Government and Municipal Loans : Income Remitted and Sums Repaid.

(£000.)

	Nominal Capital.		Income.		Repayment.	
	1937.	1936.	1937.	1936.	1937.	1936.
Dominion and Colonial Governments	1,002,100	1,016,000	38,972	42,344	19,597	74,711
Dominion and Colonial Municipalities	86,500	84,200	3,903	4,020	1,279	2,438
Foreign Governments	308,300	312,600	10,842	11,685	5,613	8,850
Foreign Municipalities	28,300	28,400	872	868	1,245	1,547
	1,425,200	1,441,200	54,589	58,917	27,734	87,546

The most surprising fact disclosed by the above figures is the fall of £4·3 million in income in 1937, compared with the previous year. As shown in the next table, this is the largest decline registered in this category of investments since these statistics were first compiled; total income at £54·6 million is actually £11·3 million below the corresponding figure for 1931. It seems perhaps even more remarkable that the highest figure should have been reached in 1931, a year of deepening depression; and the lowest in 1937, in which year recovery reached its peak. The explanation of the former is that while 1931 income fully reflected the substantial new investments in foreign loans of the preceding years, defaults arising from trade depression which first occurred in 1930 did not exert their full impact on interest payments until 1932. The comparatively severe decline that has taken place since 1935, and more especially in 1937, has been due to a number of causes. Two, the gradual increase in the proportion of Dominion sterling loans held by Dominion public authorities and the re-purchases by foreign nationals of their own low-priced foreign bonds, have already been mentioned above. Of much greater influence in the downward movement have been (*a*) the heavy repayments of recent years and (*b*) the appreciable reduction in the average rate of interest resulting from refunding and conversion operations. For example, during the period 1928–32 inclusive, repayments of Government and Municipal loans (sinking-fund payments and loans redeemed) averaged £24·3 million per annum; whereas in the period 1933–37 repayments averaged £48·8 million per annum. The 1936 figure of £87·5 million constituted a record. Similarly, conversion operations stimulated by the régime of low interest rates assumed large dimensions in 1935 and 1936.

TABLE II.

British Investments in Empire and Foreign Loans and Income Received.

(£000,000.)

	Empire Loans.			Foreign Loans.			Total.		
	Nominal Amount.	Income.	Rate, %.	Nominal Amount.	Income.	Rate, %.	Nominal Amount.	Income.	Rate, %.
1928	1,036	43·8	4·2	364	18·1	5·0	1,400	61·9	4·4
1929	1,061	46·4	4·4	351	18·2	5·2	1,412	64·6	4·6
1930	1,080	46·9	4·3	357	17·8	5·0	1,437	64·7	4·5
1931	1,104	48·4	4·4	337	17·5	5·2	1,441	65·9	4·6
1932	1,109	48·9	4·4	323	13·5	4·2	1,432	62·4	4·4
1933	1,147	49·1	4·3	333	12·0	3·6	1,480	61·1	4·1
1934	1,163	49·1	4·2	336	12·0	3·6	1,499	61·1	4·1
1935	1,157	48·2	4·2	346	12·3	3·6	1,503	60·5	4·0
1936	1,100	46·4	4·2	341	12·5	3·7	1,441	58·9	4·1
1937	1,089	42·9	3·9	336	11·7	3·5	1,425	54·6	3·8

Thus in 1937 the full effect of these operations on interest payments was felt, although in that year repayments and refunding operations were actually on a considerably smaller scale than in the two preceding years. Between the end of 1934 and the end of 1937 repayments reduced United Kingdom investments in Empire loans by £74 million, whilst refunding and conversion operations lowered the average rate of interest paid on these loans from 4·2 to 3·9 per cent. The combined effect of these factors is seen in a decline of £6·2 million in the income from Empire loans during the period. By contrast, income from foreign loans remained almost stationary,[1] although there was a fall of £0·8 million between 1936 and 1937, due principally to a reduction in payments on Greek loans.

A comparison of the sterling loans of the principal Dominion Governments outstanding at the end of 1930 with the position at the end of 1937 shows clearly the progress made in the conversion and consolidation of Dominion external debt.

TABLE III.

Number of Dominion Government Sterling Loans Outstanding at the End of 1930 *and* 1937.

	4½% or under.	Over 4½%.	Total.
		1930.	
Australia	35	34	69
Canada and Newfoundland	39	5	44
India	5	4	9
South Africa	11	4	15
New Zealand	8	6	14
	98	53	151
		1937.	
Australia	34	10	44
Canada and Newfoundland	32	4	36
India	8	1	9
South Africa	8	3	11
New Zealand	10	5	15
	92	23	115

Thus, although the total capital invested in Empire loans has, on balance, remained almost unchanged, the number of Dominion loans outstanding has been reduced from 151 to 115. Australia has made the greatest progress in its conversion operations; the

[1] Suggesting that by the end of 1934 the area of default had virtually reached its maximum.

number of its loans bearing interest in excess of 4½ per cent. is only ten, as compared with thirty-four in 1930. India has now only one loan carrying interest of more than 4½ per cent. as compared with four in 1930. No similar operations were possible with Canadian loans, since these were mostly issued in pre-war years during periods of low interest rates.

There are few loans maturing in the next two years in respect of which refunding or conversion operations will be possible. In fact, there has already been a sharp reduction in Dominion repayments in 1937—at £19·6 million compared with £74·7 million in 1936. The 1937 figure is, indeed, the lowest, with the exception of 1934, recorded in the past six years. Early in the new decade, however, numerous loans bearing comparatively high rates of interest will fall within the scope of such operations if market conditions are favourable. It may be anticipated that at any rate one powerful factor making for further conversions will continue to remain in operation for many years. For good or ill, the present régime of low interest rates, brought about largely by general abandonment of the gold standard and consequent relaxation of limitations imposed by the size of Central Bank gold reserves, but maintained instead by a gradually improving monetary technique, seems destined to continue for some time. Hence, although income from oversea Government and Municipal loans may be expected to remain stable at its present low level during the next few years, a further appreciable reduction somewhat later would not be at all surprising. This possibility is of importance, since both the stability and size of income from public loans have hitherto acted as a cushion, and reduced the fluctuations to which oversea income as a whole would otherwise have been subject. Should the former be permanently reduced below £50 million per annum, variations in total investment income may in consequence increase considerably, and a further important influence be added to the many factors which have in recent years intensified cyclical fluctuations in trade and production. The significance of this possibility is further enhanced by a noticeable trend in new investment away from fixed interest securities in favour of equities.[1]

Although total British investments in overseas Government and Municipal bonds show little net change between 1930 and 1937 (see Table II), a geographical analysis discloses appreciable changes in the nominal amounts invested in some territories and particularly in the Dominions.

[1] A discussion of recent trends in new investment follows later.

TABLE IV.

Comparison of British Capital Invested in Oversea Government and Municipal Loans[1] *at the End of* 1937 *and* 1930 *respectively.*

(£000,000.)

	1937.	1930.
Australia	434	432
India and Ceylon	251	261
Canada and Newfoundland	115	97
South Africa and Rhodesia	106	118
New Zealand	124	110
Other British Territories	59	65
Total Empire	1,089	1,083
Europe	120	120
Argentine	34	33
Brazil	72	73
Chile	20	21
China	26	26
Japan	43	57
Rest of World	21	27
Total Foreign Countries	336	357

Investments[2] in Canada and Newfoundland have risen by £18 million, and those in New Zealand by £14 million. On the other hand, repayments have reduced investments in South Africa and Rhodesia by £12 million, India and Ceylon by £10 million, and those of other British territories by £6 million. At first sight the smallness of the changes in respect of foreign countries seems rather surprising. Except for Japan, where repayments have diminished British loans by £14 million, and for some reductions in unimportant areas, there has been virtually no decline in foreign bonds held in the United Kingdom. The explanation is that during the past few years large new lines of foreign bonds have appeared on the market which were issued either in lieu of unpaid interest, frozen financial claims or in settlement of commercial arrears. The volume of such bonds outstanding at the end of 1937 is shown below.

Funding Bonds Outstanding at the End of 1937 *Issued since* 1930 *in Respect of Unpaid Interest, Commercial and Financial Arrears, etc.*

(£000.)

Argentina	13,526
Brazil	10,842
Colombia	143
Costa Rica	224
Germany	7,727
Total	32,462

[1] Excluding Russian, Mexican and other bonds in default long before 1930.

[2] *I.e.*, in this category.

United Kingdom holdings of these bonds now constitute approximately 7 per cent. of the total invested in foreign Government and Municipal bonds. Under the terms of the Anglo-German Payments Agreement of 1934, German funding bonds increased at the rate of about £2 million per annum. The revised Payments Agreement arrived at this year, however, provides for the cessation of these issues and for partial resumption of interest payments on German loans other than Dawes and Young which have been paid throughout. If we except Brazil, no further issues of funding bonds by foreign debtor countries seems likely for the time being. On the other hand, final settlement of questions relating to defaulted bonds still appears distant, and some further conversion of unpaid interest into long-term debt may have to be accepted.[1]

We now proceed to an examination of our commercial investments abroad, dealing with :

(*a*) Companies registered in the United Kingdom.
(*b*) Companies registered overseas.

The separate treatment resorted to in these articles is based on the fact that, despite a number of borderline cases, the differences between the two types of companies as regards ownership of capital, managerial control, taxation,[2] etc., are on the whole fairly distinct. Changes in the proportion of the securities held in the United Kingdom are determined by totally different factors for these two types of companies. For example, it is common knowledge that the high rate of British income tax is an effective deterrent to foreign purchases of the shares of British registered companies. As a result, foreign participation in these companies is seldom more than fractional. During the early part of 1937, however, it is probable that buying of British securities for foreign account was rather above normal, the combination of a rising London stock market with high dividend possibilities proving in many instances a sufficient counter-attraction to Continental quarters anxious to place funds abroad. Nevertheless, virtually the only cases where foreign holdings are conspicuously high occur when, for special reasons, substantial or controlling interests are

[1] An arrangement entered into with the Rumanian Government provided for the issue of Funding Bonds in respect of certain portions of interest, but so far no bonds have been issued.

[2] The country of registration is not necessarily the only criterion in connection with liability to British income tax. Under recent legislation the country from which decisions governing the company's policy emanate may be the determining factor.

acquired outright by foreign companies or Governments. On the other hand, the extent of British participation in foreign companies in the control of which the British investor can have no voice is governed entirely by his expectations either of comparatively high dividends over a long period or of rapid appreciation of capital. In recent years the hazards, political and other, have, except in the case of Dominion companies, made genuine long-term investment too risky a venture, so that most purchases of foreign shares have been of a purely speculative nature.

British Companies Operating Abroad.

The table set out below relates to the securities of British registered companies whose fixed assets are exclusively or mainly abroad. The overseas assets of the limited number of important companies conducting their principal business in the United Kingdom are covered separately later in an approximate estimate of private and unquoted investments.

TABLE V.

United Kingdom Capital Invested in British Companies Operating Abroad: Dividends and Interest Received and Capital Repaid.

Share Capital (£000).

	1937.		1936.	
	Nominal Amount.	Dividends.	Nominal Amount.	Dividends.
Dominion and Colonial Rails	1,500	3	1,500	3
Indian Rails	20,400	1,559	20,600	1,507
U.S. Rails	800	24	800	16
Foreign Rails	222,300	2,681	226,700	1,208
Banks	31,500	2,464	27,100	2,009
Breweries	6,300	850	6,100	665
Canals and Docks	600	22	600	12
Commercial and Industrial *	64,700	3,797	57,800	2,372
Electric Light and Power	9,900	719	11,600	775
Financial Land and Investment	85,300	4,160	87,700	2,572
Gas	7,400	552	7,800	634
Iron, Coal and Steel	2,500	12	3,600	66
Mines	116,600	13,416	108,200	9,532
Nitrates	1,300	—	2,600	—
Oil	106,300	16,068	106,800	13,795
Rubber	81,900	6,532	84,600	3,782
Shipping	7,800	342	7,200	189
Tea and Coffee	40,500	2,572	40,400	2,213
Telegraphs and Telephones	24,900	1,651	24,200	1,502
Tramways	10,400	276	10,600	308
Waterworks	4,100	236	3,900	203
	847,000	57,936	840,400	43,363

* See next footnote.

TABLE V (*continued*).

Loan Capital (£000).

	1937.			1936.		
	Nominal Amount.	Interest.	Repayment.	Nominal Amount.	Interest.	Repayment.
Dominion and Colonial Rails	28,600	1,256	11,608	27,500	1,381	149
Indian Rails and Annuities	66,600	2,810	2,867	63,100	2,695	3,663
U.S. Rails	800	32	—	800	32	—
Foreign Rails	175,400	5,802	272	177,800	5,465	1,410
Breweries	900	47	2	900	47	8
Canals and Docks	3,200	195	21	2,800	185	27
Commercial and Industrial *	10,600	388	1,528	17,100	598	1,650
Electric Light and Power	3,600	212	995	4,700	250	439
Financial Land and Investment	28,400	1,157	1,803	34,600	1,372	3,558
Gas	2,000	93	96	2,000	94	24
Iron, Coal and Steel	500	20	620	1,300	72	21
Mines	4,000	341	3,670	8,200	423	340
Nitrates	1,700	62	22	1,400	—	—
Oil	1,600	38	22	1,800	41	84
Rubber	4,600	266	371	4,700	223	270
Shipping	3,900	123	264	3,800	137	359
Tea and Coffee	2,600	115	100	2,600	93	168
Telegraphs and Telephones	4,400	189	7	4,200	176	202
Tramways and Omnibus	17,500	267	130	17,800	252	63
Waterworks	2,100	88	108	2,200	97	90
	363,000	13,501	24,506	379,300	13,633	12,525

* See next footnote.

As explained above, in the absence of new issues, no great changes can be expected in this section of United Kingdom investments. There was, however, a rise of £8·4 million in capital invested in mines between 1936 and 1937, due mainly to new flotations. It may, in fact, be affirmed that mining companies have really been the only concerns to attract fresh capital on an important scale since the depression. This has, of course, been brought about first of all by the rise in the price of gold following abandonment of the gold standard; whilst further investments have been encouraged, notably in South Africa, British West Africa and Australia, by the maintenance of that price. In more recent years the rise in base metal prices has induced a flow of capital to Rhodesia, where copper-mining operations have expanded considerably, whilst substantial sums of money have been raised to finance the development of lead mines in Yugoslavia and Australia. Since 1930, United Kingdom capital invested in the shares of British registered mining companies has risen from £66·0 million to £116·6 million, an advance of 77 per cent. Apart from railways, these investments now constitute the largest single category, exceeding even oil investments. Changes in other sections between 1936 and 1937 were not of great significance, and, where noticeable, were due mainly to company re-organisation and to a certain amount of re-classification.[1] A decline in United Kingdom holdings of the shares of rubber companies, however, is worthy of note, confirming as it does the rather unusual interest taken by Continental quarters in this market last year.

Repayments of loan capital in this category, at £24·5 million in 1937, were nearly double those of the previous year. Practically half this amount, however—viz. £11 6 million in the case of Dominion Rails—represented a refunding operation in connection with Rhodesia and Mashonaland railway companies. Loan capital of mining companies now outstanding is only £4 million, both the Roan Antelope and Mufulira Copper Companies having redeemed their debentures in 1937.

Turning now to income, it will be observed that dividend payments advanced from £43·4 million in 1936 to £57·9 million in 1937, the largest rise recorded since the compilation of these statistics. The average rate of dividend rose from 5·2 to 6·8 per cent., the latter figure being only slightly lower than that for 1930. The rapid expansion in dividend payments in 1937 was in accordance with expectations, since such dividends reflected profits earned during a period which covered the second half of 1936 and the early part of 1937, in which industrial activity, foreign trade and commodity prices attained their highest levels in the recent recovery. The largest rises were the following: mines £3·9 million, rubber £2·7 million and oil £2·3 million. Base-metal companies, and more particularly those engaged in copper and tin production, provided the main increase in the mining section, although receipts from gold mines were also larger, owing to the greater capital invested compared with the preceding year. Rubber dividends, at £6·5 million, were actually back to the level of 1929, a development which was not at all surprising, since the profits producing these dividends in 1937 were earned during a period in which rubber quotas represented full productive capacity and rubber prices rose to high levels,

[1] An increase of £6·9 million in share capital and a decline of £6·5 million in loan capital in the case of Commercial and Industrial represent a purely technical change for statistical purposes.

touching a peak of 1*s.* 2*d.* per lb. The general improvement in economic conditions throughout the world resulted in appreciable rises in most of the other sections. The advance of £1·5 million in dividends from foreign Railways deserves special mention, not only because of the improved earnings of the railway companies, but also because it reflected the greatly strengthened exchange position of some of the South American countries, making possible increased remittances and the liquidation of arrears of preference dividends.

A table showing the trend since 1929 of United Kingdom investments in British companies operating abroad and of receipts by way of dividends and interest is given below:

TABLE VI.

British Companies Operating Abroad. Capital Outstanding; Dividends and Interest Received.

(£000,000.)

	Share Capital.			Loan Capital.			Total Dividends and Interest.
	Nominal Amount.	Dividends.	% of Capital.	Nominal Amount.	Interest.	% of Capital.	
1929	802	67·7	8·4	385	18·3	4·7	86·0
1930	815	59·0	7·1	390	17·5	4·5	76·5
1931	813	33·3	4·1	397	15·5	3·9	48·8
1932	816	29·0	3·6	389	13·5	3·5	42·5
1933	823	29·5	3·6	387	12·5	3·2	42·0
1934	840	32·4	3·9	388	13·1	3·4	45·5
1935	849	37·8	4·5	388	14·0	3·6	51·8
1936	840	43·4	5·2	379	13·6	3·6	57·0
1937	847	57·9	6·8	363	13·5	3·7	71·4

The table shows that although dividends have doubled since 1932, interest payments have remained unchanged. In 1932 interest disbursements amounted to 32 per cent. of the total remittances in respect of British companies operating abroad; in 1937 they accounted for only 19 per cent. Although continuing default on numerous industrial bonds is still partly responsible for the absence of recovery in these payments, conversion operations have, as in the case of Government bonds also, been an important influence in recent years in reducing the average rate of interest. Taken in conjunction with the circumstance that since 1932 share capital investments have expanded by £31 million and loan capital investments have declined by £26 million, this trend supports the view that the comparatively stable income derived from investments in fixed interest-bearing securities may become a gradually declining proportion of total income from oversea investments (see p. 615).

In view of the probability that the year 1937 will appear as that in which industrial activity and world trade reached a peak, a review of the outlook for income from British companies operating abroad for the year 1938 is not without interest. Industrial securities declined severely in the second half of 1937, and the fall continued in 1938, although not quite so steeply. Commodity prices followed a similar course, and since the larger part of the dividends from these investments is derived from commodity trade, the effect on profits will have been pronounced, particularly as, in addition to the fall in prices, output was more than halved in the cases of rubber and tea, and substantially reduced in that of copper, by the various international bodies administering restriction schemes. Nevertheless there are a number of reasons for believing that income accruing to investors will not be less than in 1937. Dividends in 1938 will still partly reflect the high earnings of early 1937. Secondly, the fall in profits in 1937–38 was probably not as pronounced as the decline in prices and industrial activity. For example, it is common knowledge that commodity producers took advantage of the facilities afforded by the futures markets to sell their output, both actual and potential, at the inflated prices ruling in early 1937. They were thus able to maintain their profits despite the deterioration in the industrial outlook. This is confirmed by a study of the quarterly earnings of some of the base-metal-producing companies, which disclose only a small decline in profits for the first half of 1938. Incidentally it may be observed that although the futures market thus enables raw-material producers to prolong their period of high earnings during the beginning of a trade recession, the effect on the consumers of these materials is the reverse, since they find that they have engaged themselves to hold or acquire large stocks at unprofitable prices and with diminishing orders. This, together with a tendency for business trends to be discounted earlier than in former times, is an important factor contributing to the rapidity of modern price fluctuations. A third reason for the view that there will not be a pronounced fall in dividend payments in 1938, is to be found in the highly conservative policy adopted by most companies during the recovery. The increasing proportion of annual profits appropriated to reserve since 1934 has placed the majority of leading companies in a strong financial position, and thus ensured a continuation of reasonable dividend payments.

These considerations suggest that the investor in British companies operating abroad may have continued to benefit in 1938 from the high level of industrial activity in 1936 and 1937. The unfavourable effects of a sharp decline in profits cannot, however, be postponed indefinitely. Failing a substantial recovery from the present recession, a considerable drop in receipts may be anticipated in 1939 and 1940.

Companies Registered Abroad.

The securities of companies registered abroad, but dealt in on the London market, vary considerably, from those in which United Kingdom holdings are insignificant to others in which they are substantial. In some instances virtually the whole of the capital is held in the United Kingdom, the companies in question being registered abroad largely for convenience. A number of the securities analysed below enjoy an international market which often displays great activity on occasions when, for one reason or another, substantial movements of funds take place between financial centres. American, Canadian, South African and certain Dutch and Swedish securities form the basis of this international market, purchases and sales being mainly of a speculative or of a short-term nature, frequently as a hedge against currency risks. South African gold-mining shares are, of course, especially popular on the Continent in periods of currency uncertainties. Dominion securities other than South African and Canadian are not held to any important extent by foreigners. There are, however, appreciable United Kingdom holdings of securities of Australian, New Zealand and Indian companies.

The international market in many of the securities of companies registered abroad principally explains the substantial changes shown from year to year in the United Kingdom holdings Indeed, these securities have constituted in recent years the only variable element in the otherwise static total of Britain's oversea security investments.

The flow of British capital into international and American securities during 1937 was governed largely by stock-market prospects. The rapid rise in Wall Street in the early part of that year undoubtedly stimulated British participation in the American market, as was evidenced by increased dealing in U.S. securities in the London market and large orders placed directly in New York. Published estimates of the increase in British holdings of American securities, however, are generally excessive, since

TABLE VII.

United Kingdom Capital invested in Companies Registered Abroad : Dividends and Interest Received and Capital Repaid.

Share Capital (£000).

	1937.		1936.	
	Nominal Amount.	Dividends.	Nominal Amount.	Dividends.
Dominion and Colonial Rails	66,900	404	67,000	148
U.S. Rails	44,300	343	38,000	415
Foreign Rails	9,700	72	8,700	75
Banks	25,000	1,348	27,800	1,440
Canals and Docks	700	1,838	700	2,440
Commercial and Industrial	77,400	10,653	77,600	9,850
Electric Light and Power	22,100	1,623	19,000	1,520
Financial Land and Investment	12,100	354	14,600	356
Iron, Coal and Steel	13,500	614	12,400	370
Mines	77,500	17,785	63,000	16,012
Oil	16,000	1,400	18,000	1,483
Shipping	5,400	271	7,200	304
Telegraphs and Telephones	5,800	370	6,300	373
Tramways	10,600	326	10,600	105
Breweries, Gas, Waterworks	3,400	364	6,100	231
	390,400	37,765	377,000	35,122

Loan Capital (£000).

	1937.			1936.		
	Nominal Amount.	Interest.	Repayment.	Nominal Amount.	Interest.	Repayment.
Dominion and Colonial Rails	153,200	6,222	964	148,000	6,415	800
U.S. Rails	7,500	344	—	10,800	535	—
Foreign Rails	33,700	1,082	296	37,100	1,210	492
Banks	15,800	569	255	16,500	522	953
Breweries	200	11	15	200	5	—
Canals and Docks	2,700	25	—	3,200	27	—
Commercial and Industrial	32,200	1,214	1,308	25,600	1,197	962
Electric Light and Power	31,300	1,354	1,929	32,600	1,404	1,674
Gas	400	22	—	400	21	—
Financial Land and Investment	17,600	670	286	14,400	600	100
Iron, Coal and Steel	6,800	322	1,012	7,900	375	530
Mines	5,100	297	2,458	5,800	390	175
Nitrates	7,700	197	304	8,000	146	220
Oil	100	7	121	—	—	485
Shipping	1,600	96	182	1,900	105	51
Telegraphs and Telephones	3,600	81	84	4,300	114	67
Tramways and Omnibus	8,400	337	71	9,000	352	17
	327,900	12,850	9,285	325,700	13,418	6,526

there is reason to believe that some of the purchases made in London were in reality for account of U.S. investors. During the second half of 1937 the sharp fall in Wall Street led to a reversal of the movement, and it seems probable that by the end of the year the net increase in British holdings was only of small dimensions. Investments in U.S. railway shares, however, increased from £38 million to £44·3 million, this figure comparing with £17·3 million in 1933.[1] Rises of £3·1 million in electric light and power and £1·1 million in iron, coal and steel shares were similarly due to enlarged holdings in Canadian and American securities. The case of the United States Steel Corporation is worth special mention, since the price of this company's stock is often taken as a guide to the market's estimate of the industrial situation in the United States. United Kingdom ownership of this Company's shares rose from £5·4 million at the end of 1936 to £7·3 million at the end of 1937. The most conspicuous rise took place in mines, and amounted to £14·5 million. This resulted partly from the formation of new companies for the exploitation of goldfields and the raising of fresh capital for the development of existing mines, and partly from an increase in British participation in the shares of established mining companies. United Kingdom share capital invested in mining companies registered abroad has now risen by over 36 per cent. since 1932.[2]

Despite larger repayments in 1937, amounting to £9·3 million, compared with £6·5 million in 1936, investments in loan capital at the end of 1937 were slightly higher than in the preceding year, such repayments as occurred having been financed out of the proceeds of new loans.

As regards the income involved, it will be observed that the rise in dividends between 1936 and 1937, at £2·6 million, was small compared with the increase in the case of British companies operating abroad. Mining dividends, indeed, rose by £1·8 million, but this was due to larger capital. This category includes all the South African gold-mining companies, whose dividend distributions were on the whole slightly lower than in 1936, but excludes the copper mines, which paid handsome dividends in 1937 and were mainly responsible for the large addition to income obtained from British registered mining companies. Rising costs in the U.S.A. following social legislation adversely affected net revenues

[1] We may remind the reader that these are nominal, not market values.

[2] Declines in other sections—viz. £2·8 million in banks and £2·0 million in oil—reflect partly a diminution in British holdings, but principally company reorganisation and a continuation of the process of writing-down of capital which has been going on for some years.

of American railways and public utilities. This movement is reflected in a decline in dividends from U.S. rails, despite a rise in British investments in these companies in 1937. Oil dividends of companies registered abroad are largely dominated by the earnings of Canadian and Mexican Eagle Oil Companies. During 1936 these companies paid off all arrears of preference dividends with distributions of 17½ per cent. on preference capital outstanding, and in 1937, therefore, no payment beyond the regular dividend of 7 per cent. was made.

The reduction of £0·6 million in dividends received from the Suez Canal Company is also of interest. It will be recalled in this connection that traffic through the canal had reached a high level in 1935–36 as a result of the Italian invasion of Abyssinia.

Income from loan capital showed only slight changes from the preceding year, the net decline of £0·6 million being due principally to weaker Canadian and American dollar exchange rates, which had the effect of lowering the value of sterling remittances.

The following table summarises the results since 1929 for companies registered abroad.

TABLE VIII.

Companies Registered Abroad : Nominal Amounts of British Capital Outstanding : Dividends and Interest Received.

(£000,000.)

	Share Capital.			Loan Capital.			Total Dividends and Interest.
	Nominal Amount.	Divi-dends.	% of Capital.	Nominal Amount.	In-terest.	% of Capital.	
1929	436	42·0	9·6	403	19·7	4·9	61·7
1930	391	31·7	8·1	391	19·3	4·9	51·0
1931	376	22·7	6·0	384	18·2	4·7	40·9
1932	344	22·1	6·4	375	17·1	4·6	39·2
1933	345	20·5	5·9	350	14·7	4·2	35·2
1934	352	26·0	7·4	335	13·8	4·1	39·8
1935	370	29·7	8·0	328	13·7	4·2	43·4
1936	377	35·1	9·3	326	13·4	4·1	48·5
1937	390	37·8	9·7	328	12·8	3·9	50·6

As in the case of British registered companies, the table reflects the remarkable contrast between the trends in share capital and dividends on the one hand and loan capital and interest on the other. Since 1933 dividends have increased by nearly 85 per cent. to a point not far short of the 1929 figures. In fact, the average rate of dividend was actually higher in 1937 than in 1929;

but this was, in many instances, more apparent than real, owing to drastic writing down of capital and more conservative valuation of no par shares of American and Canadian companies. Interest payments on debentures, however, which suffered a sharp fall between 1930 and 1933 through default, have continued to decline steadily despite recovery in economic conditions. The gradual diminution in recent years has been caused partly by repayments, which have reduced the amount of British owned loan capital, and partly by refunding and conversion operations, lowering the average rate of interest from 4·6 per cent. in 1932 to 3·9 per cent. in 1937.

Reversing a decline of £92 million in United Kingdom holdings of share capital of companies registered abroad between 1929 and 1932, due mainly to winding up of companies and writing down of capital, share capital has once more risen, principally owing to investment in gold mines and larger purchases of American securities. Between 1932 and 1937 share holdings increased by £46 million, whilst loan capital fell by £47 million. Thus, as with British registered companies, a strong trend appears to be in operation as a result of which not only is income from debentures being gradually reduced in absolute amount through a lowering of the average rate of interest, but the proportion of its contribution to total income is also being reduced by a growing preponderance of equity investments.

The following tables summarise the results for quoted securities.

Table IX.

Nominal Amount of British Oversea Investments in Quoted Securities: Interest and Dividends Received and Loan Capital Repaid.

(£000,000.)

	Capital.	Income.	Repayment.
		1936.	
Oversea Governments and Municipalities	1,441	58·9	87·5
British Companies abroad	1,220	57·0	12·5
Foreign and Colonial Companies	703	48·5	6·5
	3,364	164·4	106·5
		1937.	
Oversea Governments and Municipalities	1,425	54·6	27·7
British Companies abroad	1,210	71·4	24·5
Foreign and Colonial Companies	718	50·6	9·3
	3,353	176·6	61·5

TABLE X.

Income from Britain's Oversea Investments in Securities quoted on or known to the London Market, 1929–37.

(£000,000.)

	Oversea Governments and Municipalities.	British Companies Registered in the U.K.	Companies Registered Abroad.	Total.
1929	64·7	86·0	61·7	212·4
1930	64·7	76·5	51·0	192·2
1931	65·9	48·8	40·8	155·5
1932	62·4	42·5	39·2	144·1
1933	61·1	41·9	35·3	138·3
1934	61·1	45·5	39·8	146·4
1935	60·5	51·8	43·4	155·7
1936	58·9	57·0	48·5	164·4
1937	54·6	71·4	50·6	176·6

Detailed comment has already been made in the preceding pages on the trend of income from investments in each of the three categories: Oversea Governments and Municipalities, British registered companies operating abroad and companies registered abroad. Total income from these sources by way of dividends and interest payments amounted to £176·6 million in 1937, compared with the low level of £138·3 million in 1933 and the high figure of £212·4 million in 1929. Thus, slightly more than half the ground lost between 1929 and 1932 had been regained by 1937.

We have seen that in the absence of a comprehensive settlement of the problem of defaulted bonds, no recovery in interest on Government and Municipal loans can be anticipated, whilst, on the other hand, there is reason to believe that conversion operations may result in a further reduction in later years. Earnings of British companies operating abroad, derived mainly from the production and sale of commodities like oil, base metals, rubber and tea, are so dependent on the course of commodity prices that a severe setback of dividends in 1939 and 1940 seems scarcely avoidable, in view of the precipitate fall in prices since early 1937. The earnings of foreign companies, although somewhat less directly affected by prices, will be adversely influenced by the shrinkage in world trade, by the sharp fall in the profits of American concerns and by special circumstances such as the expropriation of the Mexican Eagle Oil Company. Remittance of dividends and interest in general will again be impeded by the exchange position of South American countries, which, after a considerable improvement, has again undergone unfortunate deterioration.

If, however, the optimistic forecast of trade revival, based upon indications of incipient recovery in the United States, is borne out, the impending decline in income from oversea investments may well be of considerably smaller dimensions than the fall sustained between 1929 and 1933.

Private and Unquoted Investments.

The results presented above have dealt exclusively with securities quoted or unofficially dealt in on the London market. These, of course, constitute the main block of Britain's oversea investments. There are, however, other important miscellaneous investments abroad, less readily susceptible to accurate or even approximate measurement. For example, in addition to the considerable amount of unquoted securities, there are the numerous subsidiaries, branches and establishments abroad of one kind or another, of companies whose main assets are situated at home; the large number of small private companies or partnerships engaged in manufacturing or trading abroad; estates and property abroad owned by private individuals residing in the United Kingdom, etc.

Investments in securities quoted *abroad*, but not in the United Kingdom, are undertaken principally by investment trusts and insurance companies, the latter in deference to the laws of some foreign countries which require a certain proportion of all insurance funds to be deposited as a reserve against contingent and maturing liabilities. During the last few years, however, interest in foreign securities, notably American, has considerably broadened, although, as already remarked, transactions have been largely of a speculative nature. Judging from the information available regarding the holding of American securities quoted in London, there seems little doubt that the amount of British capital invested in non-quoted American securities increased slightly on balance during 1937.

Again, a number of important domestic concerns have, during the past few years, expanded their sphere of operations by opening up branches or factories abroad. This form of new investment, although of considerable significance, has not yet attained dimensions equivalent to those of quoted securities. Moreover, against this must be set the substantial losses suffered in 1937 by British property as a result of the hostilities in Spain and China. Damage to property in the Shanghai area in particular was very heavy, although most of this loss was probably borne by British nationals permanently resident in China.

Private and unquoted investments held in the United Kingdom were approximately estimated at £400 million at the end of 1936. Changes in these investments during 1937, where ascertained, do not indicate that there was any appreciable modification of the total. This estimate which, as has been repeatedly observed, is necessarily of a temporary nature, is left unaltered for 1937. For the sake of completeness, the approximate income produced by these investments is appended in a footnote.[1]

New Issues, Repayment and Trends in Oversea Investments.

A full survey of long-term capital movement is not possible in the absence of a comprehensive inquiry into the subject. Information is, however, available concerning two important items—viz. the subscription of money on the London market to new oversea issues, and the repayment of capital through the operation of sinking funds and maturities; whilst statistics of the past ten years indicate a trend towards a significant qualitative change in Britain's oversea investments which is worth detailed discussion.

New Issues and Repayments.[2]

(£000,000.)

	British Subscription to New Issues.	Repayments to the U.K.	Difference.
1929	96	49	+47
1930	98	39	+59
1931	41	27	+14
1932	37	48	−11
1933	83	67	+16
1934	63	42	+21
1935	51	81	−30
1936	61	107	−46
1937	60	61	− 1

United Kingdom subscriptions to new issues in 1937 still remained at the comparatively low level of £60 million. If refunding

[1]

	1937.	1936.
Unquoted investments	£400 million	£400 million
Income	21·1 ,,	19·6 ,,

Adding these figures to the statistically more reliable estimates for quoted securities we obtain :—

Total U.K. oversea investments . .	£3,753 million	£3,764 million
,, income	197·7 ,,	184·0 ,,

[2] Repayments comprise all cash remittances to United Kingdom holders, whether or not these payments were effected from the proceeds of new issues. Similarly, United Kingdom subscriptions to new oversea issues include all cash subscribed, although in some instances the proceeds may have been applied to the redemption of maturing loans.

operations are excluded, the figure is further reduced to approximately £29 million, of which by far the larger portion was for industrial requirements, chiefly for the extension of gold and base-metal-mining operations. Repayments in 1937, at £61 million, were still conspicuously high, although not as large as the record figure of 1936. In post-war years up to 1931 new issues were almost always substantially in excess of repayments, whilst from 1929 to 1931 the difference in favour of new issues was £120 million. In the period 1932–37, however, repayments exceeded new issues by £51 million. Moreover, as far as can be judged, political and economic difficulties connected with the flotation of oversea loans on the London market may persist for some time, so that even if repayments fall to a lower level, there seems little prospect of any appreciable increment in Britain's oversea investments by way of new foreign loans.

For some years it has been necessary to allude in these paragraphs to a dismal record of default by an increasing number of debtor countries on their obligations towards United Kingdom investors. With few exceptions, however, as it is fair to recall, failure to meet these obligations has been due to adverse economic circumstances or actual distress; and investors on the whole have recognised this situation and patiently refrained temporarily from pressing for the fulfilment of their legitimate claims.

The high-handed action taken for purely political reasons by the Mexican Government against the Mexican Eagle Oil Co. Ltd. is in a totally different category. It would be difficult to find in our past financial records an example of so deliberate a violation of the acknowledged rights of foreign investors, without any attempt at its justification on economic grounds, and in spite of the large contribution to the economic well-being of the country made by this company.

Reliable information goes to show that the total assets of the Mexican Eagle Co. expropriated by the Mexican Government, so far without payment, amount to £60 million. In view of the magnitude of this sum and the methods employed by the Mexican Government, it would seem that the time has now arrived for our Authorities to concern themselves seriously with the problems which these circumstances present. The most pressing would appear to be :—

1. The decline in the standards of financial morality in some foreign countries.

2. The danger of the Mexican example stimulating similar expropriations in other countries.

3. The effect of dishonest defaults and expropriations on our oversea capital and income and therefore on our balance of payments.

4. The deterrent effect of such experiences on fresh investment in foreign countries.

Attention has already been called to the steady reduction in income from our loan investments abroad and the gradual decline in the proportion of these investments to our total stake abroad. The following table shows the extent to which these trends have already affected the position of our security investments.

TABLE XI.

Security Investments: Share and Loan Capital and Income from these Investments in 1937 *and* 1930.

	1937.	1930.
A. *Capital:*		
Share capital	£1,237 million	£1,206 million
Loan capital	2,116 ,,	2,218 ,,
Total	£3,353 ,,	£3,424 ,,
Ratio share to loan capital	58·5%	54·4%
B. *Income:*		
Share income	£95·7 million	£90·7 million
Loan income	80·9 ,,	101·5 ,,
Total	£176·6 ,,	£192·2 ,,
Ratio share to loan income	118·3%	89·4%

These figures, referring to years in which world trade, production and industrial earnings were approximately of similar dimensions, show that income from loan investments has been reduced not only by default and conversion to lower rates of interest, but also as a result of the trend away from fixed interest into variable dividend securities; this trend operating on the one hand by a reduction in loan capital through sinking funds and maturity payments, and on the other by the predominantly equity character of our new investments.

It is not proposed to discuss whether in the long run the tendency to replace loan by equity investments is or is not a healthy development. But the question may well be of fundamental importance, since it is common knowledge that the difficulties experienced by many countries in meeting contractual obligations in times of depression have greatly obstructed the task of making adjustments rendered imperative by trade recession and price fluctuations. It is clear, however, that individual investors, at any rate, have reacted markedly to political and economic conditions prevailing in recent years. Continued default on foreign bonds, weakened respect for the sanctity of contract, the possibility of expropriation or warfare, have undermined the security offered to the bondholder to such an extent that he has now to envisage risks that were formerly borne by shareholders. It is not, therefore, surprising that the investor should be displaying a radical change in his attitude towards bond investments. This change, furthermore, is not merely confined to a trend away from fixed interest to variable dividend securities, but is also apparent in the character of new equity investments. For the same conditions that have rendered the position of the bondholders precarious have virtually ruled out any other form of genuine long-term investment. Consequently, new investment abroad is now of a kind on which returns, while conditions are temporarily favourable, are so large that ultimate loss of capital may be contemplated with equanimity; or else of a short-term character in respect of which income is of minor importance as compared with the expectation of a rapid appreciation of capital. In the former category may be included a good deal of the recent investment by British companies through the setting up of branches and establishments abroad under the shelter of foreign tariffs, as well as some of the investment in gold mines and base-metal shares. In the latter category may be placed the main bulk of the recent investment in American equities and the money that has flowed into some of the less assured gold-mining enterprises in other regions. Thus, paradoxically enough, the very conditions that have made investment abroad in general a perilous venture, have caused investors to prefer those forms which in previous years would have been regarded as the most speculative.

These circumstances not only foreshadow the possibility of undesirably wide fluctuations in income from foreign investments about a level whose long-term tendency is downwards, but also a disturbing instability both in the total and in the structure of the investments themselves. It is well to recall that a more-than-negligible proportion of the reduced total of foreign loan investments already consists of bonds which—at any rate as regards their origin—must be considered unsatisfactory if not unpromising, such as issues tendered in lieu of unpaid interest, in settlement of commercial and financial arrears or, more generally, embodying the enforced conversion of immediate into long-term claims. Furthermore, the purchases of foreign equities by British investors are not, as used to be generally the case, made with the intention of holding them as long-term investments; and do not, therefore, provide the same steady support as formerly for our export trade. Their principal merit is to be found in the ease with which they can be realised. It is, no doubt, convenient to keep a fairly large stock of foreign assets which, being readily saleable, can in times of national emergency provide a reservoir of foreign exchange. But the continued decline in those British oversea securities held for more permanent investment, from which a steady and substantial income has accrued over many years, is nevertheless a matter for serious concern; for it is this income, before all else, that has enabled the United Kingdom to secure a volume of imports greatly in excess of exports, and thus to maintain a standard of living higher than that of almost any other European country.

The prospect is rendered worse by the possibility that political and economic pressure from abroad accompanied by rising costs at home may continue to restrict the outlet for exports; while requirements for intensified rearmament may make it difficult to bring about a corresponding reduction in imports. Should present trends continue, as seems likely, this situation can be met adequately only by a consciously directed national effort aiming at an improvement in efficiency of management and a substantial increase in output per head of the population. In any event, the strain on our social and financial structure must be severe; without a collective effort a considerable lowering in the general standard seems inevitable. The problem has indeed become as urgent as it is grave.

R. M. KINDERSLEY

BRITISH OVERSEAS INVESTMENTS, 1938

Robert M. Kindersley

BRITISH OVERSEAS INVESTMENTS, 1938

THE present article is the eleventh of a series which has appeared in the ECONOMIC JOURNAL containing the results of my annual surveys of British Investments abroad.

This year, owing to the outbreak of hostilities and the long period of international tension prior to it, it has not been possible to furnish much detailed comment on the trends shown by the figures, and the tables are consequently presented here with a minimum of text. Nevertheless the statistical data on this occasion have been extended to include figures relating to certain other receipts in the United Kingdom derived, as in the case of dividends and interest payments, from the gross earnings of British companies abroad, but which are deducted from such earnings in published estimates of net profits. The collection of this material has been made possible by the further collaboration of some hundreds of British companies, and I wish to take this opportunity to express once again my thanks for the continued assistance given to me by these companies, as well as by the London banks and issuing houses.

My study of Britain's oversea investments has now extended over a period during which slump has been followed by boom and again by recession. Income from these investments has undergone a corresponding fluctuation, sinking to a low level in 1933 and rising again to a peak in 1937. The recession which began in the latter part of 1937 and continued throughout most of 1938 naturally impaired the ability of some Foreign Governments to meet commitments in respect of external debt, and halted the upward trend in earnings of commercial enterprise abroad. This development is, of course, reflected in the results for the year now principally under consideration, although neither fully nor uniformly throughout every category of investments. For, owing to forward commitments entered into by producers of leading commodities, the fall in profits was not as pronounced in some instances as the decline in prices or industrial output, while the high earnings in 1937 helped to maintain dividend payments in 1938. Requirements for rearmament also tended to alleviate recession, particularly in the base-metal-producing industries. An increase in the price of gold helped to stabilise gold-mining profits and dividends. Nevertheless, despite these mitigating factors, income from oversea investments fell by 6½ per cent., returning to the level of 1936.

The flow of capital, both on long and short term, was influenced by the recession which continued in the United States in the first half of 1938 and by the deterioration in the international situation. It will be recalled that the year 1936 and the early part of 1937 witnessed a considerable expansion in United Kingdom holdings of American securities. This trend, however, was reversed with the severe decline in American security markets, but the repatriation of capital slackened as soon as these markets began to recover. Moreover, political apprehensions resulted in a considerable influx of short-term funds to New York and a corresponding substantial export of gold to the United States. On balance the capital that found its way to New York consisted mainly of money deposited or invested on short term. Actual returns from United States companies show, in fact, that the amount of British holdings of American securities was slightly lower at the end of 1938 than at the end of 1937.[1]

We now pass to the detailed results.

Oversea Government and Municipal Stocks and Bonds.

As explained in previous articles, loans of oversea Governments and municipalities issued in London are by no means wholly held in the United Kingdom. Firstly, because tranches of sterling issues have been frequently placed abroad; secondly, because foreign Governments and nationals have found it convenient to repurchase bonds issued in London; and, thirdly, because sterling loans are convenient for the investment of resources accumulated in sinking funds by Dominion Governments and public bodies.

A rough measure of the proportions of oversea public sterling loans held in the United Kingdom and abroad is given in the following table.

Dominion, Colonial and Foreign Sterling Loans; Interest Payments in London to United Kingdom and Oversea Residents in 1938.

	United Kingdom, %.	Abroad, %.
Dominion and Colonial Governments	88·0	12·0
Dominion and Colonial Municipalities	85·9	14·1
Foreign Governments	57·5	42·5
Foreign Municipalities	71·6	28·4

[1] Owing to the rise in security prices, however, British holdings were worth substantially more at the end of 1938.

The percentage of foreign Government bonds held abroad has been very high for many years. The low quotations of many defaulted bonds during the depression of 1930–33 and of German loans in a later period stimulated their repurchase by foreign Governments and their nationals. More recently, however, the issue of large amounts of funding bonds to United Kingdom holders in lieu of unpaid interest has tended to raise slightly the proportion of foreign sterling bonds held in the United Kingdom.

TABLE I.

British Nominal Capital Invested in Oversea Government and Municipal Loans ; Income Remitted and Sums Repaid.

(£000.)

	Nominal Capital.		Income.		Repayment.	
	1938.	1937.	1938.	1937.	1938.	1937.
Dominion and Colonial Governments	993,200	1,002,100	38,754	38,972	14,165	19,597
Dominion and Colonial Municipalities	87,600	86,500	3,951	3,903	1,255	1,279
Foreign Governments	292,700	308,300	8,861	10,842	4,942	5,613
Foreign Municipalities	24,900	28,300	757	872	1,001	1,245
	1,398,400	1,425,200	52,323	54,589	21,363	27,734

Since 1934 (see next table) the amount of Empire loans outstanding has progressively fallen, due to the fact that some of the Dominions and Colonies, notably South Africa, have been able to meet their capital requirements from their own resources, and consequently to redeem sterling debt. There was a further drop of £8·9 million in 1938, largely owing to the redemption of Australian loans. The corresponding refunding issue was not fully paid up until early 1939, and is consequently not entirely accounted for in the above figures.

Foreign Government and municipal bonds held in the United Kingdom declined by a further £19·0 million, principally due to repayments on maturity and the operations of sinking funds. In view of the low prices of foreign bonds, the sums spent in their purchase for sinking fund are, of course, considerably smaller than the reduction effected in the face value of these bonds.

Income obtained from the investments specified in Table I showed little change in 1938, except for another striking fall of £2·0 million in the amount received from foreign Government bonds. For this, the complete default on Brazilian loans in that year was chiefly responsible. As will be observed from the next table, interest remitted on all foreign loans in 1938 was barely more than half the amount obtained in 1929. Empire loans also yielded 8·0 per cent. less income than in 1929, but whereas this was a normal development resulting from conversion to lower rates of interest, the reduction in foreign bond income is attributable entirely to default.

Table II.

British Investment in Empire and Foreign Public Loans and Income Received.

(£000,000.)

	Empire Loans.			Foreign Loans.			Total.		
	Nominal Amount.	Income.	Rate. %.	Nominal Amount.	Income.	Rate, %.	Nominal Amount.	Income.	Rate, %.
1929	1,061	46·4	4·4	351	18·2	5·2	1,412	64·6	4·6
1930	1,080	46·9	4·3	357	17·8	5·0	1,437	64·7	4·5
1931	1,104	48·4	4·4	337	17·5	5·2	1,441	65·9	4·6
1932	1,109	48·9	4·4	323	13·5	4·2	1,432	62·4	4·4
1933	1,147	49·1	4·3	333	12·0	3·6	1,480	61·1	4·1
1934	1,163	49·1	4·2	336	12·0	3·6	1,499	61·1	4·1
1935	1,157	48·2	4·2	346	12·3	3·6	1,503	60·5	4·0
1936	1,100	46·4	4·2	341	12·5	3·7	1,441	58·9	4·1
1937	1,089	42·9	3·9	336	11·7	3·5	1,425	54·6	3·8
1938	1,081	42·7	3·9	317	9·6	3·0	1,398	52·3	3·7

Thus, although the average rate of interest *payable* on foreign bonds is considerably higher than on Empire loans, the average rate actually paid was only 3·0 per cent. in 1938, compared with 3·9 per cent. on Empire loans. Of a total of £52·3 million of income received from these investments in 1938, 81·6 per cent. came from the Empire, as compared with 71·8 per cent. in 1929.

A more detailed geographical classification of the above is given in the next table.

In view of the restrictions on foreign lending and the natural reluctance of investors to subscribe to foreign loans, it is at first sight somewhat surprising that the total of these investments declined by only £42 million between 1930 and 1938. This reduction has, of course, occurred mainly in foreign bonds: £13 million in the case of European countries and £15 million in the case of Japan. Owing, however, to the inability of numerous foreign Governments to remit funds, many loans have not been redeemed at maturity, drawn bonds have not been paid, while finally the issue of funding bonds, of which some £35 million are still outstanding, has helped to maintain the nominal total of our investments in purely foreign bonds at the still considerable, if somewhat fictitious level of £317 million.

Table III.

Comparison of British Capital Invested in Oversea Government and Municipal Loans at the end of 1938 *and* 1930.

(£000,000.)

	1938.	1930.
Australia	430	432
India and Ceylon	245	261
Canada and Newfoundland	116	97
South Africa and Rhodesia	109	118
New Zealand	122	110
Other British Territories	59	65
Total Empire	1,081	1,083
Europe	107	120
Argentine	35	33
Brazil	72	73
Chile	19	21
China	25	26
Japan	42	57
Rest of World	17	27
Total of Foreign Countries	317	357
Grand Total	1,398	1,440

Commercial Investment.

Commercial investment abroad has followed three main lines, although in recent years, owing to the inter-relation of political and economic problems, a fourth and important line of development has emerged.

The oldest and principal type of commercial investment undertaken is found in the operation of purely British companies abroad, of which the leading examples are British railway companies in the Argentine and other parts of South America, rubber- and tea-plantation companies in Malay and India, base-metal-mining companies in Rhodesia and Nigeria and oil companies in Iran, Iraq, Venezuela, Trinidad and elsewhere. In these enterprises the management and control are entirely British, the capital required has been raised wholly in the United Kingdom, and there is consequently little foreign interest in the shares of these companies, particularly since dividends are subject to high British income tax. Occasionally the entire property of a company is sold outright, as in the case of a railway recently disposed of to the Argentine Government for cash and Government securities; or sometimes foreign interests may obtain control by the purchase of a preponderant block of shares. Otherwise there is, as a rule, no market for the shares of British companies except in the United Kingdom.

Investment in securities of purely foreign or Dominion companies is of less ancient origin, although in the nineteenth century and up to the outbreak of the last war a large amount of British money had been invested in the bonds of American railway companies. British investments in the United States are still substantial, though equities, not bonds, now form the larger part of these investments. British investments in Canadian Railways have always been considerable, and in late years electrical power and mining companies have become an important field of investment. More recently South Africa has jumped into prominence with the further expansion in her gold-mining industry, which has attracted more funds from the United Kingdom. Except in the case of South African gold-mining shares, share issues in general are not made on the London market, British participation taking the form of direct purchases of these securities on oversea markets. Where, however, such issues are made, the securities in question are nearly always payable in sterling only, or at sight rate of exchange in London; and dividends are subject to British income tax.

Owing to the growth of tariffs and other forms of economic nationalism since 1929, the obstacles to trade have become so numerous that many British companies have found it more convenient to establish subsidiaries or branches in foreign countries for the manufacture of finished products than to export the finished products themselves. The companies have as a rule raised the necessary funds for this purpose from their own resources. This form of investment, although far short of similar American foreign investment of this type, has attained important dimensions. Unfortunately, owing to its nature, no reliable estimate of the actual amount involved can be made.

More recently, and particularly during the few months preceding the outbreak of present hostilities, the British Government has afforded considerable assistance to the export trade through facilities granted by the Export Credits Guarantee Department; and credits have been granted not only in respect of actual exports, but also for the execution of works abroad, the materials for which were to be obtained from this country. Most of the credits arranged are, of course, of a short-term nature, but some, as for example in the case of Russia and Turkey, cover long periods.

British Companies Operating Abroad.

The table below shows the nominal value of United Kingdom capital invested in British companies operating abroad, dividend and interest payments received and repayments of loan capital.[1] The companies dealt with in the table are those whose fixed assets are exclusively or mainly abroad. The oversea assets of a number of companies conducting their principal business in the United Kingdom are not shown here, but are embraced in an approximate estimate of private and unquoted investments given later.

The total amount of British capital in this type of investment is £1,208 million, *i.e.* £190 million less than that invested in oversea Government and municipal bonds. Over 70 per cent. is in the form of ordinary or preference shares and the balance in debenture stocks or bonds. No great change is observable from year to year in the aggregate of these investments, a moderate expansion in oil

TABLE IV.

United Kingdom Capital Invested in British Companies Operating Abroad; Dividends and Interest Received and Capital Repaid.

Share Capital.

(£000.)

	1938.		1937.	
	Nominal Amount.	Dividends.	Nominal Amount.	Dividends.
Dominion and Colonial Rails	1,400	18	1,500	3
Indian Rails	20,100	1,501	20,400	1,559
U.S. Rails	800	—	800	24
Foreign Rails	221,600	642	222,300	2,681
Banks	31,600	2,591	31,500	2,464
Breweries	6,300	779	6,300	850
Canals and Docks	600	30	600	22
Commercial and Industrial	64,800	3,783	64,700	3,797
Electric Light and Power	9,800	705	9,900	719
Financial Land and Investment	83,400	3,605	85,300	4,160
Gas	7,400	527	7,400	552
Iron, Coal and Steel	2,300	9	2,500	12
Mines	118,600	13,302	116,600	13,416
Nitrates	1,500	—	1,300	—
Oil	115,900	18,383	106,300	16,068
Rubber	80,700	5,972	81,900	6,532
Shipping	7,300	397	7,800	342
Tea and Coffee	40,700	3,115	40,500	2,572
Telegraphs and Telephones	25,300	1,680	24,900	1,651
Tramways	10,400	228	10,400	276
Waterworks	4,100	220	4,100	236
	854,600	57,487	847,000	57,936

[1] Share capital repayments are also included, but these as a rule do not amount to an important sum.

TABLE IV—(*continued*)

Loan Capital.

(£000.)

	1938.			1937.		
	Nominal Amount.	Interest.	Repayment.	Nominal Amount.	Interest.	Repayment.
Dominion and Colonial Rails	28,200	1,151	306	28,600	1,256	11,608
Indian Railways and Annuities	60,500	2,690	5,679	66,600	2,810	2,867
U.S. Rails	800	32	—	800	32	—
Foreign Rails	174,900	5,130	286	175,400	5,802	272
Breweries	900	46	54	900	47	2
Canals and Docks	3,700	226	272	3,200	195	21
Commercial and Industrial	10,700	350	804	10,600	388	1,528
Electric Light and Power	3,700	163	550	3,600	212	995
Financial Land and Investment	27,000	955	1,021	28,400	1,157	1,803
Gas	2,000	92	79	2,000	93	96
Iron, Coal and Steel	400	—	70	500	20	620
Mines	4,300	214	214	4,000	341	3,670
Nitrates	1,600	63	24	1,700	62	22
Oil	1,500	37	22	1,600	38	22
Rubber	4,500	256	161	4,600	266	371
Shipping	3,100	116	846	3,900	123	264
Tea and Coffee	2,500	79	49	2,600	115	100
Telegraphs and Telephones	4,000	175	454	4,400	189	7
Tramways	17,500	223	41	17,500	267	130
Waterworks	2,100	87	17	2,100	88	108
	353,900	12,085	10,949[1]	363,000	13,501	24,506

[1] Including share capital repayment, the total of which amounts to £577,000.

and mining shares in 1938 being counterbalanced by a reduction through the operation of sinking funds or redemption at maturity. British-owned oil concerns have experienced a period of comparative prosperity, and the expansion of capital in this section has been as much due to bonus issues as to new issues for cash.

Dividend payments, except in the case of Foreign Rails, were on the whole unaffected by the fall in commodity prices and the adverse trade developments in 1937–38. This was partly because the earlier years had enabled companies to strengthen their financial position sufficiently to ensure the continuation of steady dividends, and partly because forward contracts facilitated the sale of output at fairly high prices. Oil dividends, in fact, rose by £2·3 million and payments by tea-producing companies by £0·5 million. Remittances from the Argentine by British-owned railways, however, fell sharply, owing mainly to a poor wheat crop and the lower wheat prices prevailing. This is reflected in a fall in receipts from Foreign Railways of £2·0 million dividends and £0·7 million interest.

The next table shows the trend of receipts by way of dividend and interest from British companies operating abroad since 1929.

TABLE V.

British Companies Operating Abroad; Capital Outstanding; Dividends and Interest Received.

(£000,000.)

	Share Capital.			Loan Capital.			Total Dividends and Interest
	Nominal Amount.	Divi-dend.	% of Capital.	Nominal Amount.	In-terest.	% of Capital.	
1929	802	67·7	8·4	385	18·3	4·7	86·0
1930	815	59·0	7·1	390	17·5	4·5	76·5
1931	813	33·3	4·1	397	15·5	3·9	48·8
1932	816	29·0	3·6	389	13·5	3·5	42·5
1933	823	29·5	3·6	387	12·5	3·2	42·0
1934	840	32·4	3·9	388	13·1	3·4	45·5
1935	849	37·8	4·5	388	14·0	3·6	51·8
1936	840	43·4	5·2	379	13·6	3·6	57·0
1937	847	57·9	6·8	363	13·5	3·7	71·4
1938	855	57·5	6·7	354	12·1	3·4	69·6

Receipts at £69·6 million in 1938 were 19 per cent. lower than the high figure recorded in 1929 and 65·7 per cent. higher than the lowest level reached in 1933.

Other Receipts Associated with the Operations of British Companies Abroad.

In addition to dividends and interest, miscellaneous funds from earnings are remitted to the United Kingdom by British companies abroad. Of these the principal items are receipts to meet:

(*a*) expenses of head offices maintained in the United Kingdom;

(*b*) the remuneration and other fees of directors resident in the United Kingdom;

(*c*) payments in connection with the purchase of stores or materials in the United Kingdom and their shipment to the oversea countries where British companies conduct their enterprise;

(*d*) interest on bank loans or overdrafts payable to British banks in London;

(*e*) payments to the dependents in the United Kingdom of the staff of companies employed abroad.

Although these receipts do not constitute part of the income accruing to the investor, they must, of course, be taken into account in an estimate of the United Kingdom's balance of payments. Stores shipped abroad are, of course, included in the ordinary figures of export trade, while receipts in respect of freights, insurance and salaries of oversea staffs remitted to London are no doubt embraced in the annual official estimate of the balance of payments. The information collected on this subject has, therefore, been restricted, as far as possible, to office expenses, directors' remuneration and payment in respect of bank loans and overdrafts. No great precision is claimed for the estimates given below, since in some instances it has not been possible to separate clearly the various items under the above headings. Nevertheless the data obtained have been sufficient to make possible a fairly reliable estimate.

TABLE VI.

Head Office and Other Expenses of British Companies Operating Abroad in 1938.

(£000.)

	Total Share and Loan Capital.	Expenses.	% of Capital.
Dominion and Colonial Rails	29,600	64	0·2
Indian Rails	80,600	92	0·1
U.S. Rails	1,600	—	—
Foreign Rails	396,500	609	0·2
Banks	31,600	—	—
Breweries	7,200	88	1·2
Canals and Docks	4,300	15	0·4
Commercial and Industrial	75,500	475	0·6
Electric Light and Power	13,500	93	0·7
Financial Land and Investment	110,400	1,032	0·9
Gas	9,400	129	1·4
Iron, Coal and Steel	2,700	4	0·1
Mines	122,900	1,584	1·3
Nitrates	3,100	2	0·1
Oil	117,400	617	0·5
Rubber	85,200	408	0·5
Shipping	10,400	171	1·6
Tea and Coffee	43,200	199	0·4
Telegraphs and Telephones	29,300	113	0·4
Tramways	27,900	152	0·5
Waterworks	6,200	48	0·8
	1,208,500	5,895	0·5

A number of companies are able to meet their expenditure under this heading from revenue derived from the United Kingdom. This applies with particular force to Dominion and Colonial banks, as well as to numerous important industrial companies. Nevertheless sums remitted to the United Kingdom in connection with such expenses aggregated £5·9 million in 1938, or just under

½ per cent. of the total share and loan capital held in the United Kingdom. This compares with £69·6 million, or 5·7 per cent., in the case of receipts by way of dividends and interest.

Sums expended in maintaining head offices bear little relation to the capitalisation of the companies concerned. A moderate-sized but profitable concern may allocate as large an amount for this purpose as a heavily capitalised company. For example, the London office expenses of British railways in foreign countries with an aggregate share and loan capital of £396 million amount to only £609,000, or 0·2 per cent. of the capital employed. These companies are comparatively few in number, with extremely large capitals. In recent years, moreover, they have experienced much difficulty in remitting funds to London. On the other hand, mining companies with a total capital of £123 million have spent £1,584,000 on London offices, or 1·3 per cent. of their capital. There are several hundreds of these companies, and although some have not even reached the producing stage, a considerable number of medium-sized concerns have been progressively expanding, and their high earnings have enabled them to provide for home expenditure with some liberality.

Mines, financial and land companies (also largely concerned with the exploitation of mining property) and oil concerns contribute between them 55 per cent. of the total United Kingdom expenditure of British companies operating abroad.

Companies Registered Abroad.

The amount of British capital involved in our third category of investments is substantially smaller than that held in the form of oversea Government and municipal bonds, or in securities of British companies abroad. Its importance, however, is considerable, since a large part of these securities can be sold in foreign markets to provide free exchange. Not all the securities concerned are purely foreign or Dominion in character. Some are sterling bonds of foreign or Dominion companies, such as the sterling bonds of the Canadian National Railways or French railway companies. These are not as a rule saleable in oversea markets, although in some cases indirect use of them might be made to acquire free exchange. American, Canadian, Dutch and Swedish securities are the most readily realisable abroad, many of them enjoying an international market. South African gold-mining shares are in a separate category, since their market is in the main limited to London, Paris and Johannesburg, although some interest in them is occasionally shown in the United States.

Purchases and sales between British and foreign holders of these securities have at times attained considerable dimensions, since not only have they provided opportunities for quick speculative profits on rising markets, but they have also been a very convenient means of hedging against exchange risks. It is therefore natural that considerable changes should be recorded from year to year in the amounts of British capital in this category of investment.

The next table covers all the securities of companies registered abroad that are quoted on, unofficially dealt in or otherwise known to the London market.[1]

The Dow Jones index of United States industrial securities fell from 128·97 at the commencement of 1938 to a low point for the year of 98·95 on March 31. Investors in this country consequently tended to lighten their commitments, both in these and in international securities. In the latter part of 1938, however, the United States market made an appreciable recovery, the Dow Jones index rising to 154·76 at the end of December. This development, together with the heightening of political tension in Europe and a moderate depreciation of sterling, caused investors to renew their interest in the American market. Nevertheless on balance holdings were in most cases reduced on the year, although the market value of these diminished holdings was probably higher. U.S. Railway investments were lower by £4·1 million, Miscellaneous Commercial and Industrial investments by £4·9 million and investments in Iron and Steel by £2·3 million. South African gold mines, however, still continued to attract capital, Mining investments showing a rise of £1·0 million.

Loan capital was also noticeably reduced by repayments of a cash value of £6·9 million, and a fall in holdings of Canadian National Railway bonds.

The severity of the recession in the United States caused a considerable shrinkage in her imports from raw-material-producing countries. In view also of the lower level of commodity prices prevailing, the general fall in dividends and interest payments derived from these investments is not surprising. The total reduction in dividends was £6·2 million, representing a decline of over 16 per cent., the principal falls being Commercial and

[1] Sufficient information, however, has been obtained to make possible a reliable estimate of all securities of United States railways (whether quoted or not) held in this country.

Table VII.

United Kingdom Capital Invested in Companies Registered Abroad; Dividends and Interest Received and Capital Repaid.

Share Capital.

(£000.)

	1938.		1937.	
	Nominal Amount.	Dividends.	Nominal Amount.	Dividends.
Dominion and Colonial Rails	65,200	670	66,900	404
U.S. Rails	40,200	140	44,300	343
Foreign Rails	10,700	47	9,700	72
Banks	22,700	1,211	25,000	1,348
Canals and Docks	700	1,751	700	1,838
Commercial and Industrial	72,500	7,943	77,400	10,653
Electric Light and Power	21,500	1,376	22,100	1,623
Financial Land and Investment	13,400	529	12,100	354
Iron, Coal and Steel	11,200	244	13,500	614
Mines	78,500	15,573	77,500	17,785
Oil	15,200	1,022	16,000	1,400
Shipping	4,500	234	5,400	271
Telegraphs and Telephones	5,800	380	5,800	370
Tramways	10,600	348	10,600	326
Breweries, Gas, Waterworks	3,400	131	3,400	364
	376,100	31,599	390,400	37,765

Table VII—(*continued*)

Loan Capital.

(£000.)

	1938.			1937.		
	Nominal Amount.	Interest.	Repayment.	Nominal Amount.	Interest.	Repayment.
Dominion and Colonial Rails	146,400	5,824	1,234	153,200	6,222	964
U.S. Rails	7,400	287	—	7,500	344	—
Foreign Rails	33,900	585	278	33,700	1,082	296
Banks	15,500	540	184	15,800	569	255
Breweries	200	12	35	200	11	15
Canals and Docks	2,700	16	—	2,700	25	—
Commercial and Industrial	27,700	1,232	2,716	32,200	1,214	1,308
Electric Light and Power	29,500	1,237	414	31,300	1,354	1,929
Gas	400	22	—	400	22	—
Financial Land and Investment	16,600	588	617	17,600	670	286
Iron, Coal and Steel	4,400	188	360	6,800	322	1,012
Mines	4,700	253	166	5,100	297	2,458
Nitrates	7,400	184	198	7,700	197	304
Oil	—	7	294	100	7	121
Shipping	1,300	79	217	1,600	96	182
Telegraphs and Telephones	3,800	105	133	3,600	81	84
Tramways and Omnibus	7,200	289	40	8,400	337	71
	309,100	11,448	6,886	327,900	12,850	9,285

Industrial £2·7 million and Mines £2·2 million. The average price of gold was actually 1*s*. 9*d*. per oz. higher in 1938 than in the previous year, but owing to the large share of mining profits taken by the South African Government in the form of taxation and the judicious policy followed by mining companies in working a lower grade of ore, dividends distributed were somewhat reduced. Reduced earnings in the United States and in the Dominions are mainly responsible for small declines in other sections. The following table summarises the trend in receipts of dividends and interest from investments in companies registered abroad.

TABLE VIII.

Companies Registered Abroad ; Nominal Amount of British Capital Outstanding ; Dividends and Interest Received.

(£000,000.)

	Share Capital.			Loan Capital.			Total Dividends and Interest.
	Nominal Amount.	Divi-dends.	% of Capital.	Nominal Amount.	In-terest.	% of Capital.	
1929	436	42·0	9·6	403	19·7	4·9	61·7
1930	391	31·7	8·1	391	19·3	4·9	51·0
1931	376	22·7	6·0	384	18·2	4·7	40·9
1932	344	22·1	6·4	375	17·1	4·6	39·2
1933	345	20·5	5·9	350	14·7	4·2	35·2
1934	352	26·0	7·4	335	13·8	4·1	39·8
1935	370	29·7	8·0	328	13·7	4·2	43·4
1936	377	35·1	9·3	326	13·4	4·1	48·5
1937	390	37·8	9·7	328	12·8	3·9	50·6
1938	376	31·6	8·4	309	11·4	3·7	43·0

The marked upward trend in receipts that began in 1934 was abruptly checked in 1938, the total falling to slightly below the level of 1935, though it was still considerably higher than the lowest level attained in 1933. The average rate of dividends paid was 8·4 per cent. compared with 5·9 per cent. in 1933 and 9·6 per cent. in 1929.

Interest payments, in contrast to receipts by way of dividends, have steadily declined, even in the comparatively good years from 1934 to 1937. In the earlier years they were adversely affected by numerous defaults on industrial bonds, while in the later years refunding and conversion operations also lowered the average rate of interest payable. Moreover, owing to the poor treatment meted out to the bondholders in recent years, issues of foreign bonds on the London market have been negligible. Consequently redemption of loans at maturity and the reduction of other loans outstanding through the operation of sinking funds have gradually caused a decline since 1929 of nearly £100 million, or 25 per cent. in the total amount of loan investments outstanding. This factor has, of course, also contributed substantially to reduce bond income.

The next tables summarise the results for all the quoted securities analysed in the present article.

TABLE IX.

Nominal Amount of British Oversea Investments in Quoted Securities ; Interest and Dividends Received and Loan Capital Repaid.

(£000,000.)

	Capital.	Income.	Repayment.
		1937.	
Oversea Governments and Municipalities.	1,425	54·6	27·7
British Companies abroad	1,210	71·4	24·5
Foreign and Dominion Companies	718	50·6	9·3
	3,353	176·6	61·5
		1938.	
Oversea Governments and Municipalities.	1,398	52·3	21·4
British Companies abroad	1,209	69·6	10·9
Foreign and Dominion Companies	685	43·0	6·9
	3,292	164·9	39·2

Income from Britain's Oversea Investments in Securities quoted on or known to the London Market, 1929–38.[1]

(£000,000.)

	Oversea Governments and Municipalities.	British Companies Registered in the United Kingdom.	Companies Registered Abroad.	Total.
1929	64·7	86·0	61·7	212·4
1930	64·7	76·5	51·0	192·2
1931	65·9	48·8	40·8	155·5
1932	62·4	42·5	39·2	144·1
1933	61·1	41·9	35·3	138·3
1934	61·1	45·5	39·8	146·4
1935	60·5	51·8	43·4	155·7
1936	58·9	57·0	48·5	164·4
1937	54·6	71·4	50·6	176·6
1938	52·3	69·6	43·0	164·9

Total income obtained from these investments in 1938 was £164·9 million, £11·7 million lower than in the previous year,

[1] With the exception of U.S. railways, for which an estimate has been obtained covering both quoted and unquoted securities.

and only slightly above that in 1936. Thus the immediate effect of the recession was to cancel out the improvement that was recorded between 1936 and 1937, a result which is on the whole in accordance with expectations.

There is, of course, considerable investment abroad in securities not quoted in London (held in the main by insurance companies and investment trusts). Subsidiaries and branches of companies whose main assets are situated at home; a large number of small private companies or partnerships engaged in manufacturing or trading abroad; and estates and property abroad owned by private individuals residing in the United Kingdom together constitute the other category of our unquoted investments. Because of their nature, these investments are not capable of exact measurements, but some indication is available of the trend in United Kingdom holdings of non-quoted securities of purely foreign companies. For example, it has been established that a moderate decline took place in 1938 in the amount of railway and other quoted American securities held in London, and it is believed that this also occurred in the case of non-quoted securities. On the other hand, the market value of these securities was undoubtedly higher at the end of 1938 than at the close of 1937, while the less conspicuous form of investment through the medium of subsidiaries and branches of British companies was still continued in 1938.

Private and unquoted investments held by persons resident in the United Kingdom were estimated approximately at £400 million at the end of 1937. On balance these may have slightly declined during the year under consideration, but in any event the fall, if any, was clearly not of considerable dimensions. The estimate is, therefore, left unaltered for 1938, with the proviso that no precision is claimed for this figure. For the sake of completeness, the approximate income produced by these investments is appended in a footnote.[1]

[1]

	Capital.	Income.
1937.		
Quoted Investments	£3,353 million	£176·6 million
Unquoted Investments	400 ,,	21·1 ,,
Total	£3,753 ,,	£197·7 ,,
1938.		
Quoted Investments	£3,292 million	£164·9 million
Unquoted Investments	400 ,,	20·0 ,,
Total	£3,692 ,,	£184·9 ,,

Long-Term Capital Movements.

Although these investigations are not designed for the purpose of estimating capital movements, the material collected and the results obtained indirectly provide some indication of the main trend. For instance, it has been ascertained that the nominal value of investments in quoted securities declined by £61 million during 1938. This, of course, does not imply that an equal amount of cash was received by the United Kingdom by the sale of such investments. Part of the reduction was only apparent, due in some instances to company reorganisation, which resulted in writing down nominal values. In most cases, moreover, sale prices of securities are still substantially below their par value so that proceeds of such sales are considerably smaller than the nominal value of the securities realised. This applies at least with equal force to the redemption of foreign bonds. Nevertheless, the figure indicates that the repatriation of long-term capital which appeared to begin at the end of 1931 had not ceased in 1938.

The final table gives figures showing the amount of money [1] subscribed annually to new oversea issues on the London market compared with the sums effectually repaid each year since 1929 through sinking-fund operations and redemptions at maturity.

TABLE X.

New Oversea Issues and Repayments.

(£000,000.)

	British Subscription to New Issues.	Repayments to the U.K.	Difference.
1929	96	49	+47
1930	98	39	+59
1931	41	27	+14
1932	37	48	−11
1933	83	67	+16
1934	63	42	+21
1935	51	81	−30
1936	61	107	−46
1937	60	61	− 1
1938	29	39	−10

Prior to 1932 new issues regularly exceeded repayments by substantial sums. The surplus during the three years 1929–31 aggregated £120 million. Since 1931, however, with the exception of the years 1933 and 1934, the balance has been considerably

[1] Including money subscribed for the purpose of reducing loans at maturity.

adverse, and the total deficit on this account during the last seven years of this period has amounted to £61 million.

It must be repeated that the evidence of repatriation of capital disclosed by these figures is not entirely complete. In particular, account must be taken of the considerable purchase of unquoted United States securities by British institutions and nationals during 1935 and 1936. Nevertheless there is little doubt that the steady and traditional growth of Britain's investments was not maintained after 1931. Official restrictions on foreign lending have no doubt partly contributed to this result, but even in the absence of these restrictions, political uncertainties and the difficulties which have beset the conduct of international trade would have made substantial lending impossible.

The importance of Britain's oversea investments has once more been emphasised by the measures which the Government has taken since the commencement of the war to compel holders of many securities to register their holdings with the Bank of England. It is impossible to say in what direction these securities may be utilised by the Government in connection with the financing of this country's war effort, but in any event considerable changes in some categories are likely to take place during the coming years. It would, however, be a mistake to suppose that the whole, or even the major part of our Oversea Investments will be thus affected. As the figures in this article show, more than 70 per cent. consist either of sterling bonds of oversea Governments or securities of British companies operating abroad; and few, if any, of these securities have a ready market outside the United Kingdom.

While I hope to continue these investigations, and every effort will be made to do so, it is, however, possible that the difficulties which may arise in connection with the compilation of the figures, due to a variety of reasons, will be insuperable and may, therefore, necessitate their abandonment for the time being.

R. M. KINDERSLEY

UNITED KINGDOM
OVERSEAS INVESTMENTS, 1938 TO 1948

Bank of England

UNITED KINGDOM OVERSEAS INVESTMENTS 1938 to 1948

Estimates covering a large part of the Overseas Investments of the United Kingdom outstanding in the years 1938 to 1948 have been compiled in the Statistics Office of the Bank of England. They are designed, in the main, to provide a continuation of the series of studies, covering the years 1926 to 1938, which were prepared under the direction of Lord Kindersley and were published in the *Economic Journal* each year between 1929 and 1939[1]. In 1940 Lord Kindersley had collected much of the material for 1939 but he was unable, in the circumstances of the time, to carry the work to completion. Later he was good enough to hand over his material to the Bank, to assist their study of Balance of Payments problems, and facilitated the continued co-operation of the institutions which had formerly supplied him with information. The Bank for their part, while necessarily compelled for some time to limit their work to immediate requirements, intended that when opportunity offered they would prepare and publish complete estimates covering the war years similar to Lord Kindersley's earlier figures, and thus ensure the maintenance of a valuable statistical investigation.

The continuance of the work has only been made possible by the voluntary assistance of a long list of registrars—banks, issuing houses and public companies of all kinds. Their co-operation in the enquiry must here be warmly acknowledged.

Scope of the Investigation : (i) *Capital*

In conformity with Lord Kindersley's work, the Bank's estimates cover the nominal capital value of, and the interest and dividends distributed on, the overseas investments of U.K. residents through the medium of securities quoted on, unofficially dealt in, or otherwise known to the London Stock Exchange. These securities fall into three main classes, viz. the loans of central and local governments, shares and debentures of U.K.-registered companies operating entirely or almost entirely abroad and those of companies registered abroad. The Bank have been able to widen the list of securities studied by Lord Kindersley by including a large block of U.S. and Canadian dollar securities not quoted in the Stock Exchange Official List or recorded in the Stock Exchange Official Year Book although undoubtedly known to the London Market: particulars of the U.K.

---

(1) Articles in the *Economic Journal* as follows :—

Vol. XXXIX No. 153 — March, 1929 — A New Study of British Foreign Investments.
" XL " 158 — June, 1930 — British Foreign Investments in 1928.
" XLI " 163 — Sept., 1931 — British Foreign Investments in 1929.
" XLII " 166 — June, 1932 — British Foreign Investments in 1930.
" XLIII " 170 — June, 1933 — British Overseas Investments in 1931.
" XLIV " 175 — Sept., 1934 — British Overseas Investments in 1932 and 1933.
" XLV " 179 — Sept., 1935 — Britain's Oversea Investments in 1933 and 1934.
" XLVI " 184 — Dec., 1936 — British Overseas Investments in 1934 and 1935.
" XLVII " 188 — Dec., 1937 — British Oversea Investments in 1935 and 1936.
" XLVIII " 192 — Dec., 1938 — British Oversea Investments, 1937.
" XLIX " 196 — Dec., 1939 — British Overseas Investments, 1938.

holdings of these securities have been registered with the Bank under Exchange Control regulations[2]. The estimates also include U.S. market securities (but not direct investments) pledged with the Reconstruction Finance Corporation as collateral security for the loan made to H.M. Government in July, 1941.

Representation of the capital amount of overseas investment by nominal values gives little indication of the actual realisable value of the investment but is a convenient basis for investigating the relative capital movements. For the sake of comparability, U.S. and Canadian dollar securities have been valued at rates of \$4·03 and \$4·45, respectively, from the beginning of the series in 1938; but the revaluation of the Canadian dollar to \$4·03 in 1946 and variations in other exchange rates from time to time are responsible for movements, not of relatively great magnitude, in the apparent amount of U.K. investment. In securities denominated in sterling possible revaluations due to gold clauses or currency options have been ignored. Company shares of no par value have been entered at balance-sheet values. All the estimates give the position at or near the end of the year.

(ii) *Interest and Dividends*

The figures of interest and of dividends paid on U.K. holdings of shares of overseas-registered companies represent the sums actually received and retained in the U.K. during the year, whether by the investor or by the Commissioners of Inland Revenue on account of the relative income tax. This description also applies to dividends paid by U.K.-registered companies up to early in 1946. Subsequently, in accordance with regulations made under section 52 of the Finance (No. 2) Act, 1945, dividends taxed in the U.K. at rates less than the full standard rate under Double Taxation Relief agreements are declared at levels which allow for deduction of tax at the full rate, i.e. they include a certain amount of overseas taxation, for which no practicable method of elimination can be found. In order, however, that the figures may represent as far as possible actual cash receipts by the U.K., the few examples of dividends paid free of income tax have been written up by the estimated amount of the tax and the various non-resident taxes levied by certain overseas countries on dividends earned there have, where applicable, been deducted. Dividends paid by U.K.-registered companies have been allocated to the year in which they were earned; those paid by overseas-registered companies to the year in which they were paid to shareholders—this being to some extent a change from Lord Kindersley's practice. No attempt is made in this investigation to provide estimates of the additional profits brought home by U.K. companies operating abroad in excess of the amounts distributed as interest or dividends, and utilised to meet management expenses at home, to pay U.K. taxation, or to increase reserves in this country.

---

(2) Figures for total U.K. holdings of these securities are used with the permission of H.M. Treasury.

Description of Main Classes and Methods of Compilation:

(i) *Government and Municipal Loans*

Loans of overseas Governments and Municipalities denominated in sterling, or on which interest is payable in sterling, are extensively owned by non-residents of the U.K.(3). Estimates of the amounts in U.K. ownership are based upon figures of interest payments made, non-residence being identified by exemption from payment of U.K. income tax. Exceptionally, foreign holdings coming under the control of the Custodian of Enemy Property have had their tax exemptions cancelled and require separate enumeration. Some non-resident bondholders are not able, or do not choose, to secure exemption at source on interest payments to them, but obtain subsequent refund of tax from the Inland Revenue: for this reason there is a slight overestimation of the U.K. holdings, which cannot be eliminated. The necessary particulars of capital outstanding and interest and redemption payments made during each year were supplied to the Bank by all the London paying agents. The number of Government and Municipal loans examined individually by this method was 730 in 1938, falling to 687 in 1943 and to 534 in 1948. In addition the Bank have brought into the survey 52 Irish loans, and they are indebted to Irish paying agents for information about the extent of U.K. ownership. U.K. holdings in some 700 U.S. and some 1,100 Canadian dollar loans were covered by collective figures extracted from Exchange Control records. The U.S. dollar loans are largely non-domestic and have been classified in the tables under the relative debtor countries.

(ii) *U.K.-Registered Companies*

The selection of U.K.-registered companies to be considered as operating abroad is a matter of judgment. Investment and financial trusts are excluded because their holdings of overseas securities must be largely covered elsewhere in the investigation. In fact overlapping in general, caused by companies investing in the shares of other companies, is where possible eliminated. Also excluded are those companies which operate both at home and abroad, owing to the difficulty of isolating the part of their capital that should be considered as invested abroad, or of obtaining information on the proportion of their profits derived from abroad. Among these are many important commercial companies, all insurance companies (their investment business being for the present purpose parallel to that of an investment trust) and shipping companies. It has seemed logical to omit the few U.K. shipping companies included by Lord Kindersley, thus avoiding the possibility of an overlap with any independent estimate of the national shipping income.

(iii) *Companies Registered Overseas*

In the enumeration of those overseas-registered companies that are quoted on the London Stock Exchange, no part of the capital is brought in that is known to be owned by an overseas company or by a U.K. company already included.

(3) Of interest paid in London in 1948 by Commonwealth countries on government loans, 24% was paid to non-residents of the U.K., and on municipal loans 20%. Corresponding proportions for payments by foreign countries were 59% and 49%.

The effect of this is to bring U.K.-controlled overseas companies largely into the class of U.K. companies operating abroad, i.e. under the controlling company: but some controlled investments remain in the overseas-registered category. It should be clear that the investigation does not include direct investment abroad by a U.K. company whose main business is at home, whether in the form of an overseas branch or of the ownership of an overseas-registered company outside the range of those here considered.

In the analysis by geographical areas overseas companies have been classified by the country of operation, not (as by Lord Kindersley) by the country of registration. Companies operating in more than one area have been divided according to the evidence available, which includes in the case of a holding company the field of operation of its subsidiaries.

(iv) *Companies—Method of Sampling*

U.K. investors hold the bulk of the shares of U.K.-registered companies. In companies registered overseas but quoted on the London market U.K. holdings are in normal times inclined to fluctuate from year to year, many of the securities in question having an international market. To enable the amount of U.K. investment in both classes to be ascertained, a large and representative selection of companies are good enough each year to inform the Bank how much of their capital is owned by residents of the U.K. U.K. ownership in companies not supplying this information is estimated as being the same proportion of their total capital as that of known companies of the same type. For example, the 1948 estimates take account of 1,403 U.K.-registered companies of whom 336 (24%) made a return to the Bank, covering 72% of the total nominal share and loan capital of all 1,403 companies. Similarly, 466 overseas-registered companies were included of whom 301 (65%) made a return, covering 80% of the total capital. To these figures were added, from Exchange Control sources, £117 million nominal of U.K. investment in some 2,900 U.S.A. companies and £70 million nominal in some 760 Canadian companies.

The Estimates: (i) *Capital Outstanding*

The results of the investigation are set out in detail in 22 tables below; a summary of the figures of nominal capital is as follows:—

£ millions : end of year	*1938*	*1940*	*1942*	*1944*	*1946*	*1948*
Government and Municipal Loans ...	1,521	1,458	1,186	978	859	797
U.K. Companies: Share Capital ...	817	806	792	768	748	596
,, : Loan Capital ...	367	335	322	279	255	119
Overseas Companies: Share Capital ...	473	422	351	327	303	304
,, : Loan Capital ...	368	318	219	192	164	144
In Commonwealth Countries	1,998	1,889	1,532	1,325	1,199	1,111
In Foreign Countries	1,455	1,352	1,241	1,122	1,035	749
Not Classifiable by Area	93	97	97	97	95	99
Total	3,545	3,338	2,871	2,544	2,329	1,960

Over the ten years surveyed the nominal value of U.K. investments abroad has thus fallen by £1,585 million, 45% of the total at the beginning of the period. The following table shows where the reductions have been concentrated and expresses them as percentages of the nominal totals held in 1938(4) :—

	Decrease 1938 to 1948			*Decrease 1938 to 1948*	
	£ millions	*% of 1938*		*£ millions*	*% of 1938*
India and Pakistan...	319	82	Argentina	317	86
Canada	258	61	U.S.A....	193	72
Australia	123	24	Brazil	82	50
South Africa ...	72	36	Europe	50	23
New Zealand ...	68	51	Mexico	36	55
Other Commonwealth Countries... ...	26	8	Other Foreign Countries	47	13
All Commonwealth Countries... ...	866	43	All Foreign Countries	725	50

Although the United Kingdom still held substantial overseas assets at the end of 1948 it will be remembered in any assessment of the international capital position that these are more than outweighed by overseas indebtedness incurred during and after the war. No attempt is made to compare the figures presented here with figures officially published from time to time of external liabilities of the United Kingdom, because the present figures are expressed in nominal values and, as stated above, they make no pretence of covering the whole of U.K. direct investment overseas.

(ii) *Repayment*

Table 21 gives the net reductions in nominal capital that have been identified as due to redemptions by sinking funds or at maturity (any new issues that have been made appearing as negative figures); sales or redemptions, in advance of maturity, of requisitioned securities; private sales under permit of registered securities; liquidations of company capital owing to officially arranged disposals of the relative commercial assets, e.g. railways or utility undertakings; also changes arising from the ordinary run of company reorganisations or liquidations. The total, £1,447 million in the ten years, represents net repatriation, nominal, by the debtor countries and in Table 22 is shown the corresponding net cash receipt by the U.K., viz. £1,244 million. The unidentified residual decreases in the amounts outstanding each year indicate net sales to non-residents through the market and, of course, errors and omissions(5). They amounted to £138 million nominal and their realisation is estimated to have brought in £108 million cash. In general the purchaser is not identifiable, but a large part was probably repatriation and some of this, especially in the case of South American bonds, official. Some sales of Commonwealth government loans represented the investment of various Colonial

(4) The table excludes changes caused by the classification of Burma and Palestine as Foreign Countries instead of Commonwealth Countries in 1948. The total decrease differs from that shown in the previous table owing to the small increase in investments not classifiable by area.

(5) Some changes may have arisen out of migration by investors.

reserve funds—the fund and the investment not necessarily relating to the same territory. The total cash received from the U.K. disinvestment of £1,585 million nominal was thus £1,352 million.

It is not necessary to enlarge here on the relation of these changes to the financing of the 1939–45 war. The disposal of securities readily realisable in the U.S.A. in the main preceded the passing of the Lease-Lend legislation in March, 1941: and of the remainder those which were of most value were utilised as collateral for the R.F.C. Loan of July, 1941. In 1948 the interest and dividends on pledged securities—which were earmarked for the service of the loan—amounted to £5·4 million out of the total of £7·9 million from the U.S.A. In Canada official operations continued until mid-1942, after which investments remaining were not specifically pledged but the proceeds of any sales were to be used towards repayment of the $700 million interest-free loan. The repayment of South African government sterling debt was also effected by official action by the end of 1943; in India the repatriation of the government debt and the U.K.-owned railway shares and debentures was not completed until 1944.

Large-scale repatriation of debt by other countries was related to the accumulation of short-term sterling assets. From 1944 onwards repayments of maturing debt by Australia and New Zealand were very large and there were similar operations on a smaller scale by certain Colonial territories. A special scheme for the repayment of Brazilian bonds entailing some reductions in capital values and cuts in interest rates—the successor to a series of temporary arrangements—was arranged in 1943 and came into force in 1944. Subsequent repayment of debt by the Brazilian Government has been on a larger scale than was originally planned. A writing down of Mexican Government bonds, long in complete default, was accepted in 1943 and since then there have been repatriations of Mexican railway bonds at special prices. At the beginning of 1948 the railways and other assets in the Argentine of the U.K.-registered railway companies, of which the nominal value of United Kingdom holdings was put in at £248 million, were sold for £150 million cash, a price to be related to market values, of course, rather than to nominal values.

During the period under review many sinking funds were regularly maintained and in 1945 and 1946 accumulated war-time arrears were paid up by several countries which had been in enemy occupation. These repayments were not, as in the past, offset by the flow of new investment. From the outbreak of war to 1946 new commercial investment abroad through Stock Exchange securities was negligible and in 1946 and 1947 it was practically limited to South Africa and Rhodesia. The purchase of South African shares shown by this survey represents only a part of the estimated capital flow to that country in the two years in question: the movement continued throughout the greater part of 1948 but, although there were substantial transactions in shares covered by the survey, the U.K. holding was not increased on balance. A few issues of shares by U.K.-registered oil companies in 1948 appear in the tables under " Rest of South America " and " Not Classifiable."

(iii) *Interest and Dividends*

The income distributed in respect of U.K. investments overseas (as explained earlier, a smaller figure than income from investments abroad in the national balance of payments) was £155 million in 1938, falling by 25% to £116 million in 1948. The corresponding totals of nominal capital outstanding, it will be remembered, decreased by 45%. Apart from investments in the U.S.A. and the assets of the Argentine railway companies, investments disposed of were, in general, fixed-interest loans of good quality and therefore paying relatively low interest rates. Share capital, more profitable on the average than loans, made up 36% of the total in 1938 and 46% in 1948, and dividends were on the average higher in the later year. Among the investments remaining in 1948 there were nevertheless, in round figures, some £225 million mainly in Europe and the Far East on which no income was being distributed and, mainly in South and Central America, £130 million on which the return was under 1% and £80 million on which it was between 1 and 1½%.

The following table shows income in 1939 and 1948 from the main classes of investments expressed as percentages of nominal capital. Because of the distortion that arises when income is paid during the year on securities which by the end of the year have been disposed of, the capital figure used is the average of the amounts outstanding at the end of the year and at the end of the preceding year. The figures are not yields in the ordinary sense, as no account is taken of market prices, and their value as a measure of the profitability of overseas investment is limited by such considerations as those set out above.

Per cent.	*In Commonwealth Countries*		*In Foreign Countries*	
	1939	*1948*	*1939*	*1948*
Government Loans	3·9	3·6	2·7	1·2
Municipal Loans	4·6	4·4	2·6	1·8
U.K. Companies : Share Capital	8·0	10·0	2·2	5·1
,, : Loan Capital	3·9	3·8	2·6	3·6
Overseas Companies : Share Capital	8·8	9·7	2·3	10·9
,, : Loan Capital	3·7	3·4	2·0	1·6

Appendices

Lord Kindersley published figures for 1938 which are not identical with those here given for that year. The nature of the difference is explained in Appendix I. Appendix II relates the present estimates to figures of disinvestment and of overseas income which have been published from time to time in Command Papers.

Appendix I.—Comparison between the Bank's Estimate and Lord Kindersley's for 1938

Lord Kindersley's total of £3,692 million consisted of £3,292 million for quoted investments plus £400 million for unquoted investments, "with the proviso that no precision is claimed for this figure" (*Economic Journal*, XLIX, p. 693). Allowance will have been made in the £400 million for some of the dollar securities included in full by the Bank in the light of later knowledge.

	£ millions
Lord Kindersley's quoted investments	3,292
Add for revaluation of U.S. and Canadian dollar securities at U.S. \$4·03 and Can. \$4·45	32
	3,324
U.S. dollar securities added by the Bank, at \$4·03	258
Lord Kindersley's figure adjusted	3,582
Bank's estimate	3,545

The difference of £37 million is explained by minor additions or exclusions of securities, by adjustments to eliminate double counting, or by revision of the estimated proportion of U.K. holdings of companies' capital.

Appendix II.—Comparison between the Present Estimates and Other Published Figures

Estimates of the Realisation of External Capital Assets were given in "Statistical Material presented during the Washington Negotiations" (Cmd. 6707, December, 1945) for the period September, 1939, to June, 1945, and continued for the years 1945 and 1946 in "National Income and Expenditure of the U.K., 1938–46" (Cmd. 7099, April, 1947). These estimates may be compared with the annual change in the Bank's present estimates :—

£ millions	*Cmd. 6707/7099*	*Present Estimates*
1939 September–December ...	58	—
,, Year	—	55
1940	164	152
1941	274	243
1942	227	224
1943	189	181
1944	143	146
1945	110	127
1946	70	88
1939–46 ...	1,235	1,216

Cmd. 6707 also included some geographical detail for the period September, 1939, to June, 1945, which may be compared with the present estimates for the whole years 1939–44 and 1939–45 :—

£ millions	Cmd. 6707 Sept. 1939–June 1945	Present Estimates 1939–44	Present Estimates 1939–45
Australia, New Zealand, South Africa, Eire ...	201	152	204
India, Burma, Middle East	348	317	324
Colonies and Other Sterling Area	15	17	22
Sterling Area	564	486	550
U.S.A.	203	169	180
Canada	225	195	212
South America	96	110	122
Europe	14	19	30
Rest of World	16	23	33
Non-Sterling Area	554	515	578
Total	1,118	1,001	1,128

The principal differences between the Cmd. 6707/7099 estimates and the present estimates are :—

(1) the former show the proceeds of sales and redemptions less the cost of purchases and new issues, the latter changes in outstanding nominal amounts ;

(2) the former cover all investments as far as known, the latter quoted securities only ;

(3) the former classify non-sterling securities by currency denomination, the latter by debtor country.

The discrepancy in the Sterling Area is predominantly due to (2) : in Canada to (1) and (2) : in the U.S.A. to (2) and (3)—South American U.S. dollar securities are included in Cmd. 6707 under U.S.A., not under South America. In Europe and the Rest of World (1) played a larger part, securities having been disposed of at less than their nominal value.

The same three differences affect comparisons for 1946–8, plus the fact that in the present estimates the Canadian dollar has been revalued from \$4·45 at the end of 1945 to \$4·03 at the end of 1946. Thus " United Kingdom Balance of Payments, 1946–8 " (Cmd. 7520, September, 1948) gives figures of Sales and Redemptions of U.S. and Canadian Securities (net) of £36 million in 1946 and £21 million in 1947. The present estimates give corresponding figures of £27 million and £22 million, but the former is reduced by the revaluation of all outstanding Canadian dollar holdings.

Similarly, "United Kingdom Balance of Payments, 1946–9, No. 2" (Cmd. 7928, April, 1950) gives figures of Sales and Redemptions of Overseas Investments in the Non-Sterling Area of £67 million in 1946, £54 million in 1947 and £181 million in 1948. The present estimates give £63 million, £44 million and £286 million, the large difference for 1948 being mainly due to the Argentine railway transaction.

Turning to annual income, a comparison is possible for 1945 between "Dividends, Interest, etc." in Cmd. 6707 and the present estimates :—

£ millions	*Cmd. 6707*	*Present Estimates*
Australia, New Zealand, South Africa, Eire	45	37·2
India, Burma, Middle East	11	9·4
Colonies and Other Sterling Area	17	11·6
Unallocated	22	—
Sterling Area	95	58·2
U.S.A.	9	6·9
Canada	14	9·1
South America	28	15·9
Europe	12	5·5
Rest of World	—	7·0
Rest of World and Unallocated	12	—
Non-Sterling Area	75	44·4
Non-Classifiable	—	6·2
Total	170	108·8

It should be clear that the estimates in Cmd. 6707 cover a wider field than the quoted investments now under review, and represent total earnings remitted, including for U.K. companies management expenses at home, allocations to reserves and Excess Profits and Profits Taxes. They also include payments on sterling loans remitted through London to overseas holders (Cmd. 6707, p. 10, footnote 1).

Estimates of "Interest, Profits and Dividends" are available for some other years in Cmd. 7928; broadly the same considerations apply, although the Cmd. 7928 figures do not include the overseas earnings of U.K. oil companies.

£ millions	*Cmd. 7928*	*Present Estimates*
1938	205	155·4
1946	153	110·1
1947	171	115·9
1948	174	116·4

TABLES

GENERAL NOTES TO THE TABLES

All figures are given correct to the nearest final digit ; for this reason the sum of the separate items will sometimes differ from the total as shown.

* indicates a figure less than £50,000. — signifies nil.

"Commonwealth Countries" include Protectorates, Trust Territories, Mandated Territories and Territories under Condominium. Burma and Palestine are included in Commonwealth Countries up to 1947 and in Foreign Countries in 1948. Eire, which did not become the Irish Republic until April, 1949, is included in the Commonwealth throughout. Newfoundland is included under Canada. Poland, Czechoslovakia and Danzig are included in "Rest of Europe" throughout.

Some of the geographical areas need definition, as follows :—

British West Africa	Comprises Nigeria (including Cameroons), Gambia, Gold Coast (including Togoland) and Sierra Leone.
British East Africa	Comprises Kenya, Uganda, Tanganyika, Zanzibar.
British Central Africa ...	Comprises S. Rhodesia, N. Rhodesia, Nyasaland.
South Africa (Union of) ...	Includes S.W. Africa Territory but not Bechuanaland, Basutoland or Swaziland.
Malaya	Comprises Singapore and the Federation of Malaya.
British North Borneo ...	Includes Sarawak and Brunei.
British West Indies	Includes British Honduras, British Guiana and Bermuda.
Australia	Includes Papua and New Guinea.
Rest of Europe	Includes the whole of Turkey and U.S.S.R.
Central America	Comprises Costa Rica, Guatemala, Salvador, Honduras, Nicaragua and Panama.

The classification by types of company is that of the Stock Exchange Official Year Book, except that Mines have been sub-divided into Mines, Gold, and Mines Other. A classification of U.S.-registered companies is not available in such detail.

In the case of the Austrian 4½% Guaranteed Sterling Loan, 1934–59, on which the Austrian Government is in default but on which payments of interest and redemption money have been made by guarantor governments, some in part and at irregular intervals, only those interest payments received from abroad have been included and are shown as receipts from Austria. Payments made by the U.K. Government have been excluded. The nominal capital has been reduced by the full amount of the bonds redeemed but the cash receipts shown are only those received from abroad.

The Austrian 3% Guaranteed Sterling Loan, 1933–53, is wholly guaranteed by H.M. Government : the nominal capital has been reduced by redemptions but no cash receipts of either capital or interest are shown.

LIST OF TABLES

1—ALL SECURITIES: NOMINAL CAPITAL, BY COUNTRIES

£ millions

End of year	1938	1939	1940	1941	1942	1943	1944	1945	1946	1947	1948
COMMONWEALTH COUNTRIES											
Eire	16	18	18	19	19	19	18	18	18	19	20
British West Africa ...	55	54	54	53	53	52	51	49	49	48	47
Anglo-Egyptian Sudan...	17	14	14	13	13	13	12	12	12	11	11
British East Africa ...	24	24	24	24	22	22	21	21	19	19	15
British Central Africa ...	73	72	72	71	70	71	70	70	69	82	79
South Africa	199	206	197	161	155	111	110	111	118	127	127
India ... ... }	388	379	365	295	194	112	88	82	77	63	60
Pakistan... ... }										10	9
Burma	20	20	20	20	17	16	16	15	14	14	
Ceylon	28	27	26	26	26	26	26	25	25	25	26
Malaya	67	65	64	64	64	64	64	64	64	64	64
Australia	520	522	516	506	499	496	477	429	429	411	397
New Zealand	134	144	128	126	121	117	112	107	83	74	66
Canada	420	395	355	313	242	234	225	208	189	171	162
British West Indies ...	21	22	22	22	21	21	20	18	18	18	21
Other	18	18	17	17	17	16	16	16	15	14	8
	1,998	1,978	1,889	1,730	1,532	1,389	1,325	1,244	1,199	1,170	1,111
FOREIGN COUNTRIES											
France	11	11	10	10	10	10	10	8	8	7	7
Germany	45	47	44	44	43	43	43	43	43	43	43
Austria	11	11	11	11	11	10	10	10	9	9	8
Denmark	14	14	14	14	14	14	14	11	8	7	7
Norway	11	10	9	9	9	8	8	7	6	4	4
Hungary	16	16	15	15	15	15	15	15	14	14	14
Roumania	19	16	16	16	16	16	16	16	16	16	1
Greece	26	26	26	26	25	25	25	24	24	24	2
Rest of Europe	64	67	67	70	67	62	56	52	50	47	4
Burma											1
China	37	37	37	37	37	37	37	37	37	37	3
Japan	50	48	47	46	46	46	46	46	46	46	4
Netherlands East Indies	24	24	24	23	23	23	23	23	23	23	2
Persia	34	34	34	34	34	34	34	34	34	34	3
Egypt	10	11	11	11	9	7	4	4	4	6	[illegible]
U.S.A.	268	250	201	124	120	112	100	88	80	76	7
Mexico	66	65	65	65	62	53	52	44	32	31	3
Cuba	28	28	28	28	28	27	26	26	25	25	2
Argentina	368	355	353	351	346	343	321	318	312	305	5
Brazil	164	163	162	158	154	149	115	108	103	98	8
Chile	63	62	60	58	57	56	55	54	53	50	4
Peru	25	25	25	24	24	24	24	23	23	23	2
Uruguay...	23	23	23	24	23	22	23	22	22	22	2
Rest of South America...	37	37	34	34	34	33	33	33	33	32	3
Other	40	40	39	38	37	35	33	32	31	30	3
	1,455	1,417	1,352	1,268	1,241	1,205	1,122	1,077	1,035	1,010	74
NOT CLASSIFIABLE ...	93	96	97	97	97	96	97	96	95	95	9
TOTAL	3,545	3,490	3,338	3,095	2,871	2,690	2,544	2,417	2,329	2,274	1,96

2—ALL SECURITIES: INTEREST AND DIVIDENDS, BY COUNTRIES

£ millions

	1938	1939	1940	1941	1942	1943	1944	1945	1946	1947	1948
COMMONWEALTH COUNTRIES											
Eire	·8	·8	·8	·8	·9	·9	·9	·8	·8	·9	·9
British West Africa ...	4·3	4·1	3·6	3·6	3·3	3·5	3·1	3·0	3·9	4·0	3·6
Anglo-Egyptian Sudan...	·9	·9	·7	·7	·7	·8	·9	1·0	1·1	1·0	1·0
British East Africa ...	1·0	1·0	1·0	1·0	1·0	1·0	·9	·9	1·0	·9	1·3
British Central Africa ...	5·9	5·0	4·7	4·0	3·8	3·6	3·7	3·9	5·4	6·9	7·4
South Africa	17·5	18·0	18·4	17·1	14·7	12·7	12·3	12·2	12·8	14·5	15·0
India ... ... }	18·5	18·5	18·1	14·9	12·7	8·6	7·3	7·7	7·7	7·2	5·7
Pakistan... ... }										·6	·6
Burma	2·1	2·4	2·3	1·7	*	*	*	*	·4	·4	
Ceylon	1·7	1·8	1·8	1·7	1·8	1·8	1·8	2·2	2·3	2·4	2·4
Malaya	4·0	4·0	6·3	3·5	·8	·6	·6	·6	·9	2·1	3·8
Australia	22·2	22·3	22·2	21·7	20·5	20·4	20·4	19·7	17·4	17·2	17·3
New Zealand	5·8	5·7	5·9	5·5	5·3	5·2	4·8	4·5	4·0	3·5	3·1
Canada	15·9	15·4	13·7	12·8	9·3	9·0	9·6	9·1	8·4	7·5	7·6
British West Indies ...	1·3	1·2	1·1	1·2	1·2	1·1	1·2	·9	1·2	1·4	1·5
Other	·9	·9	·9	·9	·8	·6	·6	·6	·7	·7	·5
	102·7	102·1	101·4	91·1	77·0	69·6	68·0	67·0	68·2	71·2	71·7
FOREIGN COUNTRIES											
France	·4	·4	·1	*	*	—	—	1·6	·2	·2	·4
Germany	2·0	1·4	*	*	—	—	—	—	—	—	—
Austria	·5	·7	·2	*	*	*	·1	·5	·3	·3	·7
Denmark	·6	·5	·3	·2	·2	·2	—	1·9	·9	·3	·3
Norway	·4	·4	·3	·3	·2	·2	·3	·2	·4	·4	·4
Hungary	·4	·3	·3	·2	·1	—	—	—	—	—	—
Roumania	·4	·4	*	*	—	—	—	—	—	—	—
Greece	·4	1·0	·6	·1	*	—	*	*	*	*	*
Rest of Europe	2·4	2·0	1·8	1·7	1·5	1·4	1·6	1·2	1·6	1·3	1·8
Burma											·5
China	1·5	·9	·4	·3	·2	·1	·1	*	·1	·1	·1
Japan	2·6	2·6	2·5	2·0	*	—	—	—	—	*	·1
Netherlands East Indies	1·2	1·1	1·3	·6	·1	·1	·1	·1	·1	·1	·1
Persia	5·2	2·2	2·2	2·7	5·2	5·2	5·2	5·2	7·2	7·2	7·2
Egypt	·6	·6	·6	·6	·5	·5	·3	·3	·4	4·5	2·1
U.S.A.	7·1	5·6	10·7	6·3	5·9	5·3	5·6	6·9	5·6	6·2	7·9
Mexico	·4	·2	·2	·2	·5	·6	·5	·5	·6	1·0	·9
Cuba	·1	·1	·1	·1	·2	·4	·1	·1	·1	·2	·1
Argentina	7·8	7·8	7·6	6·5	7·0	8·4	6·6	8·0	7·2	6·4	5·2
Brazil	1·6	1·0	2·2	2·5	3·1	3·3	4·3	4·1	3·9	3·4	2·6
Chile	·9	1·2	1·0	·9	·9	·9	·8	·8	·9	·9	·7
Peru	·4	·2	·3	·3	·4	·4	·5	·5	·5	·5	·3
Uruguay...	·4	·4	·5	·5	·5	·4	·4	·5	·5	·5	·4
Rest of South America...	1·7	1·8	1·6	1·5	1·6	1·6	1·8	2·0	2·2	2·1	2·4
Other	1·5	1·5	1·4	1·4	1·2	1·1	1·0	1·1	1·4	1·8	1·7
	40·3	34·3	36·1	28·8	29·4	30·4	29·5	35·6	34·1	37·3	36·0
NOT CLASSIFIABLE ...	12·5	7·5	5·8	5·7	4·8	4·8	4·9	6·2	7·8	7·4	8·6
TOTAL	155·4	143·8	143·4	125·6	111·2	104·9	102·4	108·8	110·1	115·9	116·4

3—GOVERNMENT AND MUNICIPAL LOANS: NOMINAL CAPITAL, BY COUNTRIES

£ millions

End of year	1938	1939	1940	1941	1942	1943	1944	1945	1946	1947	1948
COMMONWEALTH COUNTRIES											
Eire	11·2	12·5	12·5	13·8	13·7	13·9	13·4	13·4	13·9	14·3	15·2
British West Africa	18·9	17·7	17·6	17·5	17·0	16·7	16·2	14·4	14·1	12·3	11·6
British East Africa	15·3	15·1	15·2	15·2	14·3	14·1	13·7	13·4	11·2	10·8	6·5
Br. Central Africa	12·4	11·9	11·9	12·0	11·7	12·0	11·7	11·7	12·3	42·1	42·1
South Africa ...	99·1	104·3	97·5	67·8	61·9	23·0	21·7	20·9	21·1	20·6	20·3
India ... }	239·7	234·1	221·8	155·2	61·5	6·4	5·3	5·2	4·3	3·8	3·7
Pakistan ... }										·2	·2
Ceylon	5·9	5·2	4·2	4·2	4·0	4·0	4·0	4·0	3·9	3·7	3·5
Malaya	1·4	1·4	1·4	1·4	1·3	1·4	1·5	1·5	1·5	1·4	1·3
Australia	455·5	458·4	453·0	443·2	437·0	434·4	419·9	374·0	373·9	356·8	345·3
New Zealand ...	122·2	131·7	116·3	114·7	110·3	106·0	101·6	96·3	73·4	64·7	56·5
Canada	125·1	107·1	91·4	60·4	50·1	47·3	44·7	40·1	32·9	26·5	24·2
British West Indies	5·4	5·7	5·7	6·2	5·1	5·0	4·7	4·7	4·6	4·4	6·6
Other	14·9	12·5	12·4	12·2	11·5	11·0	10·7	10·3	9·9	9·5	6·4
	1,127·0	1,117·6	1,060·9	923·8	799·4	695·2	669·3	609·8	576·6	571·1	543·5
FOREIGN COUNTRIES											
Germany	36·8	36·9	36·9	36·9	36·9	36·8	36·8	36·8	36·8	36·2	36·2
Austria	11·0	10·3	10·8	10·8	10·5	10·1	9·8	9·6	9·3	8·9	8·4
Denmark	8·6	8·3	8·3	8·3	8·3	8·3	8·3	6·4	5·4	4·6	4·8
Norway	5·2	4·8	4·8	4·6	4·3	4·1	4·0	3·9	3·5	2·9	3·1
Hungary	10·2	10·3	10·1	9·9	9·6	9·6	9·6	9·6	9·6	9·6	9·6
Roumania ...	11·4	11·2	11·2	11·2	11·2	11·2	11·4	11·6	11·3	11·3	11·3
Greece	21·5	21·6	21·5	21·4	21·1	20·9	20·8	19·6	19·6	19·6	19·6
Rest of Europe ...	26·1	28·5	28·5	33·1	30·8	27·3	23·8	21·1	19·9	18·2	17·0
China	33·1	33·0	32·9	32·8	32·8	32·8	33·3	33·3	33·3	33·3	33·3
Japan	43·0	41·2	40·9	40·7	40·7	40·7	40·6	40·6	40·6	40·6	40·6
Egypt	5·9	6·4	6·3	6·5	5·1	3·2	·3	·3	·3	·3	·3
Mexico	7·9	7·9	7·9	7·9	7·9	1·7	1·6	1·4	1·2	1·2	1·2
Central America ...	4·1	4·1	4·1	4·0	4·0	4·0	3·4	2·9	2·8	2·4	2·1
Argentina... ...	40·2	49·0	48·3	47·8	44·7	42·4	21·3	20·1	15·4	9·7	5·5
Brazil	82·8	81·6	80·8	79·9	77·5	74·1	45·6	40·2	37·9	33·9	27·6
Chile	24·8	24·1	24·2	24·2	24·5	24·3	23·9	23·5	23·0	21·0	19·5
Uruguay	5·5	5·4	5·9	6·4	6·2	5·3	5·7	5·0	5·0	4·9	5·4
Rest of S. America	6·9	6·9	6·9	6·9	7·0	6·6	6·1	5·9	5·4	5·2	4·2
Other	8·7	7·8	6·3	4·6	3·3	2·5	2·5	2·3	2·1	1·4	3·8
	393·7	399·3	396·6	397·9	386·2	365·9	308·8	293·9	282·4	265·2	253·5
TOTAL	1,520·7	1,516·9	1,457·5	1,321·7	1,185·6	1,061·1	978·0	903·7	859·1	836·3	797·0

4—GOVERNMENT AND MUNICIPAL LOANS: INTEREST, BY COUNTRIES

£ millions

	1938	1939	1940	1941	1942	1943	1944	1945	1946	1947	1948
COMMONWEALTH COUNTRIES											
Eire	·4	·5	·5	·5	·6	·6	·6	·6	·6	·6	·6
British West Africa ...	·9	·9	·9	·9	·8	·8	·8	·7	·7	·6	·5
British East Africa ...	·7	·7	·7	·7	·7	·7	·7	·6	·6	·5	·4
British Central Africa ...	·5	·5	·5	·5	·5	·5	·5	·4	·5	·5	1·2
South Africa	3·9	4·0	4·2	3·9	2·3	1·1	·8	·9	·8	·8	·8
India ... ... }	8·7	8·5	8·3	5·2	3·0	·4	·4	·3	·2	·2	·2
Pakistan... ... }										*	*
Ceylon	·2	·2	·2	·1	·1	·1	·1	·1	·1	·1	·1
Malaya	*	*	*	*	*	*	*	*	*	*	*
Australia	18·4	18·6	18·7	18·6	17·7	17·4	17·5	16·7	13·8	13·3	12·7
New Zealand	5·2	5·0	5·2	4·9	4·8	4·6	4·3	4·0	3·4	2·9	2·6
Canada	4·5	4·8	3·5	3·3	2·0	1·8	1·7	2·1	1·5	1·1	·8
British West Indies ...	·2	·2	·2	·3	·2	·2	·2	·2	·2	·2	·2
Other	·8	·8	·6	·6	·6	·5	·4	·4	·4	·4	·3
	44·4	44·6	43·4	39·3	33·3	28·6	28·0	27·1	22·8	21·2	20·5
FOREIGN COUNTRIES											
Germany	1·6	·9	—	—	—	—	—	—	—	—	—
Austria	·5	·7	·2	*	*	*	·1	·5	·3	·3	·7
Denmark	·4	·3	·3	·2	·2	·2	—	·8	·5	·3	·2
Norway	·2	·2	·1	·1	·1	·1	·2	·1	·2	·1	·1
Hungary	·3	·3	·2	·2	·1	—	—	—	—	—	—
Roumania	·3	·2	—	—	—	—	—	—	—	—	—
Greece	·3	·9	·5	·1	*	—	—	—	—	—	*
Rest of Europe... ...	1·2	1·2	·9	1·0	·8	·8	·6	·7	·6	·3	·3
China	1·1	·4	*	*	—	—	—	—	—	—	—
Japan	2·2	2·1	2·1	1·8	—	—	—	—	—	—	—
Egypt	·2	·2	·2	·2	·2	·2	*	*	*	*	*
Mexico	—	—	—	—	—	*	·1	·1	·1	·1	·1
Central America ...	·1	*	*	*	*	*	*	*	*	*	*
Argentina	1·7	1·8	2·0	2·0	1·9	1·7	·3	·8	·6	·5	·3
Brazil	·2	*	·9	1·0	1·0	1·0	1·6	1·4	1·4	1·0	·8
Chile	·2	·5	·4	·4	·4	·4	·3	·3	·3	·3	·2
Uruguay...	·2	2	·2	·3	·3	·2	·2	·2	·2	·2	·2
Rest of South America...	*	*	*	*	*	*	·2	·1	·1	·1	*
Other	·3	·3	·3	·2	·1	·1	*	*	*	·3	·2
	10·7	10·5	8·3	7·6	5·1	5·0	3·7	5·0	4·2	3·4	3·2
TOTAL	55·1	55·1	51·7	46·9	38·4	33·6	31·7	32·2	27·0	24·6	23·7

5—U.K.-REGISTERED COMPANIES: NOMINAL SHARE CAPITAL, BY COUNTRIES

£ millions

End of year	1938	1939	1940	1941	1942	1943	1944	1945	1946	1947	1948
COMMONWEALTH COUNTRIES											
Eire	1·3	1·3	1·3	1·3	1·3	1·3	1·3	1·3	1·3	1·3	1·3
British West Africa ...	35·1	35·1	35·4	35·3	35·4	34·8	33·9	33·5	35·3	35·6	35·2
British East Africa ...	6·4	6·3	6·3	6·3	5·9	5·9	5·8	5·7	5·7	6·0	5·8
British Central Africa ...	29·2	29·1	29·0	28·7	28·6	29·1	28·9	28·6	28·2	30·0	29·1
South Africa	21·8	21·8	21·1	20·9	20·5	20·5	20·6	20·5	20·5	22·5	22·1
India ... ... }	72·6	73·1	73·0	72·4	68·8	63·3	53·2	51·6	50·5	40·5	40·8
Pakistan... ... }										8·3	8·2
Burma	10·9	10·4	10·4	10·5	10·3	10·0	10·4	10·4	10·4	10·5	
Ceylon	21·0	21·0	21·1	21·0	21·0	20·9	20·8	20·8	21·0	21·1	21·8
Malaya	61·0	59·0	58·6	58·6	58·4	58·3	58·5	58·5	58·8	58·7	58·6
British North Borneo ...	4·5	4·5	4·5	4·5	4·5	4·5	4·6	4·6	4·3	4·1	4·0
Australia	38·0	37·4	37·3	37·1	37·2	37·2	33·3	32·8	33·1	32·1	29·3
New Zealand	6·4	6·4	6·4	6·3	6·3	6·3	6·2	6·2	6·2	6·0	5·6
Canada	9·9	10·1	10·1	10·1	10·1	9·7	9·8	9·5	8·7	7·6	8·0
British West Indies ...	10·6	11·2	11·5	11·5	11·4	11·3	11·4	9·3	9·5	9·6	10·4
Other	6·7	6·7	6·3	6·3	6·3	6·2	6·1	6·6	6·2	6·1	5·7
	335·4	333·4	332·3	330·8	326·0	319·3	304·8	299·9	299·7	299·9	285·8
FOREIGN COUNTRIES											
Europe	28·1	25·8	24·7	23·7	23·7	23·8	23·2	23·0	23·0	21·9	20·1
Burma											10·3
China	3·0	3·1	3·1	3·1	3·1	3·2	3·1	3·2	3·2	3·3	2·3
Netherlands East Indies	21·1	21·1	20·9	20·7	20·5	20·5	20·6	20·5	20·5	20·5	20·7
Persia	33·6	33·7	33·7	33·7	33·7	33·8	33·7	33·8	33·7	33·7	33·8
Egypt	2·9	2·7	2·7	2·7	2·7	2·7	2·6	2·6	2·5	2·7	3·2
Mexico	16·6	16·5	16·3	16·3	13·7	13·3	13·3	9·2	3·0	2·9	2·8
Cuba	10·9	10·9	10·9	10·9	10·8	10·8	10·9	11·0	11·0	11·0	10·9
Central America ...	2·4	2·4	2·4	2·4	2·4	2·4	2·4	2·4	2·4	2·4	2·4
Argentina	181·2	180·7	179·7	179·1	178·4	178·9	178·8	177·9	176·6	176·2	27·9
Brazil	33·8	33·8	33·8	33·8	32·5	32·0	28·8	27·9	27·2	27·6	23·3
Chile	12·2	12·2	12·2	12·2	12·2	12·2	12·3	12·3	12·3	12·4	12·1
Peru	15·5	15·5	15·3	15·1	15·1	15·1	15·1	15·1	15·1	15·1	15·1
Uruguay...	10·0	10·0	10·0	10·0	10·0	10·0	10·0	10·0	10·0	10·0	9·5
Rest of South America...	22·2	21·8	20·1	20·3	20·1	20·3	20·4	19·8	19·9	19·9	20·2
Other	13·1	13·1	12·4	12·4	11·6	11·5	11·4	11·5	11·0	12·2	13·7
	406·6	403·3	398·2	396·4	390·5	390·3	386·6	380·1	371·6	371·9	228·3
NOT CLASSIFIABLE ...	75·3	75·3	75·3	75·5	75·6	75·5	76·3	76·3	76·2	76·2	82·0
TOTAL	817·3	812·0	805·8	802·7	792·1	785·1	767·7	756·2	747·5	748·0	596·1

6—U.K.-REGISTERED COMPANIES: SHARE DIVIDENDS, BY COUNTRIES

£ millions

	1938	1939	1940	1941	1942	1943	1944	1945	1946	1947	1948
COMMONWEALTH COUNTRIES											
Eire	·1	·1	·1	·1	·1	·1	·1	·1	·1	·1	·1
British West Africa ...	3·3	3·3	2·7	2·7	2·5	2·7	2·3	2·3	3·3	3·4	3·1
British East Africa ...	·1	·1	·1	·2	·2	·2	·2	·2	·3	·3	·8
British Central Africa ...	3·8	2·9	2·6	1·9	1·8	1·5	1·5	1·8	3·2	4·6	5·8
South Africa	2·2	2·0	2·0	2·0	1·9	2·0	1·9	2·1	2·3	2·9	2·6
India ... ... } Pakistan... ... }	6·9	7·3	7·0	7·0	7·1	6·3	5·5	6·1	6·5	6·3	4·7
(Pakistan)										·5	·5
Burma	1·3	1·6	1·6	1·0	—	—	—	—	·4	·4	
Ceylon	1·4	1·5	1·5	1·5	1·6	1·6	1·6	2·0	2·1	2·3	2·2
Malaya	3·5	3·6	5·8	2·9	·5	·4	·4	·4	·8	1·9	3·5
British North Borneo ...	·2	·2	·3	·1	*	*	*	*	*	·1	·1
Australia	2·2	2·1	2·0	1·8	1·4	1·7	1·7	1·8	2·5	2·7	2·8
New Zealand	·4	·4	·4	·4	·4	·3	·3	·3	·3	·4	·4
Canada	·2	·2	·2	·3	·3	·3	·4	·2	·5	·4	·4
British West Indies ...	·9	·9	·8	·9	·8	·9	·9	·6	1·0	1·2	1·2
Other	·4	·4	·4	·4	·5	·5	·7	·8	·9	·9	·9
	27·0	26·6	27·6	23·1	19·1	18·4	17·4	18·7	24·2	28·3	29·4
FOREIGN COUNTRIES											
Europe	·7	·5	·5	·4	·4	·4	·4	·4	·5	·8	1·1
Burma											·4
China	·2	·2	·2	·1	*	*	*	*	·1	·1	—
Netherlands East Indies	1·0	1·0	1·2	·4	·1	·1	·1	·1	·1	·1	·1
Persia	5·1	2·2	2·2	2·6	5·1	5·2	5·2	5·2	7·2	7·2	7·2
Egypt	·3	·3	·3	·3	·3	·3	·3	·3	·4	·4	·4
Mexico	·1	·1	·1	·1	·3	·3	·1	·2	·3	·3	·4
Cuba	·1	·1	·1	·1	*	·1	*	·1	·1	·1	·1
Central America ...	*	*	—	—	—	—	—	*	—	—	—
Argentina	1·8	1·7	1·7	1·8	1·8	1·8	1·8	1·9	1·2	1·2	1·5
Brazil	·5	·6	·6	·7	·7	·8	·9	·9	·7	·6	·6
Chile	·2	·1	·1	·1	·2	·2	·2	·2	·2	·3	·3
Peru	·2	·1	·1	·1	·1	·1	·1	·2	·2	·2	·2
Uruguay...	·1	·1	·1	·2	·2	·2	·2	·3	·3	·2	·2
Rest of South America...	1·5	1·5	1·4	1·2	1·3	1·4	1·5	1·6	1·9	1·9	2·0
Other	·6	·5	·5	·6	·5	·5	·5	·6	·8	·9	1·0
	12·2	9·0	9·1	8·7	11·0	11·1	11·2	12·0	13·8	14·2	15·3
NOT CLASSIFIABLE ...	9·4	4·4	4·9	4·6	4·3	4·4	4·5	5·8	6·1	6·2	7·5
TOTAL	48·6	40·1	41·5	36·4	34·4	34·0	33·2	36·5	44·1	48·8	52·1

7—U.K.-REGISTERED COMPANIES: NOMINAL LOAN CAPITAL, BY COUNTRIES

£ millions

End of year	1938	1939	1940	1941	1942	1943	1944	1945	1946	1947	1948
COMMONWEALTH COUNTRIES											
British West Africa ...	·6	·8	·6	·6	·7	·7	·7	·5	·1	—	—
British East Africa ...	·5	·4	·4	·4	·4	·2	·1	·1	·1	·1	·1
British Central Africa ...	23·1	22·9	22·5	22·2	22·0	21·6	21·8	21·5	21·2	1·5	3·3
South Africa	2·6	2·5	2·5	2·5	2·5	2·5	2·4	2·4	2·4	1·7	1·7
India ... ... }	70·9	68·4	66·2	63·7	59·7	39·0	25·6	22·0	19·1	15·1	12·2
Pakistan... ... }										1·1	·9
Burma	1·8	1·8	1·7	1·7	1·7	·5	·5	·4	·6	·5	
Ceylon	1·1	1·1	1·1	1·1	1·0	1·0	·8	·6	·5	·5	·5
Malaya	2·8	2·7	2·6	2·5	2·4	2·3	2·2	2·1	2·4	2·3	2·2
British North Borneo ...	1·0	1·0	·9	·9	·9	·9	·9	·9	·9	·1	*
Australia	11·2	11·3	11·1	11·0	10·6	10·5	10·1	9·1	8·2	7·5	7·4
New Zealand	3·2	3·4	3·3	3·2	3·0	2·8	2·6	2·2	2·2	2·2	2·3
Canada	7·8	7·8	7·7	7·7	7·6	7·2	7·0	6·3	5·9	4·1	4·2
British West Indies ...	1·6	1·5	1·5	1·5	1·5	1·5	1·4	1·4	1·2	1·2	1·2
Other	4·1	4·0	3·7	3·5	3·5	3·4	3·1	2·9	2·8	2·6	2·5
	132·3	129·6	125·8	122·5	117·5	94·1	79·3	72·6	67·7	40·6	38·4
FOREIGN COUNTRIES											
Europe	10·7	10·7	10·5	8·7	8·4	7·9	7·6	6·4	5·2	4·1	4·0
Burma											·3
Netherlands East Indies	2·8	2·6	2·5	2·3	2·3	2·2	2·1	2·1	2·1	2·1	2·2
Mexico	7·5	7·4	7·3	7·2	7·0	7·0	6·7	4·1	1·2	1·2	1·2
Central America ...	1·8	1·7	1·7	1·6	1·6	1·6	1·6	1·6	1·6	1·6	1·6
Argentina	140·7	119·4	118·6	118·1	117·9	117·5	116·7	115·6	115·3	115·0	13·0
Brazil	17·0	17·0	17·0	17·0	16·8	16·4	15·7	15·5	15·0	14·7	11·1
Chile	7·3	7·1	5·9	5·7	5·6	5·4	5·3	5·1	5·0	4·8	4·4
Peru	4·1	4·1	4·0	4·0	4·0	4·0	4·0	4·0	4·0	4·0	4·1
Uruguay...	7·8	7·7	7·6	7·6	7·6	7·5	7·5	7·5	7·5	7·5	7·3
Rest of South America...	7·2	6·8	5·8	5·8	5·8	5·6	5·7	5·6	5·4	5·3	8·7
Other	24·6	24·4	23·3	22·9	22·7	22·3	22·0	21·1	21·1	20·2	17·2
	231·6	209·0	204·3	200·8	199·6	197·5	194·9	188·5	183·4	180·5	75·2
NOT CLASSIFIABLE ...	2·6	5·0	5·2	5·1	5·1	5·1	4·7	4·5	4·2	4·1	5·1
TOTAL	366·5	343·6	335·3	328·4	322·2	296·7	278·9	265·6	255·3	225·1	118·7

8—U.K.-REGISTERED COMPANIES: LOAN INTEREST, BY COUNTRIES

£ millions

	1938	1939	1940	1941	1942	1943	1944	1945	1946	1947	1948
COMMONWEALTH COUNTRIES											
British West Africa ...	*	*	*	*	*	*	*	*	*	*	*
British East Africa ...	*	*	*	*	*	*	*	*	*	*	*
British Central Africa ...	1·0	1·0	·9	·9	·9	·9	·9	·9	·9	·9	·1
South Africa	·1	·1	·1	·1	·1	·1	·1	·1	·1	·1	·1
India ... ... }	2·7	2·6	2·5	2·5	2·3	1·7	1·2	1·0	·8	·7	·5
Pakistan... ... }										*	*
Burma	·1	·1	·1	·1	·1	—	—	—	—	—	
Ceylon	·1	·1	·1	·1	·1	·1	*	*	*	*	*
Malaya	·2	·2	·2	·1	·1	·1	·1	·1	·1	·1	·1
British North Borneo ...	·1	·1	*	*	*	*	*	*	*	*	—
Australia	·4	·4	·4	·4	·4	·4	·4	·4	·3	·3	·3
New Zealand	·1	·1	·1	·1	·1	·1	·1	·1	·1	·1	·1
Canada	·1	·2	·2	·2	·2	·3	·2	·2	·1	·1	·1
British West Indies ...	*	*	*	*	*	*	*	*	*	*	*
Other	·2	·2	·2	·2	·2	·2	·2	·1	·1	·1	·1
	5·2	5·1	5·0	4·8	4·7	4·0	3·3	3·1	2·7	2·5	1·5
FOREIGN COUNTRIES											
Europe	·2	·2	·2	·2	·2	·2	·5	·1	·4	·1	·1
Burma											*
Netherlands East Indies	·2	·1	·2	·1	·1	*	*	*	*	*	*
Mexico	*	*	*	*	*	*	*	*	—	—	—
Central America ...	·1	·1	*	·1	·1	·1	·1	*	*	*	*
Argentina	4·2	4·1	3·7	2·5	3·1	4·8	4·5	5·2	5·3	4·6	3·4
Brazil	·2	·2	·5	·4	·7	·6	·7	·7	·6	·6	·2
Chile	·3	·3	·2	·2	·2	·2	·2	·2	·2	2	·1
Peru	·1	·1	·1	·1	·2	·2	·2	·2	·2	·2	·1
Uruguay...	·1	·1	·1	·1	·1	*	*	·1	·1	*	*
Rest of South America...	·2	·2	·2	·2	·2	·2	·2	·2	·2	·1	·2
Other	·6	·5	·5	·5	·5	·4	·4	·3	·3	·4	·3
	6·1	5·8	5·6	4·4	5·3	6·7	6·9	6·9	7·3	6·3	4·6
NOT CLASSIFIABLE ...	·1	·1	·2	·2	·2	·2	·2	·2	·2	·2	·2
TOTAL	11·4	11·1	10·8	9·5	10·2	10·9	10·4	10·1	10·1	8·9	6·3

9—U.K.-REGISTERED COMPANIES: NOM. SHARE CAPITAL, BY TYPES OF COMPANY

£ millions

End of year	1938	1939	1940	1941	1942	1943	1944	1945	1946	1947	1948
Dominion & Col. Rails...	1·7	1·7	1·7	1·7	1·7	1·7	1·7	1·7	1·7	1·6	1·6
Indian Rails †	19·4	18·9	18·9	18·0	14·6	9·3					
Foreign Rails	214·9	213·7	213·7	213·7	213·2	213·3	213·0	208·5	202·4	202·3	53·8
Banks	33·8	33·8	33·7	33·7	33·7	33·8	33·8	33·9	33·9	36·3	34·9
Breweries, &c.	5·1	5·2	5·2	5·2	5·2	5·2	5·2	5·2	5·2	5·2	5·2
Canals & Docks ...	·7	·7	·3	·3	·3	·3	·3	·3	·3	·3	—
Commercial, Industrial	62·9	62·1	60·4	60·2	59·2	59·1	59·2	58·8	57·5	57·3	54·9
Electric Light & Power	10·0	10·9	10·9	11·1	11·1	10·9	10·8	10·3	10·0	8·3	8·2
Financial Trusts, Land...	77·8	77·6	77·0	75·4	72·9	72·3	68·6	67·8	66·5	64·8	63·5
Gas	10·3	10·2	10·2	10·2	10·2	10·3	10·3	10·3	10·3	9·8	9·7
Iron, Coal & Steel ...	2·4	2·3	2·3	2·3	1·4	1·4	1·4	1·4	1·3	·6	·9
Mines, Gold	44·8	44·0	44·2	44·0	43·2	42·8	37·8	36·7	38·4	38·2	37·0
Mines, other than Gold...	67·0	66·6	66·6	66·1	65·6	65·4	65·2	64·1	63·1	66·4	61·7
Oil	109·1	108·5	106·8	107·5	107·0	107·1	107·7	105·6	105·7	105·6	114·4
Rubber	77·2	75·5	74·9	74·8	74·7	74·5	74·5	74·1	74·5	74·5	74·3
Tea & Coffee	39·9	39·9	39·9	39·9	39·8	38·9	38·5	38·4	38·3	38·4	38·5
Telegraphs, &c.... ...	23·0	23·0	22·9	22·9	22·7	22·7	22·7	22·4	22·2	22·2	22·0
Tramways, &c.... ...	10·8	10·7	10·3	9·8	9·8	10·3	10·3	10·8	10·6	10·6	10·3
Waterworks	4·3	4·4	4·4	4·4	4·3	4·3	4·2	3·4	3·4	3·4	2·9
Other †	2·3	2·3	1·5	1·5	1·5	1·5	2·3	2·3	2·3	2·4	2·2
	817·3	812·0	805·8	802·7	792·1	785·1	767·7	756·2	747·5	748·0	596·1

10—U.K.-REGISTERED COMPANIES: SHARE DIVIDENDS, BY TYPES OF COMPANY

£ millions

	1938	1939	1940	1941	1942	1943	1944	1945	1946	1947	1948
Dominion & Col. Rails...	*	*	*	*	*	*	*	*	*	—	—
Indian Rails †	1·4	1·3	1·3	1·3	1·2	·5					
Foreign Rails	·8	·7	·6	·6	·6	·6	·6	·6	·6	·6	·5
Banks	2·6	2·6	2·6	2·4	2·2	2·2	2·3	2·4	2·8	3·2	3·5
Breweries, &c.	·8	·8	·7	·8	·7	·7	·6	·7	·9	·9	·7
Canals & Docks.... ...	*	*	*	*	*	*	*	*	*	*	—
Commercial, Industrial	3·4	2·7	2·8	2·7	2·4	2·4	2·6	3·4	4·2	4·5	4·8
Electric Light & Power	·9	·8	·9	1·0	·8	·8	·7	·7	·7	·6	·6
Financial Trusts, Land...	2·7	2·5	2·7	2·6	2·6	2·6	3·1	3·1	3·1	3·4	4·5
Gas	·8	·6	·2	·2	·2	·2	·3	·7	·7	·6	·5
Iron, Coal & Steel ...	*	*	*	*	*	*	*	*	*	*	*
Mines, Gold	4·6	5·0	4·0	3·5	3·3	3·2	2·4	2·6	2·6	2·6	2·2
Mines, other than Gold...	5·9	5 3	6·1	4·5	2·9	3·0	2·9	3·2	5·9	8·2	10·4
Oil	16·7	9·3	9·7	9·8	11·9	12·0	12·2	12·7	15·6	15·8	16·6
Rubber	3·2	3·8	5·2	2·1	·8	·8	·7	·8	·9	1·7	2·2
Tea & Coffee	3·2	3·2	3·0	3·2	3·2	3·1	3·2	3·6	4·4	4·8	3·9
Telegraphs, &c.... ...	1·1	1·1	1·1	1·1	1·0	1·1	1·1	1·3	1·1	1.1	1·0
Tramways, &c.... ...	·3	·2	·2	·2	·2	·2	·2	·2	·2	·2	·2
Waterworks	·2	·2	·2	·2	·2	·2	·2	·2	·2	·2	·2
Other †	—	—	—	—	·1	·1	·1	·1	·1	·1	·1
	48·6	40·1	41·5	36·4	34·4	34·0	33·2	36·5	44·1	48·8	52·1

† "Other" comprises the residue of Indian Rails after 1943, U.S. Rails and Nitrate Companies.

11—U.K.-REGISTERED COMPANIES: NOM. LOAN CAPITAL, BY TYPES OF COMPANY

£ millions

End of year	**1938**	**1939**	**1940**	**1941**	**1942**	**1943**	**1944**	**1945**	**1946**	**1947**	**1948**
Dominion & Col. Rails...	28·2	27·9	27·3	27·0	26·7	26·3	26·0	25·2	24·8	4·6	5·5
Indian Rails	68·9	66·5	64·3	61·9	57·9	36·2	23·1	20·5	17·8	15·0	12·0
Foreign Rails	180·1	158·5	156·1	155·7	155·3	154·8	154·1	149·6	146·5	145·7	41·9
Breweries, &c.	·8	·8	·8	·8	·8	·8	·8	·8	·8	·8	·8
Canals & Docks... ...	3·7	3·6	3·6	3·5	3·5	3·4	3·4	3·3	3·2	3·1	—
Commercial, Industrial	9·8	9·9	9·6	9·4	9·2	8·6	7·6	6·3	5·2	3·9	3·3
Electric Light & Power	3·6	3·4	3·4	3·3	3·2	3·2	3·1	2·9	2·7	1·6	·8
Financial Trusts, Land...	29·6	29·4	28·3	26·0	25·4	24·4	23·9	21·4	20·9	19·2	19·3
Gas	1·5	1·4	1·3	1·1	1·0	1·0	·6	·6	·5	·5	·4
Iron, Coal & Steel ...	·5	·5	·5	·5	·5	·5	·5	·5	·5	—	—
Mines, Gold	·8	·9	·8	·8	·9	·9	·7	·6	·3	·1	·1
Mines, other than Gold...	5·3	4·9	4·6	4·4	4·3	3·8	3·8	3·7	3·4	2·7	3·0
Oil	1·1	3·7	3·7	3·7	3·7	3·7	3·5	3·4	3·3	3·1	7·7
Rubber	4·6	4·5	4·3	4·1	3·9	3·8	3·7	3·6	3·7	3·8	3·8
Tea & Coffee	2·5	2·4	2·4	2·4	2·3	2·1	1·4	1·2	1·0	1·0	·9
Telegraphs, &c.... ...	2·2	2·1	2·3	2·3	2·3	2·1	1·9	1·6	1·4	1·4	1·4
Tramways, &c.... ...	17·0	16·9	16·8	16·7	16·6	16·5	16·5	16·2	15·8	15·5	15·4
Waterworks	1·8	1·7	1·6	1·6	1·5	1·5	1·3	1·2	1·2	1·0	·7
Other †	4·2	4·4	3·5	3·3	3·2	3·1	3·1	2·9	2·3	2·1	1·7
	366·5	343·6	335·3	328·4	322·2	296·7	278·9	265·6	255·3	225·1	118·7

12—U.K.-REGISTERED COMPANIES: LOAN INTEREST, BY TYPES OF COMPANY

£ millions

	1938	**1939**	**1940**	**1941**	**1942**	**1943**	**1944**	**1945**	**1946**	**1947**	**1948**
Dominion & Col. Rails...	1·1	1·1	1·1	1·1	1·1	1·2	1·1	1·0	1·0	1·0	·2
Indian Rails	2·6	2·5	2·4	2·3	2·2	1·5	1·0	·9	·7	·6	·5
Foreign Rails	4·7	4·6	4·2	3·1	4·0	5·5	5·4	6·0	6·2	5·4	3·8
Breweries, &c.	*	*	*	*	*	*	*	*	*	*	*
Canals & Docks... ...	·2	·2	·2	·2	·2	·2	·2	·2	·2	·2	·2
Commercial, Industrial	·3	·4	·3	·3	·3	·3	·6	·2	·4	·1	·1
Electric Light & Power	·2	·1	·2	·2	·2	·1	·1	·1	·1	·1	·1
Financial Trusts, Land...	1·0	·9	·9	·9	1·0	1·0	1·0	·9	·9	·8	·6
Gas	·1	·1	·1	·1	*	*	*	*	*	*	*
Iron, Coal & Steel ...	—	—	—	—	—	—	—	—	—	—	—
Mines, Gold	*	*	*	*	*	*	*	*	*	*	*
Mines, other than Gold...	·2	·2	·2	·1	·1	·1	·1	·1	·1	·1	·1
Oil	—	·1	·1	·1	·1	·1	·1	·1	·1	·1	·3
Rubber	·3	·3	·3	·2	·2	·1	·1	·1	·1	·1	·1
Tea & Coffee	·1	·1	·1	·1	·1	·1	·1	·1	·1	*	*
Telegraphs, &c.... ...	·1	·1	·1	·1	·1	·1	·1	·1	·1	·1	·1
Tramways, &c.	·2	·2	·3	·2	·2	·2	·2	·2	·2	·1	·1
Waterworks	·1	·1	·1	·1	·1	·1	·1	·1	·1	·1	*
Other †	·2	·2	·2	·1	·1	·1	·1	·1	·1	·1	·1
	11·4	11·1	10·8	9·5	10·2	10·9	10·4	10·1	10·1	8·9	6·3

† U.S. Rails, Banks and Nitrate Companies.

13—COMPANIES REGISTERED ABROAD: NOMINAL SHARE CAPITAL, BY COUNTRIES

£ millions

End of year	1938	1939	1940	1941	1942	1943	1944	1945	1946	1947	1948
COMMONWEALTH COUNTRIES											
Eire	2·5	2·5	2·5	2·4	2·4	2·4	2·1	1·6	1·5	1·6	1·5
British East Africa ...	1·5	1·7	1·6	1·6	1·3	1·2	1·2	1·6	1·6	2·3	2·5
British Central Africa ...	8·6	8·1	8·0	8·0	8·0	7·9	7·8	7·9	7·8	8·1	4·2
South Africa	65·8	67·8	66·9	61·0	61·4	60·3	60·6	63·4	70·4	79·8	80·1
India	1·6	1·5	1·5	1·5	1·8	1·8	1·9	1·9	1·3	2·1	2·0
Malaya	1·4	1·3	1·4	1·4	1·4	1·4	1·4	1·4	1·4	1·4	1·5
Australia	9·7	10·0	10·0	10·0	9·8	9·6	9·0	9·0	8·9	9·2	11·4
New Zealand	1·8	1·8	1·8	1·7	1·7	1·7	1·9	1·8	1·3	1·3	1·2
Canada	106·0	104·4	102·1	101·3	99·0	97·1	93·1	86·5	82·9	79·4	76·0
British West Indies ...	2·3	2·3	2·3	2·3	2·3	2·3	2·4	2·4	2·5	2·5	2·5
Other	10·5	10·5	10·5	10·5	8·3	8·4	8·1	6·8	5·4	5·9	·2
	211·7	211·9	208·6	201·7	197·5	194·1	189·4	184·1	185·1	193·5	183·2
FOREIGN COUNTRIES											
Europe	8·5	9·3	9·8	10·1	10·1	9·4	9·9	8·3	7·3	8·0	7·9
Japan	·8	·8	·8	·8	·8	·5	·5	·5	·5	·5	·5
Egypt	·8	·8	·8	1·0	·7	·7	·5	·6	·6	3·0	2·9
U.S.A.	203·9	188·8	153·3	96·7	94·4	89·5	80·6	72·7	66·5	63·9	63·8
Mexico	7·3	7·1	7·3	7·2	7·2	7·1	7·1	7·3	5·9	5·5	5·1
Cuba	1·4	1·4	1·4	1·3	1·3	1·3	·6	·3	·3	·3	·3
Argentina	1·8	1·8	1·9	1·9	1·7	1·4	1·4	1·4	1·4	1·4	1·3
Brazil	14·9	14·9	14·9	14·9	14·9	14·9	14·9	14·9	14·6	14·6	14·6
Rest of South America...	3·5	3·5	3·5	3·5	3·5	3·1	3·1	3·1	3·3	3·3	3·4
Other	4·2	4·2	4·2	4·2	4·2	4·2	3·8	3·8	3·7	3·7	9·1
	247·1	232·6	197·9	141·6	138·8	132·1	122·3	112·8	104·0	104·1	108·9
NOT CLASSIFIABLE ...	13·8	14·3	15·0	15·1	15·1	15·0	15·6	15·6	14·2	14·2	12·2
TOTAL	472·6	458·8	421·5	358·4	351·4	341·2	327·3	312·5	303·3	311·9	304·3

14—COMPANIES REGISTERED ABROAD: SHARE DIVIDENDS, BY COUNTRIES

£ millions

	1938	1939	1940	1941	1942	1943	1944	1945	1946	1947	1948
COMMONWEALTH COUNTRIES											
Eire	·1	·1	·1	·1	·1	·1	·2	·1	·1	·1	·1
British East Africa ...	·1	·1	·1	·1	·1	·1	·1	·1	·1	·1	·1
British Central Africa ...	·6	·7	·6	·7	·7	·8	·7	·7	·8	·9	·3
South Africa	10·9	11·4	11·7	10·7	10·0	9·2	9·2	8·8	9·4	10·6	11·3
India	·1	·1	·2	·2	·2	·2	·2	·2	·1	·1	·2
Malaya	·3	·2	·3	·4	·1	—	—	—	*	·1	·2
Australia	·9	·9	·9	·7	·8	·7	·7	·6	·7	·8	1·3
New Zealand	·1	·1	·1	·1	·1	·1	·1	·1	·1	·1	·1
Canada	4·6	4·1	4·4	4·4	4·2	4·0	4·5	3·6	3·9	3·7	4·5
British West Indies ...	*	*	*	*	*	*	*	*	*	*	·1
Other	1·0	·8	·8	·9	·2	·2	·2	·2	·3	·3	·1
	18·8	18·6	19·4	18·4	16·6	15·4	16·0	14·6	15·6	16·7	18·3
FOREIGN COUNTRIES											
Europe	·6	·4	·2	·2	·2	·1	·2	·3	·2	·2	·5
Japan	·1	·1	·1	·1	*	—	—	—	—	*	·1
Egypt	*	*	*	*	*	*	*	*	*	4·1	1·7
U.S.A.	6·0	4·5	9·4	5·5	5·4	5·0	5·3	6·5	5·3	6·0	7·7
Mexico	·1	·1	·1	·1	·1	·1	·1	·1	·2	·3	·2
Cuba	—	—	—	—	—	—	—	—	—	—	—
Argentina	·1	·1	·1	·1	·1	·1	*	·1	*	*	*
Brazil	·4	*	*	·2	·4	·8	1·0	1·0	1·0	1·0	1·0
Rest of South America...	*	*	*	—	*	*	—	—	*	*	·1
Other	·3	·3	·3	·3	·2	·1	·1	·1	·2	·3	·3
	7·6	5·6	10·2	6·5	6·6	6·2	6·7	8·1	7·1	12·0	11·6
NOT CLASSIFIABLE ...	2·9	2·8	·7	·8	·1	·1	·2	·3	1·5	1·0	·9
TOTAL	29·3	27·0	30·3	25·7	23·4	21·8	22·8	23·0	24·2	29·6	30·8

15—COMPANIES REGISTERED ABROAD: NOMINAL LOAN CAPITAL, BY COUNTRIES

£ millions

End of year	1938	1939	1940	1941	1942	1943	1944	1945	1946	1947	1948
COMMONWEALTH COUNTRIES											
Eire	1·4	1·4	1·4	1·4	1·4	1·4	1·3	1·5	1·5	1·4	1·7
South Africa	9·5	9·1	8·8	8·3	8·1	5·0	4·3	3·8	3·7	2·8	3·0
India	2·7	2·3	2·2	2·1	2·1	1·9	1·8	1·6	1·4	1·3	1·2
Australia	5·2	5·1	4·8	4·6	4·5	4·2	4·2	4·6	4·4	5·2	4·0
Canada	170·8	165·6	143·1	133·3	74·7	72·7	70·2	65·2	58·8	53·2	49·8
Other	1·8	1·6	1·1	1·0	·9	·7	·6	·6	·4	·3	·2
	191·3	185·1	161·4	150·7	91·7	85·9	82·4	77·3	70·2	64·4	60·0
FOREIGN COUNTRIES											
Europe	37·7	37·7	34·1	34·0	33·6	33·4	32·4	30·0	27·3	26·0	25·0
Japan	6·2	6·2	4·8	4·8	4·8	4·6	4·6	4·6	4·6	4·6	4·6
Egypt	·7	·6	·7	·8	·7	·3	·1	·1	*	*	*
U.S.A.	57·4	55·1	44·3	25·7	24·3	22·0	18·0	14·1	12·5	11·5	10·5
Mexico	26·7	26·1	26·1	26·1	25·9	23·9	23·2	22·5	20·7	20·5	20·1
Cuba	3·0	3·0	3·0	3·0	3·0	3·0	2·2	1·9	1·8	1·7	1·6
Argentina	4·5	4·5	4·4	4·4	3·2	3·1	3·1	3·2	3·2	2·9	3·0
Brazil	14·8	15·2	15·0	12·2	12·0	11·8	9·9	9·6	8·1	6·7	5·3
Chile	19·1	18·6	17·5	15·7	14·4	13·9	13·2	13·0	12·5	11·8	10·9
Rest of South America...	3·2	3·1	3·0	2·9	2·6	2·3	2·5	2·5	2·5	2·4	2·3
Other	2·3	2·2	1·9	1·7	1·7	1·2	·3	·3	·2	·2	·2
	175·6	172·3	154·9	131·3	126·2	119·5	109·4	101·6	93·5	88·3	83·5
NOT CLASSIFIABLE ...	1·4	1·7	1·5	1·5	1·4	·6	·6	·2	·2	·2	·1
TOTAL	368·3	359·1	317·8	283·5	219·3	206·0	192·4	179·1	163·9	153·0	143·6

16—COMPANIES REGISTERED ABROAD: LOAN INTEREST, BY COUNTRIES

£ millions

	1938	1939	1940	1941	1942	1943	1944	1945	1946	1947	1948
COMMONWEALTH COUNTRIES											
Eire	·1	·1	·1	·1	·1	·1	·1	·1	*	*	·1
South Africa	·4	·4	·4	·4	·3	·3	·2	·2	·2	·2	·2
India	·1	·1	·1	·1	·1	·1	·1	·1	·1	·1	*
Australia	·2	·2	·2	·2	·2	·2	·2	·2	·2	·2	·1
Canada	6·4	6·2	5·4	4·7	2·6	2·5	2·8	2·9	2·5	2·1	1·7
Other	·1	·1	·1	*	*	*	*	*	*	*	*
	7·3	7·0	6·2	5·3	3·4	3·2	3·4	3·5	3·0	2·6	2·1
FOREIGN COUNTRIES											
Europe	1·3	1·3	·5	·1	·1	·1	·1	2·5	·8	·4	·6
Japan	·3	·3	·3	·1	—	—	—	—	—	—	—
Egypt	*	*	*	*	*	*	*	*	*	*	*
U.S.A.	·9	·9	1·1	·6	·5	·4	·3	·3	·2	·2	·2
Mexico	·2	*	*	*	*	·2	·2	·1	·1	·3	·2
Cuba	*	*	—	—	·2	·4	·1	·1	*	*	·1
Argentina	·1	·1	·1	·1	·1	*	*	*	*	*	*
Brazil	·2	·3	·2	·2	·2	·2	·2	·2	·3	·2	·1
Chile	·3	·3	·3	·2	·2	·2	·1	·2	·2	·1	·1
Rest of South America...	·1	·1	·1	·1	·1	*	·1	·1	·1	*	*
Other	·1	·1	·1	·1	·1	·1	*	*	*	*	*
	3·6	3·4	2·8	1·6	1·4	1·5	1·0	3·5	1·7	1·4	1·3
NOT CLASSIFIABLE ...	·1	·1	·1	·1	·1	*	*	*	*	*	*
TOTAL	11·0	10·6	9·0	7·0	4·8	4·7	4·4	7·0	4·6	4·0	3·5

17—COMPANIES REGISTERED ABROAD: NOMINAL SHARE CAPITAL, BY TYPES OF COMPANY

£ millions

End of year	1938	1939	1940	1941	1942	1943	1944	1945	1946	1947	1948
EXCLUSIVE OF U.S.A.											
Dominion & Col. Rails ...	50·9	50·9	50·9	50·9	49·7	49·7	47·5	44·9	41·4	38·3	36·4
Foreign Rails	8·7	8·7	8·7	8·7	8·7	8·2	7·1	6·8	5·0	5·0	5·0
Banks	11·2	11·2	11·1	11·6	11·6	11·6	11·4	11·3	11·1	11·3	10·9
Breweries, &c.	1·4	1·4	1·3	1·2	1·2	1·1	1·1	1·1	1·2	1·2	1·1
Canals & Docks ...	2·8	2·7	2·7	2·7	2·7	2·7	2·7	2·7	2·7	2·4	2·3
Commercial, Industrial	59·2	60·0	61·0	60·5	59·1	57·6	58·8	55·3	56·2	62·9	64·9
Electric Light & Power	22·4	22·6	22·4	22·0	21·5	21·1	20·1	19·2	19·0	18·9	13·9
Financial Trusts, Land...	8·8	8·1	8·0	8·1	7·8	7·6	7·4	7·0	6·7	6·3	6·9
Gas	·8	·8	·8	·8	·8	·8	·8	·8	·8	·8	·8
Iron, Coal & Steel ...	5·4	5·1	4·9	4·9	4·8	4·6	4·3	4·6	4·7	5·3	4·8
Mines, Gold	44·0	45·1	43·4	37·4	39·1	38·0	37·5	39·2	41·8	46·6	45·6
Mines, other than Gold...	22·1	22·2	22·1	22·0	19·5	18·6	18·0	17·0	15·9	16·8	18·5
Oil	13·6	13·8	14·1	14·2	14·1	14·0	14·0	13·9	14·4	16·3	13·6
Rubber	·1	·1	·1	·1	·1	·1	·1	·1	·1	·1	·1
Shipping...	2·2	2·2	2·2	2·2	1·9	1·6	1·4	1·4	1·4	1·4	1·3
Telegraphs, &c.... ...	1·6	1·6	1·0	·9	·9	·9	·9	·9	·8	·8	·8
Tramways, &c.... ...	13·5	13·5	13·5	13·5	13·5	13·5	13·5	13·3	13·4	13·4	13·4
TOTAL EXCLUSIVE OF U.S.A.	268·7	270·0	268·2	261·7	257·0	251·7	246·7	239·8	236·8	248·0	240·5
U.S.A.											
Rails	39·8	38·3	30·7	18·4	17·7	16·0	13·1	10·7	10·3	10·2	8·4
Financial	8·7	8·4	7·3	6·1	6·0	5·8	5·4	4·8	4·7	4·5	4·4
Utilities	33·5	32·1	24·0	18·2	17·5	16·8	14·8	12·9	10·2	9·6	9·9
Industrial	121·9	110·0	91·3	54·0	53·2	50·9	47·3	44·3	41·3	39·6	41·2
TOTAL U.S.A.	203·9	188·8	153·3	96·7	94·4	89·5	80·6	72·7	66·5	63·9	63·8
TOTAL	472·6	458·8	421·5	358·4	351·4	341·2	327·3	312·5	303·3	311·9	304·3

18—COMPANIES REGISTERED ABROAD: SHARE DIVIDENDS, BY TYPES OF COMPANY

£ millions

	1938	1939	1940	1941	1942	1943	1944	1945	1946	1947	1948
EXCLUSIVE OF U.S.A.											
Dominion & Col. Rails ...	·7	·1	·6	1·0	1·0	1·0	1·9	1·8	1·7	1·5	1·4
Foreign Rails	·2	·1	·1	*	*	*	—	·1	·2	·2	*
Banks	1·0	1·0	1·0	·9	·7	·5	·5	·5	·8	·9	1·1
Breweries, &c.	·1	·1	·1	·1	·1	·1	*	*	·1	·1	·1
Canals & Docks ...	1·7	1·8	·5	·7	—	—	—	—	·8	4·1	1·7
Commercial, Industrial	6·0	6·1	5·8	5·3	5·0	5·0	4·7	3·6	4·1	5·1	6·7
Electric Light & Power	1·2	1·2	1·1	1·2	1·2	1·2	1·2	1·3	1·5	1·5	1·1
Financial Trusts, Land...	·1	·1	·1	·1	·1	·1	·2	·2	·4	·4	·7
Gas	·1	·1	·1	*	*	*	*	*	*	*	*
Iron, Coal & Steel ...	·3	·2	·3	·3	·3	·3	·3	·3	·3	·3	·3
Mines, Gold	8·4	8·7	8·8	7·1	6·8	6·1	5·3	5·2	5·4	5·0	5·1
Mines, other than Gold...	2·0	1·8	2·0	2·8	1·8	1·4	1·9	1·9	2·2	2·8	3·2
Oil	·7	·7	·2	·2	·2	·2	·2	·2	·4	·7	·5
Rubber	*	*	*	*	*	—	—	—	—	*	*
Shipping...	·2	·1	·2	·2	·2	·2	·1	·1	·1	·1	·1
Telegraphs, &c.... ...	·1	·1	*	*	*	*	—	·1	*	*	*
Tramways, &c.... ...	·4	*	*	·2	·4	·8	1·0	1·0	1·0	1·0	1·0
TOTAL EXCLUSIVE OF U.S.A.	23·3	22·5	21·0	20·2	18·0	16·8	17·5	16·5	18·9	23·6	23·1
U.S.A.											
Rails	*	*	*	*	*	*	*	*	*	*	*
Financial	·3	·3	·4	·3	·3	·3	·3	·3	·3	·3	·3
Utilities	·1	·1	·1	·1	·1	·1	·1	·1	·1	·1	·1
Industrial	5·5	4·0	8·8	5·1	5·0	4·6	4·9	6·1	4·9	5·6	7·2
TOTAL U.S.A.	6·0	4·5	9·4	5·5	5·4	5·0	5·3	6·5	5·3	6·0	7·7
TOTAL	29·3	27·0	30·3	25·7	23·4	21·8	22·8	23·0	24·2	29·6	30·8

19—COMPANIES REGISTERED ABROAD: NOMINAL LOAN CAPITAL, BY TYPES OF COMPANY

£ millions

End of year	1938	1939	1940	1941	1942	1943	1944	1945	1946	1947	1948
EXCLUSIVE OF U.S.A.											
Dominion & Col. Rails...	147·7	147·4	129·7	120·2	62·1	61·6	59·1	55·7	50·4	47·1	44·4
Indian Rails	·3	·3	·3	·3	·3	·3	·3	·3	·3	·3	·3
Foreign Rails	43·0	42·8	42·4	39·5	39·0	38·4	35·4	33·3	30·8	29·9	29·2
Banks	17·2	13·0	12·5	12·5	12·3	11·4	11·0	10·6	10·5	10·1	9·1
Canals & Docks ...	2·2	2·2	2·2	2·2	2·2	2·2	2·2	2·2	1·8	1·5	1·1
Commercial, Industrial	27·5	24·5	20·5	19·8	19·5	16·6	16·1	14·5	13·7	11·2	10·8
Electric Light & Power	30·2	29·0	23·7	23·4	22·8	20·9	20·9	19·9	19·3	19·0	18·9
Financial Trusts, Land...	11·4	13·2	12·8	12·6	12·3	10·8	10·5	10·4	8·0	7·4	5·4
Iron, Coal & Steel ...	3·8	3·4	3·1	3·1	3·1	2·9	2·2	2·1	1·9	1·9	2·0
Mines, Gold	1·4	1·6	1·5	1·4	1·3	·6	·4	·3	·3	·2	·3
Mines, other than Gold...	1·9	1·8	1·7	1·7	1·5	·8	·6	·6	·5	·4	·5
Nitrate	16·1	15·7	14·7	12·9	11·7	11·2	10·5	10·2	9·8	9·1	8·6
Telegraphs, &c.... ...	·9	·9	·8	·8	·7	·7	·6	·5	·5	·5	·5
Tramways, &c.... ...	4·7	5·4	5·4	5·3	5·3	5·1	4·3	4·1	3·4	2·4	1·7
Other†	2·6	2·8	2·2	2·1	·8	·5	·4	·4	·4	·4	·3
TOTAL EXCLUSIVE OF U.S.A.	310·9	304·0	273·5	257·8	195·0	184·0	174·4	165·0	151·5	141·4	133·1
U.S.A.											
Rails	32·6	31·3	25·6	14·4	13·6	11·9	8·4	5·0	4·1	3·7	3·0
Financial	2·5	2·5	2·1	1·8	1·8	1·8	1·6	1·4	1·3	1·1	1·1
Utilities	19·7	18·9	14·6	8·5	8·0	7·5	7·2	6·9	6·6	6·2	6·0
Industrial	2·6	2·4	2·0	1·0	·9	·8	·8	·8	·5	·5	·5
TOTAL U.S.A.	57·4	55·1	44·3	25·7	24·3	22·0	18·0	14·1	12·5	11·5	10·5
TOTAL	368·3	359·1	317·8	283·5	219·3	206·0	192·4	179·1	163·9	153·0	143·6

† Breweries, &c., Gas, Oil and Shipping Companies.

20—COMPANIES REGISTERED ABROAD: LOAN INTEREST, BY TYPES OF COMPANY

£ millions

	1938	1939	1940	1941	1942	1943	1944	1945	1946	1947	1948
EXCLUSIVE OF U.S.A.											
Dominion & Col. Rails ...	5·5	5·5	4·9	4·1	2·1	2·1	2·4	2·3	2·1	1·9	1·5
Indian Rails	*	*	*	*	*	*	*	*	*	*	*
Foreign Rails	·5	·5	·2	·1	·3	·4	·1	1·4	·3	·3	·3
Banks	·5	·4	·3	·2	·2	·1	·1	·5	·3	·3	·4
Canals & Docks ...	*	—	—	—	—	—	—	—	—	—	*
Commercial, Industrial	1·1	1·0	·8	·6	·5	·5	·4	·6	·4	·2	·2
Electric Light & Power	1·1	·9	·7	·5	·3	·5	·3	·3	·3	·4	·4
Financial Trusts, Land...	·4	·4	·3	·2	·2	·2	·2	·9	·6	·2	·2
Iron, Coal & Steel ...	·2	·1	·1	·1	·1	·1	·2	·2	·2	·2	·1
Mines, Gold	·1	·1	·1	·1	·1	·1	·1	*	*	*	*
Mines, other than Gold	·1	·1	*	*	*	*	*	*	*	*	*
Nitrate	·2	·2	·3	·2	·1	·1	·1	·1	·1	·1	·1
Telegraphs, &c.... ...	*	*	*	*	*	*	—	·1	*	*	*
Tramways, &c.	·2	·2	·2	·2	·2	·2	·2	·1	·2	·2	*
Other†	·1	·1	·1	·1	·1	*	*	*	*	*	*
TOTAL EXCLUSIVE OF U.S.A.	10·0	9·6	7·9	6·4	4·3	4·3	4·1	6·7	4·4	3·8	3·3
U.S.A.											
Rails	·3	·4	·4	·3	·2	·1	·1	·1	·1	·1	*
Financial	·1	·1	·1	*	·1	·1	*	·1	*	*	*
Utilities	·4	·4	·5	·3	·2	·2	·2	·1	·1	·1	·1
Industrial	·1	·1	·1	·1	*	*	*	*	*	*	*
TOTAL U.S.A.	·9	·9	1·1	·6	·5	·4	·3	·3	·2	·2	·2
TOTAL	11·0	10·6	9·0	7·0	4·8	4·7	4·4	7·0	4·6	4·0	3·5

† Breweries, &c., Gas, Oil and Shipping Companies.

21—ALL SECURITIES: NET CAPITAL REPAYMENT, NOMINAL

£ millions

Commonwealth Countries	1939	1940	1941	1942	1943	1944	1945	1946	1947	1948
Eire	−1·3	·1	−1·1	·2	·1	·1	·3	·6	·1	−1·1
British West Africa	−1·5	−·1	·1	−·1	·4	·1	1·8	−1·1	1·1	−·1
Anglo-Egyptian Sudan... ...	3·2	·4	·3	·3	·3	—	·2	·3	·3	·3
British East Africa	−·1	·1	·1	·5	·3	·1	−·2	1·8	−·6	3·6
British Central Africa	·8	·2	·2	·2	·7	·1	−·1	·1	−12·4	−1·2
South Africa	−4·6	7·4	28·4	4·6	37·7	·1	1·7	−3·2	−6·3	2·4
India ... ... Pakistan... ... ... }	2·8	14·4	67·6	98·7	79·7	22·7	5·0	2·8	4·3 ·1	2·9 ·1
Burma	·5	·1	*	*	1·2	·1	—	—	—	
Ceylon	·2	1·4	*	*	·1	·3	·2	—	—	−·1
Malaya	·1	·1	·1	·2	·1	·1	·1	−·3	·2	−·1
Australia	−4·7	3·3	5·9	1·2	8·5	15·9	41·5	1·6	14·2	10·2
New Zealand	−12·0	15·0	1·6	3·1	3·8	2·8	4·2	21·2	8·6	10·7
Canada	24·5	40·6	42·2	71·5	7·0	9·0	20·4	25·1	20·8	5·7
British West Indies	−·5	−·2	*	·5	·2	·3	·2	·1	—	−2·3
Other	·2	·7	*	·5	*	·6	·4	·6	1·0	*
	7·4	83·7	145·5	181·5	140·1	52·4	75·8	49·5	31·4	31·0
Foreign Countries										
France	·2	1·0	—	—	—	—	1·8	−·2	·3	1·0
Germany	·2	—	—	—	—	—	—	—	—	—
Austria	·8	1·0	·4	·4	·3	·2	·6	·6	·4	·3
Denmark	·2	—	—	—	—	—	·3	3·0	·8	·4
Norway	·6	·1	—	·1	·2	·2	·9	·7	1·8	·1
Hungary...	·3	·3	·3	—	—	—	—	—	·1	·1
Roumania	—	—	—	—	—	—	—	—	—	—
Greece	*	·1	·1	—	—	—	·2	—	·1	—
Rest of Europe	−1·7	·2	−·9	1·9	3·3	3·6	3·1	1·5	2·6	·3
Burma										·3
China	·7	*	*	*	—	—	—	—	—	—
Japan	2·1	·8	·4	—	·4	—	—	—	—	—
Netherlands East Indies ...	·1	·1	·2	·1	·1	·1	—	—	*	−·2
Persia	*	*	*	*	*	*	*	*	*	·4
Egypt	·3	·2	·2	·2	1·1	3·1	*	*	−·2	·1
U.S.A.	18·0	48·9	76·9	4·7	7·4	12·9	13·9	7·6	3·6	·9
Mexico	·2	·3	·1	2·8	7·9	·7	5·9	11·6	·4	·1
Cuba	—	—	·2	—	*	1·4	*	*	·7	·2
Argentina	13·8	2·1	1·9	3·7	3·0	20·8	3·7	5·6	6·7	251·7
Brazil	1·3	·5	3·2	1·4	2·5	23·3	3·8	3·4	1·4	7·1
Chile	1·0	1·7	2·0	1·1	·4	·2	·6	·8	1·6	2·2
Peru	·1	·1	·1	·1	*	·5	·1	*	*	*
Uruguay...	·1	·1	·1	·1	·2	·1	·1	·1	·1	·1
Rest of South America	1·0	3·2	*	·1	·1	−·1	·7	−·1	·3	−3·4
Other	·3	·6	·7	1·1	1·5	1·5	1·1	·2	1·0	3·6
	39·5	61·3	85·9	18·0	28·4	68·5	36·8	34·8	21·8	265·2
Not Classifiable	−3·6	*	·1	*	·9	*	*	·2	−2·2	−7·4
Total	43·3	145·0	231·5	199·4	169·5	120·9	112·6	84·6	51·0	288·8

22—ALL SECURITIES: NET CAPITAL REPAYMENT, CASH

£ millions

	1939	1940	1941	1942	1943	1944	1945	1946	1947	1948
COMMONWEALTH COUNTRIES										
Eire	-1·3	·1	-1·1	·3	·1	·1	·1	·6	·1	-1·1
British West Africa	-1·0	·2	*	-·1	·3	·1	1·6	-2·2	-·1	-1·1
Anglo-Egyptian Sudan... ...	3·5	·4	·3	·3	·3	·3	·4	·3	·3	·3
British East Africa	-·3	*	*	·1	·1	·1	-·4	1·7	-·8	3·7
British Central Africa	·3	·8	·6	·2	·7	-·2	·3	-·2	-12·1	-1·1
South Africa	-4·7	6·6	30·6	4·9	40·0	-·3	-·4	-6·7	-14·5	10·1
India ... ... }	2·8	14·4	72·5	90·7	83·9	26·5	6·5	3·0	6·6	2·8
Pakistan... ... ... }									·2	·1
Burma	*	*	*	·1	1·0	·1	—	*	*	
Ceylon	·2	1·4	*	*	·2	·3	·1	*	·1	-·1
Malaya	-·2	·1	·1	·2	·2	·1	·1	-·3	*	-·2
Australia	-5·0	3·3	6·0	·8	8·5	15·8	38·6	2·9	12·3	9·9
New Zealand	-11·9	15·0	1·6	3·2	3·6	2·9	4·1	21·6	8·6	10·7
Canada	24·6	40·8	42·3	71·6	5·4	10·5	21·0	27·8	20·7	6·4
British West Indies	-·5	-·2	*	·9	·1	·3	*	*	-·1	-1·0
Other	·2	·6	—	·6	*	·4	*	·1	1·8	*
	6·7	83·5	152·8	173·8	144·4	56·9	72·0	48·6	22·9	39·4
FOREIGN COUNTRIES										
France	·2	·1	—	—	—	—	1·8	·4	·5	·4
Germany	·1	—	—	—	—	—	—	—	—	—
Austria	·4	·8	*	*	*	*	·3	·1	·1	·1
Denmark	·2	—	—	—	—	—	·3	2·8	·8	·4
Norway	·6	·1	·1	·1	·2	·2	·9	·9	1·0	·1
Hungary...	·3	·3	·3	*	—	—	—	—	—	—
Roumania	—	—	—	—	—	—	—	—	—	—
Greece	*	*	*	—	—	—	—	—	—	—
Rest of Europe...	-2·0	-·5	-3·9	2·0	3·5	3·2	2·8	1·3	2·9	1·0
Burma										·3
China	·7	*	*	*	—	—	—	—	—	—
Japan	1·8	·7	·4	—	—	—	—	—	—	—
Netherlands East Indies ...	·1	·1	·1	·1	·1	·1	·1	—	*	-·2
Persia	*	*	*	*	*	*	*	*	*	·4
Egypt	·4	·2	·2	·2	1·1	3·1	*	-·1	-·5	·1
U.S.A.	25·1	50·8	74·0	4·4	5·5	10·9	11·4	10·1	4·7	-1·8
Mexico	*	—	*	·1	·2	·3	·3	1·3	·8	·2
Cuba	—	—	·2	—	*	·5	*	*	·3	·1
Argentina	1·8	2·0	1·8	3·8	2·6	20·7	3·6	5·2	6·6	153·6
Brazil	·9	·4	1·4	1·1	1·2	8·0	1·9	1·4	1·2	8·6
Chile	·8	1·5	·8	1·0	·4	·2	·4	·7	1·1	1·3
Peru	·1	·1	*	*	*	·1	·1	·1	·1	*
Uruguay...	*	·1	·1	·1	·1	·1	·1	·1	·1	·1
Rest of South America	·1	1·1	·3	*	-·4	-·4	-·9	-1·8	·2	-3·4
Other	·3	·4	·4	·1	1·3	1·2	1·0	·2	·5	3·3
	32·0	58·1	76·1	13·0	15·7	48·2	24·0	22·7	20·4	164·5
NOT CLASSIFIABLE	-3·7	*	*	*	·8	-·1	·1	·7	-2·3	-27·3
TOTAL	35·0	141·6	228·9	186·8	160·9	105·0	96·1	72·0	41·0	176·7

EUROPEAN BUSINESS

Four Centuries of Foreign Expansion

An Arno Press Collection

Anstey, Vera, *The Economic Development of India* 1952

Baster, A. S. J. *The Imperial Banks.* 1929

Baster, A. S. J. *The International Banks.* 1935

Blount, Edward. *Memoirs of Sir Edward Blount.* 1902

Braake, Alex L. Ter. *Mining in the Netherlands East Indies.* 1944

British Electrical and Allied Manufacturers' Association. *Combines and Trusts in the Electrical Industry.* 1927

Brode, Heinrich. *British and German East Africa.* 1911

Burden, William A. M. *The Struggle for Airways in Latin America.* 1943

Calvert, Albert F. *Nigeria and Its Tin Fields.* 1910

Crouchley, Arthur Edwin. *Investment of Foreign Capital in Egyptian Companies and Public Debt.* 1936

Davies, A. Emil. *Investments Abroad.* 1927

Deterding, Henri. *An International Oilman.* 1934

Ferns, Henry S. *Britain and Argentina in the Nineteenth Century.* 1960

Fitzgerald, Patrick. *Industrial Combination in England.* 1927

Gregory, Theodore. *Ernest Oppenheimer and the Economic Development of Southern Africa.* 1962

Henry, James Dodds. *Baku.* 1906

Hussey, Roland Dennis. *The Caracas Company, 1728-1784.* 1934

Jucker-Fleetwood, Erin Elver. *Sweden's Capital Imports and Exports.* 1947

Korthals-Altes, J. *Sir Cornelius Vermuyden.* 1925

Laves, Walter Herman Carl. *German Governmental Influence on Foreign Investments, 1871-1914.* 1977

Levy, Herman. *Monopoly and Competition.* 1911

Liefmann, Robert. *Cartels, Concerns and Trusts.* 1932

Marcus, Edward and Mildred Rendl Marcus. *Investment and Development Possibilities in Tropical Africa.* 1960

Meakin, W. *The New Industrial Revolution.* 1928

Michell, Lewis. *The Life and Times of the Right Honourable Cecil John Rhodes, 1853-1902.* Two vols. in one. 1910

Miller, Benjamin L. and Joseph T. Singewald. *The Mineral Deposits of South America.* 1919

Mulhall, Michael G. *The English in South America.* 1878

Nordyke, Lewis. *Cattle Empire.* 1949

Nute, Grace Lee. *Caesers of the Wilderness.* 1943

Patterson, E. M., editor. *America's Changing Investment Market.* 1916

Pinner, Felix. *Emil Rathenau und das Elektrische Zeitalter.* 1918

Riesser, J. *The German Great Banks and Their Concentration in Connection with the Economic Development of Germany.* 1911

Rippy, J. Fred. *British Investment in Latin America, 1822-1949.* 1959

Rondot, Jean. *La Compagnie Française des Pétroles.* 1962

Roth, Cecil. *The Sassoon Dynasty.* 1941

Senior, Nassau W. *A Journal Kept in Turkey and Greece in the Autumn of 1857 and the Beginning of 1858.* 1859

Siemens, Georg. *History of the House of Siemens.* Two vols. 1957

Southworth, Constant. *The French Colonial Venture.* 1931

Spender, John A. *Weetman Pearson, First Viscount Cowdray, 1856-1927.* 1930

Thorner, Daniel. *Investment in Empire.* 1950

U. S. Department of Commerce, Bureau of Foreign and Domestic Commerce. *Investments in Latin America and the British West Indies.* 1918

U. S. Federal Trade Commission. *Report of the Federal Trade Commission on Foreign Ownership in the Petroleum Industry.* 1923

U. S. Office of the Alien Property Custodian. *Alien Property Custodian Report.* 1919

U. S. Office of the Alien Property Custodian. *Annual Reports.* Four vols. in one. 1943/45/46/47

Van Oss, S. F. *American Railroads as Investments.* 1893

van Winter, Pieter J. *American Finance and Dutch Investment, 1780-1805.* 1977

Vlekke, Bernard H. M. *Nusantara.* 1943

Wallace, Donald H. *Market Control in the Aluminum Industry.* 1937

Wellington, Dorothy Violet Wellesley. *Sir George Goldie, Founder of Nigeria.* 1934

Wheeler, John. *A Treatise of Commerce.* 1931

Wilkins, Mira, editor. *British Overseas Investments, 1907-1948.* 1977

Wilkins, Mira, editor. *European Foreign Investments, As Seen by the U. S. Department of Commerce.* 1977

Wilkins, Mira, editor. *Foreign Investments in the United States.* 1977

Wilkins, Mira, editor. *Issues and Insights on International Investment.* 1977

Williamson, John W. *In a Persian Oil Field.* 1930

Wilson, Arnold T. *The Suez Canal.* 1933

Wilson, Charles Henry. *Anglo-Dutch Commerce and Finance in the Eighteenth Century.* 1941

Wood, Gordon. *Borrowing and Business in Australia.* 1930

Wortley, B. A. *Expropriation in Public International Law.* 1959